Consumer Incentives for Health Care

EDITED BY SELMA J. MUSHKIN

New York · 1974

Published for the Milbank Memorial Fund by

PRODIST

PRODIST
a division of
Neale Watson Academic Publications, Inc.
156 Fifth Avenue
New York, New York 10010
© 1974 Milbank Memorial Fund
Manufactured in the U.S.A.

Second printing   1977

Library of Congress Cataloging in Publication Data

Mushkin, Selma J   1913–
    Consumer incentives for health care.

    Includes bibliographies.
    1. Medical care—Public opinion. 2. Health
attitudes. 3. Consumers. I. Milbank Memorial Fund.
II. Title. [DNLM: 1. Consumer participation.
2. Delivery of health care. WB50 M987c 1974]
RA418.M87   362.1   74-6170
ISBN 0-88202-057-9

Consumer
Incentives
for Health Care

Stage of Illness	Age of Patient	Sociology	Economics	Psychology	Medicine	Ethics	Demography	Biology
Preprevention (nutrition, exercise, "no smoking")								
Prevention (immunization)								
Acute care (infectious diseases, accidents)								
Chronic illness (arthritis)								
Rehabilitation								
Terminal illness								

Study Area

The Structure of Demand

Interuniversity Advisory Committee on Health Incentives Research

KENNETH ARROW, Ph.D.
Project on Efficiency of Decision Making in Economic Systems
Harvard University
Cambridge, Massachusetts

S. J. AXELROD, M.D.
Department of Medical Care Organization
School of Public Health
University of Michigan
Ann Arbor, Michigan

PAUL M. DENSEN, Ph.D.
Director, Center for Community Health and Medical Care
Harvard University
Cambridge, Massachusetts

JACK ELINSON, Ph.D.
Head, Division of Sociomedical Sciences
School of Public Health and Administrative Services
Columbia University
New York, New York

ROBERT R. HUNTLEY, M.D.
Chairman, Community Medicine and International Health
Georgetown University
Washington, D. C.

RICHARD F. MANEGOLD, M.D.
Associate Chief
Department of Medicine
Georgetown University
Washington, D. C.

MATTHEW F. McNULTY, JR., Sc.D.
Vice President
Medical Center Affairs
Georgetown University
Washington, D. C.

SELMA J. MUSHKIN, Ph.D.
Director
Public Services Laboratory
Georgetown University
Washington, D. C.

MARK V. PAULY, Ph.D.
Associate Professor of Economics
Northwestern University
Evanston, Illinois

GEORGE A. SILVER, M.D.
Professor of Public Health
Department of Epidemiology and Pub-
    lic Health
Yale University
New Haven, Connecticut

CHARLES I. SCHOTTLAND, Ph.D.
Florence Heller Graduate School for
    Advanced Studies in Social Welfare
Brandeis University
Waltham, Massachusetts

KARL D. YORDY, Ph.D.
Senior Program Officer
Institute of Medicine
National Academy of Sciences
Washington, D. C.

Contents

Incentives by Stage of Illness

Socioeconomic Incentives in Consumer Use

Directions for Health Services Research

Contributors

KATHARINE G. BAUER
Associate
Center for Community Health and
  Medical Care
School of Public Health and Medical
  School
Harvard University

JAMES E. BILLINGS
Economics Section Head
Minnesota Systems Research, Inc.

PATRICIA J. BUSH
Research Consultant
Department of Community Health
Georgetown University

MARIE-PAULE DONSIMONI
Research Associate
Bell Museum of Pathology
University of Minnesota Medical
  School

DAVID DUNLOP
Assistant Professor
Department of Family and Commun-
  ity Health and Division of Health
  Care Administration and Planning
Meharry Medical College
  and
Assistant Professor
Department of Economics
Vanderbilt University

DIANA B. DUTTON
Research Associate
Urban Studies and Political Science
Massachusetts Institute of Technology

PAUL M. GERTMAN
Chief, Evans Memorial Section of
  Health Care Research
Boston University Medical Center

MICHAEL GROSSMAN
Senior Research Staff
National Bureau of Economic
  Research
  and
Associate Professor of Economics
City University of New York

CHARLES P. HALL, JR.
Professor and Chairman
Department of Health Administration
School of Business Administration
Temple University

LESTER B. LAVE
Head, Department of Economics
Graduate School of Industrial
  Administration
Carnegie-Mellon University

JOHN B. McKINLAY
Professor
Department of Sociology
Boston University

SELMA J. MUSHKIN
Director
Public Services Laboratory
Georgetown University

MARK V. PAULY
Associate Professor of Economics
Northwestern University

ELIZABETH H. RAND
Senior Research Analyst
National Bureau of Economic
   Research

MARIAN OSTERWEIS RIVKIN
Assistant Professor
Department of Community Medicine
   and International Health
Georgetown University

STUART O. SCHWEITZER
Associate Professor
Department of Community Medicine
   and International Health
Georgetown University

MICHAEL ZUBKOFF
Associate Professor of Health
   Economics
Meharry Medical College
   and Vanderbilt University
   and
Associate Chairman
Department of Family and
   Community Health
Meharry Medical College

Preface

The papers which make up this volume were prepared for the Conference on Consumer Incentives in Health Care Uses, supported by a grant from the Milbank Memorial Fund, held by the Public Services Laboratory in Washington, D. C., June 8–9, 1973. The papers cover incentives by stages of illness, and are presented from perspective of a number of fields of study and disciplines. In each instance the authors were asked to review the "state of the art" of research and analysis on the topic addressed, and the followup studies that should be considered. Overall, the papers provide not only a summary of what is known about consumer incentives in the use of health care, but also illuminate the deficiences in knowledge about critical problems of health care.

The intent of the Conference was to bring together a group of experts to consider the current state of the art on consumer incentives in health care and to suggest new study areas. Those in attendance attested to the quality of the conversation by their continued participation throughout the Conference. The usual dropoff in attendance as the sessions continued did not occur. And it must be underscored that the discussions were continually lively and good despite the heat of Copley Lounge, in which the meeting took place, and the government-surplus wooden chairs. For all of the inconvenience my apologies go to everyone in attendance. Yet perhaps the "poverty" in modern equipment contributed to the intellectual wealth of the discussion. It was certainly a reminder for some old friends of the gains from an earlier collaborative effort that facilitated an advance from poverty in research support on the economics of health.

I wish to express my deep appreciation to the many who contributed to the work of the Conference. My special thanks go to the members of the Ad Hoc Committee on Health Care Incentives who helped to conceptualize the meeting's main concerns, gave of their guidance, and lent their experience at each stage of the planning and carrying out of the work of the Conference.

This volume will, I know, help those who are concerned with health policy to identify an agenda for further study. The findings set forth throw light on the problems and processes that remain still to be understood.

The general sessions of the Conference were chaired by Dr. S. J. Axelrod, Dr. Paul Densen, Dr. Matthew F. McNulty, and Dr. George A. Silver.

I am happy to acknowledge the cooperation of the authors of the papers who gave of their time so willingly during the process of readying this volume for publication. Violet Gunther, Angela Murray, Robin Raphel, Cindi Rose, and Jim Grotberg carried a good deal of the responsibility for processing the essays in preparation for publication.

No thanks would be complete without mention of the work of those who carried out the Conference planning, particularly the expert work of Violet Gunther, Ann Guillot, and Stephen Stageberg.

SELMA J. MUSHKIN

Foreword

Whenever health policy is assessed, consideration turns to the incentives that guide consumers and producers of care. The present volume concerns itself with consumer incentives.

Incentives that cause consumers to seek care and choose to spend for health services are not well understood. Why, for example, do some persons turn away from free health services such as screening for selected diseases? Why do others use care "excessively?" Or, alternatively, what guides the choices that are made between providers of care? How do persons select physicians? And why is hospital care often encouraged in place of care at home?

It is generally agreed that financial incentives play a major role in consumer decisions. But existing financial incentives designed to facilitate administration and cut costs have worked perversely. Cost to the patient of institutional care at the time of illness as a result of insurance coverage has stimulated use of high-cost hospitalization and deterred others from seeking uninsured care at home. While steps are being taken to broaden the scope and range of prepaid health services so as to remove undue financial encouragement for hospital care and to reduce imbalances in health-services utilization, the research base on which to draw for fact and analysis is inadequate.

The Milbank Memorial Fund in its meeting developed a set of priorities for its program support. Incentives in health care use were high on the agenda adopted. The selection was guided by the apparent critical concern about incentive structures in the design and implementation of a national health insurance program for the United States.

Within the Fund guidelines and in pursuit of those purposes,

support was granted to the program of research planning at Georgetown University suggested by the Public Services Laboratory (PSL).
The research planning proposed the promise of defining the factual
and analytical gaps about incentives in health care.

The symposium on consumer incentives in use of health care
carried out by the Public Services Laboratory of Georgetown University has identified an agenda for research that should prove useful
not only in assisting the Fund in its selection among research proposals, but also other foundations concerned with health care.

Several notable contributions were made by the work of the
Conference. Attention is directed to differences in the critical determinants of demand depending upon stage of illness. Cost of care, for
example, appears to be a greater obstacle to preventive services than
to care for terminally ill. Family structure, age, income, and physician
perception all work differently to determine amounts of use.

A second contribution is the example offered by the interuniversity
group of scholars who guided the work on the design and the carrying out of the Conference. Their collaborative efforts brought to bear
the knowledge and experience not only of persons from many universities, but also from a range of disciplines, including physical
medicine, community medicine, sociology, physiology, medical care
administration, economics, demography, biostatistics, and public
administration.

Public Services Laboratory, within the School of Foreign Service,
worked closely with the Medical School, the Jesuit Social Study Center, and the Department of Community Medicine in carrying out the
work of the Conference; this cooperative effort is itself exemplary
and responsive to the widely recognized need for interdisciplinary
research.

A special word of thanks is gratefully extended to Selma Mushkin
for her original idea of the conference and her usual capable organization and management which assured a successful outcome.

L. E. BURNEY, M.D.

PRESIDENT

MILBANK MEMORIAL FUND

Incentives
by Stage of
Illness

Averting

the Self-Inflicted

Nemeses (Sins) from Dangerous

Driving, Smoking, and Drinking

KATHARINE G. BAUER

Long before cost-benefit analysis was able to furnish the documentation, most people recognized that an ounce of prevention was worth a pound of cure. Today almost everyone also recognizes that by far the largest share of premature death and avoidable sickness and disability in advanced industrial countries comes from peoples' own self-destructive behavior and that the consequences of such behavior place enormous burdens on health and welfare systems. The prime examples considered in this paper are dangerous driving, excessive drinking, and smoking.

How society should respond to those situations is far from clear. To what extent is it justifiable to interfere with peoples' values and life styles in order to ward off nemesis for a relatively small proportion of their number? Most people, after all, use cars, alcohol, and even cigarettes in ways and for purposes they perceive to be personally useful and satisfying. The right to drive is often an economic necessity, even for the heavy drinker; mood alterants of one sort or another have been with us throughout history. Even if it is agreed that interventions may be desirable, given the past failures of both legal prohibitions and health education to modify human behavior, is it hopeless to try? What external and internal forces influence the individual's decision to act in such and such a way, and what are the barriers to change? Have we learned enough to construct new incentive strategies that may yield greater payoffs? Finally, what new kinds of research are needed to help design and implement such strategies?

This paper will review these questions, suggesting both the complexities of the issues they raise and some general contexts in which attempts at "preprevention" may be approached.

Should Society Attempt to Prevent Self-Destructive Practices?

If people are informed about the potential consequences of their risky habits, such as driving without seat belts or smoking, but nevertheless choose to continue them, is it anyone's business but their own? Herbert Packer, as quoted by Wilson, holds that a desirable aspect of liberalism is that it allows people "to choose their own roads to hell if that is where they want to go" (Wilson et al., 1972). Yet while begging the moral question, "Am I my brother's keeper?" even the most libertarian thinkers would probably agree with humanists that interventions would seem to be justified in circumstances:

—where the harmful consequences of the action are likely to devolve on other people, either as threats to health or to pocketbook
—when the potential victim or offender is being deliberately subjected to other types of communications that promote or reinforce his possibly harmful behavior
—when he indicates the desire to change, but has trouble doing so.

In the cases of dangerous driving, alcohol abuse, and smoking, at least one and usually several of the three conditions apply. The facts, though generally familiar, merit a brief review.[1]

Dangerous Driving

The National Safety Council tells us that each year approximately fifty-five thousand people die in motor-vehicle accidents (about the same number as all United States military personnel killed in nine years of the Vietnam war) and that, of the two million people injured, one hundred seventy thousand are left with permanently disabling injuries. Much of that loss of life and limb involves completely innocent victims. In any case, their families and society at large pick up the pieces, at an annual cost conservatively estimated at $11.0 billion. In 1971 the reported attendant medical expenses alone were $1.1 billion (National Safety Council, 1972).

Young males, for whom deaths from car accidents are almost seven times the number from the next leading cause, are particularly subjected to communications that downplay safe driving as a desirable social value and that stimulate the risk-taking proclivities that society for the most part condones and often encourages for their age group. Many segments of the peer group youth culture still associate machismo with prowess at the wheel in conditions of danger (Rommel, 1959). Car model names, such as Mustang, Jaguar, and Cougar, presumably reinforce the message. Not surprisingly, young males make up the age and sex group found least likely to use seat belts (Council, 1969).

Seat belts, if everyone wore them, might save an estimated eight to ten thousand lives annually. Although their installation has been required in new cars since 1968, studies show that even in cars so

[1] Most of the figures quoted in this section are those commonly disseminated by national organizations as part of their information-alert campaigns. Many are approximations, subject to either upward or downward revisions depending on the definitions employed, reliability of measurements, etc. These questions of methodology, while important, are not discussed here, since the measures are used merely to suggest the overall dimensions of the various problems with which the paper deals.

equipped only one of every three drivers on the road actually fastens them. Many more people apparently think of themselves as conscientious seat-belt users than is the actual case. A field study followed by telephone interviews found that, of the drivers who reported that they always used seat belts on long trips, fewer than half had actually been wearing them when observed at toll booths on open highways (Robertson et al., 1972).

Dangerous Drinking

The National Commission on Marihuana and Drug Abuse in its final report calls alcohol dependence "without question the most serious drug problem in this country today" (1973:143). Here is another case where the individual—the drinker—harms many others besides himself, where he is subjected to a variety of powerful social communications reinforcing his practice, and where he often wants to modify his behavior but fails.

Alcohol users, about ninety-five million persons, far outnumber the users of other drugs. (In this paper, alcohol and tobacco are defined as drugs. See National Commission on Marihuana and Drug Abuse, 1973; and Brecher, 1972.) About nine million are estimated to be alcohol abusers and alcoholics (U.S. Department of Health, Education, and Welfare, 1971:vi).[2] The visible victims found on skid rows make up only three to five percent; the remainder, while beset with problems and inflicting them on others, manage to remain in the working, homemaking, and driving population.

Heavy drinking and alcoholism are implicated as primary or related causal factors in many pathological conditions, and alcoholics

[2] The National Institute on Alcohol Abuse and Alcoholism stresses that the line between alcohol abuse and alcoholism cannot be clearly drawn. "The difference is mostly a matter of degree and consequence, or purpose and pattern. . ." (National Institute on Alcohol Abuse and Alcoholism, n.d.). In the 3 surveys of drinking practices conducted in the 1960s the definition of heavy drinking was: "Drink nearly every day, with 5 or more per occasion at least once in a while, or about once weekly with usually 5 or more per occasion." By that definition, 12 percent of the adult population are heavy drinkers (U.S. Department of Health, Education, and Welfare, 1971: 22).

frequently fall victim to all sorts of illnesses not directly connected with alcoholism (Barcha et al., 1968). Alcohol plays a major role in half of all highway fatalities, is associated with one out of every three suicides and with one out of every two homicides and criminal assaults, and is highly implicated in deaths by fire, drowning, and home accidents (Palola et al., 1962; Wolfgang, 1958; Brenner, 1967; Wechsler et al., 1969). All told, the U.S. Department of Health, Education, and Welfare (USDHEW) reports alcohol abuse reduces an individual's average life span by an average of about ten to twelve years (1971:45).

Alcohol abuse and alcoholism, according to the same report, drain the economy of an estimated fifteen billion dollars a year—ten billion dollars in worktime lost in business, industry, civilian government, and the military; two billion dollars in health and welfare services provided to alcoholic persons and their families; and three billion dollars or more in property damage, medical expenses, and other overhead costs.

Few people deliberately choose to end their days as alcoholics. The end result here, as for smokers, comes in consequence of myriad small, intermediate decisions made over considerable periods of time. While the individual may appreciate the possibilities of danger in the long run, the short-term risk attached to each of his intermediate decisions is inconsequential. Furthermore, as the National Commission on Marihuana and Drug Abuse states.

> The risk of individual involvement is accentuated by the pervasive sentiment which tends to exclude alcohol from classification as a drug, thereby eliminating it from the concept of drug abuse and the social problems which go by that name (1973:143).

The alcoholic beverage industry's yearly advertising expenditures of more than two hundred fifty million dollars presumably help to reinforce that view (Brecher, 1972:252). In comparison, the Division of Prevention hopes to obtain three million dollars out of the total budget of eighty-seven million dollars of the National Institute for Alcohol Abuse and Alcoholism for 1974.

As with seat-belt use, there seems to be considerable ambivalence between what many people think is sensible drinking behavior and how they actually drink. A national survey was conducted in 1964–1965 that measured drinking practices and attitudes in the adult household population of the United States. It found that three-fourths of the sample, including a majority of male heavy drinkers, said they thought drinking "does more harm than good," and three-fourths of them believed alcoholism to be a serious public health problem. Nine percent of all alcohol users reported that they worried about their own drinking—almost the same proportion that serious problem drinkers represent of all drinkers (USDHEW, 1971:29).

Dangerous Smoking

Since the release of the Surgeon General's report in 1964 on the effects of smoking on health, the high volume of excess deaths from heart disease, lung cancer, and emphysema has been widely publicized. In addition to dramatic differences between the life expectancies of smokers and nonsmokers, with total excess deaths estimated at two hundred thousand annually, cigarette smokers have higher rates of disability of all kinds than do nonsmokers (Public Health Service, 1970). A National Health Survey analysis calculated that in a single year cigarette smoking causes an excess over the expected burden from disability of seventy-seven million mandays lost from work, eighty-eight million mandays spent ill in bed, and three hundred-six million mandays of restricted activity (National Clearinghouse for Smoking and Health, 1967).

Except for a significant risk of damage to her unborn child from the pregnant woman smoker, the physical harm done by smokers to others is small compared with that from dangerous driving and drinking. Nevertheless, there is again a substantial burden of lost productivity and economic dependency created by the avoidable long-term chronic illnesses and premature deaths associated with smoking.

At the risk of being repetitious, we must again observe that the smoker is reinforced in his practice by advertising, for which more than two hundred million dollars is spent annually (Hicks, 1972). Following the ban on television commercials at the end of 1970, cigarette advertising in other media rapidly increased. Within the first quarter of 1971 it tripled in newspaper and increased eleven-fold on billboards (Read, 1972:130).

Nevertheless, sizable proportions of smokers want to stop and try to stop. A national survey in 1970 found that eighty-seven percent of the male smokers said they had thought seriously about giving it up and that seventy-one percent had tried to do so (Horn, 1972:61).

The driving, drinking, and smoking problems outlined in this summary review appear to justify attempts at intervention, according to the criteria we have established. A further question is the relation of costs and benefits of such actions, or of failures to act.

Costs and Benefits of Prevention

In view of the magnitude of the problems, surprisingly little work has been done to weigh the benefits that might be expected from diminishing the harmful consequences of the abuse of cars, alcohol, and cigarettes against the expected economic costs to industry, government, and the general economy. Questions of definition, including the difficulty of setting a monetary value on human life and inability to put price tags on the costs of successful preventive measures, greatly handicap all such efforts.

Despite the difficulties, some beginnings have been made. A study by Hedrick, extrapolating from a Canadian study, estimated that in 1966 in the United States the costs of smoking consequences were twenty percent greater than the total consumer expenditures, excluding taxes, for cigarettes. The estimates were based on a number of tentative assumptions, however, and conclusions are subject to a large margin of error (Hedrick, 1971).

Simon has calculated that abolishing cigarette advertising might reduce consumption five percent a year, with further five-percent drops in subsequent years. He figures that, when the loss of wages and salaries from such reductions is taken into account, the trade-off is between an incremental shortrun decrease of one dollar in wages and an increase of ninety-nine hours in human life (Simon, 1968).

Another study sought to estimate the marginal benefits and costs of treating alcoholics and suggested that, even if the probability of success falls below 0.10, expenditures could still be justified on grounds of economic efficiency (Holtman, 1964). Ubell (1972) looks more specifically at cost savings from prevention and notes that treatment programs for three million persons with alcohol problems would cost $3 billion a year. If $100 million a year were spent just for behavior change and achieved only a ten-percent success rate, society would still "save" $2.9 billion in treatment costs alone, not to mention savings in time lost from work, illness related to alcoholism, and so on.

Hopefully, necessary methodologies and information will be developed that will permit more refined types of projections along those lines. As the final example suggested, a necessary input to many such analyses is estimates of the relationship of input costs to varying probabilities of success from different kinds of preventive efforts. Unfortunately, except perhaps in the area of highway safety, such estimates are now almost completely unobtainable.

Before looking at some types of preventive measures, it is important to consider the larger societal context in which they are being proposed or tried. Are the barriers to change so formidable that it is unrealistic to hope for significant modification of the present situation? Such barriers, both those external to the individual and those within him, must be identified if effective counterpolicy and incentives are to be mounted.

External Barriers to Change

Ernest Wynder (1972) reminds us that in 1849 John Snow urged the adoption of his recommendations on water treatment to prevent cholera because "they do not involve any commercial intercourse." The same argument cannot be advanced today for the cases we are considering. The alcoholic beverage, tobacco, and automotive industries are among the nation's largest. While, like the gun manufacturers, they may deplore the misuse of their products, their overriding obligation to their stockholders is to increase sales. Clearly, they must be expected to continue actively pressing consumers to buy and use.

The extent to which sales pressures contribute to the problems of misuse is not known. At a minimum they reinforce the user in his practice. It seems plausible that they also influence the attitudes of potential users among the young, although research that could successfully test this proposition has not been carried out. Kramer, after an extensive review of the effect of mass media on drug use and abuse, states that:

> On the one hand, available data do not support the conclusion that mass communication has a decisive effect upon the behavior patterns of its audience. On the other hand, many observers, including practical men of business as well as students of communication theory, believe that the media are highly influential, even if measurement of their impact remains an imprecise art (1973:587–588).

In view of the nature of the trade-offs noted above, it would seem to be good policy to ban all forms of cigarette advertising and display until their lack of influence can be conclusively proved, rather than the opposite. Similar bans on alcoholic beverage advertising should also be considered.

Governments, which spend massively to prevent the sale of illicit psychoactive drugs, act schizophrenically about the sale of licit drugs, perhaps because of the substantial revenues they bring. In 1971 the federal government received $5.05 billion from taxes on the sale of alcoholic beverages; state and local governments received $3.2 billion (National Commission on Marihuana and Drug Abuse, 1973:382). New Hampshire derives about twelve percent of its total revenue from liquor taxes. Cigarettes likewise have enormous tax yields. Thus, while the White House is conducting Crusades Against Cancer and Heart Disease and USDHEW is promoting antismoking campaigns, tobacco growers are receiving federal subsidies and the Economic Research Service of the U.S. Department of Agriculture is not unhappily informing the tobacco industry that domestic cigarette consumption in 1972 rose nearly three percent from the 1971 level, and that:

> . . . with favorable economic prospects, above average population increases for 25–44 year olds and a low level of anti-cigarette announcements, . . . U.S. cigarette output for calendar 1972 will set a record high (Economic Research Services, 1972:4).

Although cost-benefit analyses such as those already noted would undoubtedly show that the aggregate dollar benefits to government from reduced consumption of alcohol and cigarettes would exceed the tax revenues lost, the difficulty is that different entities within government stand to gain or lose.

The public's general ambivalence on issues connected with drinking, smoking, and bad driving creates another type of barrier to change, since it results in unclear objectives for preventive programs. Everyone would like to prevent the consequences flowing from the present state of affairs and would agree on the global objective of preventing overtly dangerous behavior. But there is a notable reluctance to specify the particular points on the long continuum between harmless recreation and dangerous abuse at which lines should be drawn. In view of our limited knowledge in those areas, and the possibilities of harm from ill-considered action, such reluctance may be not only understandable but wise. Nevertheless, without some intermediate goals it is difficult to pinpoint the precise types of behavior to be changed and by whom they should be changed, and thus to design and implement focused regulatory actions or preventive programs. Nor can results of such measures be properly evaluated. Accordingly, after a cursory examination of the personal and interpersonal barriers to change, some surrogate intermediate goals will be suggested.

Personal and Interpersonal Barriers to Change

Extensive epidemiological and behavioral research in motor vehicle accidents and alcohol and smoking practices over the past decade has begun to identify many of the demographic and personality characteristics of subgroups of the population for whom the risk of engaging in dangerous behavior seems to be high, as well as patterns of use and danger. (Findings from the studies are referred to in various sections of this paper.) Yet we still know very little about how to predict which individuals among the high-risk groups are especially prone over time to develop harmful patterns of use. Nor, in spite of an encouraging level of ongoing research, do we know enough about the interplay of social, biological, and psychological factors that pushes people to adopt such patterns, creates barriers to their changing, or leads to modifications of behavior before it becomes too late. We only know enough to be certain that, in addition to external pressures, the habits and attitudes of family, mentors, friends, and associates, situations of particular stress, and special personality traits all contribute importantly to the total context in which the individual makes his personal decisions and thus create the framework within which counterincentives must be designed.

There is a related question, crucial in the design of preventive programs. In what proportion of the high-risk populations is it reasonable to expect positive behavior change? At the pessimistic extreme, there is evidence that harmful behavior of various types often appears in constellations within a small segment of the population. The vast majority of drivers with crashes or citations associated with alcohol, for example, are usually known to the police or community-service agencies before they reach age twenty-five or thirty (Waller, 1967). The very small proportion of youths under age seventeen who use illicit drugs with relatively high frequency and intensity are most likely to be multidrug users and to escalate to the more dangerous drugs (National Commission on Marihuana and Drug Abuse, 1973:92). Most had begun using tobacco and alcohol at early ages. Among the small proportion of cured narcotics addicts reported by followup studies from the federal narcotics hospital at Lexington, almost half became either alcoholics or barbiturate addicts. Others became compulsive overeaters (O'Donnell, 1969). In a New York methadone clinic, of the 181 people being maintained, 98.0 percent smoked, many heavily, in comparison with a national rate of 36.7 percent for the same age group (Berger and Schweigler, 1972). Heavy smoking is also highly prevalent among members of Alcoholics Anonymous.

The National Commission on Marihuana and Drug Abuse suggests that there may be a maximum penetration level of drug dependence in any society.

> Even in Hong Kong where heroin is available and inexpensive the prevalence of intensified and compulsive use does not exceed 4% of the entire population, although this proportion is higher among males over 20 years of age, about 11%. Similarly, heroin and opium are easily secured in Thailand but the proportion of chronic smokers does not exceed 2% of the entire population, or 10% of the adult male population. In the U.S. the proportions are roughly the same for chronic alcohol use; about 5% of the total population and about 15% of the middle aged population (1973:142).

Some observers believe that there are no addictive substances but only people with a high predilection to dependency and compulsive behavior (Peele, in press). Although the issue is highly debatable and not likely to be settled soon, for purposes of designing effective interventions it is essential that the charactristics of "addictive" users be better understood and the policy implications faced. For this small fraction of the population, prevention may not be a realistic goal, only mitigation and containment of the consequences.

At the other extreme, many people do successfully change their smoking and drinking behavior. Of the forty-nine million people who were smokers in 1966, for example, about thirteen million had stopped and were still off cigarettes in 1970 (Horn, 1972). Many more millions had stopped but resumed.

The 1964–65 American Drinking Practices Survey (Cahalan et al., 1969) found that, among the thirty-two percent of the adult population who were nondrinkers, one-third said they once used to drink. A 1967 survey found that as many persons had had fairly severe drinking problems in an earlier three-year period as within the past three years (Cahalan, 1970). The retrospective reports on past changes in drinking behavior were borne out by separate measurements. During the short period between the two surveys, fifteen percent of the persons interviewed had either moved into or out of the group reporting heavy drinking (USDHEW, 1971:35).

These facts suggest that, though problems may be almost intractable for some small proportion of the population, behavior change is indeed a realistic goal for a far larger proportion.

Somewhere between the two extremes are people who might go either way, depending on the forces of external and personal circumstances that push both towards dangerous patterns and their modification. Among them are the millions of smokers and heavy drinkers who recognize their problems but can't seem to handle them unaided.

Given the varying degrees of tractability, the realistic goals for preventive programs appear to be:

—to attempt to stop outright the most extreme forms of dangerous behavior (such as driving while drunk)

—to mitigate the harmful consequences to and from the dangerous user who cannot change in time to avert them

—to prevent recidivism among people who have managed to change

—to strengthen the resolve of people who would like to change but have not been able to do so

—to alert those at risk to the benefits of risk avoidance.

Current preventive efforts are largely geared to prohibitions and mitigations at the one end of the list and information about the nature of the risks at the other. Except for the efforts of such groups as Alcoholics Anonymous (which is perhaps better categorized as a treatment than a preventive program), only spotty activity is presently geared towards preventing recidivism or buttressing resolve.

Current Preventive Efforts

For dangerous driving, drinking, and smoking, as for other health threats, preventive actions may try to change the environment, the agent, or the host. Respecting the theme of this conference, the focus here is on the third approach—intervention designed to influence the host's behavior. But the manifold efforts being made both to provide a safer environment for him and to improve the safety of the products he uses are the principal means of mitigating the consequences of his ongoing, potentially dangerous actions. Safer road design and construction, for example, are credited with almost halving the rate of deaths per miles traveled on limited-access highways (National Safety Council, 1972:13).[3]

Attempts to intervene in the process between the formation of people's drinking, smoking, and driving habits and the onset of their destructive consequences have employed both direct and indirect means to influence behavior with respect to the potentially harmful agent. Society has commonly imposed rules to prohibit or circumscribe the conditions of its use and has signaled warnings. Less often, indirect means of persuasion are sought through tax and pricing policies and through the influence of exemplars and peer groups that might affect the individual's decision-making.

Indirect Incentives

The effect of pricing and tax policies on cigarette and alcohol consumption is imperfectly understood. On army posts, where both products are available at low prices, consumption is much higher than it is in the general population. But in the particular circumstances of military life men may well have been willing to pay higher prices to ensure the same consumption. Counterproductive effects may flow from overpricing, such as encouraging the user to smoke his cigarette to its shortest, most hazardous point or to resort to illegal sources for his liquor (Simon, 1968).

The influence of mentors and peers can be positive as well as

[3] It can be argued that the ultimate goal of preventing harmful end results is most likely to be reached by such lines of future research and application. A mechanically safe car that won't start for a drunk driver, an easily fastened seat belt, a genuinely safe cigarette, a beverage that would give the drinker all the satisfactions he presently derives from alcohol without any of its harmful effects, all would seem to hold better promise of adoption than would drastic changes in people's customary attitudes and daily habits.

negative. The smoking rate among physicians has fallen substantially below that of the general population, presumably because of their direct clinical observations of end results. Since people rely on doctors for their perception of good health practices, their example may influence the general public. But parents of children under age twelve, who provide important role models, report a high degree of desire to stop smoking but unfortunately have a low success rate (Allen and Fackler, 1967; Eisinger, 1971). The success of the American Cancer Society's antismoking campaigns with members of influential community groups, such as Jaycees and Rotarians, is again not known.

In one of the few well-evaluated studies of the success of peer group and threat measures, a program on a military base that publicly labeled driving while drunk "sick behavior" and grounds for discharge was associated with a marked reduction in crashes, compared with the record for a control base without the program (U.S. Department of Transportation, 1968:84).

High school clubs have been formed in some areas that have made abstention from smoking and other types of drugs a central condition of membership. Other forms of antidrug peer group pressure are generated by the many new meditative and religious groups appearing as part of the current youth culture. How much long-lasting change in behavior will result remains conjectural. Their activities, however, illustrate another type of incentive that has up to now been perhaps insufficiently explored—deliberate efforts to provide equally satisfying but less hazardous alternative forms of life activity tailored to suit the needs of the individuals potentially at risk.

Prohibitions

Attempts at prohibitions have a long history. Brecher (1972) reminds us that in 1633 Sultan Murad IV in Constantinople decreed the death penalty for smoking. Offenders were punished by beheading, hanging, or quartering. Yet a contemporary writer observed that "even the fear of death was of no avail with the passionate devotees of the habit" (Brecher, 1972: 210–212).

After the 20th Century prohibitions on sales of cigarettes and alcohol were repealed in the United States, bans remained on controlled drugs, sales of licit drugs to minors, and on some types of driving. In 1921, fourteen states had cigarette prohibition laws and prohibition bills were under consideration by an additional twenty-eight (Brecher, 1972:231). Their deterrent effects are not known.

Despite state age restriction laws, the 1972 survey conducted for the National Commission on Marihuana and Drug Abuse (1973:29, 47) found that among youth aged twelve to seventeen about four million (seventeen percent) had smoked cigarettes and about six million (twenty-four percent) had consumed alcohol during the week preceding the survey. Though the extent of use is considerably less than that reported by adults, it is certainly substantial.

The failure of state laws attempting to prohibit the use of cars by underage or dangerous drivers is revealed in the nation's high car-theft and driving-while-drunk accident statistics. Even the revocation of driving licenses may not prove effective. A California study that analyzed the records of drivers whose licenses had been suspended or revoked for serious offenses found that a third of the former group and two-thirds of the latter were known not only to have been driving but to have had citations or crashes during the penalty periods (U.S. Department of Transportation, 1968:85).

That simple prohibitions against tobacco, alcohol, and other drugs and dangerous driving will always be ineffective with their most "passionate devotees" is well recognized, as are the harmful by-products—disrespect for the law, criminal behavior, and high enforcement costs. Nevertheless, their advocates argue that increased accessibility leads to increased demand and use and thus that prohibitions may at least contain the size of the particular problem (Wilson et al., 1972). If heavy users of mood alterants, for example, always constitute ten to fifteen percent of all users, in line with the speculations offered earlier, it follows that the absolute numbers at the dangerous end of the use curve will increase in rough proportion to the increased total consumption.

The proportionate increase appears to be true among users of alcohol. The annual per capita consumption of distilled spirits rose from 1.96 gallons in 1935—two years after the repeal of the Volstead Act—to 2.63 gallons in 1971 (USDHEW, 1971:10; U.S. Statistical Abstract, 1972:716). Problems relating to alcoholism appear to have increased at an even greater rate.

The question then becomes not whether prohibition "doesn't work" but rather on whom it does work, and the size and nature of the trade-offs between its societal costs and benefits. The public appears to have decided the issue in regard to the manufacture and sale of cigarettes and alcohol; the debate over other drugs and driving regulations continues.

Unfortunately there are almost no studies to indicate the effectiveness of different forms of activities prohibiting or regulating either driving or the sale of alcohol and cigarettes, despite the natural laboratory provided by the diversity of state laws.

Reinforcements and Other Direct Attempts to Change Behavior

With the exception of the network of Alcoholics Anonymous groups, most attempts to reinforce the drinker or smoker who wants to stop or modify his habits are confined to small-scale efforts, locally organized. Smoking clinics and other group-therapy and support methods have demonstrated short-term successes, but their graduates have high rates of recidivism (Eisinger, 1971). Longer term social and emotional reinforcements for exsmokers are now being advocated. The various forms of help to individuals include techniques of operant conditioning, hypnosis, aversive therapy, and psychotherapy. Despite their variety, both group and individual approaches remain for the most part scattered, poorly funded, and underevaluated.[4]

New products to aid the would-be quitter are constantly being explored, such as a tobaccoless cigarette and chewing gum with a nicotine additive, but results have so far been disappointing. Nevertheless, in a 1972 survey more than six percent of a general population sample, or about one in six smokers, reported that they had

---

[4] Some evaluations have been undertaken. See National Clearinghouse for Smoking and Health (1972) and the *Quarterly Journal of Studies on Alcohol,* Rutgers University, New Brunswick, New Jersey.

bought some type of commercially marketed aid to smoking cessation (National Analysts, Inc., 1972).

Having the offender directly confront the possible consequences of his dangerous behavior is another type of incentive to change. Examples are the requirements by some local jurisdictions that persons convicted of driving while drunk observe the results of accidents in hospital clinics and emergency rooms. Again, we do not know how successful such methods have been.

Warnings—the Health Education Approach

Health education, primarily directed to teenagers in school, is still the principal vehicle for most preventive programs. In the 1960s, however, organizations such as the Public Health Service, the American Cancer Society, and the National Safety Council began using the mass media to reach first community audiences and then people of all ages in their homes. Some employers organized or arranged alcoholism programs for their employees.

As with other types of prevention efforts, little hard data are available by which to judge the actual results. For example, after reviewing all retrievable published studies on drinking-driving and safety campaigns, Haskins (1970) found only two that conformed to all the requirements for valid evaluation. Similarly, the National Commission on Marihuana and Drug Abuse found that no information was available from the current school drug-education programs that would permit systematic appraisal, although about forty million dollars was spent on the programs in 1972 (1973:355). After raising the possibility that some of the programs, by whetting curiosity and perhaps providing misinformation, may actually do more harm than good, the Commission recommended an immediate moratorium on the production and dissemination of new information materials.

A fundamental problem in all traditional school education efforts concerning use of cigarettes, alcohol, and other types of drugs appears to lie in confusion of objectives. What precise behavior is to be prevented? Is all experimentation with any psychoactive substance to be discouraged, or just some? If some use is condoned, which substances, by whom, at what age? And how much is too much? Finally, should the criteria for the recommendations be based on the substance's potential harm to the individual's health, its propensity to be habit-forming, or its current "moral" or legal status? Because few government or school authorities want to be held accountable for making such judgments, even the programs designed to prevent only high-risk use, or dependence, or use of some one particular substance usually end up trying to curtail all use (National Commission on Marihuana and Drug Abuse, 1973:351). In the eyes of children and youth, such a sweeping prohibition may raise serious questions of credibility, as witness the case of marihuana.

The new credo of the Division of Prevention of the National Institute of Alcohol Abuse and Alcoholism provides a welcome contrast. The thrust is to educate for responsible drinking, rather than for abstention (Chafetz, 1970–1971). There is also a general movement within school health education towards trying to strengthen children's general skills in making decisions about their own personal conduct, instead of trying to proscribe particular forms of behavior. We may hope that the new approaches will be more rigorously evaluated than those they are designed to replace.

Traditional health education programs for both youth and adults are also criticized both for the type of information they seek to communicate and the way they communicate it. Typically, they assume that, once given the necessary facts, people will either forego or stop their potentially dangerous behavior. Ignoring or discounting powerful social influences and the personal satisfactions associated with various drug uses and driving practices, programs are offered on the premise that all but neurotic risk-takers reach decisions on their daily actions through logical processes that take into account the entire range of possible consequences.

Such a simplistic premise flies in the face of all the evidence about the differences between what people understand intellectually, what they believe, and how they actually act that has been gained in laboratory and field studies by social psychologists since the end of World War II (McGuire, 1969). It results too often in fear-rousing or "commonsense" appeals, usually offered without ei-

ther a pre- or post-testing of their effects. Many of the classic
health warnings may be counterproductive. Evidence from a prospective smoking study, for example, indicates that smokers' perceived importance of the health factor contributes significantly to
their thinking about stopping, and trying to stop, but makes no contribution whatever to the success of those who actually do stop
(Horn, 1972:62). The finding makes sense if we remember that
when messages arouse anxiety or fear in a confirmed smoker, he
can always fall back on a trusted help in coping—his cigarette.

Whether in school programs or through the media, most health
messages are beamed at heterogeneous audiences. Tailoring to the
special receptivities of different target groups is thus precluded.
The constraints can be illustrated, as shown above, by the fact that
fear-rousing messages can, after all, be successfully employed for
some audiences—those for whom an appropriate response creates
no problems (Janis, 1971). Thus, while warning messages may fail
to persuade the true smoker, they may prevent the smoking habit
among nonsmokers or casual experimenters for whom the cigarette
has not yet become a strong source of pleasure, relaxation, or support.

The antismoking television counteradvertisements are generally
considered to represent a breakthrough in health education applica-
tions. Unfortunately their volume has been sharply reduced. But
again, their messages have had to be directed to broad audiences. A
study (O'Keefe, 1971) of the effects of such telecasts in central
Florida reports that nonsmokers were highly reinforced in their behavior by the messages, that more than half the smokers who wanted to quit said the messages had helped them to do so, or to cut
down, but that among the confirmed smokers—those smoking two
to three packs a day—they made no impact.

In the early years of the smoking counteradvertisements, fear-
arousal techniques were commonly employed. More recently, responding to findings from communications research, the campaigns
have become more subtle in their appeals: "For someone you love,
stop smoking." Seat-belt use and safe-driving media campaigns
have followed suit.

Another challenge to health education is to have the message delivered by a trustworthy source. The 1972 survey conducted by the President's Commission on Health Education (National Analysts, Inc., 1972) not surprisingly reports that most people find the physician the most persuasive conveyor of health information. (The media are second.) At one level, the American Cancer Society has been successful in mobilizing physician speakers for school and community lectures. It may be assumed that direct advice from the physician to his patients about their health-threatening smoking and drinking habits might be even more effective. According to a recent study of medical practice by Coe and Brehm (1972:60), however, that type of counseling is not usual. Among the nearly 1,600 physicians they interviewed, only 17.6 percent mentioned warnings against smoking among the types of counseling frequently given; none mentioned advice concerning drinking behavior. (By contrast, 65.0 percent recommended exercise, and 60.6 percent recommended diets.)

Finally, the settings in which effective communication about driving, smoking, and drinking practices take place have not been sufficiently studied. Some types of messages are presumably best received in work or peer groups, some in one-to-one talks, some in family settings, some through direct observation of the consequences, as in accident wards.

Whatever their shortcomings, the warning programs have succeeded in alerting the public to the dangers of smoking and of failure to wear seat belts—dangers that are now almost universally acknowledged. It can be argued that people's verbalization of their desire to avoid those dangers, noted at the outset, is perhaps a necessary though not a sufficient condition for changing behavior and that more time is required for the switch to new habits. Certainly even though forty-five million persons still smoke and new millions of children and youth start smoking each year, it is a hopeful sign that thirteen million smokers have stopped and that the majority of teenage smokers say they expect to stop within five years (Lieberman Research, Inc., 1969:118).

The National Commission on Marihuana and Drug Abuse

(1973:13) found, however, that both adults and youth in the population surveyed seriously misjudge and underestimate the dangers of alcohol in comparison with other drugs. Here prevention attempts have only a small base of public understanding on which to build.

In summary, the effects of the many special efforts to induce less dangerous behavior with respect to drinking, driving, and smoking are largely unknown. Because the problems they address continue almost unabated, we are tempted to discount their worth. But, except in the rare instances where evaluation has been built in, it cannot be known how much worse the present situation would have been without them.

Proposed Strategy for Interventions

It seems apparent from this review of the goals and current attempts at prevention that a major strategy in future activities must be to segment the problems as finely as possible and to design preventive programs accordingly. Simple prohibitions of behavior, on the one hand, or warning signals, on the other, cannot be expected to accomplish more than a small part of the larger purpose. It is encouraging to note that both the antismoking forces and the National Institute for Alcohol Abuse and Alcoholism are now beginning to use that strategy in their preventive efforts, recognizing that completely different types of campaigns, appeals, and supports must be directed to nonusers, moderate users, and heavy users of cigarettes and alcohol, as well as to users of different ages and socioeconomic backgrounds, ethnic groups, or whatever. When an effort is being made to change the customary behavior patterns of millions of people, such tactics appear to be essential.

If the resources devoted to prevention are to be allocated to areas where they hold promise of maximum payoff, it is suggested that the concept of segmentation be further elaborated to become the underlying framework for policy formation and for research.

The time dimension is another factor important both in planning preventive activities and evaluating them. How quickly must the attempted intervention succeed if it is to avert disastrous consequences? Can we afford to wait until the potential offender has reached a stage in life or a situation where he is receptive to change? Furthermore, at what ages or in what life situations may it perhaps be counterproductive for the outsider to attempt to influence a person's behavior? What particular types of intervention work and when? Finally, what are the effects of persuasion at time X on an individual's actions at time Y?

It is suggested here that in addition to pinpointing target populations and individuals at high risk, models be constructed that would (1) specify the time frames within which countermeasures must be introduced if harmful consequences both to the individual and to his potential victims are to be avoided and (2) plot life curves of receptivity to various approaches for changing attitudes and behavior. Such models would permit the selection of the types and timing of interventions most appropriate to a particular situation and make it possible to develop priorities for action.

Our knowledge, for example, that driving while drunk by both young and alcoholic drivers accounts for a huge proportion of our highway deaths and disabilities suggests that society cannot afford to wait for the slow processes of attitude and behavior change to take effect. Interventions, if they are to save the immediate potential victims and avert the costs, must be mounted swiftly and be of different kinds. Similarly, since young males constitute the largest group of crash victims, reaching them would seem to be the obvious priority for safety-belt campaigns. Success might be measured not only in terms of the proportion of seat-belt wearers among all drivers, but in terms of their use by that particular high-risk group.

In contrast, teenage smoking, however much it may be deplored, is not apt to cause immediate loss of life; there is more time in which to mount suitable preventive actions. We know, too, that smoking prevalence increases with age until it reaches a peak of nearly half the population in the twenty-six to thirty-four age bracket but that it then decreases. Interventions might be more cost effective if they were constructed in the light of this life use curve. Instead of the present high concentration of education efforts during the resistant teen years, facts about the consequences of smoking might be more usefully beamed at elementary school children, whose information-seeking propensities are high, and again at young adults in colleges, trade unions, etc. Physicians and other health professionals might be pressured to give special antismoking counseling in the course of all their contacts with this age group, such as at preemployment and premarital health examinations and, most especially, to expectant mothers during the course of prenatal care. To help them in their quitting efforts, the number of voluntary stop-smoking and after-smoking mutual support groups might be stepped up sharply and perhaps linked to other types of organized social activity in communities.

Whether or not these particular approaches would be feasible or effective is not the point. They are put forth merely to illustrate the need for flexibility in selecting and timing preventive measures according to some model that takes into account both the realities of the dangers and the likelihood of receptivity to incentives for behavior change.

Such a strategy, however, requires much better knowledge than we presently have about the characteristics of the high-risk groups to whom special efforts should be directed, about the natural history of developing (and diminishing) danger patterns, and about types of interventions that will work in given situations.

Future Research Directions

The rich corpus of recent research findings on the nature of drinking, smoking, and driving practices in the United States has given us a solid base on which to build. As with so many problems, however, identification of the precursors of harmful behavior patterns has been retrospective, reconstructing associated factors of cultural, situational, or personality characteristics by the tenuous wisdom of hindsight. The limitations are obvious. To what extent, for example, do people become problem drinkers because they are poor, depressed, and maladjusted, and to what extent do people become poor, depressed, and maladjusted because they are problem drinkers? Cahalan and Room (1972) who have been responsible for developing most of the national data on problem drinkers, are now following subsamples from former surveys in longitudinal studies in which changes in people's lives between two points in time can be related to subsequent changes in drinking behavior, health, and interpersonal relations. At another stage, controlled experimental studies are needed in which various remedial measures are implemented for test groups with different characteristics and degrees of drinking problems, and their effects measured over time and compared with controls.

If preventive measures are to be more finely tuned, we badly need to be able to identify predictors of populations at special risk. Beginnings are being made. A recent study in Ontario has identified several factors in the predriving histories of young applicants for licenses that were significantly associated with future accident records. The factors included failure in one or more elementary school grades; having been charged with a criminal offense; regular cigarette smoking at or before age sixteen; and having worked full-time during the school year before age seventeen, presumptive dropout (Kraus et al., 1970). If these or other accident-risk predictors can be generalized, the license application might be used to identify persons for special driver-education efforts; at the least, the benefit of the doubt on licensing examinations and after subsequent driving citations might systematically be withheld. If similar types of predictors could be developed at early ages for people at special risk for dangerous drinking and for becoming "addictive," other kinds of special preventive measures could be tailored to their apparent needs.

A final important avenue for future research is for better evaluation of the effects of all the types of preventive efforts currently being employed, as well as for the pilot testing of new ones, with appropriate feedback into planning and policy decisions. The lack of such processes, noted throughout this paper, undoubtedly leads to considerable waste of the scant budgets presently allotted to prevention.

The anticigarette forces are in the forefront of attempts to identify the factors associated with a person's success or failure in
changing his potentially harmful behavior. In longitudinal studies,
samples of smokers and nonsmokers drawn from the national
smoking surveys of 1964 and 1966 were reinterviewed in 1970; in
addition, a new national sample was surveyed in 1970. Data are
being analyzed by multivariate techniques to determine the predictors of change in smoking behavior and the interactions among
them (Horn, 1972:60).

Some preliminary findings have been mentioned above, such as
the unimportance of the health factor by itself in contributing to
stop-smoking success. Other counterintuitive findings are that the
mastery theme—the importance of being able to control one's own
destiny and be one's own decisionmaker—does not in itself contribute to any step of the process of thinking about stopping, trying to
stop, or actually succeeding. The exemplar motivation—the importance of being a good example to somebody else who is important
to you—was found to contribute significantly to thinking about
stopping but to make no contribution to trying to stop. Where the
exemplar role is important to people, it actually interferes with the
likelihood of success when they try to stop smoking, and interference applies both to short-term and long-term success. However, a
person's confidence in his ability to stop smoking, while not contributing to his thinking about stopping, does contribute significantly to his trying to stop and to his ultimate success.

Further studies revealing some of the complex motivational patterns that seem to either block or lead to changes in human attitudes and behavior are essential if consumer incentives are to be
designed that will actually accomplish their purpose. The myths underlying "common sense" approaches have been too long with us.

Summary

A review of the literature on efforts to avert the costly consequences of dangerous driving, drinking, and smoking yields a picture of many well-intentioned, often expensive, usually uncoordi-

nated, and almost entirely unevaluated activities taking place in the context of ill-defined and often contradictory public policies. On the one hand, the consumer receives many types of social reinforcements for his potentially dangerous habits; on the other, a variety of attempted prohibitions, indirect and direct incentives, and warnings are placed before him to urge that he refrain from carrying those habits to the point of abuse.

It is suggested that large human and economic savings are possible if the present levels of such abuse can be reduced. Preventive efforts might be most cost effective if goals were better delineated; if societal reinforcements of potentially harmful behavior were systematically reduced; if the target groups for whom interventions are designed were more highly segmented and their characteristics better understood; if models were constructed to permit better focused and better timed interventions; and if the effects of preventive measures were evaluated. Finally, building on the already considerable accomplishments of epidemiologic and behavioral studies in these areas, we need further research to explicate the etiology and natural history of dangerous behavior habits in populations and individuals at high risk, and to increase our knowledge about the complex of factors predisposing to positive behavior change.

References

Allen, William *and* William A. Fackler
 1967   "An exploratory survey and smoking control program conducted among parents of Philadelphia school children," Pp. 63–65 in Zagona, Salvatore V. (ed.), Studies and Issues in Smoking Behavior. Tucson: University of Arizona Press.
Barcha, R., M. A. Steward, *and* S. B. Guze
 1968   "The prevalence of alcoholism among general hospital ward patients." American Journal of Psychiatry 125: 681–684.
Berger, H. *and* M. Schweigler
 1972   "Smoking characteristics of methadone patients." Journal of the American Medical Association 222 (November 6): 705 (Letter).

Brecher, Edward M.
    1972   Licit and Illicit Drugs. Boston: Little Brown and Company.
Brenner, B.
    1967   "Alcoholism and fatal accidents." Quarterly Journal of
              Studies on Alcohol 28: 517–528.
Cahalan, Don
    1970   Problem Drinkers. San Francisco: Jossey-Bass.
Cahalan, Don, et al.
    1969   American Drinking Practices. New Brunswick: Rutgers
              Center of Alcohol Studies.
Cahalan, D. *and* R. Room
    1972   "Problem drinking among American men." Monographs of
              the Rutgers Center of Alcohol Studies, No. 7. New Bruns-
              wick, N.J.: Rutgers Center of Alcohol Studies.
Chafetz, Morris E.
    1970–1971   "The prevention of alcoholism." International Jour-
                 nal of Psychiatry 9: 329–348.
Coe, Rodney M. *and* Henry P. Brehm
    1972   Preventive Health Care for Adults: A Study of Medical
              Practice. New Haven: College and University Press.
Council, F. M.
    1969   "Seat belts: A follow-up study of their use under normal
              driving conditions." Journal of Safety Research 1:
              127–136.
Economic Research Services
    1972   Tobacco Situation. U.S. Department of Agriculture TS
              142, December.
Eisinger, Richard A.
    1971   "Psychosocial predictors of smoking recidivism." Journal of
              Health and Social Behavior 12 (December): 355–361
Haskins, Jack B.
    1970   "Evaluative research on the effects of mass communications
              safety campaigns: A methodological critique." Journal of
              Safety Research 2 (June): 86–96.
Hedrick, James L.
    1971   "The economic costs of cigarette smoking." HSMHA
              Health Reports 86 (February): 179–182.
Hicks, Nancy
    1972   "Ex-health chief hits tobacco ads." New York Times, New
              York, New York. October 25: 6.

Holtman, Alfonse G.
  1964   "Estimating the demand for public health services; the alco-
           holism case." Public Finance 19: 351–358.
Horn, Daniel
  1972   "Determinants of change." Pp. 58–76 in Richardson, R. G.
           (ed.), Second World Conference on Smoking and Health.
           New York: Pitman Publishing.
Janis, Irving L.
  1971   "When warnings fail." Pp. 123–144 in Janis, Irving L.,
           Stress and Frustration. New York: Harcourt Brace Jova-
           novich, Inc.
Kramer, Ester H.
  1973   "A review of the literature relating to the impact of the
           broadcast media on drug use and abuse." Pp. 586–611 in
           National Commission on Marihuana and Drug Abuse,
           Drug Use in America: Problem in Perspective. Appendix.
           Washington, D.C.: Government Printing Office.
Kraus, A. S., R. Steele, W. R. Ghent, *and* M. G. Thompson
  1970   "Pre-driving identification of young drivers with a high risk
           of accidents." Journal of Safety Research 2 (June):
           55–66.
Lieberman Research, Inc.
  1969   The Teenager Looks at Cigarette Smoking. Chicago: The
           American Cancer Society, September.
McGuire, William J.
  1969   "The nature of attitudes and attitude changes." Pp.
           136–314 in Lindzey, Gardner *and* Eliot Aronson (eds.),
           The Handbook of Social Psychology, 2nd ed., Vol. III.
           New York: Addison-Wesley Publishing.
National Analysts, Inc.
  1972   A Study of Health Practices and Opinions. U.S. Depart-
           ment of Commerce, PB-210 978, June.
National Clearinghouse for Smoking and Health
  1967   Smoking and Illness. Washington, D.C.: Government Print-
           ing Office.
  1972   Directory of On-Going Research in Smoking and Health.
           Washington, D.C.: Government Printing Office.
National Commission on Marihuana and Drug Abuse
  1973   Drug Use in America: Problem in Perspective. Washing-
           ton, D.C.: Government Printing Office, March.

National Institute on Alcohol Abuse and Alcoholism
    n.d.   Statement of Purpose, mimeo.
National Safety Council
    1972   Accident Facts. Chicago: The National Safety Council.
O'Donnell, John
    1969   Narcotics Addicts in Kentucky. PHS Publication No. 1881.
                Washington, D.C.: Government Printing Office.
O'Keefe, Timothy
    1971   "The anti-smoking commercials: A study of television's im-
                pact on behavior." The Public Opinion Quarterly 35 (Sum-
                mer): 242–248.
Palola, E. G., T. L. Dorpat, *and* W. R. Larson
    1962   "Alcoholism and suicidal behavior." Pp. 511–534 in Palola,
                E. G., T. L. Dorpat, *and* W. R. Larson, Society, Culture
                and Drinking Patterns. New York: John Wiley and Sons.
Peele, Stanley
    In press   Love and Addiction. Middlesex, England: Penguin
                Press.
Public Health Service
    1970   The Facts About Smoking. PHS Publication No. 1712, re-
                vised, January.
Read, C. R.
    1972   "American experience with newspapers and magazines."
                Pp. 127–131 in Richardson, R. G. (ed.), Second World
                Conference on Smoking and Health. New York: Pitman
                Publishing.
Robertson, Leon, et al.
    1972   "Factors associated with observed safety belt use." Journal
                of Health and Social Behavior 13 (March): 18–24.
Rommel, R. C. S.
    1959   "Personality characteristics and attitudes of youthful acci-
                dent-repeater drivers." Traffic Safety Research Review 3:
                13–14.
Simon, Julian L.
    1968   "The health economics of cigarette consumption." Journal
                of Human Resources 3: 111–117.
Ubell, Earl
    1972   "Health behavior change: A political model." Preventive
                Medicine 1 (March): 209–221.

U.S. Department of Health, Education, and Welfare
  1971   Alcohol and Health. Washington, D.C.: Government Printing Office, December.
U.S. Department of Transportation
  1968   1968 Alcohol and Highway Safety Report, Washington, D.C., Government Printing Office.
U.S. Statistical Abstract 1972.
Waller, J. A.
  1967   "Identification of problem drinking among drunken drivers." Journal of the American Medical Association 200 (April 10): 114–120.
Wechsler, Henry, E. H. Kasey, Denise Thum, *and* Harold Demone, Jr.
  1969   "Alcohol level and home accidents: A study of emergency service patients." Public Health Reports 84: 1043–1050.
Wilson, J. Q., M. H. Moore, *and* D. I. Wheat, Jr.
  1972   "The problem of heroin." The Public Interest 29 (Fall): 3–28.
Wolfgang, Marvin E.
  1958   Patterns in Criminal Homicide. Philadelphia: University of Pennsylvania Press.
Wynder, Ernest L.
  1972   "Preventive medicine introduction." Preventive Medicine 1 (March): 1–5.

Incentives and the Consumption of Preventive Health Care Services

STUART O. SCHWEITZER*

Definitions of Preventive Care

In its broadest form preventive medicine has been defined as "that part of medicine concerned in particular with the advancement of the purpose of promoting health and preventing illness . . ." (Clark, 1967:1). Promoting health involves planning and action at the community and the personal level in such areas as community health services and environmental health.

Preventing illness, in contrast, is disease specific, though the term "preventing" is used in different senses. Clark (1967:4–5) distinguishes between "primary prevention," meaning averting the occurrence of disease, and "secondary prevention," meaning halting or slowing the progress of a disease. Other authors add a third category, "tertiary prevention," and define it as restoring normal or nearly normal function to a person after the progress of an illness has been stopped (Leavall and Clark, 1965). It can as readily be defined as "rehabilitation," with the domain of preventive medicine restricted to either the outright prevention of an illness or its effective diagno-

* The author is grateful for the research assistance of Joseph Kane.

34

sis and treatment at an early stage. That is the approach used in this paper.

When discussing the role of incentives in the consumption of preventive health services, it is meaningful to make another distinction in the type of care given. The individual can seek medical care either on his own initiative or on referral from a health professional. Because of the willingness of consumers to delegate authority over health matters to physicians and other members of the health "team," most health care decisions are made jointly with the providers (Klarman, 1965:14–15). Decisions of an entirely separate kind are those made by consumers without the aid of professional judgment. They are the decisions to seek initial contact with the medical system and can result either from an awareness of symptoms of disease or a wish to prevent illness or obtain early diagnosis.

In studying incentives to determine the use of preventive health-care services, it is fruitful to consider principally those medical services that are initiated solely by consumers. In other situations included in this study, the patient is urged by a health professional to undergo procedures for which some of the same decision factors enter. But of central concern in our health-care system is the influence of incentives upon the individual's decision to seek professional counsel and services.

An interesting subcase of the self-initiated contact is the contact occurring without clinical symptoms of illness. The patient presumes himself to be in good health and is interested solely in continuing in that state. Physicians, of course, can and do recommend checkup visits. But the primary interest here is to study the role of incentives in the initial decision to seek medical care, especially before any specific disease symptoms occur.

Decision Scheme for Health-Care Utilization

To see the nature of the decision process inherent in preventive care it is instructive to construct a scheme of the determinants of

decision-making for the entire health system. Some elements from
Kalimo (1969:4–5) and Rabin (et al., 1972:21) have been bor-
rowed for Fig. 1.

Members of the population at risk are defined as being in a
state of either health or sickness according to objective medical criteria. But an individual is not necessarily aware that he is or is not

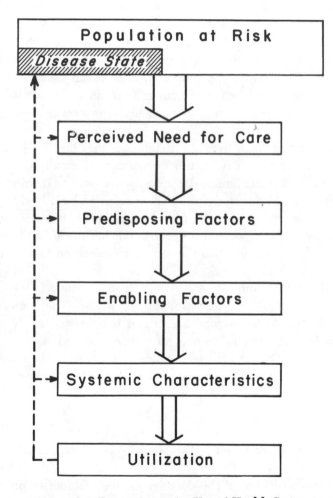

Figure 1. *Determinants for Use of Health Care*

sick. In fact, as shown in Fig. 2, there are four possible disease-perception states.

DISEASE – PERCEPTION STATES

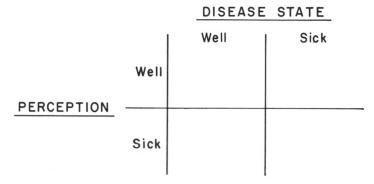

Figure 2.   *Disease-Perception States*

The diagonal elements are the "true" states: A sick person perceives himself as sick, and a well person perceives himself as well. The other two states, however, involve errors in perception: Either a well person believes he is sick, or a sick person mistakenly assumes he is well.

But perception of disease is neither necessary nor sufficient to effect medical-service utilization. It is insufficient because of the intervening influences shown in Fig. 1, and it is unnecessary because of the self-initiated, purely preventive type of visit. The incentives influencing the use of health services in general, and preventive services in particular, can be grouped according to the classifications shown in Fig. 1.

Population at Risk

The factors determining the risk of the individual are both personal and community based. The personal factors are demographic, occupational, and psychic characteristics, the person's life style, and his personal habits. A community-based factor consists of environmental conditions. The individual's medical history, of course, is a personal factor influencing his current health status. Most of the risk-determining factors fall in the pre-prevention phase of health care. The important consideration for decisions involving preventive health care, however, is the objective assessment of risk. Individuals exposed to greater risks will, other things being equal, desire more preventive care. Thus, inner-city ghetto residents would desire pediatric screening for lead poisoning to a greater extent than suburban residents.

Perception of Need

The "other things" are rarely "equal," and the perceived need for care is not equal among individuals. What are the factors determining the perceived need for preventive health care? Ludwig and Gibson (1961) suggest several variables influencing the use of preventive services. But only one—income—appears to influence perception of need for care. The income variable enters into so many studies of the use of preventive care that its importance can hardly be denied, but there is little agreement about how its influence acts (Bullough, 1972). By itself, income certainly determines ability to afford care, and it will be discussed subsequently under the heading of "enabling influences."

Correlates of income, however, affect sensitivity to health. Education, both in its broadest form and when specifically related to hygiene, is a crucial factor. Another correlate is health status and medical history. How is anyone to know he is sick unless he knows what it is like to be well? The poverty circle often limits a person's experience through exposing him to such a chain of sickness—some of it chronic in nature—that his perception of illness is considerably weakened, and he would require a much higher severity threshold to realize that medical attention is warranted.

Furthermore, whether or not an individual is actually ill, use of preventive care implies an awareness of the risk of disease. General education will ordinarily give an individual a general awareness of the concepts of health and sickness and a feeling that he has some control over his position in either state. Education related specifically to health, such as hygiene, will provide knowledge about the physiological system, agents causing sickness, and available countermeasures. An even more specific form of education will be campaigns directed toward a particular disease or screening program (e.g., "Cancer's Danger Signals") where perception is heightened and directed toward a single disease entity.

Predisposition to Seek Health Care

Perception of the need for health care can be considered a sine qua non for the use of preventive health services, but, as Fig. 1 illustrates, utilization will be effected only if individuals are predisposed to seek professional medical care. A number of factors are cited as making the individual receptive to use of health care: education, social class, anomie, culture, ethnic group, tastes, need to reinforce social status, social contact, institutional involvement, family role, and past experience with the medical system.

Education again enters the picture, this time as a determinant of respect for medical intervention. Both general physician use and use of preventive services are significantly higher for those with some education beyond high school than for others (U.S. Comptroller General, 1972:6). An educated invidivual is less likely to feel the sense of "powerlessness" mentioned by Bullough as a deterrent to seeking preventive health-care services.

We know far less, however, about the objective need or cost-effectiveness of preventive health care than we should, so that at least some of the conventional wisdom pertaining to preventive health care ought to be treated with healthy doubt (Schweitzer, 1973; Cochrane, 1969). Somers and Somers (1961:163–164) indicate their skepticism in the observation that "a 1955 NIF-NORC survey found that 80 percent of the people believe they should see a doctor for a regular check-up, even when they feel well, but only 29 percent do so."

The Kaiser Foundation health plan's change from a rigid annual schedule for physical examinations for its younger members illustrates the problem of assessing the use of preventive services.

When the standard or norm is found to be less than cost-effective, can we criticize individuals for failing to have an annual physical examination? The irony might well be that better educated individuals find it less rational to use presymptomatic preventive care than do those with less education, who have been conditioned by advertising programs sponsored by various disease prevention societies.

Cochrane illustrates our present lack of information: While the time will undoubtedly come when a wide range of conditions will be capable of early detection and amenable to early treatment, this time has yet to come for all but a very few conditions. Only if and when that situation exists can the community be approached and offered, in return for their cooperation, significant benefit to a reasonably sized proportion of those screened (1967:213).

The effect of a person's ethnic group on physician utilization has been shown (McKinlay, 1972), though it is impossible to separate the effects of social class, tastes, and cultural background. It is apparent, however, that some groups—Jews, for instance—are far more likely to use physician services for a given set of circumstances than are some other ethnic groups. The reason for their greater predisposition is not clearly understood.

Some individuals use physician services to bolster their social status among their peers (McKinlay, 1972). To them a physician is a symbol—perhaps an example of Veblen's conspicuous consumption. To people at the lower end of the socioeconomic scale, however, the physician is an integral part of the social system. Alienation from the system means less use of medical services. Several factors contribute to the feeling of separation from the health organization that some individuals experience. Certainly, physical geographic distance is one. The psychological barrier facing an inner-city ghetto resident, for example, as he thinks about visiting an affluent white section of the city for a medical examination is formidable. Even something as innocuous as architecture plays a role. We often admire a public building if it is imposing, but that characteristic itself makes the facility forbidding to someone who is insecure for other reasons. The style of architecture, the dress and manner of health-center staff, and the formality of regulations accentuate the differences between the patient and the provider.

A health center can, however, facilitate social contact among patients. A facility where the potential for such an atmosphere is recognized will be closer to the people it serves and will tend to lessen alienation.

The opposite of alienation is involvement. By institutional involvement Bullough (1972) and others mean the individual's sense of participation in the organization of the social system. Does a person feel that the means of running his life are, at least partly, under his own control? Institutional involvement is probably best understood as an underlying determinant of alienation.

Much has been written recently concerning the role of the family in influencing a person's predisposition to respond to perceived health "cues." Rivkin (1972) found that women with family and career responsibilities are more likely to seek professional medical care than are women with family responsibilities alone, for given levels of morbidity. Our social structure defines acceptable patterns of behavior, unless the need is particularly acute and use of medical services is less appropriate for non-employed family members. It is accepted, however, that other members of the same family will seek professional advice at the slightest provocation.

A final predisposing factor deserving attention is the person's medical history, which is important for a number of reasons. A past illness not only attunes perceptions to symptoms of illness but also determines willingness to delegate responsibility for the matter to a health professional. If a person were fortunate enough at one time to experience a spontaneous remission in symptoms, he is more likely to rely on "things getting better by themselves." But if in the past encounter with the symptoms the condition became worse, he is likely to feel disposed to seek medical attention early. This finding is consistent with the observation that prenatal care is more likely to be sought late in pregnancy by women who had given birth to several children (Watkins, 1968).

Enabling Influences

What determines whether an individual who is willing to use health services, is actually able to do so? As the schematic diagram (Fig. 1) illustrates, professional health care will not be sought, no matter how positive the perceptions and attitudes are, unless specific barriers to care can be overcome. Economists have given considerable attention to the effects of both price and income on utilization (Wilensky and Holahan, 1972; Rosett and Huang, 1973).

The literature is by no means consistent in either price—or income—elasticity estimates. Wilensky and Holahan (1972) use coverage elasticities (a sort of quasi-price elasticity) of -0.33 and 0.67. Rosett and Huang (1973) estimate price elasticities as ranging from -0.35 to -1.5, depending upon whether the coinsurance rate is low or high. Rosenthal (1970) estimates price elasticities for various medical and surgical services that range up to a maximum negative value of -0.7. Feldstein and Severson's (1964) estimate of price elasticity is -1.12. The range of the estimates is so broad that any single generalization is bound to be misleading. Nonetheless, if we adopt the position that the price elasticity for health services is in the neighborhood of -1.0, it follows that utilization of health care is rather responsive to price (and hence to insurance coverage).

Income-elasticity estimates, however, are considerably lower, implying that use of health services varies little with income, once other factors (such as access) are held constant. The estimates are thus in full agreement with the empirical work of Grunlick and his associates (1970a), indicating that gross differences in health-care utilization patterns that have been attributed to income differentials shrink significantly when the population is enrolled in a comprehensive, prepaid plan.

It is reasonable to expect higher price elasticities (in absolute value) for less serious (elective) procedures than for more serious (acute) procedures. Unfortunately, only Rosenthal attempts to disaggregate medical expenditures into services or procedures, but the variables he uses make the findings somewhat less than entirely useful for this study of preventive health care. The income-elasticity estimates, shown to be rather low by Rosett and Huang (1973) and others are also for an aggregate of services, and we do not know if they are applicable to preventive services.

Recently consideration has been given to the nonmonetary costs of health-care utilization. Time is the major economic factor in the possible variables. Everyone is aware of the monetary equivalency of time and money, but other noneconomic factors, such as fear, alienation, and inconvenience, are barriers too. All of them could be thought of as having an economic counterpart—as "everything has a price." That approach might not be the most useful one to take, though for economists the temptation exists.

Both Simon and Smith (1973) and Acton (1973) have found that time is a significant cost in health-care utilization. In Simon and Smith's study part of a university's student health service was moved further from campus. As one would expect, total utilization was reduced. But more interesting was the observation that time-consuming services were less affected than were visits of short duration. The increased time necessary to visit the relocated clinic was viewed in relative rather than absolute terms by potential users.

In the Acton study, the pattern of health-care utilization at the Palo Alto Clinic was noted both before and after a copayment was introduced. Here, too, the short visits were more adversely affected than the long visits. Again, time was being treated as another element in "cost," to which the new fee schedule was being added.

An important characteristic of the time factor is the payment of wages for time off from employment. Most full-time employees are granted sick leave to compensate them for the time spent seeking health care. Whether or not sick leave removed the time-cost barrier, however, depends upon a number of considerations. Is the sick-leave allowance large enough to cover the actual need? More to the point: Is the allowance perceived as adequate? If it is not, or if there is doubt, then use of the allowance is not thought of as being without cost but is saved so that it can be used "when it's really necessary." The same consideration would apply if accumulated sick leave could be transformed into vacation time—either legally or illegally.

Far less formal accounting for his time is required of a professional than of other workers. Therefore, on the surface, the cost of his time off is usually zero. Occasionally the opportunity cost is also essentially zero, but usually it is far greater than that. As a result, the high-income, salaried executives, for whom price and income considerations would be of little importance, are often the most reluctant to take time off to seek medical care. Again the need for disaggregation of service is important.

As Simon, Smith, and Acton have found, the incentive effect of lost time depends upon the expected time requirements of a health visit, and certainly the perceived urgency of the visit as well. The use of primary preventive care, especially the self-initiated, pre-symptomatic types, is thus likely to be most affected by time considerations and sick-leave policies.

Certainly an important enabling factor is knowledge of the points of access to the system. Regardless of the system's accessibility, a consumer must know the system's characteristics and how to use them. Ignorance is most serious in the scatter-site, atomistic, fee-for-service system currently prevalent in the United States. Often the consumer has no specific point of contact at which he can initiate health care. Even when a contact point exists, the site is more likely to be an institution than a specific health professional, especially for the poor (Andersen and Anderson, 1967).

Similar in nature to knowledge of the health-care system and its access points is the degree of institutional involvement. As discussed earlier, a person who is involved with the "system" can use that system to serve his needs. The alienated individual, who is passive toward institutions, is at the mercy of their maneuvers and unable to use their benefits.

The family role is a significant determinant of ability to use health services. Since sick-leave policies are strictly limited to the employed (and usually the full-time employed), nonmarket workers, such as housewives, have no means of reducing the opportunity cost of time spent seeking medical care. A housewife's tasks usually include child care—a full-time activity, especially if preschool children are in the family. Babysitters are normally hard to find during the day, when older children are either in school or are engaged in after-school activities. When sitters are most available, health services are typically unavailable except on an emergency basis. When husbands are at home to tend children, the timing is again out of phase with physicians' hours. Presently there is no organized way for a mother to acquire the services of a responsible housekeeper during an occasional daytime period. Given those constraints, it is not surprising that mothers have a higher pain threshold before seeking professional health care than employed women (Rivkin, 1972).

System Characteristics

Once a person is both predisposed and able to use preventive-care services, he must actively seek and make contact with the health-care system in order to actualize his preferences. At that point the structural and procedurial characteristics of the existing health-delivery system itself must have some effect on that actualization—i.e., on the quantity and mix of medical care demanded. The demand for care is determined in the context of the costs imposed by the system upon the user. Costs, of course, take many forms, most of which are nonmonetary but clearly real. To a certain extent there is an overlap in this discussion with the incentives discussed as predisposing and enabling factors. In the earlier discussions, however, it was intended to show the effect of those incentives on the structure of patient demand for services while this discussion really addresses the characteristics of the supply system as they affect demand. Consideration of supply incentives was not part of the specific intent of this paper, but a discussion of consumer incentives seems to necessitate at least an overview of the supply side. Previous medical history and experience, for example, are discussed as predisposing factors in consumer demand. Yet it seems that the residual predisposition to use professional health services is a direct function of the system as it functioned (or failed to function) in earlier episodes.

It seems useful, therefore, to discuss the system characteristics: the structure of and access to organization and resources. The structural characteristics of the health-care system will largely be exogenous—the independent variables determining a patient's actual status with respect to many of the predisposing and enabling factors. The price structure of services provided by the nearest medical facilities will determine the effect of money income on decisions to use services. Despite low money income, for example, university students are relatively high users of university clinics and medical facilities. (They face essentially the same decision criteria as users of prepaid group practice.) Where money charges increase (whether through fee-for-service, deductible, or copayment structure), utilization has been shown to drop significantly (Scitovsky and Snyder, 1972; Phelps and Newhouse, 1972).

Other system characteristics will also affect nonmonetary (but equally real) costs. If preventive services are provided or available, levels of utilization and predisposition to use services among the target population could well depend upon the ancillary health education and outreach services provided in conjunction with the preventive care. The relationship is particularly marked when the target population is lower-middle class or below that in socioeconomic status or is constrained by strong cultural or ethnic biases against professional medical services.

Where such constraints cause underutilization of available preventive services, a unified and effective intervention strategy involving education and outreach, possibly through the tying of health counseling to other social services, will be important in developing appropriate incentive structures. There is hardly a single incentive among the predisposing and enabling factors that could not be favorably affected by the provision of an education-outreach service. Rosenstock (1969) found a strong correlation between "health beliefs" and health behavior, and there is little evidence to indicate that subjecive beliefs could not be altered by an effective intervention strategy.

Additionally, the more psychological incentives, such as alienation and fear (conversely social involvement, knowledge and understanding) can be significantly affected by decisions made by those providing preventive services concerning the mix, location, and provision of services—that is, the circumstances of contact with the health professional. The circumstances of contact are complementary to outreach and affect the disposition of the patient as he makes contact with the health-care system. As has been noted in several studies (Ludwig and Gibson, 1961; Watkins, 1968; Mindlin and Densen, 1971), the determinants of health-care utilization are so complex that removal of financial barriers alone will not suffice to ensure desired levels of utilization. A necessary adjunct to the education-outreach effort will be the structuring of services in such a way and in such an environment that the lessons of education-outreach are reinforced rather than negated.

The considerations of intervention and delivery lead to more specific questions concerning service mix and level of services provided. Obviously, decisions in those areas must be made by the providers of preventive services within the context of limited medical resources and the demand for all other forms of medical care. Wilson (1971) and Ferrer (1968), among others, have addressed the problems of developing criteria for the decisions. Ferrer does not consider the optimal level of preventive services, other than in a brief closing chapter on future trends. Rather, he sets about to establish some criteria for assessing the effectiveness of screening procedures by looking at the state of knowledge on screening tests and their evaluation in association with health education in a comprehensive health service. His criteria, however, only suggest which individual procedures pay off, while saying little about appropriate aggregate levels of utilization. Wilson expands the analysis to examine the need for change in pattern, distribution, and use of medical resources. He describes an initial framework for decision-making about allocation of medical resources to screening as a preventive action, and he discusses the substantial need for additional research.

Decisions about service mix and levels of preventive services will also be affected by the mix of input resources available to the suppliers of preventive care and constraints on delivery of the services potentially available. The point here is that we must reconsider our decisions about producing inputs to health care (e.g., physicians) and about resources devoted to delivery simultaneously with our consideration of optimal levels of services. As Wilson points out, if optimal capacity for providing preventive care is created, there is no guarantee that the demand for the product will be sufficient or appropriate. (The way in which services are produced and distributed is as important as the decision to produce. Heretofore, preventive-care services have been produced and distributed in such a way as to find actual utilization well below expectations.)

One major consideration here is the spatial distribution of preventive-care resources. It not only affects the direct costs of services provided but also is a major determinant of the level of access that the client at risk has to the proposed service. Large centralized facilities can produce preventive and screening services at a relatively low direct cost. But, in fact, such facilities shift some direct costs to the client population at risk and increase almost all indirect costs, such as time costs and the costs of social alienation. If the increase in real cost facing the individual consumer is too great, reduced utilization could result in much higher average costs. Thus, centralized facilities compound the entry problem and can increase consumer disincentives by reducing the effectiveness of outreach, ease of access, number of entry points, and patient perception of benefits.

Utilization of Modes of Health Care

The "health-care system" has been referred to throughout the previous discussion of factors determining health-care utilization. In fact, what this country has is not a system but a "nonsystem." The private practitioner, fee-for-service organization mode is composed of a vast array of nonintegrated units, each operating independently of one another, with only casual lines of communication between them. To conclude the discussion of factors determining health-care utilization and of preventive health care in particular, the system characteristics are outlined and the components most susceptible to influence by the factors outlined above are noted.

The basic units of health-care delivery in the United States are office-based physicians, general hospitals, and extended-care facilities. Within the hospital unit are the emergency service and the out-patient departments, in addition to other acute-care services. Under a broad definition all provider units render preventive care. But office-based physicians and hospital outpatient facilities provide the bulk of primary preventive care and all the presymptomatic, self-initiated care.

Composition of the service utilization has concerned planners and others for some time, as office-based physicians and hospital outpatient clinics provide much the same type of medical care, though the costs differ widely. Furthermore, inpatient care can be substituted for some outpatient care, opening up the possibility of even greater misuse of facilities—depending upon the price structure facing consumers (Davis and Russell, 1972). It is only when we view the pattern of utilization that the importance of incentives for consumers of health services becomes clear.

Although third-party payers (government, private insurers, philanthropy, and industry) paid 63.5 percent of the total personal health care bill in 1971, coverage was far from uniform across service units. Third-party payers met 90 percent of hospital bills, but only 58 percent of physicians' bills and 30 percent of all other charges (Cooper and Worthington, 1973).

Though the actual resource cost of providing many services, such as health checkups and minor surgical procedures, are undoubtedly lower if performed for ambulatory patients, the better insurance for inpatient services distorts the relative prices facing consumers. Hospitalization therefore occurs where it is neither medically warranted nor economically efficient.

A further price-distorting effect of insurance is the frequently used distinction between "acute" and "routine" care, which is obviously based upon the belief that health care is essential only when an acute illness occurs and is otherwise elective. In a sense, that belief is well-founded. Every illness that can be either prevented or controlled at a presymptomatic stage can be treated subsequently at the clinical stage. The treatment will not necessarily be as successful, however, nor are the consequent complications or disabling effects warranted by the delay. The delay in treatment may be economically justified, but usually it is not. And yet the third-party payers hold to the notion that preventive care is a luxury that does not need to be covered through insurance. The nation does indeed have a system of "sickness" insurance rather than "health" insurance.

There are additional incentives favoring use of hospital facilities in place of physicians' offices. Convenience, a sense of camaraderie among patients, and simplicity encourage use of the nonappointment, hospital-based emergency room or "drop-in" clinic. The outpatient clinic is open twenty-four hours a day, and the location is well known. Furthermore, the lack of an appointment simplifies planning and time scheduling. Of course, the waiting period in an emergency room is often long. But if the time can be spent in conversation with a neighbor, and if the opportunity cost is low enough, it cannot be viewed as an irrational use of an individual's time, whether or not it is an efficient use of society's resources.

The problem posed for preventive care is that the arrangement precludes continuity of care and the concern for health maintenance that should be engendered. Emergency rooms and drop-in clinics are typically understaffed and overcrowded, and are not usually the setting for the degree of patience or concern that would encourage family health measures. The staff has enough problems treating patients who come in with acute and serious medical problems.

Alternative Processes to Harness Incentives

Not only can incentives influence the use of preventive health-care services at the various stages of decision-making, but there are alternative ways in which they can be employed to increase the use of preventive care and the efficiency of health-care utilization in general.

Of paramount importance are the ways in which the pricing system can be altered to bring relative prices closer to marginal rates of transformation for various services. The removal of the selective bias in health insurance is one. Certainly coverage for all ambulatory services (with or without a deductible or copayment) would increase the consumption of preventive services. The difficulty is that we do not know the most efficient combination of acute and preventive services. Vast quantities of health resources would be utilized if every adult in the country received an annual comprehensive health examination. Could we serve those needs and still meet the acute health-care problems as well? We do not know.

There should be an effort to remove the distinction between a father's paid sick leave and a mother's barriers to seeking care. At the very least, paid sick leave should be ample, with perhaps a physician's verification to prevent abuse. Perhaps sick leave could be given the wage earner that would enable his spouse to receive medical care. Again, the mechanism to prevent abuse ought to be manageable.

The psychological barriers to preventive care are difficult to attack, but there are ways of approaching the multifaceted problem. First, neighborhood clinics should be established in inner-city areas, where comprehensive primary (including preventive) care can be given. The centers should be physically accessible by car or public transportation and should become involved in the community by including a congenial, open waiting area and an area for neighborhood meetings and perhaps by serving as a site for other social services, such as food-stamp distribution, voter registration, and sale of bus tokens. The hours of the clinic should enable all groups of the population to use the system. Full staffing should be employed until mid-evening. To permit reduced activity at night, a triage screening system should be implemented, with the less seriously ill patients sent home until the next day.

Making the center easily accessible should accompany measures designed to reduce patient apprehension and anomie. If the building's architecture and the staff's appearance were made less alien to the patients, and if the day-to-day operation of the facility were controlled to some extent, at least by the community, patients would feel more a part of the system and more disposed to seek professional counsel.

The health center would also be an ideal place to hold educational meetings on such topics as lead poisoning, hypertension, and infant care. Reliance for health education on narrow, disease-oriented, philanthropic institutions, such as the Cancer Society or the March of Dimes, is an inefficient means of achieving a socially optimal mixture of preventive and acute health-care utilization.

Agenda for Further Research

We know a good deal about the role incentives play in the use of health services. The various social science disciplines have contributed much knowledge about the reasons people use (or fail to use) professional health care. Two major gaps remain, however, in our knowledge. We have an inadequate understanding of the role of incentives in the use of and choice among specific health services, and we do not fully understand the socially optimal amount of preventive health services. Both deficiencies lie largely within the domain of economics.

As pointed out before, the sociological and psychological literature abounds with information concerning use of preventive services, but the economic literature generally covers all health services or expenditure categories. It is reasonable to suppose, for example, that the demand elasticity for preventive services may be rather large, but we do not know. If it is large, then use can be affected by changes in insurance coverage and sick-leave policies.

The fundamental problem remains—our lack of a norm against which we can assess our use of preventive care. If preventive care were an unambiguous good, then (barring diminishing marginal returns) we would unhesitatingly move in the direction of providing it in greater amounts. Unfortunately, the evidence we have leads to skepticism but to no firm criterion or objective. Until that research is successful, our understanding of incentives will constitute only part of the knowledge necessary for public policy formulation.

References

Acton, Jan P.
   1973   Demand for Health Care When Time Prices Vary More than Money Prices. Santa Monica: The RAND Corporation.
American Academy of Political and Social Sciences
   1972   "The nation's health: Some issues." Annals of the Ameri-

can Academy of Political and Social Sciences 399 (January): 14–21.

Andersen, R. *and* O. W. Anderson
  1967 A Decade of Health Services. Chicago: University of Chicago Press.

Barnoon, Shlono *and* Harvey Wolfe
  1970 Measuring Effectiveness of Medical Decisions, An Operations Approach. Springfield: Charles C. Thomas.

Borsky, P. N. *and* O. K. Sagen
  1959 "Motivations toward health examinations." American Journal of Public Health 49 (April): 514–527.

Bullough, Bonnie
  1972 "Poverty, ethnic identity and preventive health care." Journal of Health and Social Behavior 13 (December): 347–359.

Clark, Duncan W.
  1967 "A vocabulary for preventive medicine." Pp. 72–109 in McMahon, B. *and* D. W. Clark (eds.), Preventive Medicine. Boston: Little Brown and Company.

Cochrane, A. L.
  1965 "Rhonda Fach–South Wales." The Milbank Memorial Fund Quarterly 43 (April): 326–332.
  1967 "A medical scientist's view of screening." Public Health 81: 207–213.
  1969 "Screening procedures in relation to disease prevention: Screening the case against it." Medical Officer 31 (January): 53–57.
  1972 Effectiveness and Efficiency: Random Reflections on Health Services. For the Nuffield Provincial Hospitals Trust, London: Oxford University Press.

Cooper, Barbara S. *and* N. L. Worthington
  1973 "National health expenditures: Calendar years 1929–1971." Social Security Administration Research and Statistical Note. Department of Health, Education, and Welfare Publication No. 73-11701.

Davies, J. B. M.
  1965 Preventive Medicine for Nurses and Social Workers, 1st ed. London: English Universities Press.
  1971 Preventive Medicine, Community Health and Social Services, 2nd ed. London: Bailliere-Lindall.

Davis, K. *and* L. B. Russell
  1972   "The substitution of hospital out-patient care for in-patient
           care." Review of Economics and Statistics 54 (May):
           109–120.

Dean, Dwight G.
  1961   "Alienation: Its meaning and measurement." American So-
           ciological Review 26 (October): 753–758.

Donebedian, Avedis
  1971   "Social responsibility for personal health services: An ex-
           amination of basic values." Inquiry 9 (June): 3–19.

Fein, Rashi
  1971   "On measuring the economic benefits of health programs."
           Pp. 179–220 in McLachlan, R. *and* T. McKoewn (eds.),
           Medical History and Medical Care. For the Nuffield Pro-
           vincial Hospitals Trust, London: Oxford University Press.

Feldstein, Martin S.
  1967   Economic Analysis for Health Service Efficiency. Amster-
           dam: North Holland Publishing Company.

Feldstein, Paul J. *and* Ruth Severson
  1964   "The Demand for Medical Care." Pp. 57–76 in American
           Medical Association, Report of the Commission on the
           Cost of Medical Care. Chicago: American Medical Asso-
           ciation.

Ferrer, H. P.
  1968   Screening for Health: Theory and Practice. London: But-
           terworth.

Greenlick, M. R., D. K. Freeborn, T. J. Colombo, J. A. Prussin, *and* E.
  W. Saward
  1970a   "Comparing the use of medical care services in a medical-
           ly indigent and a general membership population in a
           comprehensive pre-paid group practice program." Unpub-
           lished paper.

Greenlick, M. R., J. E. Weiss, *and* J. F. Jones
  1970b   "Determinants of medical care utilization: The impact of
           ecological factors." Paper presented to the 98th Annual
           Meeting of the American Public Health Association,
           Houston, Texas, October.

Grosse, Robert
  1972   "Cost benefit analysis of health services." The Annals of the

American Academy of Political and Social Sciences 399 (January): 89–99.

Hack, Elizabeth
1960 "Participation in case finding programs for cervical cancer." Washington, D.C.: Government Printing Office.

Haefner, D. P., S. S. Kegeles, J. Kirscht, *and* I. M. Rosenstock
1967 "Preventive actions in dental disease, tuberculosis, and cancer." Public Health Reports 82 (May): 451–460.

Haefner, D. P., J. Kirscht, *and* S. S. Kegeles
1966 "A rational study of health beliefs." Journal of Health and Human Behavior 7: 248–254.

Hauser, M. (ed.)
1970 The Economics of Health Care. York, England: University of York, Studies in Economics.

Heinzelmann, F.
1962 "Determinants of prophylaxis behavior with respect to rheumatic fever." Journal of Health and Human Behavior 3 (Spring): 73–81.

Huntley, Robert R.
1970 "Improving the health services system through research and development." Inquiry 7 (March): 15–21.

Jeffers, James R.
1971 "Conflicting economic pressures on health care." Hospital Administration 16 (Summer): 21–35.

Jeffers, James R. *with* Howard R. Bowen
1971 Economics of Health Services. Morrestown, New Jersey: General Learning Press.

Jeffers, James R., Bognanno, *and* J. C. Bartlett
1971 "On the demand vs. the need for medical services and the concept of shortage." American Journal of Public Health 61 (January): 46–63.

Kalimo, Esko
1969 Determinants of Medical Care Utilization. Helsinki: Finland Research Institute for Social Security, National Pension Institute.

Kegeles, S. S.
1963a "Some motives for seeking preventive dental care." Journal of the American Dental Association 67 (July): 90–98.

1963b   "Why people seek dental care." Journal of Health and Human Behavior 4 (Fall): 166–173.

Kegeles, S. S., J. P. Kirscht, D. P. Haefner, *and* I. M. Rosenstock
1965   "Survey of beliefs about cancer detection and taking papanicolaou tests." Public Health Reports 80 (September): 815–824.

Klarman, Herbert E.
1964   "The case for intervention." Medical Care 3 (January/March): 59–62.
1965   The Economics of Health. New York: Columbia University Press.
1970   Empirical Studies in Health Economics. Baltimore: Johns Hopkins University Press.

Lave, Lester B. *with* Robert Kaplan
1971   "Incentives and medical insurance." Health Services Research 6 (Winter): 288–300.

Leavall, H. R. *and* E. G. Clark
1965   "Levels of application of preventive medicine." Pp. 105–121 in Clark, E. G. *and* H. R. Leavall (eds.), Preventive Medicine for the Doctor in His Community, 3rd edition. New York: McGraw-Hill.

Leventhal, Howard
1960   "Epidemic impact on the general population in two cities." Pp. 17–31 in Rosenstock, I. M. (ed.), The Impact of Asian Influenza on Community Life. Washington, D.C.: Government Printing Office.

Leveson, Irving
1970   "The demand for neighborhood medical care." Inquiry 7 (December): 17–24.
1972   "The problems of health services for the poor." The Annals of the American Society of Political and Social Scientists 399 (January): 17–24.

Levine, Gene N.
1963   "Anxiety about illness: Psychological and social basis." Journal of Health and Human Behavior 3 (Spring): 30–35.

Ludwig, Edward G. *and* Geoffrey Gibson
1961   "Self perception of sickness and the seeking of medical care." Pp. 190–198 in Bullough, B. *and* V. L. Bullough (eds.), New Directions in Nursing. New York: Springer.

McKinlay, John B.
1972   "Some approaches and problems in the study of the uses of services: An overview." Journal of Health and Social Behavior 13 (January): 152–155.

McKoewn, Thomas *and* Associates
1968   Screening in Medical Care: Reviewing the Evidence—A Collection of Essays. For the Nuffield Provincial Hospitals Trust, London: Oxford University Press.

McLachlan, Gordon *and* Thomas McKoewn (eds.)
1971   Medical History and Medical Care. London: Oxford University Press.

McLachlan, Gordon *and* Richard A. Shegog (eds.)
1968   Computers in the Service of Medicine: Essays on Current Research and Application. For the Nuffield Provincial Hospitals Trust, London: Oxford University Press.

McLain, John O. *and* Donald C. Riedel
1973   "Screening for utilization review: On the use of explicit criteria and non-physicians in case selection." American Journal of Public Health 63 (March): 247–251.

Milio, Nancy
1967   "Values, social class and community health services." Nursing Research 16 (Winter): 26–31.

Mindlin, R. L. *and* P. M. Densen
1971   "Medical care of urban infants: Health supervision." American Journal of Public Health 61 (April): 687–697.

Mueller, Marjorie Smith
1970   "Health insurance plans other than Blue Cross, Blue Shield and insurance company plans—1969." Social Security Administration Research and Statistics, Note No. 27, December 24.
1971   "Private health insurance in 1969: A review." Social Security Bulletin 34 (February): 1–18.

Oleinich, Arthur
1971   "Pediatric utilization in the Kaiser health plan of Oregon." American Journal of Diseases of Children 122 (December): 478–480.

Pauly, Mark V.
1970   "Efficiency, incentives and reimbursements for health care." Inquiry 7 (March): 114–131.

Phelps, C. E. *and* J. P. Newhouse
    1972   "Effect of coinsurance, a multivariate analysis." Social Se-
             curity Bulletin 35 (June): 20–28.
Pole, J. D.
    1970a   "The cost-effestiveness of screening." Proceedings of the
             Royal Society of Medicine (Pathology Section).
    1970b   "The economics of mass radiography." Pp. 73–94 in Hau-
             ser, M. (ed.), The Economics of Health Care. York, Eng-
             land: University of York, Studies in Economics.
    1971   "Mass radiography: A cost-benefit approach." Pp. 55–61 in
             McLachlan, Gordon (ed.), Problems and Progress in Medi-
             cal Care: Essays in Current Research, fifth series. For the
             Nuffield Provincial Hospitals Trust, London: Oxford Uni-
             versity Press.
Rabin, D. L., J. Crawford, E. Ferrero, D. Myer, A. Ross, *and* E. Schach
    1972   "Methods." Milbank Memorial Fund Quarterly 50 (July,
             Part 2): 19–30.
Rivkin, Marion
    1972   "Contextual effects of families on female response to ill-
             ness." Unpublished dissertation, Johns Hopkins University,
             Baltimore, Maryland.
Robbins, Paul
    1962   "Some explorations into the nature of anxieties relating to
             illness." Geriatric Psychology Monographs, No. 66. Wash-
             ington, D.C.: Government Printing Office.
Rosenstock, I. M.
    1966   "Why people use health services." Milbank Memorial Fund
             Quarterly 44 (July): 94–127.
    1969   "Prevention of illness and maintenance of health." Pp.
             31–45 in Kosa, J., A. Antonovsky, *and* I. M. Zola (eds.),
             Poverty and Health: A Sociological Approach. Cambridge:
             Harvard University Press.
Rosenstock, I. M., M. Derberry, *and* B. K. Carringer
    1959   "Why people fail to seek poliomyelitis vaccination." Public
             Health Reports 74 (February): 8–10.
Rosenthal, Gerald
    1970   "Price elasticity of demand for short-term hospital ser-
             vices." In Klarman, Herbert (ed.), Empirical Studies in
             Health Economics. Baltimore: Johns Hopkins Press.

Rosett, Richard N. *and* Lien-Fu Huang
  1973   "The effect of health insurance on the demand for medical care." Journal of Political Economy 81 (March/April): 281–305.
Scitovsky, A. A. *and* N. M. Snyder
  1972   "Effect of coinsurance on use of physician services." Social Security Bulletin 35 (June): 3–19.
Schottenfeld, David
  1972   "Patient risk factors and the detection of early cancer." Preventive Medicine 3 (August): 352–371.
Schweitzer, Stuart O.
  1974   "The cost effectiveness of the early diagnosis of disease." Health Services Research (Spring), forthcoming.
Sharp, Clive *and* Harry Keen (eds.)
  1968   Presymptomatic Detection and Early Diagnosis: A Critical Appraisal. Baltimore: Williams and Wilkins.
Simon, John L. *and* D. B. Smith
  1973   "Change in location of a student health service: A quasi-experimental evaluation of the effects of distance on utilization." Medical Care 11 (January/February): 59–71.
Simpson, John
  1970   "Preventive Medicine: An Introduction. London: Heinemann.
Somers, Ann R.
  1971   "Catastrophic health insurance: A Catastrophy." Medical Economics 48 (May 10): 213–226.
Somers, Herman M. *and* Ann R. Somers
  1961   Doctors, Patients, and Health Insurance. Washington, D.C.: Brookings Institution.
Startwell, P.
  1965   Preventive Medicine and Public Health, 9th edition. New York: Appleton-Century Crofts.
U.S. Comptroller General
  1972   Study of Health Facilities Construction Costs. Washington, D.C.: Government Printing Office.
U.S. National Cancer Institute
  1966   Cancer: Cause and Prevention. Washington, D.C.: National Cancer Institute.

Watkins, E. L.
   1968   "Low-income negro mothers: Their decision to seek prenatal care." American Journal of Public Health 58 (April): 655–667.
Weisbrod, Burton A.
   1961   Economics of Public Health: Measuring the Impact of Disease. Philadelphia: University of Pennsylvania Press.
White, K. L.
   1967   "Internal comparisons of medical care utilization." New England Journal of Medicine 277: 516–522.
Wilensky, Gail R. *and* John Holahan
   1972   National Health Insurance: Costs and Distributional Effects. Washington, D.C.: The Urban Institute.
Wilson, J. M. G.
   1971   "Screening and early detection of disease." In McLachlan, Gordon (ed.), Problems and Progress in Medical Care: Essays in Current Research, 6th series. For the Nuffield Provincial Hospital Trust, London: Oxford University Press.

Consumer

Behavior in

Preventive Health Services*

MICHAEL ZUBKOFF

AND DAVID DUNLOP

Seven years ago Irwin Rosenstock (1966b) wrote a seminal article entitled "Why People Use Health Services." That same basic question is posed again—this time as the subject of a conference. In this paper we limit our remarks to consideration of the primary factors affecting consumption of those health services designed to prevent illness or detect early disease.

Health Problems and the Socio-Cultural Milieu

Although the primary focus of this paper is to identify the factors affecting the consumption of preventive health services, it is important to understand that activity in a larger context. Whereas preventive health care may have an impact on an individual's gen-

* The authors wish to express deep appreciation to Robert Metcalfe, M.D., Meharry Medical College, and Lewis Lefkowitz, M.D., Vanderbilt University Medical School, for their helpful comments and suggestions.

eral level of health, it has no ultimate value in itself but only an instrumental value that can lead to improved functions and "quality
of life." As a consequence, the strictly medical/biological systems
approach to health problems, or the prescription of one or more
preventive health services by a member of the health-care team,
may alleviate disease and illness but not have the same impact on
the "perceived quality of life." If the biological approach is indeed
inadequate, it is important to understand how social and cultural
factors affect consumer perceptions of health status and illness. In
our country today, for example, many women, perceiving their
changing role, are seeking to change the definition of the "illness"
called pregnancy by changing present maternity-leave provisions
commonly used by employers (Wilson, 1970; Zubkoff and Blumstein, 1974).

In addition to changes in the definition of illness as a result of
sociocultural forces at work in society, it should be emphasized that
preventable illness episodes may lead to degrees of functional dislocation that differ from one individual to another. (Dislocation is
defined as the extent to which an individual's or society's level of
activity or function is disrupted by an illness or accident [Blumstein
and Zubkoff, 1973].) As a result, consumption of preventive health
services by certain individuals may yield different impacts on the
qualify of life for the individual and public.

Finally, improvements in the quality of life may be achieved by
general improvements in environmental quality, with improved
health a byproduct. Three families of environmental problems fall
in that class: (a) those related to the technological process of in-
dustrialization, such as air and water pollution; (b) personal living
habits related to such activities as recreation, patterns of leisure that
contain little exercise, and smoking and other overindulgences of
various kinds; and (c) the syndrome of poverty, which has environmental components such as poor housing and sanitation. As we
point out later in the paper, a number of alternative preventive
health services may be consumed in order to improve the quality of
life by improving health.

Role of Public Intervention in the
Market for Preventive Health Services

As will become increasingly evident throughout the paper, government (federal, state, and local) has become involved in the preventive health-services market, particularly in production. It is important to understand the criteria underlying government intervention and the possible intervention strategies. Basically, two principal criteria have been used as a basis for government intervention in any activity. The first comes into play when society, through the government, decides that a particular good or service is a merit good (a right). The second group of criteria arises when the good or service (a) exhibits significant externalities, (b) exhibits characteristics of public goods, such as joint consumption, (c) is produced under monopoly conditions, or (d) when other market imperfections arise that provide a justification for public intervention.

There seems to be a growing public consensus that health care in general, and preventive health services in particular, should be given the status of a merit good (Blumstein and Zubkoff, in press). But even if society determines that preventive health services are not justifiable on merit good grounds, a persuasive argument could be made to justify government involvement based on the relationship between dislocation and preventive health services.

When there is dislocation, there exists social and economic cost well beyond the costs of medical treatment. To be sure, individuals can insure privately against most forms of dislocation, although the income-supplement plans are not normally comprehensive. Yet the impact of a mistaken choice by a head of a household has major secondary effects on his dependents. It is unrealistic, of course, to expect children to make a private choice about catastrophe or disability, given their subordinate role within the family unit and their lack of independent funds. It may also be unhealthy to saddle children with the risk preference of their parents. Clearly, the private choice by an adult between dislocation insurance and some other form of consumption can significantly affect third parties if a family is involved. Consequently, the burden of private error falls upon others besides the chooser.

Because of the severe social and economic costs that arise from dislocation, and because those costs do not fall exclusively on the person on whom the obligation to take out private insurance would devolve, a basis for government intervention may exist, particularly when the risk of dislocation might be reduced by consuming preventive services. By government action, losses resulting from dislocation can be spread among many people (interpersonal-loss spreading) and over time (intertemporal-loss spreading) (Calabresi, 1970). In that way the impact of functional dislocation on any individual or family would be reduced.

Once the criteria for intervention have been determined, the government may intervene in different ways, particularly on the supply side. At one extreme, it may do nothing at all if the market mechanism is functioning well; at the other, it may be inclined to supply directly all preventive health services. Between the extremes are the following forms of intervention: (1) piecemeal dynamic intervention aimed at restoring the market mechanism—for example, increasing the flow of information to consumers about the potential impact of consuming or not consuming preventive services; (2) ad hoc static regulation aimed at short-run symptomatic remedies—for example, utilization review and wage and price controls; and (3) regulation of output of preventive services by a regulatory commission, such as a public utility, with control of such items as product standards, pricing standards, investment standards, and cost standards.

At present, government policy primarily reflects a heavy reliance on short-run symptomatic remedies. The establishment of national health priorities will mirror the political determination about government's appropriate role. Much of the emphasis in government programs will hinge on the public's decision on whether health care is a right, a qualified right, or a privilege.

Target Populations for Preventive Health Services

There are two basic types of preventive health services: (1) those that are individually consumed, such as immunizations and vaccinations, antenatal services, family planning services, multiphasic screening services, child welfare services, health examinations, and single disease screening services for such diseases as tuberculosis and diabetes and (2) those that are publicly consumed, such as water supplies, liquid and solid waste disposal, the control of air and noise pollution, standards of food sanitation, control of substance abuse including drugs, building standards, occupational safety, control of radiological hazards, transportation safety, control of disease vectors such as rats and insects, and health education. No single preventive health service can eliminate, or even significantly reduce the incidence of all diseases. For that reason, it is necessary to determine the distribution of diseases that can be effectively addressed by each preventive service. Table I, in which diseases are grouped into fifteen categories conforming to the major disease classifications contained in the international classification of diseases, permits such an analysis (World Health Organization, 1967:3–40).

The grouping shows that there is usually more than one effective preventive service. The question then becomes one of determining which service has the greatest impact.

It is important to recognize that no single preventive health service is effective in reducing the incidence of all diseases or even one disease in every major disease classification. The incidence, for example, of many digestive or genito-urinary diseases will not be affected by the consumption of immunization or vaccination services. To design a public policy strategy for the reduction of disease incidence it is important to determine:

(a) the specific disease or group of diseases that have the greatest effect upon mortality, morbidity, and debility in the defined population and

TABLE 1 An Analysis of the Effect of Preventive Health Services by Major Disease Category

	SERVICES																		
	Individually Consumed							Publicly Consumed											
DISEASE CATEGORIES	Immunization/Vaccination	Antenatal (prenatal)	Family Planning	Multiphasic Screening	Child Welfare (weighing, etc.)	Physical/Health Examination	Single Disease Screening (chest X-rays)	Water Supply	Liquid & Solid Waste Disposal	Air Pollution Control	Food Sanitation Standards	Drug Control	Noise Pollution	Building Codes	Occupation Safety	Radiological Hazards Control	Transportation Safety	Vector Control (rats, infec. dis.)	Health Education
	1	2	3	4	5	6	7	1	2	3	4	5	6	7	8	9	10	11	12
Infectious and parasitic—TB syphilis	x			x	x	x	x	x	x	x	x			x	x			x	x
New growths (cancer)		x	x	x	x	x	x			x	x				x	x			x
Allergic, metabolic and blood	x	x	x	x	x	x	x			x					x	x		x	x
Diseases of the nervous system (mental)	x	x	x	x	x	x	x	x			x	x	x				x		x
Diseases of eye, ear, the senses	x		x	x	x	x	x					x	x		x	x			x
Circulatory heart	x	x		x	x	x	x					x							x

66

Respiratory	x		x	x				x		x		x	x
Gastro-intestinal			x	x		x					x		x
Genito-urinary	x	x	x	x		x	x	x		x		x	x
Pregnancy and puerperium (abortion)		x	x	x		x	x	x	x	x		x	x
Delivery w/o complication		x		x		x	x	x	x	x		x	x
Skin and musculo-skeletal			x	x		x	x	x	x	x	x	x	x
Diseases of the newborn	x	x	x	x		x		x	x	x		x	x
Ill defined diseases			x	x	x	x	x	x					
Injuries		x	x	x	x	x	x	x	x	x		x	x

x indicates that the incidence of disease in that catagory can be reduced by the consumption of the service.

(b) the set of preventive services having the greatest impact on the incidence of those diseases.

Third, the table indicates that individually consumed preventive services tend to have an impact on a greater number of disease classifications than those publicly consumed, with the possible exception of health education and radiological hazard control. Most of the publicly consumed health services tend to be specific for diseases or disease classifications. Before scarce resources are allocated to their delivery, it is necessary to determine the extent to which the diseases affected by them are widespread or are potentially widespread.

Fourth, only one personal preventive health service, the physician examination, has a potential preventive impact upon all disease types (although presently the actual impact is under debate). If that is the case, then it is disturbing to consider the present trend toward an increasing lack of access to physical examinations. Because of the length of time they require, such procedures are becoming less frequently consumed by the general public and often are consumed only by relatively wealthy persons (National Center for Health Statistics, 1968).

Fifth, it is disturbing to find that health education receives such a small proportion of the total health expenditure in this country, although the table shows it has potential impact among all disease types. It is likely that additional resources allocated to the production and consumption of health education should have a major positive effect on the health of the general population.

Finally, it must be recognized that the table has been drawn up to reflect existing medical technology and knowledge. Given the dynamic state of research, it is possible that new preventive health services will be introduced and that those services specified in Table I will likely be the subject of further research that may affect other diseases in the future. If the table had been developed ten years earlier, such concerns as air pollution control, noise pollution, and perhaps drug pollution would probably not have been included. Ten years from now it may include vaccines for some forms of cancer.

Consumption and production of various potential preventive health services can also be compared. Such analyses show that, although it is possible to distinguish between individual and public consumption, most preventive health services are produced publicly as well as privately. The implication of the private production activity is that incentives already exist for individual producers of preventive health services, particularly those related to young children, family planning, and antenatal care. The public generally views the benefits of its consumption of preventive health services as being greater than those accruing to individuals. Burton Weisbrod (1961) is among the writers who have suggested that as a possibility because of the nature of externalities involved.

Demand for Preventive Health Services

To understand consumer behavior with respect to individual preventive health services, the nature of such services to individual and/or collective consumers must first be examined. What is there about preventive health services, such as health examinations and immunizations, that creates individual or public demand for them? Perhaps most important is the fact that preventive services are generally consumed by the individual before an illness episode. In other words, the individual is in a state of relative healthiness at the time he consumes the service. In the case of health examinations, it may be that an individual desires to consume such a service when he is concerned about whether he is as healthy as he ought to be. Most individuals, however, are in a state of relative healthiness, and regulations actually require that the individual be healthy at the time he consumes vaccinations and immunizations.

Most analyses of the demand for health services assume that an important factor in demand is existence of a perceived health need, manifested by psychological or biological factors (Wirick and Barlow, 1964; Feldstein, 1969; Rosenstock, 1966b). When a perceived need by the individual is lacking, consumption will be severely curtailed irrespective of any other factors that may affect demand, such as economic or social variables. Since preventive health services are consumed in states of relative healthiness, without a perceived biological and/or psychological need for the services, relatively few incentives exist for individuals to consume. For that reason it is necessary to distinguish between public and individual consumer behavior with respect to health services.

Analysis of the principal factors determining public demand for the consumption of preventive health services is needed to understand, for example, the consumption of immunizations and health examinations by employers and the United States military services. Because the public usually benefits to a greater degree than individuals, the extent to which certain preventive health services will be consumed (regardless of the demand by individuals) is determined by public legislative action. For such services as food sanitation standards, building codes, occupational safety, and transportation safety, the public determines and enforces minimum consumption requirements for the general well-being of the population. In addition, legislation often determines the extent to which the public will become engaged in producing such services as water and waste disposal, as well as immunizations and antenatal and family planning services. Often, however, when service is made available as a result of the public determining the benefits that may accrue to it (particularly in situations where the externalities may be great as with such infectious diseases as smallpox, polio, and diphtheria), individuals may choose not to consume them. In those cases the public imposes legal sanctions upon individuals to force consumption of such individual preventive health services. The requirements often occur at the point of school entry, when the public school system can require that individual school children consume certain vaccinations (Jackson and Carpenter, 1972).

Certain preventive services are provided on the basis of the professional's assessment of the prognosis for his clients, particularly in the area of antenatal care, family planning, and child welfare services. To some degree, single disease multiphasic screening health services are also recommended on the basis of professional decisions. However an individual provider rarely gets involved in determining the extent to which an individual will consume public preventive health services or the extent to which the public will produce such services.

In formulating a theory of demand by individual consumers for such specific preventive health services as examinations, multiphasic screening, and immunizations, there are two types of variables to consider: constraint and behavioral. Constraint variables define the potential scope of demand (e.g., the number of individuals in the population who may be potentially eligible to consume a particular service). Behavioral variables, in contrast, affect the consumption decision of individuals who may be in the potential consuming population; they usually affect both the timing of consumption and the quantity consumed.

Age and sex are important constraint variables because they are personal parameters that often determine the extent to which there is a physiological or psychological need for consumption of any given service. A person over the age of twenty, for example, obviously has little personal demand for child welfare services. Similarly, a male has no personal demand for antenatal services. Other personal characteristics, such as occupation, also define the boundaries of demand.

The following behavioral variables are of particular importance: perceived physiological need, health education, risk of nonacquisition, income, and price. The first three variables identified —perceived physiological need, health status awareness (information) acquired through health education, and the risk of nonacquisition—are interrelated in their effect on consumption behavior. Both the degree of perception of physiological need as well as the information related to the risk of nonacquisition (consumption) are affected by the degree to which health education services are provided to and consumed by individuals. It is unlikely, however, that the consumption of preventive health services will be significantly affected by increasing perceived physiological need, since most information received by individuals about the efficacy of preventive service consumption is received during a state of relative health when the level of perceived need is low (Williams and Jelliffe, 1972:74–79). Information is most likely to have a positive impact on improving awareness of the risk of nonacquisition. The degree to which awareness levels translate into actual consumption is unclear but the relationship is generally assumed to be positive (Becker et al., 1972).

Assuming that preventive health services are normal goods (services), we would expect according to economic theory that individual demand for the services would increase as income increases. There is evidence to suggest that the consumption of certain individually consumed preventive health services conforms to that pattern (Millar, 1971; Green, 1970).

It is important to distinguish between two price variables, both of which have an impact on the consumption of preventive health services. The first price variable is the money price. It is primarily through altering the money price variable that insurance can have an impact on the demand for preventive health services.

The second price variable is the opportunity cost of time and effort. As certain factors affect the money price in one direction, the opportunity cost of consuming may possibly move in the opposite direction, and, as a result, we may observe no appreciable effect on consumption from changes in price. If, for example, government policy deems it important to increase individual consumption of preventive health services by providing free clinics and, at the same time, allows the queue to lengthen, the opportunity cost of consuming that service will rise, perhaps enough to offset the effect of reducing its money price.

Policy is often formulated without distinguishing between the two price effects at work. As a result, policies that address the money price variable separately often lead to unfortunate inconsistencies, particularly when the opportunity cost of consumption may rapidly increase because of binding supply constraints. Similarly, when determining or setting legal requirements for consumption, it is important that the government consider the potential impact on the opportunity cost of consumption.

Supply of Individual Preventive Health Services

Both behavioral and constraint variables are important primary factors affecting the supply of preventive health services. Behavioral variables include the price of the preventive service and the supply of inputs. The major constraint variables are technology and the organizational structure of the preventive health-service delivery system.

There are four distinct supply input variables: financing; manpower; supplies; and buildings, equipment, and other capital items. There may also be a fifth input, new knowledge, that we should consider, particularly how new knowledge becomes available.

If government is involved in producing individual preventive health services, we must determine the extent to which government policy affects each of the behavioral and constraint variables that influence the supply of preventive health services. With respect to price, the government, through local public health departments, has been involved in subsidizing the consumption of preventive health services, particularly immunizations and vaccinations. Similarly, antenatal clinics and family planning and child welfare clinics are often provided free.

The government also intervenes on the supply side by subsidizing the supply of inputs. Virtually all health manpower training programs today are subsidized to some degree by training grants, although the funds have been decreasing rapidly in recent months. The federal government thereby dictates the relative priorities in supplying the requisite manpower inputs. In addition to providing training grant incentives to reduce manpower shortages, the government can reduce the shortages by changing licensing and other legal requirements imposed on certain health personnel. Through such mechanisms the government is determining the extent to which manpower inputs can be substituted for one another. In particular, governments can have a major impact on the extent to which the traditional activities of physicians will be delegated to nurse practitioners, physicians' assistants, and other health-service providers.

The government has played a major role in the area of financial inputs by providing grants for the physical expansion of health facilities. In the case of drugs, the government intervenes through legislation or administrative action. In the area of family planning technology, government's role has been important in determining the methods that may be used (Blumstein, 1973).

Turning to the mechanism through which the government affects technology and the rate of technological change, the federal government is the predominant supplier of research funds. Since it wields the leverage of financial support for research, it has the power to adapt existing technology related to the delivery of preventive health services. By providing increasing research support to solving the problems of pollution—air, water, drug, noise, and radiological—it is manifesting its newest priorities to promote additional consumption of those preventive health services. It should be recognized that government intervention, including provision of research funds, will substantially determine the long-run supply of preventive health services.

Finally, the government intervenes in the area of organizational structure through numerous legal devices. It provides incentives to modify organizational structure of health-delivery systems by service reimbursement mechanisms. At the present time, health maintenance organizations are a primary example of such a mechanism. If a national health insurance bill is passed, however, its reimbursement mechanism will probably have a major impact on the organizational structure of the delivery system and thereby affect the extent to which that system responds to changes in demand for preventive health services.

Immunization

This review is undertaken to determine the principal factors affecting the demand for immunizations—a preventive health service. It should be emphasized that no study so far has formulated the research problem in terms of the basic question: Why do people consume immunization services at all?

The theoretical framework most commonly used in the literature is the "health belief model," in which three factors are identified as primary in affecting the use of preventive services. They are (1) susceptibility to disease, (2) seriousness of the disease, and (3) perceived benefits and costs of taking appropriate preventive action (Haefner and Kirscht, 1970; Rosenstock, 1969; Rosenstock, 1966b; Becker et al., 1972).

That particular model, however, does not incorporate such constraint variables as the legal factor or the social factors of age and sex. In addition, there is relatively little discussion about the specific factors that may be incorporated into a benefit-cost framework. In particular, the money price and the opportunity cost price, as well as the important linkage between information/health education as it is related to perceived physiological need and perceived risk of nonacquisition, are not incorporated into the model.

Among the research findings is a 1972 study that carefully identifies legal requirements as primary factors affecting demand (Jackson and Carpenter, 1972). The study documents the tremendous change in the level of immunization throughout the State of Oklahoma after passage of a state law requiring all children to have received diphtheria-pertussis-tetanus, polio, smallpox, and rubella immunizations before entering public school. The legal constraint was reinforced by such mass communication methods as television, radio, and direct mail advertising to inform the public of the law's passage and anticipated enforcement.

Several studies have suggested that income is a primary variable in determining consumer behavior with regard to immunizations. Many of them incorporate income within a sociological framework, utilizing a socioeconomic index that includes not only income but also education and occupation (Saxon, 1973; Stewart, 1970; Merril et al., 1958; Green, 1970; Millar, 1971). One of the studies by Green, however, suggests that it is important to examine further the potentially distinct impacts of education, income, and occupation upon the consumption rates of specific preventive health services.

With respect to the effects of information on consumption of immunization services, several studies have documented a change in behavior as the result of using mass-communication methods (Miller et al., 1972; Jackson and Carpenter, 1972). In addition to the simple utilization of mass-communication methods, however, other factors have been identified as important in understanding the extent to which information is actually consumed and believed, to the point where observable change occurs in the use of preventive health services. Stewart and Hood (1970) and Hildebrand (1970) are among the authors who suggest that the use of indigenous personnel, normally at a nonprofessional or paraprofessional level, can be most effective in persuading low-income persons who may otherwise be indifferent to consume immunization services. By using a large number of motivational personnel in the delivery of preventive health services, the production technology obviously becomes more labor intensive and has important impacts on the basic structure and cost of the delivery system.

The opportunity cost of time, as a factor, has also been discussed in the literature. Stewart and Hood's analysis (1970) of a program in Austin, Texas obliquely deals with opportunity cost in their discussion of supply problems. The opportunity cost of time was not identified as an important factor in the consumption of the initial injection in a series of three diphtheria immunization shots but became a problem for the second and third shots. The immunization program was being administered from one or two locations in the city, and long queues developed for the first injection. As a result, a relatively large number of persons were not returning for subsequent immunizations. When the problem was discovered, the organizational structure of the delivery system was redesigned to shorten the queues and thereby improve the return rates for follow-up shots. Mobile health teams, which traveled to a number of locations, both reduced travel time and increased the accessibility of the service; as a result, the return rate did significantly increase.

It should be noted at this point that immunization programs are not always found to be the most cost-effective approach to alleviating a particular disease. Moseley and his colleagues (1972), working in Bangladesh, found that the most cost-effective method to combat cholera was still treatment of existing cases rather than attempts to prevent the disease from occurring in the first place. The principal reason lies in the fact that the basic prevention technology for cholera requires a numer of repeat injections every six months, as well as large quantities of supplies, drugs, and personnel to continue the vaccination program. There was, in addition, the problem created by people who did not return for followup vaccinations and thus lowered the overall effectiveness of the vaccine as a method of preventing the disease. Unfortunately, the study did not suggest an additional possibility—namely, that it may have been cost-effective to provide a limited vaccination program to certain sections of the population who would make full use of it, such as high-income groups, civil servants, and workers in large industrial firms.

In summary, there have been relatively few studies of consumer behavior related to immunization services. Some of the important work that has been done has incorporated the factors of the health belief model, but unfortunately even those studies have not been comprehensive enough in terms of analyzing all factors affecting consumer behavior toward immunization services. Virtually no research has been conducted on the effect of changing insurance coverage for immunization services as a means of increasing consumption of certain kinds of immunizations. In addition, little is known about the extent to which professional recommendations and decisions made by doctors and other providers have an impact on the consumption of immunization services. Pediatricians, for example, may very well have a major impact on the consumption of immunization services purchased by parents for their children.

A more inclusive frame of analysis is required to determine the extent to which each of several variables has an impact on consumer demand for preventive health services such as immunization. Such a study would have important repercussions for public policy, particularly where the analysis focuses on efforts to increase the use of immunization service throughout an entire population and have actually been effective in reducing the incidence of certain diseases.

Screening

The rationale of any kind of screening for preventive health care rests on certain assumptions.

(1) The diseases under attack are serious or frequent enough in the population being screened to justify the cost of the program in money and, more critically, in personnel, particularly when the program is being carried on at the expense of other health-promoting activities.

(2) There exists sufficient knowledge of the natural history of diseases to recognize them and modify their course.

(3) Detection tests are available, administered , and interpreted with acceptable reliability and reproducibility.

(4) Forms of treatment are known and available that will favorably influence the course of the disease, and persons with the disease can actually receive the available treatment.

(5) Persons who receive treatment will ultimately be better off than those who remain untreated.

(6) Early treatment of the disease will be less costly.

(7) Tests are available at reasonable cost in terms of time, money, and inconvenience.

(8) Services are accepted by the population.

Most of the research done on these assumptions to date has neglected the last assumption (and much of it has neglected several others)—that most crucial to our investigation of consumer incentives is the utilization of screening (Collen et al., 1969; Grossman et al., 1971; Holland, 1970; Rancharan et al., 1971; Sunderman, 1971).

One study, however, which deals with patients' acceptance of the multiphasic screening examinations done in 1969 at the Kaiser Permanente Medical Care Program (KFHP) in Northern California (1,960 persons), indicates that age, distance, and "health consciousness" are significant variables (Soghikian and Collen, 1969). In comparing the age distribution of all patients who chose to be screened to the entire population of the KFHP, it was found that those screened were significantly older. It was also shown that health plan members who live close to the screening center use it more regularly than others. In addition, "health conscious" members, such as teachers and upper middle class families, show a higher level of utilization. In sum, it was seen that members of the KFHP use multiphasic screening mostly in lieu of a regular health checkup; that those over age forty-five are the most frequent users; and that the majority of patients return for repeat examinations.

To what extent are utilization rates related to differences in income? It has generally been shown that those with a low income possess less information about health and disease than those with a high income (Rosenblatt and Suchman, 1964). Apparently even when educational attainment is controlled, a marked association has been found between income and the possession of correct information about health effects (Lazarsfeld and Kendall, 1970; Bogart, 1964; Swinehart, 1968).

Other studies have indicated that the general procedure by which innovations (new practices and ideas) are diffused is such that differences among the segments of the social structure (including age groups) may exist only during the initial phases of a process. As the effectiveness of the innovation is demonstrated, utilization becomes more widespread; finally, with almost universal acceptance, no significant differences exist among the segments of the population (Ellenbogen et al., 1968). It seems to matter little whether an innovation has a great advantage over the idea it is replacing. What does matter is whether the individual perceives the advantages (Rogers, 1962). This finding is consistent with human capital theory in that the demand for screening services tends to decrease progressively from the young age groups to the old (Grossman, 1972).

As stated earlier, few attempts have been made to study incentives affecting consumer utilization of screening. The thrust of the few studies that have been conducted focus on the "belief in efficacy of procedures" rather than on determining the effect of age, sex, income, prices, education, and other factors on utilization.

Summary and Conclusions

Little attention has been paid either to understanding why consumers use preventive health services or to developing appropriate public policies for exploiting consumer incentives that may exist. As a result of legal requirements, many preventive services have either been publicly produced and consumed or publicly produced and privately consumed, and consequently little attention has been devoted to analyzing the nature and kind of incentives that affect consumer behavior. As the spectrum of preventive health services has expanded, however, and as government, at all levels, has become more involved in the financing of health, legitimate concern has developed for achieving the optimal mix of preventive, emergency, acute, rehabilitative, chronic, and terminal care.

In our examination of the literature on the utilization of preventive health services, several important factors have been identified that affect related consumer behavior. First, many studies suggested that income or a closely correlated factor, such as occupation, was positively related to the consumption of preventive health services. The correlation was particularly true for immunization services. Second, it was evident that health education as a method of disseminating information was most important in changing health beliefs. (We assume that health behavior, as it relates to the consumption of preventive health services, is highly correlated with health beliefs.) Although the process of changing health beliefs was not thoroughly understood, it was evident that research was progressing in that area. Third, there have not been any studies, systematically analyzing all the factors identified that affect the consumption of preventive services, particularly in research conducted by economists. The socio-psychological studies have, in our view, progressed farther in identifying the important factors related to the perception of susceptibility to illness and the associated risks of not taking preventive action. In this light, a number of studies have recently recognized the significant informational and motivational role played by nonprofessionals and paraprofessionals in delivering preventive health services to potential consumers.

Finally, with respect to government action, we believe that a careful study is needed of the potentially paradoxical effect on consumption that a national health insurance program may induce. It is likely that such an insurance program, which seeks to expand the consumption of preventive health services by reducing the money price to the consumer without addressing potential supply constraints, particularly the organization of the delivery system, can significantly increase the opportunity cost of consuming such services and thereby negate the initial intent of the legislation.

Implications for Future Research

It is easy to be critical and remain above the tedium of pushing back the circumscribing barriers to new knowledge related to the consumption of preventive health services. If we were to seriously work on the empirical issues, in order to provide new answers, what would be the priorities. We suggest that the following list provides a clear indication of the priorities for further action. This agenda will come as no shock to those who have read the earlier sections of this paper.

(1) The theory of the demand for health as developed by Michael Grossman (1972) must be further refined to explicitly incorporate the demand for preventive health services by individuals, in order to define more precisely from the consumer's perspective the nature of preventive health services. This activity would further assist in determining the relevant data required for an analysis of the impact of the identified economic, social, medical, and psychological factors on consumer behavior.

(2) The impact of changes in the pattern of supply on the consumption of preventive services must be analyzed, particularly the affect on the various components of the opportunity cost of consuming. In addition, insurance incentives—both public and private—for consuming preventive health services must be analyzed to determine the extent to

which they affect the length of queues and the travel distance to the nearest point of consumption. It is also important to determine the extent to which the organization of the delivery system and the inputs used to deliver the services affect queue lengths, the time required for actual consumption, and the distance traveled.

(3) There have been no quantitative estimates developed for such commonly used economic parameters as price and income elasticities of demand for preventive health services. To develop estimates, additional thought must be given to output indices for preventive health services (Dunlap, 1972).

(4) How does one sell the consumer? Although research has improved our understanding of the importance of education in affecting health beliefs and .the use of certain types of personnel for information and motivational purposes, further research is required to know whether increasing or decreasing returns to health education exist with respect to the consumption of preventive health services.

(5) What should the government do? Public discussion must resolve the issue of merit good with respect to preventive health services. It is important that any proposed health legislation be analyzed to determine the effect of legislation on the factors identified (in this and other papers) as affecting the demand and supply of preventive health services. This analysis must be conducted in such a way that the implications for equal consumption are explicit.

We look forward with anticipation for others to join with us in rolling up our sleeves, unloosening our ties, and getting our hands dirty.

References

Bates, B., et al.
    1972   "Clinical evaluation and multiphasic screening." Annals of Internal Medicine 77 (December): 929–931.

Becker, M. H., R. H. Drachman, *and* J. P. Kirscht
  1972   "Motivation as predictors of health behavior." Health Services Reports 87 (November): 852–862.
Blumstein, J.
  1973   "Foundations of federal fertility policy." Report to the Ford Foundation.
Blumstein, J. and M. Zubkoff
  1973   "Perspectives on government policy in the health sector." Milbank Memorial Fund Quarterly 51 (Summer): 395–431.
Bogart, L.
  1964   "The mass media and the blue-collar worker." Pp. 416–428 in Shostak, A. *and* W. Gomberg (eds.), Blue Collar World. Englewood Cliffs, N.J.: Prentice-Hall.
Breslow, L.
  1973   "An historical review of multiphasic screening." Preventive Medicine 2 (June): 177–196.
Brown, H.
  1972   "Multiphasic screening for preschool children." Journal of the American Medical Association 219 (March 6): 1315–1319.
Calabresi, G.
  1970   The Costs of Accidents: A Legal and Economic Analysis. New Haven: Yale University Press.
Coe, R. M.
  1967   "The impact of Medicare on the utilization of health care facilities." Inquiry 4 (December): 42–47.
Collen, M., et al.
  1970   "Dollar cost per positive test for automated multiphasic screening." New England Journal of Medicine 283 (August 27): 459–463.
  1973   "Multiphasic checkup evaluation study. 4. Preliminary cost benefit analysis for middle-aged men." Preventive Medicine 2 (June): 236–246.
Collen, M., P. H. Kidd, R. Feldman, *and* J. H. Cutler
  1969   "Cost analysis of a multiphasic screening program." New England Journal of Medicine 280 (May 8): 1043–1045.
Collver, A., et al.
  1967   "Factors influencing the use of maternal health services." Social Science and Medicine 1 (September): 293–308.

Corner, R., et al.
    1972   "Appraisal of health care delivery in a free clinic." Health
            Services Report 8F (January): 12–16.
Cutler, J., et al.
    1973   "Multiphasic checkup evaluation study. 1. Methods and
            population." Preventive Medicine 2 (June): 197–206.
Dales, L., et al.
    1973   "Multiphasic checkup evaluation study. 3. Outpatient clinic
            utilization, hospitalization, and mortality experience after
            seven years." Preventive Medicine 2 (June): 221–235.
Densen, P. M.
    1972   "The measurement of utilization in health care programs."
            Health Services Report 87 (December): 958–968.
Discher, D. *and* H. Feinberg
    1969   "Screening for chronic pulmonary disease: Survey of
            10,000 industrial workers." American Journal of Public
            Health 59 (October): 1857–1867.
Dunlap, David W.
    1972   "The development of an output concept for analysis of
            curative health services." Social Science and Medicine 6
            (Summer): 373–385.
Dyer, N. H. *and* A. H. Schultz
    1972   "Mass immunization campaigns—the successful and con-
            tinuing approach." West Virginia Medical Journal 68 (Feb-
            ruary): 35–37.
Eisner, V., et al.
    1972   "The effectiveness of health screening in a school program
            for migrant children." Pediatrics 49 (January): 128–131.
Ellenbogen, B. L.
    1968   "The diffusion of two preventive health practices." Inquiry
            5 (June): 62–71.
Feldstein, P. J.
    1966   "Research on the demand for health services." Milbank
            Memorial Fund Quarterly 44 (July, Part 2): 128–165.
Green, L. W.
    1970   "Manual for scoring socio-economic status for research on
            health behavior." Public Health Reports 85 (September):
            815–827.
Grossman, J. H., G. O. Barnett, M. T. McGuire, *and* D. B. Swedlow

1971   "Evaluation of computer-acquired patient histories." Journal of the American Medical Association 215 (February 22): 1286–1291.

Grossman, M.
1972   The Demand for Health: A Theoretical and Empirical Analysis. New York: Columbia University Press.

Haefner, D. R. *and* J. P. Kirscht
1970   "Motivational and behavioral effects of modifying health beliefs." Public Health Reports 85 (June): 478–484.

Hawthorne, V. M.
1970   "Population screening as a personalized method of health education." Social Science and Medicine 3 (April): 653–658.

Hildebrand, G. I.
1970   "Guidelines for effective use of nonprofessionals." Public Health Reports 85 (September): 773–779.

Holder, L.
1972   "Effects of source, message and audiences characteristics on health behavior compliance." Health Services Report 87 (April): 343–350.

Holland, O. B.
1970   Disease Detection by Automated Multiphasic Health Testing, Proceedings of the Annual Scientific Meeting of the Society for Advanced Medical Systems, Baltimore, Maryland. Washington, D.C.: Government Printing Office.

Howe, H.
1972   "Application of automated multiphasic health testing in clinical medicine." Journal of the American Medical Association 219: 885–889.

Jackson, C. L. *and* R. L. Carpenter
1972   "Effect of a state law intended to require immunization of school children." Health Services Report 87 (May): 461–466.

Kaplan, R. S. *and* L. B. Lave
1971   "Patient Incentives in hospital insurance." Health Services Research 6 (Winter): 288–300.

Kirscht, J. P., et al.
1966   "A national study of health beliefs." Journal of Health and Human Behavior 7: 248–254.

Lane, M. *and* J. D. Millar
   1969   "Routine childhood vaccination against smallpox reconsi-
           dered." New England Journal of Medicine 281 (November
           27): 1220–1224.
Lazarsfeld, P. F. *and* P. Kendall
   1970   "The mass communication behavior of the average Ameri-
           can." Pp. 425–437 in Schramm, W. (ed.), Mass Communi-
           cations. Urbana: University of Illinois Press.
Lessler, K.
   1972   "Health and educational screening of school-age children:
           Definition and objectives." American Journal of Public
           Health 62 (February): 191–198.
Magnuson, W.
   1972   "Congressional responsibility for preventive health care."
           Preventive Medicine 1 (August): 388–395.
McKinlay, J. B.
   1970   "A brief description of a study of the utilization of materni-
           ty and child welfare services by a lower working class sub-
           culture." Social Science and Medicine 4 (December):
           551–556.
Millar, J. D.
   1971   "Gaining public acceptance in maintaining regular pro-
           grams in the development of countries." Pp. 505–511 in
           Pan American Health Organization, International Confer-
           ence on the Application of Vaccines Against Viral Ricket-
           tsial and Bacterial Diseases of Man. Washington, D.C.: Pan
           American Health Organization.
Miller, W. A., A. K. Hottle, *and* A. E. Berwick
   1972   "Rub out rubella campaign in Lane County, Oregon."
           HSMHA Health Reports 87 (January): 12–16.
Moseley, W. A., K. M. A. Aziz, A. S. M. Rahman, A. K. M. Alauddin
   Chowhury, A. Ahmed, *and* M. Fahimuddin
   1972   "Report of the 1966–67 cholera vaccine trails in rural East
           Pakistan; No. 4. Five years of observation with a practical
           assessment of the role of a cholera vaccine in cholera-con-
           trol programs." Bulletin of the World Health Organization
           47: 229–238.
Nickerson, G. S. *and* D. L. Hochstrasser
   1970   "Factors affecting non-participation on a county-wide tu-

berculin testing program in Southern Appalachia." Social Science and Medicine 3 (April): 575–596.

Ramcharan, S., et al.
1973   "Multiphasic checkup evaluation study. 2. Disability and chronic disease after seven years." Preventive Medicine 2 (June): 207–220.

Rauscher, F.
1972   "The outlook for cancer prevention, 1972." Preventive Medicine 1 (August): 293–299.

Rogers, E.
1962   Diffusion of Innovations. Glencoe, Illinois: The Free Press.

Rosenblatt, D. *and* E. Suchman
1969   "Blue-collar attitudes and information toward health and illness." Pp. 324–333 in Shostak, A. *and* W. Gomberg (eds.), Blue Collar World. Englewood Cliffs: Prentice-Hall.

Rosenstock, I. M.
1966   "Why people use health services." Milbank Memorial Fund Quarterly 44 (July, Part 2): 94–127.
1969   "Prevention of illness and maintenance of health." Pp. 168–190 in Kosa, J. Kosa, J., A. Antonovsky, *and* I. M, Zola (eds.), Poverty and Health. Cambridge, Mass.: Harvard University Press.

Saxon, G.
1973   "Studies of behavior change to enhance public health." American Journal of Public Health 63 (April): 327–334.

Shapiro, S., et al.
1960   "Further observations on prematurity and perinatal mortality in a general population and in the population of a prepaid group practice medical care plan." American Journal of the Public Health 50 (September): 1304–1317.
1972   "A program to measure the impact of multiphasic health testing on health differentials between poverty and non-poverty group." Medical Care 10 (May/une): 207–214.
1973   "Evaluation of two contrasting types of screening programs." Preventive Medicine 2 (June): 266–277.

Soghikian, T. *and* F. B. Collen
1969   "Acceptance of multiphasic screening examinations by patients." Bulletin of the New York Academy of Medicine 45 (December): 1366–1375.

Steinfeld, J. L.
    1972   "Preventive medicine: The long-term solution." Preventive
            Medicine 1: 10–11.
Stewart, J. C. *and* W. R. Hood
    1970   "Using workers from hard-core areas to increase immuni-
            zation levels." Public Health Reports 85 (February):
            177–185.
Sunderman, S. W.
    1971   "Conceptual problems in the interpretation of multi-test
            surveys." Unpublished paper.
Swinehart, J. W.
    1968   "Voluntary exposure to health communications." American
            Journal of Public Health 58 (July): 1265–1275.
Twaddle, A. C. *and* R. H. Sweet
    1970   "Factors leading to preventable hospital admissions." Medi-
            cal Care 8 (May/June): 200–208.
Ubell, E.
    1972   "Health behavioral change: A political model." Preventive
            Medicine: 209–221.
U.S. Department of Health, Education, and Welfare
    1970   Provisional Guidelines for Automated Multiphasic Health
            Testing and Services, Vol. 1. Washington, D.C.: Govern-
            ment Printing Office.
Weisbrod, B. A.
    1961   Economics of Public Health: Measuring the Economic Im-
            pact of Diseases. Philadelphia: University of Pennsylvania
            Press.
Williams, C. D.
    1973   "The deductible in medical expenses insurance." Journal of
            the American Association of University Teachers of Insur-
            ance 20 (March): 1–7–115.
Williams, C. D. *and* D. Jelliffe
    1972   Mother and Child Health: Delivering the Services. London:
            Oxford University Press.
    1974   Framework for Government Intervention in the Health Sec-
            tor. Lexington, Massacusetts: Lexington Books, D.C. Heath
            & Company (in press).
Wirick, G. *and* R. Barlow
    1964   "The economic and social determinance of the demand for

health services." Pp. 95–124 in the Economics of Health and Medical Care, Proceedings of a Conference Held in Ann Arbor, Michigan, 1962. Ann Arbor: University of Michigan.

World Health Organization
    1972   Health Education in Health Aspects of Family Planning, Technical Report Series No. 483. Geneva: World Health Organization.

Zubkoff, M. *and* J. Blumstein
    1972   "Framework for government intervention in the health sector." Paper presented at the Seminar on Problems of Regulation and Public Utilities, Amos Tuck School of Business Administration, Dartmouth College, Hanover, New Hampshire, August.

Incentives Affecting
Use of Emergency and
Other Acute Medical Services
LESTER B. LAVE

Definition of Terms

Emergency: An emergency is any condition that—*in
the opinion of the patient*—requires immediate medical
attention. This condition continues until a determination has been *made by a health care professional* that
the patient's life or well-being is not threatened.

Emergent (patient): Requires immediate medical attention. Delay is harmful to the patient; disorder is acute
and potentially threatens life or function.

Urgent (patient): Requires medical attention within a
few hours. In danger if not attended; disorder is acute
but not necessarily severe.

Nonurgent (patient): Does not require the resources of
an emergency service. Disorder is minor or nonacute.

SOURCE: American Hospital Association (1972:vii–viii).

Intellectual imperialism in defining the domain of "emergency and
acute" medical care could easily result in including all medical care
save the relatively minor institutions giving rehabilitation or care
for the aged, the infirm, and the mentally ill. Clearly, an asthma attack is an acute situation, even if the disease is a chronic one. Routine or preventive care is a small portion of total care.

Manageability of the problem, more than this writer's modesty, compels a more limited definition—the care given in emergency rooms and transportation by ambulances. This is a small but rapidly growing part of total medical care; it has been seen as the most important way of saving lives and so has been the source of much concern in recent years (e.g., National Academy of Sciences, 1966; American Hospital Association, 1972).

It may be argued, however, that even that definition is too encompassing since only a small proportion of the care given in emergency rooms is of an emergency nature; indeed, not even all of it is of an acute nature. Therein lies the crux of the problem perceived in the literature. The medical-care system has provided what it regards as a specialized and sharpened scalpel, which it finds is being used to chop wood. Thus, complaints are legion about the stupidity and recalcitrance of people who insist on using the emergency room or public ambulance system for problems that are not emergencies and indeed often are not even medical problems.

The presence of large numbers of such "inappropriate" patients has even resulted in some hospital's turning them away without service, for fear that serving them might reinforce their bad habits. Can one wonder at the complaints concerning the medical-care system?

How can people be so unthinking as to misuse this fine instrument that the medical-care system has provided? Are there reasons other than the perversity of human nature? Is there something that can be done either to improve the performance of people or to change the system to accommodate their needs? Why is the emergency room such a sensitive indicator of problems elsewhere in the medical-care delivery system?

General Problems of Medical-Care Delivery

Why People Use the Emergency Room

A number of studies done in the past fifteen years show that many people whose problems could not remotely be classified as emergencies use the emergency room (ER). Recent studies put the proportion of true emergencies as extremely low, and even the proportion of urgent cases as being only on the order of 0.5 to 0.7. Why do people use the ER rather than seek care more conventionally through their general physician or family physician?

The simple question deserves a simple answer: People go to the ER for medical care because they find it most accessible (best known, most available, easiest to be seen at, least intimidating, lowest cost) (see particularly Vaughan and Gamester, 1966). In comparing the conventional medical-care system with the ER, many people find that the ER has preferable characteristics. The ER can attempt to become less attractive (by refusing to see nonurgent patients, by raising prices, or by having longer waiting times), but not without considerable cost.

While this author may marvel at the power and precision represented by a well-run ER, he sees the patient as the focus of the problem, and as by far the most important actor in the system. It is the patient's needs and desires that must be analyzed. The emergency-care system can succeed only by being tailored to his needs and desires, rather than to some abstract or medically defined notion of the proper role for the emergency-care system.

Demand for Medical Care

Much of the literature has focused on the "need" for medical care. An individual's environment and personal habits (as well as his age, sex, and other characteristics) tend to determine his physical-medical condition at any time. Some conditions can be corrected or cured, or their symptoms eased by medical care. Most are self-limiting or self-correcting. Unfortunately, not everyone with a condition that medical care could help actually seeks treatment, nor can the physician correct, cure, or alleviate the symptoms of all the conditions that he sees.

With few exceptions (such as children, the mentally retarded, the mentally ill, and people with certain communicable diseases), the individual himself decides whether to seek treatment. He does so by viewing his health state (symptoms) through his personal beliefs (facts and superstitions) concerning the severity of such symptoms, the extent to which they can be relieved by medical care, and the cost of seeking care—in money, time, and transportation—as well as the cost of getting information about where to go, the cost of going into an unfamiliar setting, and so on. Lave and Leinhardt (1972) focus on those costs in the course of reviewing programs designed to provide medical care for the urban poor. The relationships are not simple ones; cultural and personal factors are extremely influential in determining for what and how often an individual seeks care. They clarify much of the recent public policy by classifying programs in terms of their effect in shifting either the demand for medical services (by lowering price or other access costs) or the supply of medical services (by providing more health professionals or more institutions for care).

The price elasticity of medical care has been the particular focus of economists and has been estimated in analyses by Kaplan and Lave (1971), Hall (1966), Grossman and Benham (1973), Phelps and Newhouse (1972; 1973), and Scitovsky and Snyder (1972). Estimating the demand for medical care is difficult, and a large number of methodological quarrels have surfaced in such attempts. There is agreement that demand is inelastic, but to what degree is the issue. Phelps and Newhouse (1973) tend to find elasticities that are much lower than those of other investigators. While one hesitates to argue that any set of estimates has been satisfactorily established, the better data and more careful methods of Phelps and Newhouse tend to lend more credence to their estimates.

An offshoot of the attempts to estimate price elasticity has been a policy argument on the implications of such estimates. Many practitioners argue that price does not and should not play any role in rationing medical care. The empirical work clearly demonstrates that price does play a role; economists tend to agree that it should. Where medical care is palliative, and where people desire much more palliation than they (or society) are willing to pay for, some rationing is necessary. Economists tend to believe that rationing by price has more desirable properties than rationing by waiting, influence, or other nonmarket means.

Remarkably little has been done to investigate the other factors influencing demand. Clearly, distance has an effect. A number of studies show that distance is an important determinant of how often medical care is sought (see Weinerman, 1966; Dixon and Morris, 1971). As an extreme example, imagine the people in a small town that loses its doctor; they must now travel twenty miles to see the doctor in the next town. Clearly, the demand for medical care must fall and, in general, it takes a more alarming set of symptoms to get an individual to travel the twenty miles to seek care in the next town.

Another important factor is the time the patient must wait to be seen. Many emergency rooms or outpatient departments have substantial waiting times. Casual observation suggests that it is the expected waiting time that is the prime determinant of demand in outpatient departments. The author could find no studies, however, that document an increase in demand when something is done to lower waiting time. Our own studies in Pittsburgh suggest such a development when the screening clinic of an outpatient department was changed and three interns were substituted for a resident. The increased capacity resulted in a sharp drop in waiting time initially. But by the end of a month or two, the average waiting time was back up to its previous level, in spite of the much greater number of patients being served. Thus, there seemed to be a great deal of latent demand, ready to manifest itself when waiting time decreased.

Other factors, such as the alien setting or ease of getting information, have not been quantified to the best of this author's knowledge. Lave and Leinhardt (1972) suggest that the factors may be important, but there is little knowledge of their effect.

Effect of Insurance and Government Programs

Insurance coverage of the population against the cost of medical care has increased enormously in the past twenty to thirty years. At the same time, government programs have been instituted or broadened to extend coverage to the aged, the poor, and various categorical groups. The net result has been an increasing tendency to insulate the individual from the provider payment (the cost of paying the deliverer for his services). As a result, other aspects of care have become more important—the time cost of seeking care, for example, and the transportation cost. The rise in personal incomes has also contributed to the trend, making the provider payment less significant and emphasizing the time and other costs. In the limit, one might think of one of the proposed national health insurance systems, or of the British National Health Service where the provider payment is zero and care is rationed by other costs, especially the cost of waiting.

The most important effect of increased insurance coverage and of government intervention in the medical-care delivery system has been to lower the price faced by the consumer in seeking care. But the increase in demand (shift of the demand curve) has not been neutral. The principal increase in insurance, for example, has lowered the cost of hospitalization without affecting the cost of ambulatory-care services. As a result, consumers and physicians face changed incentives and are influenced to substitute inpatient for outpatient care.

Even where the demand shift was neutral, the end effect was not. In the short run, the supply of physicians' services is not very elastic (see Feldstein, 1970b; Sloan, 1973). In contrast, the supply of services from other groups or from equipment is much more elastic. Thus, a neutral shift in the demand curve will wind up with small, or even negative, increases in the supply of physicians' services and substantial increases in the services of nurses, hospitals, laboratories, etc.

The incentives have worked not only on patients but on every actor in the system. Medicaid in Pennsylvania, for example, reimburses four dollars for an ambulatory care visit (to a physician's office or to an outpatient department) and fourteen dollars for an ER visit. There is casual evidence that the movement of patients to the ER has been motivated by the private physician, as well as by the patient desiring the ER services. Berman and Luck (1971) argue similar motivations in Baltimore. The effect of Medicare regulations on hospital behavior has also been immense. Few hospitals had utilization-review committees or tissue-review committees before Medicare. As a result of the Hill-Burton program, many hospitals established obstetrics units, changed their physical plant, or made modifications that they would not have made in the absence of the program.

Systems Aspects of the Problem

When physicians shift the locations of their offices toward more concentrated areas (see Kaplan and Leinhardt, 1974) not only does the demand for the ER shift but so do the demands for such diverse services as those of the registered nurse and medical records clerks. Medical-care delivery takes place in a highly interdependent system, and the interactions can be ignored only in very special cases. Recent attempts have been made to model the entire medical-care delivery system.

Feldstein (1970a, 1971) and Yett and asssociates (1971a; 1971b) have constructed multiequation models of the demand and supply interactions and institutions of medical care. The models have been used to forecast both the immediate consequences of a change in the system and the total effects, once all interactions have been worked out. They represent notable theoretical contributions, since they help clarify our understanding of the medical-care delivery system. The actual estimation of the model, however, and its use in forecasting have been severely limited by the quality of the data available.

Lave, Lave, and Leinhardt (in press) have modeled the medical-care delivery system with an eye toward exploring interactions and outcomes. Defining the outcome of the system in terms of a series of health status levels, they trace the health status level and the cost of the medical care for each proposed change in the delivery system. One novelty of the model is its ability to get explicit measures of the efficacy of the medical-care system by looking at the distribution of health status across the population. One of the conclusions they reach is that making use of an inexpensive and relatively low level institution for delivering primary care is highly desirable, in terms of both the resulting cost and the resulting health status distribution.

Empirical Studies

Some evidence has been cited here concerning the framework within which consumers approach the medical-care delivery system and within which the system works. A substantial literature has presented answers to many of the questions raised, in terms of the use of both ambulances and ER's, and the results are reviewed below. Studies in addition to the references cited have been listed by the AHA (1972). Most of the literaure is focused on how to run an ambulance service or ER, or on legal, medical, or personnel problems connected with running such a service. Only recent literature reporting detailed surveys have been considered in this review.

Use Of Ambulance Services

Several papers report the results of simulation studies designed to optimize the positioning of ambulances and the number of ambulances within a city (Savas, 1969; Gordon and Zelin, 1970; Sagar and Dick, 1971). They give few statistics on the actual demand currently served.

Two studies (Aldrich et al., 1971; Gibson, 1971a; 1971b) report analysis of the demand for ambulance services. Aldrich and colleagues found that socioeconomic variables were good predictors of demand, that demand was rising substantially over time, and that demand was extremely sensitive to the price charged for the service. For 632 census tracts in Los Angeles, they were able to explain more than ninety percent of the variance in total ambulance calls per capita. The most important variables increasing demand were the proportion of people who had moved recently, the proportion over age sixty-five, the proportion of single males, the proportion of unemployed males, the proportion of the population who employed males, the total number of employed people, the proportion of children, and certain occupational categories. The most important variables lowering demand were housing density, the proportion of the population that was white, the proportion of single females, and certain occupational categories. They also analyzed six categories of reasons giving rise to the call from auto accidents to poison cases; between forty-four and eighty-seven percent of the variation in the individual categories is explained by the same set of socioeconomic variables.

Gibson (1971a) and Gibson et al. (1971) report a similar study for Chicago. They are able to explain about seventy-six percent of the variation in fire department ambulance calls per one thousand people across seventy-five areas in Chicago, seventy-one percent of police department calls, and twenty-one percent of private ambulance calls. The most important factor increasing demand is the median years of education of residents; the important factors reducing demand are the proportion of nonwhites, median family income, and household crowding. Neither the proportion recently moved nor that under age eighteen is a significant variable. The studies cannot be compared, since the omission of a series of important explanatory variables from the Gibson (1971a) study means that the remaining coefficient estimates will be biased. It might be noted, however, that the effect of nonwhites is contradictory. The only real agreement comes in the sign of the crowding variable.

In another paper, Gibson (1971b) reports the number of patients transported to Chicago hospital ER's, who make up about twelve percent of all patients treated at ER's. He also displays data on the reason for the call, including some data on whether the case was an emergency; most of the trips were classified as emergency (seventy-three percent of police department and ninety-two percent of fire department calls). For Kingston, Ontario, Sagar and Dick (1971) report a rough tabulation of average number of ambulance calls by shift (twelve-eight, eight-four, four-twelve) and by type (traffic, other, and transfer).

Dimendberg (1969) reports a number of statistics on ambulance calls in New York City in August 1966. He found between thirty-four and ninety-eight calls a year (for every thousand persons) across boroughs, or an average of 61.4. Calls with total illness accounted for about forty percent and injuries for about thirty-four percent. He also analyzes the data by shift and by borough.

Taubenhaus and Kirkpatrick (1967) report on the use of Boston City Hospital ambulances in early 1966. They tabulate trips by race and age, by distance and time, and by disposition of the case. Sixty-nine percent were admitted to the hospital, which indicates that most calls were for emergencies. The statistics are limited, since only 432 calls are reported.

A report on San Francisco indicates that the call rate for ambulances ranges from five per one thousand for children under age five to two hundred per one thousand for people over age eighty, with a mean of about thirty per one thousand per year. Forty-five percent of the trips were for accidents, and twenty percent for cardiovascular or respiratory diseases (Waller, 1965).

King and Sox (1967) investigate public ambulance calls and total emergency medical service visits in San Francisco in 1963–1964. About thirty percent of the patients were transported by ambulance. (No charge was assessed.) For ambulance and non-ambulance patients, they present cross-tabulations by age, sex, race, type of emergency, diagnosis, disposition of patient, day of week and time of day, and type of equipment used and treatment given. Children are responsible for few ambulance calls, while the aged are responsible for a larger number than their proportion in the population would suggest. Accident injury is responsible for more than half the calls, and illness for about thirty-eight percent. The greatest number of calls (16.1) come on Saturday, the fewest (13.1) on Tuesday and Wednesday. Seventy-eight percent of the patients are sent home; twenty percent are referred for further care.

Noble et al. (1971) found that from six to eight ER visits per day are transported by ambulance (representing four to ten percent of all visits) in three Boston hospitals. Christiansen (in press) presents data and an analysis of the emergency medical system in Copenhagen.

Demand for Emergency Room Service

Beginning with Shortliffe, Hamilton, and Noroian (1958), many studies have documented the increasing demand for ER services. Recent reviews by Atterbury and his associates (1968) and Noble, LaMontagne, Bellotti, and Wechsler (1971) show extensive agreement among the various studies. In particular, the reported rate of increase in visits per year ranges from eight percent to one hundred percent. The national average rate of increase has been about fifteen percent a year. Since the number of ambulatory visits per year has not risen at a rate approaching fifteen percent, it is evident that people are shifting from ambulatory care in a private physician's office to ambulatory care in an ER.

Data from the 1960s show that the proportion of cases considered nonurgent ranged from about thirty percent to about fifty-five percent across a number of studies. Only a small percentage were considered to be emergencies.

Shortliffe et al. (1958) hypothesize that the increase in ER use may be due to the unavailability of physicians on weekends, nights, and holidays. Weinerman and others (1966) have shown that the ER is a major source of care for inner-city residents.

The types of questions asked in the studies include (1) the rate of increase in utilization, (2) the proportion of urgent cases, (3) the distribution of patients (or patient visits) by race, sex, age, family income, marital status, and pay status, (4) the complaint or reason for the visit, (5) the diagnosis, (6) treatment patterns, (7) disposition of the case and status of the patient on leaving the ER, (8) differences between inner-city and suburban patterns of treatment, (9) missed appointment rate for follow-up care, (10) general pattern of medical care obtained, (11) referral pattern to the ER, (12) transportation to the ER, (13) seasonal, daily, and hourly distribution of patient visits, (14) regional differences, and (15) problems in financing the ER. The studies present a vast amount of pertinent data, but only a few prominent trends in the quality of care and the users of the ER will be pointed out here.

The use of ER's by children and adolescents has received a fair amount of atention (Wingert, 1970; Alpert et al., 1969; Hochheiser et al., 1971, Sklar and Downs, 1970; 1968; Robinson and Klonoff, 1967; Wingert et al., 1968). Robinson and Klonoff (1967) tabulate the age, season, cause, day, and disposition of visits to Vancouver (BC) General Hospital in British Columbia. Wingert, Friedman, and Larson (1968) look at visits to the Los Angeles

County Hospital ER to look at the characteristics of patients, where they get all their care, the severity of their problem, language difficulties, and disposition of the case. They find that the ER and the outpatient department are the primary source of medical care for a large number of patients. In a later paper (Wingert, 1970) that fact is recognized in the recommendation that the ER and outpatient department be set up to give comprehensive care to children. Alpert et al. (1969) find that twenty-four percent of the children visiting a Boston ER had a stable relationship with a physician, while almost half had no relationship with a physician. They present cross-tabulations by family income, race, and referral. Finally, when people were asked where they would seek various types of care, almost all answered that they would go to a private physician if they had, for example, a fever of 104.°

Hochheiser et al. (1971) find that when a comprehensive health program was established, there were fewer visits of children to the ER. Thus, the care did substitute for ER care. It is chastening to realize, however, that 15,000 to 30,000 visits per year at the health center reduced ER visits by about 228.

Sklar and Downs (1968; 1970) tabulate patient characteristics and reasons for the visits for pediatric ER visits in New York City and surrounding areas.

Gampel (1965) tabulates patient characteristics and characteristics of the visit for children visiting an ER in London. Dixon and Morris (1971) look at use of a health center and ER located in a United Kingdom housing project. They present data on a number of patient characteristics and use factors; distance is an extremely important factor in determining which facility the patient will choose.

A comparison of inner-city and suburban ER's in Pittsburgh (Solon and Rigg, 1972) disclosed quite different patterns of care. More than half of the patients in both settings had a private physician as their central source of care, but the proportion was eighty-five percent for the suburban ER and fifty-nine percent for the inner-city ER. In both settings, the ER provided only a small fraction of all medical care (two percent for the suburb and five percent for the inner city). This usage is reflected in perceptions about whether the ER is used for emergencies only (eighty-seven percent for the suburb and seventy-three percent for the inner city) and is considered of peripheral significance (seventy-eight percent for the suburb and sixty-nine percent for the inner city). Finally, there was evidence that the inner-city resident tends to use more sources and types of sources of medical care than does the suburban resident.

The most complete set of studies on ER's has been done on New Haven hospitals by Weinerman et al. (1965). They looked at patient characteristics (and have data over time), at the day, time, type of service, use of ancillary facilities, disposition, and urgency of visits. The studies are extremely thorough and detail use of the ER. They even tabulate the proportion (0.30) of referral appointments missed, by characteristics of the patient and reason given for the miss. Weinerman (1966) also finds that distance is an important characteristic, since only 30.1 percent of the patients come from New Haven and they make 63.7 percent of patient visits.

In 1963, 45 percent of the patients were discharged, 25 percent referred to the outpatient department, 13 percent to private physicians, and 9 percent admitted to the hospital; the others were in miscellaneous categories. In 1964, 6.6 percent of the visits were emergent, as defined by the AHA, and 34.7 percent were urgent. Sixty-nine percent of the problems had occurred the same day as the visit, 23 percent within the preceding week. The very young and the very old tended to have a higher proportion of urgent problems, as did whites and people who had resided at the current address for a longer period of time. All those groups are more likely to have a private physician with whom they have a relationship. And indeed, people who usually sought care from a private physician had a greater proportion of urgent visits, particularly when the patient sought help before coming to the ER or was referred to the ER by a physician. People in a higher social class as a rule used a private physician and infrequently used the ER in comparison with people in a lower social class.

In investigating the characteristics of patients whose visits are true emergencies, Lavenhar et al. (1968) find that they are people who are over age forty-five, live alone, are self-referred, have low incomes, and have no regular physician. Those characteristics, however, explain only about ten percent of the variance.

Keggi et al. (1970) present more recent data on the New Haven patients and their use of the ER's. They find no definite over-representations by age class, although they find that males are seen more often than females. Nonwhites are overrepresented in the ER, but a smaller proportion of their cases are serious trauma. People living alone are overrepresented in the ER and trauma population; married people have fewer traumas than expected. Friday, Saturday, and Sunday are the days with greatest use, and seventy-five percent of the cases show up between five p.m. and four a.m. About sixty-five percent of the trauma patients arrive by private car, eighteen percent by ambulance, and the rest walk or come by public transportation.

Reed and Reader (1967) find that distance is important in visits to a New York City ER, since thirty-three percent of the patients live within a mile of the hospital; fourteen percent travel twelve miles or more. For half the people, the ER visit was the first to any facility (in that hospital). Seventy-six percent had no ER visits in the past two years, and only four percent had three or more visits.

Torrens and Yedvar (1970) compare the ER's in four New York City hospitals and find a number of differences. The differences were great in the social class and pay status of the patients. One inner-city hospital had only eight percent of its patients with trauma, while the suburban hospital had sixty-eight percent. Suburban patients came to the ER by private car; inner-city patients tended to walk or come by public transit. The suburban problems were more severe, requiring more ancillary services and prescriptions. About a third of the inner-city patients were discharged, and an additional fifty percent were referred to the outpatient department. Only four percent of the suburban patients were discharged, and seventy-two percent were referred to a private physician. During the preceding year, almost thirty percent of both groups of patients received no medical care. Thirty-two percent of the inner-city patients had been to an ER or outpatient department (compared with fifteen percent of the suburban patients), and about twenty-five percent had seen a private physician (compared with fifty-seven percent of the suburban patients). Evidently, ER's in the inner city of New York and suburban ER's have quite different roles.

Jacobs et al. (1971) report data for Rochester, New York. They classify thirty-five percent of visits as true emergencies requiring the service of the ER and thirty-five to fifty-seven percent as acute problems that could have been handled in a physician's office. The other data are consistent with those in previous studies.

Kirkpatrick and Taubenhaus (1967) have a different classification of urgency. In a Boston ER, they found that seven percent of the nonaccident cases and fifty-eight percent of the accident cases were urgent, while twenty-one percent of nonaccident cases did not need to be seen. Sixty-one percent of the nonaccident cases and thirty-six percent of the accident cases were discharged, and fourteen percent of the nonaccident cases and fifty-three percent of the accident cases were referred to the outpatient department.

White and O'Connor (1970) studied an ER in Saginaw, Michigan. Though the proportion of urgent cases was a bit high (sixty percent), the data were generally consistent with previous data.

Vaughan and Gamester (1966) surveyed ER's in Michigan hospitals. Forty-six percent of the patients called or tried to call their physician before going to the ER: Sixteen percent were told by the physician to go to the ER, nineteen percent were instructed to meet the physician at the ER, and twelve percent failed to reach their doctor. Of those who did not try to reach their physician, twenty-three percent believed he was not available, eight percent believed that immediate help was required, nine percent were taken or ordered to go to the hospital, six percent reported the hospital was more convenient than their physician, and one percent reported that they were influenced by the fact that their insurance coverage was contingent on hospitalization. For nontraumas particularly, patients consulted their physicians or at least attempted to do so. About a fourth of the patients were treated by their physician in the ER. During ordinary work periods the physician tended to see the patient; he was likely to refer him to the hospital after hours or on weekends. Thus, Michigan physicians tended to use the hospital to cover their practice during off hours, and also tended to use the ER as an off-hours office.

Berman and Luck (1971) analyzed the case mix at a hospital that was located in a poor area but drew most of its patients from a nearby affluent area. They found "Jewish patients used the emergency service for nonurgent problems less frequently than blacks" (thirty-one percent and sixty-two percent). "Lack of physicians in black residential sections is the most obvious (factor for their seeking care in the ER)." "Many physicians in (black) areas do not accept Medicaid patients."

Perkoff and Anderson (1970) analyze data from a St. Louis hospital and report data consistent with previous studies.

Roth (1971) surveyed hospital ER's in five hospitals throughout the country. The data are generally consistent with those reported in previous studies.

Summary and Agenda for Research

The focus of an investigation of the use of emergency and acute services is the consumer. It is he who determines how the system that is presented to him shall be used. Past designs have tended to center on what was necessary to treat serious acute problems, but the vast majority of cases that are presented are not serious, and almost half are not even important enough to be classified as acute.

In determining which institution he will use, when he will use it, and how often he will use it, the consumer starts from an objective set of symptoms that he perceives. Those symptoms are filtered through his perceptions of their importance and the extent to which his perceptions alarm him. The resulting feeling of how much he desires to seek care is tempered by the cost of doing so. Whether he actually seeks care depends on the generalized cost of care, including the payment to the provider, the time and cost of travel and waiting, and the cost of going into an unfamiliar or alien setting. The effect of insurance and government programs has been to pay most or all of the provider cost and thus to make the other aspects assume predominant importance.

It is argued that incentives, financial and other, are extremely influential in determining the behavior of patients, physicians, and health-care institutions. Monetary incentives have played a major role in determining how much treatment the patient seeks and where he seeks it. Physicians have modified their treatment patterns and hospitals their capacity, range of services, and general procedures.

The systems aspects of medical-care delivery must be stressed, since an attempt to modify one part of the system, such as emergency-room service, inevitably leads to changes throughout the rest of the system. Some examples of current models of the delivery system are shown in this paper, and it is argued that more must be done to develop our conceptual understanding of the system.

The second part of this paper reviews empirical studies of the demand for emergency ambulatory services and of the use patterns of emergency rooms. Price and distance are found to be important. There is substantial evidence that emergency rooms are a major source of care for inner-city residents, but that upper class whites continue to use private physicians for most service. Private physicians tend to use the emergency room as an after-hours office and to "cover" themselves when they do not want to be on call. The growth of emergency room services means that the ER is asssuming a greater share of the supply of ambulatory services, particularly during periods other than the standard working hours.

The ER is clearly offering a service that people desire despite waiting times, which are often long, and despite refusal by many hospitals to treat patients without serious acute problems or to give them only preliminary treatment and then refer them to a private physician or to the outpatient department. The potential growth in ER services is high if the service were made more pleasant, if staffing were changed to reflect demand patterns (and thus minimize waiting), and if the service were organized to give complete care for those problems. Patients do seem to desire a "no appointment" service where problems can be treated as they occur. The reduction in the absolute number of primary care physicians (and the vast reduction in primary care physicians per capita) means that the classical image of the family physician and close relationship with him is not a reality for a substantial proportion of the population. They think of their problems as episodic, and they seek episodic care at an institution they can easily gain information on and use with a minimum of planning.

If we are not to remain in the position of reacting to changes in consumer demand with no advance planning, we must do more to investigate consumer desires and the current ways in which they are being met. Commendable attention is finally being given to estimating the price elasticity of medical care. Careful attention must also be given to estimating the effect of travel time and distance, of waiting time, and of various factors—including the difficulty of acquiring information and psychological barriers to entering the sterile setting of modern, professional medical care.

A second area requiring research is the interaction between various parts of the medical-care delivery system. Much needs to be done to increase our understanding of the effect of changing one part of the system.

The role of incentives on physicians and health-care institutions demands much greater attention. Lare, Lare, and Silverman (1973) have argued that incentive reimbursement for hospitals would do much to curb the exorbitant rate of cost increase. Clearly, past incentives have caused physicians and health-care institutions to modify their behavior (often in pernicious ways); we must learn enough so that we can anticipate consequences and design systems that use incentives to advantage.

Finally, it is the individual who decides whether to seek care and when to seek it. And it is the individual who decides whether he has been helped and whether he should stop seeking care. No matter how effectively medical science can intermediate in a particular disease, no matter what the physician thinks about the patient adhering to his treatment regime or leaving the system with an untreatable problem, it is not the health professional who makes the decisions. In an age of massive government intervention into the medical-care delivery system, it is about time that we stopped focusing our attention on the health professional and the way some health professionals want the system to be structured. We ought to try to make the system work.

References

Aldrich, C. A. C. Hisserich, *and* L. B. Lave
     1971   "An analysis of the demand for emergency ambulance service in an urban area." American Journal of Public Health 61 (June): 1156–1169.
Alpert, J., J. . Kosa, R. Haggerty, L. Robertson, *and* M. Heagarty
     1969   "The types of families that use an emergency clinic." Medical Care 7 (January–February): 55–61.
American Hospital Association
     1972   Emergency Services. Chicago: American Hospital Association.
Atterbury, C. E., T. P. Weil, *and* H. D. Donnell, Jr.
     1968   "Factors affecting emergency room utilization." Southern Medical Journal 61 (October): 1061–1067.
Barry, R., E. Shortliffe, *and* H. Wetstone
     1960   "Case study predicts load variation patterns." Hospitals, Journal of the American Hospitals Association 34: 34–36.
Berman, J. I. *and* Elizabeth Luck
     1971   "Patients' ethnic backgrounds affect utilization." Hospitals, Journal of the American Hospitals Association 45 (July): 64–68.
Christiansen, U.
     in press "Demand for energy health care and regional systems for provision of supply." In Perlman, M. (ed.) Economics of Health and Medical Care. Washington, D.C.: International Economics Association.
Dimendberg, D.C.
     1969   "Emergency ambulance service in the City of New York." New York Medicine 25 (March): 124–129.
Dixon, P. N. *and* A. F. Morris
     1971   "Casual attendances at an accident department and a health centre." British Medical Journal 4 (October): 214–216.

Feldstein, M. S.
   1970a   "An aggregate planning model of the health care sector."
           Pp. 309–328 in Paelink, . H. P. (ed.), Programming for
           Europe's Collective Needs ASEPELT. Amsterdam: North-
           Holland Publishing Co.
   1970b   "The rising price of physicians' services." The Review of
           Economics and Statistics 52 (May): 121–133.
   1971   "An econometric model of the medicare system." The
           Quarterly Journal of Economics 85 (February): 1–20.

Gampel, B.
   1965   "Attendances for a new complaint at casulty department
           of two childrens' hospitals in London." Medical Care 3:
           222–230.

Gibson, G.
   1971a   Letter to the Editor. American Journal of Public Health
           61 (November): 2158–2160.
   1971b   "Status of urban services—2." Hospitals, Journal of the
           American Hospitals Association 45 (December): 62–66.

Gibson, G., G. Bugbee, *and* O. W. Anderson
   1971   Emergency Medical Services in the Chicago Areas. Chica-
           go: University of Chicago, Center for Health Administra-
           tion Studies.

Gordon, G. *and* K. Zelin
   1970   "A simulation study of emergency ambulance service in
           New York City." Transactions of the New York Academy
           of Sciences 32 (April): 414–427.

Grossman, M. *and* L. Benham
   1973   "Health, hours and wages." Paper presented before the To-
           kyo Conference on Economics of Health and Medical
           Care, International Economic Association, Tokyo, Japan,
           April 2–7.

Hall, Charles
   1966   "Deductibles in health insurance: An evaluation." Journal of
           Risk and Insurance 33: 253–263.

Hochheiser, L. I., K. Woodward, *and* E. Charney
   1971   "Effect of the neighborhood health center on the use of pe-
           diatric emergency departments in Rochester, New York."
           New England Journal of Medicine 285: 148–152.

Jacobs, A. R., J. W. Gavett, *and* R. Wersinger
  1971   "Emergency department utilization in an urban communi-
           ty." Journal of the American Medical Association 216:
           307–312.
Kaplan, R. S. *and* L. B. Lave
  1971   "Incentives and medical insurance." Health Services Re-
           search 6 (Winter): 288–300.
Kaplan, R. S. *and* S. Leinhardt
  1974   "Determinants of physician office location." Medical Care.
Keggi, K. J., S. B. Webb, Jr., *and* E. J. Broadbent
  1970   "A methodology for studying the emergency care of the
           trauma patient: Results of the Yale Trauma Study." Con-
           necticut Medicine 34 (February): 107–114.
Kerr, T. A., D. W. K. Kay, *and* L. P. Lassman
  1971   "Characteristics of patients, type of accident, and mortality
           in a consecutive series of head injuries admitted to a neuro-
           surgical unit." British Journal of Preventive and Social
           Medicine 25: 179–185.
King, B. G. *and* E. D. Sox
  1967   "An emergency medical service system—analysis of work-
           load." Public Health Reports 82 (November): 995–1008.
Kirkpatrick, J. R. *and* L. J. Taubenhaus
  1967   "The non-urgent patient on the emergency floor." Medical
           Care (January–February): 19–24.
Lave, J. R., L. B. Lave, *and* L. Silverman
  1973   "A proposal for incentive reimbursement of hospitals." Med-
           ical Care 11: 25–34.
Lave, J. R. *and* S. Leinhardt
  1972   "The delivery of ambulatory care to the poor: A literature
           review." Management Science 19 (December): 78–99.
Lavenhar, M. A., R. S. Ratner, *and* E. R. Weinerman
  1968   "Social class and medical care: Indices of nonurgency in
           use of hospital emergency services." Medical Care 6
           (September–October): 368–381.
Lee, S. S., J. A. Solon, *and* C. G. Sheps
  1960   "How new patterns of medical care affect the emergency
           unit." Modern Hospital 94 (May): 97–101.
National Academy of Sciences, National Research Council
  1966   Accidental Death and Disability. Washington, D.C.: Na-
           tional Academy of Sciences.

Noble, J. H., M. E. LaMontagne, C. Bellotti, *and* H. Wechsler
  1971   "Variations in visits to hospital emergency care facilities: Ritualistic and meteorological factors affecting supply and demand." Medical Care 9 (September–October). 415–427.

Perkoff, G. T. *and* M. Anderson
  1970   "Relationship between demographic characteristics, patient's chief complaint, and medical care destination in an emergency room." Medical Care 8 (July–August): 309–323.

Phelps, C. E. *and* J. P. Newhouse
  1972   "Effects of coinsurance: A multivariate analysis." Social Security Bulletin 35 (June): 20–28.

  1973   "Coinsurance and the demand for medical services," R-964-OEO/NC. Santa Monica: The RAND Corporation (April).

Reed, J. I. *and* G. G. Reader
  1967   "Quantitative survey of New York hospital emergency room, 1965." New York State Journal of Medicine 67 (May): 1335–1342.

Robinson, G. C. *and* H. Klonoff
  1967   "Hospital emergency services for children and adolescents." Canadian Medical Association Journal 96 (May): 1304–1308.

Roth, J. A.
  1971   "Utilization of the hospital emergency department." Journal of Health and Social Behavior 12 (December): 312–320.

Sagar, R. G. *and* L. K. Dick
  1971   "A computer simulation of ambulance services." Canadian Hospital 48 (May): 23–26.

Savas, E. S.
  1969   "Simulation and cost-effectiveness analysis of New York's emergency ambulance service." Management Science 15 (August): B608–B627.

Scitovsky, A. A. *and* N. M. Snyder
  1972   "Effect of coinsurance on use of physician services." Social Security Bulletin 35 (June): 3–19.

Shortliffe, E., T. Hamilton, *and* E. Noroian
  1958   "The emergency room and the changing pattern of medical care." New England Journal of Medicine 258: 20.

Sklar, H. S. *and* E. F. Downs
  1968   "Acute medical problems of suburban adolescents." Clini-
            cal Pediatrics 7 (April): 220–225.
  1970   "Emergency room utilization patterns of adolescents." New
            York State Journal of Medicine 70 (March): 643–649.
Skudder, P. J. M. *and* P. Wade
  1961   "Hospital emergency facilities and services, a survey." Bul-
            letin of the American College of Surgery 46:44.
Sloan, F. L.
  1973   "Supply responses of young physicians," R-1131-OEO. San-
            ta Monica: The RAND Corporation (March.)
Solon, J. A. *and* R. D. Rigg
  1972   "Patterns of medical care among users of hospital emergen-
            cy units." Medical Care 10 (January–February): 60–72.
Taubenhaus, L. J. *and* J. R. Kirkpatrick
  1967   "Analysis of a hospital ambulance service." Public Health
            Reports 82 (September): 823–827.
Torrens, P. R. *and* D. G. Yedvar
  1970   "Variations among emergency room populations: A com-
            parison of four hospitals in New York City." Medical Care
            8 (January–February): 60–75.
Vaughan, H. F., Jr. *and* C. E. Gamester
  1966   "Why patients use hospital emergency departments." Hos-
            pitals, Journal of the American Hospitals Association 40
            (October): 59–61.
Waller, J. A.
  1965   "Ambulance service: Transportation or medical care?"
            Public Health Reports 82 (October): 847–853.
Weinerman, E. R.
  1965   "Yale studies in ambulatory medical care—IV. Outpatient-
            clinic services in the teaching hospital." The New England
            Journal of Medicine 272: 947–954.
  1966   "Yale studies in ambulatory medical care—III. Innovation in
            ambulatory services." Journal of Medical Education 41
            (July): 712–721.
Weinerman, E. R., R. S. Ratner, A. Robbines, *and* M. A. Lavenhar
  1966   "Yale studies in ambulatory medical care—V. Determi-
            nants of use of hospital emergency services." American
            Journal of Public Health 57 (July): 1037–1056.

Weinerman, E. R., S. R. Rutzen, *and* D. A. Pearson
    1965   "Effects of Medical 'triage' in hospital emergency service." Public Health Reports 80 (May): 389–399.
Weinerman, E. R. *and* H. R. Edwards
    1964   " 'Triage' system shows promise in management of emergency department load." Hospitals, Journal of the American Hospitals Association 38 (November): 55–62.
White, H. A. *and* P. A. O'Connor
    1970   "Use of the emergency room in a community hospital." Public Health Reports 85 (February): 163–168.
Wingert, W. A.
    1970   "Changing trends and opportunities in pediatric emergency care." Medical Times 98 (May): 146–153.
Wingert, W. A., D. B. Friedman, *and* W. R. Larson
    1968   "The demographical and ecological characteristics of a large urban pediatric outpatient population and implications for improving community pediatric care." American Journal of Public Health 58 (May): 859–876.
Yett, D., L. Drabek, M. Intrilligator, *and* L. Kimbell
    1971a   "A macro-economic model for regional health planning." Economic and Business Bulletin 24 (Fall): 1–21.
    1971b   "The use of an econometric model to analyze selected features of national health insurance plans." Paper presented before the American Economic Association Meeting, New Orleans, Louisiana, December 28.

Consumer

Incentives for Health

Services in Chronic Illness

MICHAEL GROSSMAN

AND ELIZABETH H. RAND

As acute illness has been increasingly controlled and deaths from infectious and parasitic diseases nearly eliminated, and as the population has grown both larger and older, the problem of chronic disease has increased in importance. In 1901 only 46 percent of all deaths were attributable to chronic disease, by 1955 the percentage was 81.4 (Bright, 1966). And though those figures independently indicate the importance of chronic illness in the medical-care needs of the nation, they in no way indicate the burden of illness and disability preceeding death (Lilienfeld and Gifford, 1966:4). Consumer incentives in the use of medical-care services by the chronically ill are considered in this paper. Most studies of utilization have implicitly or explicitly dealt with the acutely ill population—studying, for example, an individual's most recent episode of illness or utilization of short-stay hospitals. As the dominant form of illness shifts from acute to chronic, it is important to study factors associated with utilization specific to the chronically ill.

Because of the paucity of theoretical and empirical studies in the area, a major purpose here is to suggest a framework for future research. Since we are economists and true believers in "economic imperialism," our framework emphasizes the roles of economic variables in the demand curve for medical care by the chronically ill. It also examines how that curve is likely to differ from demand curves for medical care by other groups. Our emphasis on economic factors does not mean that we ignore variables, such as attitudes, perceptions, demographic characteristics, and education, that other disciplines might consider important. What it does mean is that we make predictions about the effects of those variables in an economic context.

The first section defines chronic illness first broadly and then more specifically, as it is applied in most statistical data available. Some limitations of the prevailing classification system are discussed. Published national data on the incidence and types of chronic illness for the population and certain subgroups are presented. The second section deals with theoretical considerations in analyzing the demand for medical care by the chronically ill. Grossman's model (1972a; 1972b) of the demand for health and the derived demand for medical care serves as the point of departure. The final section contains a selective review of the literature on the utilization behavior of the chronically ill. Although only a few of the studies cited actually estimate demand curves, they all present data and findings that suggest issues and areas for future research.

Definition and Prevalence of Chronic Illness

Definition

The Commission on Chronic Illness formulated the broad definition of chronic disease that still prevails:

> All impairments or deviations from normal which have *one or more* of the following characteristics: are permanent; leave residual disability; are caused by nonreversible pathological alterations; require special training of the patient for rehabilitation; may be expected to require a long period of supervision, observation or care (1951:14).

Such a definition is useful in distinguishing the chronically ill from the acutely ill and comprehends the total population in need of long-term care. It can also be transformed readily into the specific categories of diagnosis that have traditionally formed the basis of prevalence studies. The Health Interview Survey, for instance, which provides the largest body of ongoing descriptive data on the chronically ill, counts as chronic any condition on a checklist of chronic conditions and impairments, or any other current condition first noticed more than three months earlier (National Center for Health Statistics, 1971:59).

The classification and measurement of chronic illness are important issues in an analysis of consumer incentives in the use of medical-care services among this population. Tyroler suggests that the category-of-diagnosis approach may not be particularly useful in the study of utilization among the chronically ill because of "the apparent multicausal etiology of the chronic disease; the marked and varied range of manifestations; the long-term course of their development, often with asymptomatic and chronically non-detectable pathologic evolutions . . .; and the wide range of responses to the [therapeutic] modalities which are available (1969:45)." Thus, the heterogeneity of the population subsumed under the broad working definition of chronic illness diminishes the definition's usefulness in utilization studies.

Of the 94.9 million persons reported in 1965–1967 as having one or more chronic illnesses, 76.8 percent reported no limitation of activity and 93.3 percent reported no mobility limitation (National Center for Health Statistics, 1971:19–20).[1] Although they might not currently be utilizing medical service because of their chronic conditions, since most chronic illnesses progress with time, they can be expected to use the service later. The 23.2 percent (22.0 million persons) indicating one or more limiting chronic conditions ranged from 26 percent reporting some "limitation, but not in major activity" to 18 percent "unable to carry on major activity." Of the 6.3 million persons with some mobility limitation, 50 percent reported "having trouble getting around" and 22 percent were

[1] Limitation in activity refers to a person's major activity as well as leisure activities. Limitation of mobility refers to a person's ability to move around freely.

"confined to the house." The variation in restricted activity and mobility exists within given diagnoses, e.g., arthritis, as well as across
diagnoses.

Two additional aspects of heterogeneity within the chronically
ill population concern the issues of treatability and multiplicity of
conditions. Certain chronic illnesses or impairments, such as blind-
ness, can be classified as nontreatable (Hurtado and Greenlick,
1971; and Hurtado and Greenlick, n.d.) (although, of course, they
may indicate demand for personal care or special education), while
for others treatment ranges from merely palliative (in the case of
emphysema) to definitive (as with pernicious anemia) (Blum and
Keranen, 1966). The average number of reported chronic conditions is 2.2 (National Center for Health Statistics, 1971:3). For
persons with some activity limitation the average is 3.4, and for
persons with some mobility limitation it is 4.1. Thus, there will
be various combinations, stages, and complexities of disease. For further discussion of the heterogeneity of the chronically ill population,
see Katz et al. (1969).

According to some authorities, the most desirable approach to
the control of many chronic illnesses is through prevention (see, for
instance, Blum and Keranen, 1966:2; Commission on Chronic Illness, 1957b:4). Measures for preventing the occurrence of illness
would be included, as well as such measures as periodic health examinations, multiphasic screening, and diagnostic services to assist
in arresting disease in its early, often undiagnosed stages. In fact, in
1957, the Commission on Chronic Illness estimated that, in nearly
40 percent of the cases, unnecessary suffering and disability could
be avoided by earlier diagnosis and treatment (Commission on
Chronic Illness 1957a:59). There is still controversy, however, over
the usefulness of even some of the most accepted forms of early
detection, such as the Papanicolaou Test for cervical cancer. A recent study in England indicates that, though the test is successful in
detecting cases in earlier stages, death rates are not lower for
groups that receive the test (Cochrane, 1972).

Consumer incentives for utilization of medical services will
clearly be composed of variables related to health status itself as

well as to the patient's socioeconomic characteristics, including variations in interpretation of health status. Thus Tyroler (1969:10) suggests that, at a minimum, studies of health-service utilization require the inclusion of both the provider's and the population's perspectives in the classification system. Certainly users and providers differ in their feelings about need for medical care. The National Center for Health Statistics (1971:4–5) notes, for example, that nearly 10 percent of those with some activity limitation claimed it was due to aging rather than to any specific chronic illness. Coe et al. (1967) point out that perceptions of illness as well as definition of symptoms as illness in need of professional services will vary from individual to individual. They suggest that chronic, as opposed to acute, illnesses may be normative rather than deviant in that they are, by definition, long-term and often permanent.

Some researchers are currently formulating and testing classification systems for chronic illness that do not abandon the categories of disease but refine or group them. Katz et al. (1969) are particularly concerned with problems of heterogeneity, diagnosis, and levels of illness. They propose a classification system that attempts to combine measurements of all three aspects of chronic illness. Hurtado and Greenlick (n.d.) are concerned with behavioral as well as clinical aspects of disease. Their classification system was devised for the ongoing utilization study being made of all aspects of the Kaiser Foundation Hospitals service in Portland. They first classified conditions into forty-six clinical subgroups and then combined those into ten behavioral classes, each of which is composed of clinical subgroups expected to produce similar medical-care utilization from persons with similar background characteristics. The method resulted in two chronic disease classifications: one "with no symptoms or non-treatable symptoms" and the other "with treatable symptoms."

Given the usual long-term progression of chronic illness, the importance of early detection, and the wide range of resulting limitation of activity and mobility, the variety of services used by the population is enormous. They include not only the usual treatment

services, but screening and other casefinding services as well as rehabilitation, long-term institutional, and personal and medical home
services.

Prevalence

Despite the limitations of the current classification system, prevalence of chronic illness is useful as a variable to explain demand
for services or utilization, or as a variable to be controlled in measuring determinants of utilization other than disease. (Tyroler,
1969:39). It has already been cited that 22.0 million persons in
1967–1969 reported having one or more chronic conditions causing
limitation of activity, and 6.3 million persons reported a condition
causing some mobility limitation. Table 1 lists the ten leading

**TABLE 1 Percentage Distribution of Persons with Limitation of Activity
or Limitation of Mobility, by Selected Chronic Conditions
Causing Limitation, United States, July 1965–June 1967**

Selected Chronic Conditions Causing Activity Limitation	Percentage Distribution	Selected Chronic Conditions Causing Mobility Limitation	Percentage Distribution
All limiting conditions	100.0%	All limiting conditions	100.0%
Heart conditions	16.4	Arthritis and rheumatism	24.4
Arthritis and rheumatism	14.8	Heart condition	12.6
Impairments (except paralysis) of back or spine	8.2	Impairments (except paralysis or absence) of lower extremities and hips	11.4
Mental and nervous conditions	7.8	Paralysis, complete or partial	10.9
Impairments (except paralysis and absence) of lower extremities and hips	6.1	Visual impairments	10.4
Visual impairments	5.6	Impairments (except paralysis) of back or spine	5.2
Hypertension without heart involvement	5.4	Mental and nervous conditions	4.9
Asthma-hay fever	4.8	Other conditions of circulatory system	3.9
Paralysis, complete or partial	4.2	Hypertension without heart involvements	3.4
Conditions of genito-urinary system	4.1	Other diseases of muscles, bones and joints	3.3

Source: National Center for Health Statistics (1971: 21–22).

chronic conditions causing activity limitation and mobility limitation for the noninstitutionalized civilian population.[2]

There are notable differentials in prevalence of chronic conditions across demographic and other variables. The strongest variations occur with age: as age increases the prevalence of chronic conditions increases correspondingly for all degrees of limitation. Although the aged (sixty-five years or over) are more likely to have one or more limiting chronic conditions than younger persons, they rarely account for more of the cases of any given illness (with the exception of arthritis and rheumatism and visual impairments). Because of the strong variations across age groups, it is most useful to look at age-adjusted differentials for other characteristics.

Table 2 shows that, on an age-adjusted basis, more males than females report limitation in their major activity, while more females than males report chronic conditions with minor or no limitation. Similarly, limitations in major activity are reported by more non-whites than whites, and more whites than nonwhites report conditions with minor or no limitation of activity. As family income rises, the age-adjusted prevalence of one or more conditions remains remarkably stable, but there is an increasing prevalence of reported conditions involving no activity limitation and a decreasing prevalence of more severely limiting conditions. The relationships are even more accentuated for increasing educational levels.

The net result is that the chronically ill have lower average family income than others, partly because income itself is a function of chronic illness. Since chronic conditions are, by definition, permanent rather than temporary, so is the difference in income. As would be expected, the employed population has fewer chronic conditions and less limitation of activity than the unemployed population or those not in the labor force. Among regions the West has

---

[2] The data in tables 1 and 2 refer to the civilian, noninstitutionalized population. In 1960 the U.S. Census reported 1,887,000 inmates of institutions, nearly 75 percent of whom were in medical institutions, such as mental hospitals, homes for the aged, and homes for the mentally and physically handicapped. Thus, presumably, nearly all such persons are chronically ill (U.S. Department of Commerce, 1972).

the highest prevalence of minor conditions, and the South has the highest prevalence of more seriously limiting conditions. The relationships differ somewhat but appear to be generally true for mobility limitation as well.

To the extent that prevalence of chronic illnesss represents demand for services, and since prevalence is highly associated with age, it is of some interest to examine the degree to which the population is getting older. Twaddle (1968) points out that increases in chronic illness result both from the aging of the population and from medical advances in the fight against disease mortality. He predicts that from 1960 to 1985, while the population will get older, the prevalence of chronic conditions (among older persons) will increase even more rapidly and disability related to chronic disease will increase still faster.

Theoretical Considerations

What can economic theory say about the demand curve for chronic medical care—that is, care for the chronically ill? (By the term "demand curve" for chronic medical care is meant the demand curve by persons with chronic conditions. The theory outlined in this section will be more applicable to persons whose chronic conditions result in some limitation of activity or mobility.) How is that demand curve likely to differ from the curve for care for acute cases or preventive care? There has been little theoretical or empirical work, at least in the United States, on estimating and interpreting separate demand curves for the three types of care. Consequently, the main purpose of this section is to suggest a framework for future work. The theoretical treatment is most relevant for studies of variations in utilization among persons who use positive amounts of medical care.

Most of the analysis draws heavily on Grossman's model (1972a; 1972b) of the demand for health and the derived demand for medical care. In the context of Grossman's model, the rate of depreciation in the stock of health capital can be viewed as a meas-

TABLE 2 Age-Adjusted [a] Percentage Distribution of Persons by Degree of Chronic Activity Limitation, According to Selected Characteristics

SELECTED CHARACTERISTIC	PERSONS WITH NO CHRONIC CONDITIONS	PERSONS WITH ONE OR MORE CHRONIC CONDITIONS			
		With No Limitation of Activity	With Limitation but Not in Major Activity [b]	With Limitation in Amount or Kind of Major Activity [b]	Unable to Carry on Major Activity [b]
Sex					
Male	50.9	36.4	2.6	6.8	3.3
Female	50.2	39.4	3.3	6.0	1.1
Color					
White	49.8	39.0	3.0	6.2	2.0
All other	55.6	30.6	2.2	7.9	3.6
Family income					
Under $3,000	48.2	33.6	3.5	10.6	4.1
$3,000–$4,999	51.8	35.6	2.8	7.5	2.3
$5,000–$6,999	51.9	37.8	2.7	5.9	1.8
$7,000–$9,999	50.1	40.3	3.0	5.1	1.6
$10,000–$14,999	49.2	41.8	3.0	4.5	1.4
$15,000 and over	50.0	42.2	3.1	3.5	1.3
Educational level					
Under 5 years	30.4	36.7	3.7	18.3	10.9
5–8 years	33.9	44.5	4.3	13.2	3.9
9–11 years	37.8	46.8	3.9	9.3	2.2
12 years	38.3	48.9	3.9	7.3	1.7
13–15 years	35.9	52.4	3.8	6.4	1.6
16 years and over	35.5	55.2	3.3	4.7	1.3

Employment status

Currently employed	38.4	49.7	3.5	8.1	0.3
Currently unemployed	36.6	44.0	4.6	12.7	2.1
Not in labor force	32.7	45.6	4.6	11.3	5.9

Geographic region

Northeast	54.1	36.2	2.3	5.6	1.8
North Central	50.8	38.3	3.2	6.0	1.8
South	48.9	37.5	2.8	7.9	2.9
West	47.2	41.5	3.7	5.8	1.8

Sources: For sex, color, family income, employment status, and geographic regional characteristics: National Center for Health Statistics (1971: 7,17); for educational level characteristics: National Center for Health Statistics (1970:12).

[a] Adjusted to the age distribution of the total civilian, non-institutional population of the United States for sex, color, income, and regional characteristics. Adjusted to the similar population age seventeen and over for education and employment characteristics.

[b] Major activity refers to ability to work, keep house, or engage in school-preschool activities.

ure of the "loss" due to illness. Persons with chronic conditions are likely to have above-average rates of depreciation. The analysis therefore focuses on the effects that variations in the depreciation rate have on the demand for medical care and on interactions between that rate and other variables in the demand curve, such as income and price. It also shows how the predictions of the model are altered when preventive and curative medical care are introduced as separate inputs in the health-production function. Empirical studies that are directly related to the theoretical development are also discussed.

Grossman's Model

Grossman's model (1972a; 1972b) of the demand for medical care is based on the fundamental proposition that what consumers demand when they purchase medical services are not those services per se but rather "good health." According to his proposition, the demand for medical care must be derived from the more basic demand for health. The household-production function approach to demand theory serves as the point of departure for his specific model of the demand for health (see, for example: Becker, 1965; Michael and Becker, in press; Lancaster 1966; Muth, 1966). In that approach, consumers produce all their basic objects of choice, called commodities, with inputs of market goods and services and their own time. Since goods and services are inputs into the production of commodities, the demand for goods and services may be viewed as derived demand for a factor of production.

Within the context of the household-production function framework, Grossman treats health as a durable item. Thus, individuals inherit an initial stock of health capital that depreciates with age and can be increased by investment. By definition, net investment in the stock of health equals gross investment minus depreciation. Direct inputs into the production of gross investments in health include the consumer's own time, medical care, proper diet, exercise, recreation, housing, and other market goods as well.

In the Grossman model, health is demanded by consumers for two reasons. As a consumption commodity, it directly enters their utility functions; put differently, illness is a source of disutility. As an investment commodity, it determines the total amount of time available for work in the market sector of the economy, where consumers produce money earnings, and for work in the nonmarket or household sector, where they produce commodities that enter their utility functions. The investment motive for demanding health is present because an increase in the stock of health lowers the amount of time lost from market and nonmarket activities as a result of illness and injury. Grossman develops in detail two extreme versions of the general demand-for-health model: a pure investment version and a pure consumption version. In the former, health does not enter the utility function directly, while in the latter the monetary rate of return on an investment in health equals zero.

One main advantage of his model is that it makes strong predictions about the effects of shifts in variables other than income and the price of medical care on the demand for care. The predictions are based on the proposition that the "shadow price" of health depends on many variables besides the price of medical care. In particular, it rises with age if the rate of depreciation in the stock of health rises over a person's life cycle and falls with schooling if more schooling makes him a more efficient producer of health. An increase in the shadow price of health would generally lower the quantity of health demanded. If, however, the price elasticity of demand for health were less than one, the quantity of medical care demanded would rise. (For a proof of this proposition, see Grossman, 1972b:15–19, 24–28.)

It should be noted that Grossman does not explicitly deal with uncertainty in his analysis. He does indicate, however, that uncertainty can be introduced into the model by assuming that each person faces a probability distribution of depreciation rates at any given age. Using Grossman's framework, Phelps (1973) has developed a model of the joint determination of the demand for medical care and the demand for health insurance under uncertainty. He shows that the introduction of uncertainty does not alter the basic properties of the demand curve for medical care that Grossman derives from his model.

Effects of Variations in Depreciation Rates

Within the context of Grossman's model, the demand for chronic medical care may be studied by assuming that persons with chronic conditions have higher rates of depreciation or higher losses due to illness in their stocks of health capital than other persons. To be sure, this is an oversimplification. As indicated in the first section, some chronic conditions cause no limitations in amount or kind of usual activity. Moreover, certain acute conditions may be associated with higher rates of depreciation, at least temporarily, than certain chronic conditions.[3] Despite those qualifications, it is extremely probable that persons with chronic conditions will have higher depreciation rates on the average.

Grossman shows that an increase in the depreciation rate would raise the shadow price of health and would cause the quantity of health capital demanded to fall. At the same time, the quantity of medical care demanded would rise if the price elasticity of demand for health were less than 1. The proposition is summarized by the formula for the elasticity of medical care M with respect to the depreciation rate δ. (Equation (1) assumes that the rate of interest is equal to zero. For a proof and a complete discussion of the equation, see Grossman, 1972b.

$$\frac{\partial \ln M}{\partial \ln \delta} = e_\delta = 1 - \epsilon, \tag{1}$$

where ϵ is the price elasticity of demand for health capital. (The price elasticity of demand for health capital is defined as the abso-

---

[3] Strictly speaking, the presence of an acute condition can be associated with a temporary increase in the rate of depreciation, while the presence of a chronic condition can be associated with a permanent increase in the rate of depreciation. In a model that permitted lagged responses to an increase in the rate of depreciation, the distinction between permanent and temporary variations would be very important. Since Grossman's model does not permit such responses, the distinction is much less relevant. It may be relevant, however, in considering interactions between the rate of depreciation and the wage rate in the demand curve for medical care.

lute value of the percentage reduction in the quantity of health capital demanded for a one-percent rise in the shadow price of health.
It is important to distinguish that elasticity from the price elasticity
of demand for medical care, discussed later in this section.)

The interpretation of equation (1) is that a rise in the rate of
depreciation lowers the quantity of health capital supplied to consumers by a given amount of medical care. If the demand curve for
health is relatively inelastic, consumers would have an incentive to
offset part, although not all, of the reduction in health capital by
using more medical care. From now on, it is assumed that the price
elasticity of health is in fact less than one. (In the context of his
pure investment model, Grossman shows that the price elasticity of
health should be in theory smaller than one. See Grossman,
1972b:17–18.) On that premise, the model predicts a positive correlation between the loss to the stock of health caused by illness and
medical care. Thus, with other variables in the demand curve for
medical care held constant, consumers with chronic conditions
should demand more medical care than others.

Grossman's empirical estimates of demand curves for medical
care do not directly measure the rate of depreciation in health
capital.[4] Newhouse and Phelps (1973) and Acton (1973) have,
however, included proxy variables for the rate of depreciation in
demand curves that are estimated on data for individuals. Newhouse and Phelps measure the rate of depreciation by the number
of disability days and by self-rated health status, and Acton uses the
number of chronic conditions that limit activity. Both studies assess
the effects that their indexes of health status have on medical care,
with wage and nonwage income, the price of medical care, age,
schooling, and other variables held constant. The two studies report
strong positive effects for number of disability days and of chronic
conditions on the demand for medical care and a strong negative ef-

---

[4] Grossman assumes that the rate of depreciation is a positive function of age.
His demand functions do contain an age variable, but he does not control for
variations in the rate of depreciation that are uncorrelated with age. If such
variations were uncorrelated with the independent variables in the demand
function, the parameter estimates that he obtains would be unbiased.

fect for self-rated health status (see, for example, Andersen, 1968; Richardson, 1971).[5]

A difficulty arises when the number of disability days, the number of chronic conditions, or self-rated health status is used as a proxy for the rate of depreciation in health capital. Differences in those variables partly reflect not only differences in the rate of depreciation but also in health capital itself. Since health capital and medical care are determined simultaneously in Grossman's model, it is not entirely appropriate to hold health capital constant when, for example, the income elasticity of medical care is estimated.[6] Of course, this criticism is mitigated to the extent that there is no direct measure of the depreciation rate. It does suggest, however, that future research might consider whether certain characteristics of a person are more closely related to his rate of depreciation than those used in past studies.

Interaction Effects

The conclusion reached in the preceding section that illness and utilization of medical services should be positively correlated is not particularly striking. But the analysis used to reach that conclusion also provides a framework for examining differences in the parameters of the demand curves for preventive, acute, and chronic medical care. In comparing the demand curves for the three kinds of care, the detection of parameter differences is crucial.

[5] The studies by Newhouse and Phelps and by Acton are cited in the text because they are based on Grossman's model of the demand for health. Moreover, in measuring the effect of health status on medical care, they hold constant variables that are not included in other studies, such as the wage rate and the coinsurance rate associated with a consumer's health insurance policy.

[6] With health held constant and with income interpreted as a measure of the value of time, the estimated income elasticity of medical care would simply reflect substitution of medical care for the consumer's own time in the production of health as the value of time rises. If health were not held constant and if income and the quantity of health demanded were positively correlated, the income elasticity of medical care would reflect both a substitution effect and an expansion effect.

In general, parameter differences may be traced to two types of interaction that involve the rate of depreciation in health capital. First, a given parameter in the demand curve for medical care may be a function of the depreciation rate. Second, characteristics other than the rate of depreciation may distinguish the chronically ill from other groups. Those distinguishing characteristics may, in turn, enter the demand curve for medical care in a nonlinear fashion, or the parameters of the function may depend on them.[7]

Depreciation rate parameter. What are the sources of the interaction? According to equation (1), the elasticity of medical care with respect to the depreciation rate is inversely related to the price elasticity of demand for health capital. Therefore, if persons with chronic conditions had a less elastic demand curve for health than other persons, their utilization of medical services would rise more in response to a given percentage increase in the rate of deprecia-

---

[7] Let the demand curve for medical care be

$$\ln M = a_0 + a_1 \ln X_1 + a_2 \ln X_2 + a_3 \ln X_3 + a_4 \ln X_4 + a_5 \ln \delta,$$

and let

$$a_5 = a'_5 + b_1 \ln \delta$$
$$a_1 = a'_1 + b_2 \ln \delta$$
$$\ln X_3 = (\ln X_2)^2$$
$$a_4 = a'_4 + b_3 \ln Z.$$

Then if $\ln M_\delta$ and $\ln M_i$ denote partial derivatives of $\ln M$ with respect to $\ln \delta$ and $\ln X_i$ ($i = 1, 2, 3, 4$),

$$\ln M_\delta = a_5' + 2b_1 \ln \delta$$
$$\ln M_1 = a'_1 + b_2 \ln \delta$$

$$\ln M_2 = a_2 + 2a_3 \ln X_2$$
$$\ln M_4 = a_4 + b_3 \ln Z,$$

where the last two derivatives are evaluated at the mean of $\ln X_2$ and the mean of $\ln Z$, respectively. It is obvious that the first two derivatives depend on δ. Suppose that individuals are grouped according to their observed values of δ, and suppose that separate demand curves are estimated for each group. If $\ln X_2$ and $\ln Z$ depend on δ, the estimates of $\ln M_2$ and $\ln M_4$ would differ among groups.

tion. At an empirical level, if disability days or self-rated health status is used as an index of the depreciation rate, the regression coefficient of the variable should be larger in the demand curve for chronic medical care than it is in the demand curve for preventive or acute care.

Although Grossman's pure investment model of the demand for health does not suggest a relationship between the depreciation rate and the price elasticity of health, his pure consumption model does. The relationship between the two variables arises because the share of income spent on health will rise as the depreciation rate rises. The model does not, however, specify the sign of the relationship. In the pure consumption model, by definition,

$$\epsilon = (1 - s)\sigma_c + s\eta, \tag{2}$$

where s is the share of income spent on health,[8] σ_c is the elasticity of substitution in consumption between health and other commodities in the utility function, and η is the income elasticity of demand for health. It follows that

$$\frac{d\epsilon}{d\delta} = (\eta - \sigma_c)\frac{ds}{d\delta}, \tag{3}$$

provided η and σ_c are constant. The price elasticity of health would fall with the rate of depreciaftion if σ_c exceeded η, and it would rise with δ if η exceeded σ_c.[9] (See Phelps and Newhouse, 1973:29.)

Equations (1) and (2) also imply that the depreciation-rate effect may vary with income. From equation (1), a negative correla-

---

[8] The variable s is not simply equal to the share of income spent on medical care. Since the own time of the consumer is an input in the production of health, s equals medical outlays plus the monetary value of time spent producing health divided by income.

[9] Charles E. Phelps and Joseph P. Newhouse have pointed out that s and δ are positively correlated. Their discussion of the effect of the correlation on ϵ emphasizes its impact on the term $s\eta$ in the formula for ϵ but ignores its impact on the term $(1 - s)\sigma_c$.

tion between income and the price elasticity of health would cause
the elasticity of medical care with respect to the depreciation rate to
rise with income. From equation (2), if the share of the income
spent on health fell as income rose, ϵ would fall with income provided the income elasticity exceeded the elasticity of substitution.
(See, for example, Andersen and Benham, 1970; Fuchs and Kramer, 1972. The share of income spent on health would fall with
income if income elasticity of health were less than one. Existing
studies indicate that the income elasticity is smaller than 1. An additional factor that would produce the same result is a drop in the
elasticity of substitution as income rises. As Table 2 indicates, persons with chronic conditions have lower permanent or long-run income than others and would be less sensitive to increases in the rate
of depreciation for that reason alone.[10]

---

[10] The net effect on the elasticity of M with respect to $\delta(e_\delta)$ of a nefiative correlation between ϵ and δ and a negative correlation between ϵ and income y
is ambiguous. Let the demand curve for medical care be

$$\ln M = \eta \ln y + e_\delta \ln \delta,$$

where

$$e_\delta = 1 - \epsilon.$$

In addition let

$$e_\delta = e'_\delta + b_1 \ln \delta + b_2 \ln y$$

Then if e_δ is evaluated at the means of $\ln \delta$ and $\ln y$,

$$\overline{e_\delta} = \overline{e'_\delta} + 2b_1 \overline{\ln \delta} + b_2 \overline{\ln y}$$

Since $\overline{\ln y}$ rises as $\overline{\ln \delta}$ falls, $\overline{e_\delta}$ may be larger or smaller for consumers with
chronic conditions than for other consumers. It should be noted that the
income-depreciation rate interaction effect is relevant in examining the
responses of different income groups to a given increase in the rate
of depreciation. For example, the model would predict that an increase
in the rate of depreciation associated with a given acute condition would
cause a greater increase in utilization of medical services at higher income levels. The income-depreciation rate interaction may be more relevant in studying
this issue than it is in comparing the utilization behavior of the chronically ill
to that of other groups.

Age and schooling parameters. When the price elasticity of health varies with the rate of depreciation, the effects of age and schooling will be different in the demand curve for chronic care than in demand curves for other types of care. Grossman assumes that the rate of depreciation in health capital rises with age, at least after some point in the life cycle. He shows that the parameter of age A in the demand curve for medical care is given by

$$\frac{\partial \ln M}{\partial A} = M_A = \tilde{\delta}(1 - c), \qquad (4)$$

where $\tilde{\delta}$ is the percentage rate of increase in the rate of depreciation caused by a one-year increase in age (for proof of equation (4), see Grossman, 1972b:13–17). It should be clear that equation (4) can be interpreted in the same manner as equation (1). Since it is still assumed that ϵ_S is less than 1, M_A is positive.

Equation (4) implies that M_A would be larger for persons with chronic conditions if the demand curve for health is less elastic for them than for others. An added consideration that would generate a different age effect for the chronically ill is that the rate of depreciation in their stock of health may increase at a faster or slower rate.

Grossman postulates that years of formal schooling completed enters the demand curve for medical care because more schooling makes a person a more efficient producer of health. In other words, a rise in schooling raises the amount of health obtained from given amounts of medical care and other inputs, lowers the shadow price of health, and raises the quantity of health demanded. The parameter of years of formal schooling completed S in the demand curve for medical care equals

$$\frac{\partial \ln M}{\partial S} = M_S = r(\epsilon - 1), \qquad (5)$$

where r is the percentage increase in health productivity caused by a one-year increase in schooling (for complete discussion, see

Grossman, 1972b:24–28, 35–37)[11] Equation (5) reflects the same forces as equations (1) and (4). When the demand curve is relatively inelastic, those with more schooling would have an incentive to offset part of the resulting increase in health by using less medical care. Therefore, with other variables in the demand curve for medical care held constant, the regression coefficient of schooling should be negative.

A literal interpretation of equation (5) would suggest that, if the presence of chronic conditions causes ϵ to fall, schooling should have a larger negative effect on utilization for consumers with such conditions. One factor, however, goes in the opposite direction. It is probable that the productivity effect of schooling is greater in preventive or acute medical care than in chronic care. If the presence of chronic conditions causes r to fall then the negative effect of schooling on utilization of medical care should be smaller in absolute value for the chronically ill.

Income and price elasticities. The two fundamental parameters of any demand curve are its income and price elasticities. Therefore, in comparing the demand curve for medical care by persons with chronic illness with the demand curves for care by other persons, the crucial question to answer is: What is the effect of chronic illness on the income and price elasticities of medical care?

Grossman's model does not answer the question definitely, but it does suggest the relevant factors that must be considered. The analysis of variations in income and price elasticites due to chronic illness is based on three propositions. First, income and the value of time—measured, say, by the hourly or the weekly wage rate—are highly correlated. Second, under certain conditions, variations in income or wage and price elasticities will be related to variations in the wage rate. Finally, persons with chronic conditions have lower actual or potential wage rates than other persons.

In the health-production function in Grossman's model, the two

---

[11] The discussion in the text assumes essentially that schooling raises efficiency in the production of health but not in the production of other nonmarket commodities.

most important direct inputs are medical care and the consumer's own time. It follows that the basic formulas for analyzing variations in income and price elasticities are (Grossman, 1972b:22–24, 90–92)

$$\frac{\partial \ln M}{\partial \ln W} = e_W = (1 - k)\epsilon + k\sigma, \qquad (6)$$

$$\frac{\partial \ln M}{\partial \ln P} = \epsilon_P = -[(1 - k)\epsilon + k\sigma]. \qquad (7)$$

In these equations, W is the hourly or weekly wage rate, P is the price of medical care, σ is the elasticity of substitution between medical care and time in the production of health, k is the fraction of the total cost of producing health accounted for by time, and $1 - k$ is the fraction of total cost accounted for by medical care.[12]

Equation (6) gives a formula for the wage elasticity of demand for medical care. It is not identical with the income elasticity of demand for medical care, and Grossman's model says little about variations in the "pure" income elasticity of medical care, defined as the income elasticity that would be observed if income varied with the wage rate held constant. Indeed, equation (6) is based on Grossman's investment model, where the pure income elasticity would equal zero.[13] Equation (6) reveals that, as the wage rate rises, the quantity of medical care demanded rises for two reasons. An increase in the wage raises the monetary rate of return on an investment in health and causes the quantity of health demanded to rise. The effect is represented by the term $(1 - k)\epsilon$. Consumers have an incentive, moreover, to substitute medical care for their rel-

---

[12] If T is the own time input, then $k = WT/(WT + PM)$ and $1 - k = PM/(WT + PM)$.

[13] If income were held constant as the wage rate varied or if the pure income elasticity were constant, then the wage elasticity would behave in the same manner in the consumption model as it does in the investment model.

atively more expensive own time in the production of health. That effect is represented by the term $k\sigma$.[14]

Equation (7) gives a formula for the price elasticity of demand for medical care. The price of medical care is the "net" price, defined as $P = cP^*$, where c is the coinsurance rate associated with a consumer's health insurance policy and P^* is the "nominal" price of medical care. The implication is that the elasticities of medical care with respect to c and P^* are identical. (For justification of this definition of price, see, for example, Newhouse and Phelps, 1973; and Phelps, 1973.) As the net price rises, the shadow price of health rises, and the quantity of health demanded falls, as shown by the negative term $-(1 - k)\epsilon$ in equation (7). In addition, there is an incentive to substitute own time for medical care in the production of a given amount of health, which is shown by the negative term $-k\sigma$.

Equations (6) and (7) indicate that the wage and price elasticities of medical care would be related to the wage rate if the fraction of the total cost of health accounted for by time k varied with the wage. Differentiating equation (6) and the absolute value of equation (7) with respect to $\ln W$ and assuming the ϵ and σ are constant, one obtains

$$\frac{de_W}{d\ln W} = (\sigma - \epsilon) \frac{dk}{d\ln W}, \tag{8}$$

$$\frac{de_P}{d\ln W} = (\sigma - \epsilon) \frac{dk}{d\ln W}. \tag{9}$$

If it is assumed that the elasticity of substitution in production

---

[14] This analysis is relevant even for persons who are not in the labor force. For such individuals, the value of time would be measured by the monetary equivalent of the marginal utility of time. That variable in turn would be related to property and other nonearnings income. For discussions of the concept of the monetary equivalent of the marginal utility of time, see, for example, Gronau (1973) and Heckman (in press).

between medical care and own time σ were smaller than one, then k would rise with the wage.[15] Wage and price elasticities would then fall with the wage rate if ϵ exceeded σ, and they would rise with the wage rate if σ exceeded ϵ.[16] Provided the wage rate and the incidence of chronic illness were negatively correlated, the demand curve for chronic care would have larger wage and price elasticities than the demand curve for other types of care if ϵ exceeded σ. The demand curve for chronic care would, however, have smaller elasticities if ϵ were smaller than σ.[17]

Differences in wage or income elasticities between demand curves may also be caused by "omitted variable bias." Suppose that

[15] Let $v = k/(1 - k)$, and note that v is a monotonically increasing function of k. Since $v = WT/PM$,

$$\frac{\partial \ln v}{\partial \ln(W/P)} = 1 + \frac{\partial \ln(T/M)}{\partial \ln(W/P)},$$

or

$$\frac{\partial \ln v}{\partial \ln(W/P)} = 1 - \sigma \gtrless 0 \text{ as } \sigma \lessgtr 1.$$

For some rough evidence that σ is less than one, see Grossman (1972b: 102–105).

[16] For a similar analysis of the effect of changes in the wage rate on wage and price elasticities, see Newhouse and Phelps (1973:6). Their discussion is not as complete as ours because they assume that ϵ exceeds σ.

[17] Let the dependence of wage and price elasticities on the wage rate be summarized by a demand curve of the form

$$\ln M = b_1 \ln W + b_2 (\ln W)^2 + b_3 \ln P + b_4 \ln P \ln W,$$

where b_2 and b_4 are negative if $\sigma < 1$ and $\epsilon > \sigma$ and are positive if $\sigma < 1$ and $\epsilon < \sigma$. If wage and price elasticities are evaluated at the mean values of $\ln W$ and $\ln P$, then

$$e_W = b_1 + 2b_2 \overline{\ln W} + b_4 \overline{\ln P}$$
$$e_P = b_3 + b_4 \overline{\ln W}.$$

Since $\overline{\ln W}$ is lower for persons with chronic conditions, $\overline{e_W}$ and the absolute value of e_P would be higher for such persons provided $b_2 < 0$ and $b_4 < 0$ and would be lower provided $b_2 > 0$ and $b_4 > 0$.

there is no good measure of the rate of depreciation in health capital, and suppose that this variable is more highly correlated with the wage or with permanent income for the chronically ill than for others. To take an extreme example, let permanent income and the depreciation rate be negatively correlated for the chronically ill but uncorrelated for other persons. Then if lnδ were omitted from the demand curves, the income elasticity of medical care would be biased downward for the chronically ill but not for other groups.[18]

Distance parameter. One of the most important time inputs in the health-production function is the time it takes the consumer to travel to his or her usual source of medical care. In general, the quantity of medical care demanded should be negatively related to the amount of travel time required to obtain a unit of care. Clearly, travel time depends on the distance between the consumer and the usual source of care. In turn, distance depends on the "availability of care," measured, say, by the number of physicians per capita in an area.

If a direct measure of travel time is available, it can be entered as an independent variable in the demand curve for care.[19] There is no particular reason to expect an interaction between that variable and chronic illness. Suppose, however, that one simply has a measure of distance to usual source of care. Since the chronically ill are undoubtedly less mobile than other groups, the amount of time it takes them to travel a given distance should be greater. Therefore, the regression coefficient of distance should be larger in absolute value in the demand curve for chronic care, which implies that "shortages" of physicians would have a greater impact on the utilization behavior of the chronically ill than that of other groups. Hence government policies that are designed to increase the utilization of medical services by the chronically ill should pay particular

[18] The above argument could be used to explain William C. Richardson's finding (1970) that income is a better predictor of utilization in the case of nonserious illness than in the case of serious illness.

[19] For an excellent study that emphasizes the effects of travel and waiting time on the demand for medical care, see Acton (1973).

attention to inequalities in the distribution of physicians among areas.

Preventive and curative medical care. So far, we have distinguished demand curves for different types of medical care by the average value of the rate of depreciation for the group demanding care. According to our analysis, groups with low depreciation rates primarily demand preventive care, and groups with high rates primarily demand curative or remedial care. We have, however, treated medical care itself as a single homogeneous input in the production function of gross investment in health. We now modify this treatment by assuming that the production function depends on curative or remedial medical care M_1 and preventive medical care M_2. (For simplicity, inputs other than preventive and remedial medical care are omitted from the production function.)

One way to distinguish between the two types of medical care is to postulate that their relative productivity is a positive function of illness level or the rate of depreciation in health capital. To take a concrete example, let the production function of gross investment in health I be

$$I = M_1^{a} M_2^{1-a},\qquad(10)$$

and let $\alpha = b\delta$. Then the ratio of the marginal product of curative care to the marginal product of preventive care is

$$\frac{\partial I/\partial M_1}{\partial I/\partial M_2} = \frac{b\delta}{1 - b\delta}\frac{M_2}{M_1}.\qquad(11)$$

With M_2/M_1 held constant, the ratio of marginal products obviously rises as δ rises.

Since the relative productivity of curative care increases with the depreciation rate, the share of curative medical expenditures in total medical expenditures also increases with that variable. Therefore, own and cross-price elasticities of curative care vary as the depreciation rate varies. The own-price elasticity of curative care is defined as the elasticity of curative care with respect to the price of curative care. The cross-price elasticity is defined as the elasticity of curative care with respect to the price of preventive care. The two elasticities are given by

$$\frac{\partial \ln M_1}{\partial \ln P_1} = e_{11} = -[k_1 \epsilon + (1 - k_1)\sigma_{12}] \qquad (12)$$

$$\frac{\partial \ln M_1}{\partial \ln P_2} = e_{12} = (1 - k_1)(\sigma_{12} - \epsilon), \qquad (13)$$

where P_1 is the price of curative care, P_2 is the price of preventive care, k_1 is the share of curative expenditures in total medical expenditures, ϵ is the price elasticity of health, and σ_{12} is the elasticity of substitution in production between curative and preventive care. It is reasonable to assume that σ_{12} exceeds ϵ. It follows that own and cross-price elasticities of curative care fall in absolute value as k_1 rises. It also follows that own and cross-price elasticities of preventive care rise in absolute value as k_1 rises.[20]

Our model of preventive and curative medical care is by no means definitive. A more comprehensive treatment, for example, would allow both the loss associated with a given health hazard and the probability of incurring that loss to be a negative function of preventive care. (For a model along these lines, see Ehrlich and Becker, 1972.) Nevertheless, our model does capture an essential aspect of the trade-off between curative and preventive care. The model suggests that a health insurance plan that provided benefits for curative services would only cause consumers to substitute such services for preventive services. More importantly, it suggests that groups with relatively high medical outlays, such as the chronically ill, may have a

---

[20] The own and cross-price elasticities of preventive care are given by

$$\frac{\partial \ln M_2}{\partial \ln P_2} = e_{22} = -[(1 - k_1)\epsilon + k_1\sigma_{12}]$$

$$\frac{\partial \ln M_2}{\partial \ln P_1} = e_{21} = k_1(\sigma_{12} - \epsilon).$$

lower price elasticity of demand for curative services. Thus, they would be less responsive than other groups to a given reduction in the price of medical care associated with the enactment of a national health insurance plan. Most discussions of optimal health insurance conclude that benefits should increase as outlays increase with income held constant. (See, for example, Pauly, 1971.) If those with relatively high outlays have inelastic demand curves, then the coinsurance rate would have to fall as outlays rise in order to produce the optimal result.

Selective Review of the Literature

Demand Curve Estimates

Using data for Finland, Kalimo (1969) has estimated demand curves for various types of medical care (physician visits, hospital stays, prescribed and nonprescribed drugs, etc.) by persons with acute conditions and by persons with chronic conditions. The independent variables in his multiple regressions include age, sex, schooling, income, distance to nearest physician, and the possibility of obtaining inexpensive medical care. His results are not easy to summarize, partly because he considers many different factors in explaining utilization behavior, but one striking finding is that distance to nearest physician has a much larger negative effect in the demand curve for number of physician visits by the chronically ill than in the corresponding demand curve for the acutely ill. As Kalimo is the only researcher who has divided a national sample into the acutely and the chronically ill and has estimated separate demand curves for each group, his work can serve as a guide for future research with United States data.

On a small scale, Leveson (1972) has obtained an approximation to a demand curve for chronic care with United States data. His data consist of all residents of the Queensbridge Housing Project in New York City who were at least sixty years old in 1963 and who reported that they had heart conditions. Leveson examines the data to discover whether the members of that population used the

Health Maintenance Service established in the project in 1961 by the New York City Departments of Health, Hospitals, and Welfare. He makes his determination by fitting a multiple regression with a dichotomous dependent variable that equals one if the person used the Health Maintenance Service. Predictor variables include age, race, sex, schooling, income, mobility status, self-rated health status, and alternative sources of medical care.

Leveson's most important finding is that mobility limitations reduce the probability of participation. He proposes the interesting hypothesis that this variable acts as a proxy for the inconvenience costs of obtaining medical care. Other results are somewhat ambiguous, since estimated effects are often statistically insignificant and contradict a priori hypotheses. Nevertheless, Leveson has developed a useful methodology for larger scale studies of the utilization behavior of the chronically ill.

Socioeconomic and Demographic Characteristics of Users

Bice and his associates (1972) present the number of physician visits per capita for all age-income groups and then for similar (though not identical) groups by chronic-disability status. The data sources are published and unpublished statistics from the National Center for Health Statistics for 1969. They find that, in general, this measure of health status does not change the relationship of income and utilization. Income is positively related to use for children in all disability groups. Adults aged seventeen to sixty-five show no clear relationship between income and physician visits except in the most disabled group, where the correlation is positive. Persons over age sixty-five show no clear pattern except that the highest income class has a higher rate of visits than the lowest class.

The Bice study reveals that the positive correlation between age and utilization for each income group in the general population does not hold for the chronically ill. For each of the three income classes the pattern is unclear, except among the most disabled, where age tends to be negatively associated with utilization. One possible explanation is that the effect of age on the rate of depreciation in health capital may be smaller for the chronically ill. Another possibility is that the positive age effect in the general population may represent the effect of health status on utilization—an effect that should be diminished when the chronically ill are examined as a separate group.

Greenlick and his colleagues (1972) have compared use of Kaiser Foundation Health Plan services in Portland, Oregon, by a medically indigent population served by the Office of Economic Opportunity (OEO) and a cross-section of the general membership. Obviously, the OEO population has a lower average family income than the general membership of the Kaiser plan. An advantage of the study is that it controls for differential access to medical care. A disadvantage is that the populations compared differ in several characteristics: The OEO group is younger, has a higher percentage of females, has larger families, and is more likely to reside in the core city.

Data are presented on doctor office visits per person per year by age, sex, and disease classification for the two income groups. For all persons in the disease classification, "chronic disease, treatable," there is no relationship between income and visits for children and a negative correlation for the age groups nineteen to forty-four and forty-five to sixty-four. When the data are further subdivided by sex, the only change is that there is a positive income effect for women aged nineteen to forty-four. The negative income effect is also observed in tabulations that do not control for disease classification, possibly because of the positive correlation between income and the value of time. As the value of time rises, quantity of services per visit may rise, while the number of visits falls. Alternatively, some high-income consumers may go outside the Kaiser system to obtain less "time-intensive" sources for routine medical care.

Greenlick and his colleagues show the same positive effect of age on utilization for the general population, as do Bice and his associates. Greenlick also shows a positive age effect for the chronically ill subgroup, but Bice finds either no effect or a negative one. Finally, the Greenlick data indicate that among the chronically ill, as well as among all users of health services, females in every age-income group have higher utilization rates than males.

A study by Tagliacozzo and her associates (1972) suggests that there may be a negative relationship between education and utilization under certain conditions. It examines the role of prescriptions in preventing premature terminations of treatment among the chronically ill. The entire population was black, largely low income, already embarked on a course of treatment, and not advised to terminate treatment. As hypothesized, the presence of prescriptions for either medication or diet prolongs attendance for both high and low education groups. The level of premature terminations is, however, greater for the group with high education. The result is consistent with Grossman's treatment of education as an efficiency variable in the health-production function. If the more educated are more efficient and if the price elasticity of health is less than one, that group would demand more health but less medical care.

Type of Service

The chronically ill probably differ from the acutely ill in the specific types of medical services demanded. Greenlick and others at the Health Services Research Center of the Kaiser Foundation Hospitals in Portland are publishing an ongoing series of articles examining various determinants of medical-care use. "The study will test the hypothesis that the determinants of utilization for chronic disease, for communicable acute disease, for trauma, for diseases with a high emotional component, and for preventive services are different and operate in different ways" (Greenlick et al., 1968:298). Their research includes a look at the role of the telephone in medical care, and some findings are presented by disease classification (1973). Telephone calls to physicians concerning symptoms from persons with treatable chronic illness tend to have a slightly higher proportion resulting in prescription of medication than in discussion or instruction to visit the physician. Persons in all disease classes, in contrast, are most likely to simply discuss their problem. A preliminary study in the series on the use of laboratory services indicates that the ratio of lab tests to doctor's office visits is lower for the chronically ill, and especially for those with treatable symptoms, than for the general population (Freeborn et al., 1972).

Another aspect of the type of services demanded by the chronically ill is the place of the services—whether they will be demanded in the market or in the household. Put differently, what determines whether a person with chronic conditions that cause activity or mobility limitations will seek admission to a nursing or personal-care home? Data from the National Center for Health Statistics (1969) indicate that among persons over age sixty-five a smaller percentage of residents in nursing and personal-care homes than of the noninstitutionalized population are married. In addition, current residents of such homes who lived with spouses or children before admission have a higher mean number of chronic conditions than residents who lived alone. The data suggest that some substitution possibilities do exist between care in the household and care in institutions.

Work by Chiswick (in progress) presents additional evidence on that point. He is studying differences in the percentage of the population over age sixty-four in nursing and personal-care homes in Standard Metropolitan Statistical Areas. One preliminary finding is that the percentage of the population in personal-care homes is positively correlated with the labor-force participation rate of married women, but the percentage in nursing homes is not correlated with that variable. Since personal-care homes offer both nursing and custodial services, the result implies that substitution between the household and the market is easier when the patient requires a smaller fraction of "pure" medical services.

Decision to Obtain Care

In constructing theoretical models to explain consumer utilization of medical services, sociologists and psychologists have emphasized "predisposing factors," such as attitudes and perceptions. (For a review of these models, see Bice et al., 1972:266–268.) Often those factors are applied to the decision to use or not use care. We believe that it is more revealing to examine that decision in an economic context. Two important variables are income and knowledge about the efficacy of medical care. It is well known that, if a good has a positive income elasticity, a consumer's entry price (the minimum price at which he or she would be willing to consume a positive amount of the good) would be a positive function of income. Thus, at any given price, the percentage of consumers who use no medical care should fall as income rises.

The tendency to seek medical care for a given health condition should also be a positive function of the rate of return on investment. The higher the marginal product of medical care in the production of gross investments in health, the lower is the shadow price of health and the higher the rate of return. If knowledge about the marginal product of medical care varied among consumers, then so would the "perceived" rate of return. Since knowledge itself depends on education, the decision to seek care should be related to that variable, although the direction of the relationship is ambiguous. The less educated might be too optimistic, for example, about the efficacy of medical care. With other relevant variables held constant, the result would be a negative relationship between education and the percentage of consumers who use medical care.

There are no studies that deal directly with the decision by the chronically ill to use care. Some issues, however, can be raised from related work and from what is known of the characteristics of the chronically ill. In the first section, we mentioned the possibility that a certain percentage of the aged view their activity and mobility limitations as a result of aging rather than illness and thus not treatable. Recovery is not generally a possibility in chronic illness, but less disability and less limitation of activity are possible. In a study of delay in the initiation of treatment among a population over age forty-five, Battistella (1971) finds that delay increases with increasingly poor perception of chances for recovery. Similarly, Hulka et al. (1972) show that, with the number of symptoms held constant, perception of the doctor's ability to relieve symptoms is important in predicting who uses physicians' services.

Delay is an issue that may hold some significance among the chronically ill. On the one hand, delay in initiation of treatment may be more possible than in acute illness and certainly in trauma. On the other hand, delay is probably not desirable because the disease is allowed to progress into what may be a more difficult stage of treatment. Battistella (1971) finds that the proportion of persons delaying least is negatively correlated with income, negatively correlated with health insurance, and positively correlated with medical indigency. Since a higher proportion of the chronically ill than of the entire population probably have little income or health insurance and are medically indigent, delay might be a more important factor for them.

Implications for Future Research

The implication of almost everything we have said is that much more research is necessary to get a better understanding of the demand curve for medical care by the chronically ill. At the theoretical level, if we had more knowledge about the basic parameters in the demand curve for health and in the production function of health, we could make more powerful predictions about the nature of the demand curve for chronic medical care. Examples of the basic parameters include the price elasticity of demand for health and the elasticity of substitution between medical care and the person's own time in the production of health.

At the empirical level, studies must be undertaken that divide random samples of the U.S. population into the acutely ill and the chronically ill. Some of the heterogeneity in the latter population could be eliminated by distinguishing those with treatable symptoms from others. Separate demand curves should be estimated for each group. At present, there are no estimates of prices and income elasticities of demand for medical care for chronic illnesss. We are not even sure about the effects of certain variables on the utilization behavior of the chronically ill based on two- or three-way cross-tabulations. The Greenlick study, for example, finds a positive effect of age on utilization, while the Bice study finds age has no effect. To assess the impact of national health insurance and other government policies on the demand for medical care by the chronically ill and to design optimal insurance policies for them, much more must be known about their utilization behavior.

References

Acton, Jan P.
  1973   Demand for Health Care Among the Urban Poor, With Special Emphasis on the Role of Time. Santa Monica: The RAND Corporation, R-1151-OEO/NYC.

Andersen, Ronald
  1968   A Behavioral Model of Families' Use of Health Services. Chicago: Center for Health Administration Studies, University of Chicago.

Andersen, Ronald *and* Lee Benham
  1970   "Factors affecting the relationship between family income and medical care consumption." In Klarman, Herbert E. (ed.), Empirical Studies in Health Economics. Baltimore: Johns Hopkins University Press.

Battistella, Roger M.
  1971   "Factors associated with delay in the initiation of physicians' care among late adulthood persons." American Journal of Public Health 61 (July): 1348–1361.

Becker, Gary S.
  1965   "A theory of the allocation of time." Economic Journal 75 (September): 493–517.

Bice, Thomas W., et al.
  1972   "Socioeconomic status and use of physician services: A reconsideration." Medical Care 10 (May/June): 261–271.

Blum, H. L. *and* George M. Keranen
  1966   Control of Chronic Diseases in Man. Washington, D.C.: American Public Health Association.

Bright, Margaret
  1966   "Demographic background for programming for chronic diseases in the United States." In Lilienfeld, A. M. *and* A. J. Gifford (eds.), Chronic Diseases and Public Health. Baltimore: Johns Hopkins University Press.

Chiswick, Barry R.
  In progress   "Nursing home utilization." New York: National Bureau of Economic Research.

Cochrane, A. L.
  1972   Effectiveness and Efficiency: Random Reflections on
          Health Services. For the Nuffield Provincial Hospitals
          Trust, London: Oxford University Press.
Coe, Rodney M., et al.
  1967   "The impact of Medicare on the utilization and provision
          of health care facilities: A sociological interpretation." In-
          quiry 4 (December): 42–47.
Commission on Chronic Illness
  1951   Proceedings of the Conference on Preventive Aspects of
          Chronic Disease, March 12–14, 1951. Baltimore: Commis-
          sion on Chronic Illness.
  1957a   Chronic Illness in the United States. Volume IV, Chronic
          Illness in a Large City. Cambridge: Harvard University Press.
  1957b   Chronic Illness in the United States. Volume I, Prevention
          of Chronic Illness. Cambridge: Harvard University Press.
Ehrlich, Isaac *and* Gary S. Becker
  1972   "Market insurance, self-insurance and self-protection."
          Journal of Political Economy 80 (July/August): 623–648.
Freeborn, Donald K., et al.
  1972   "Determinants of medical care utilization: Physicians' use
          of laboratory services." American Journal of Public Health
          62 (June): 846–853.
Fuchs, Victor R. *and* Marcia Kramer
  1972   Determinants of Expenditures for Physician Services in the
          United States 1948–68. Washington, D.C.: National Center
          for Health Services Research and Development and Na-
          tional Bureau of Economic Research.
Greenlick, Merwyn R., et al.
  1968   "Determinants of medical care utilization." Health Services
          Research 3 (Winter): 296–315.
  1972   "Comparing the use of medical care services by a medically
          indigent population and a general membership population
          in a comprehensive prepaid group practice program." Med-
          ical Care 10 (May/June): 187–200.
  1973   "Determinants of medical care utilization: The role of the
          telephone in total medical care." Medical Care 11
          (March/April): 121–134.

Gronau, Reuben
>   1973   "The effect of children on the housewife's value of time."
>   Journal   of   Political   Economy   81   (March/April):
>   S168–199.

Grossman, Michael
>   1972a   "On the concept of health capital and the demand for
>   health." Journal of Political Economy 80 (March/April):
>   223–255.
>   1972b   The Demand for Health: A Theoretical and Empirical In-
>   vestigation. New York: Columbia University Press for the
>   National Bureau of Economic Research.

Heckman, James J.
>   In press "Shadow prices, market wages, and labor supply." Econ-
>   ometrica.

Hulka, Barbara S., et al.
>   1972   "Determinants of physician utilization: Approach to a ser-
>   vice-oriented classification of symptoms." Medical Care 10
>   (July/August): 300–309.

Hurtado, A. V. *and* M. R. Greenlick
>   n.d.   "The clinical-behavior disease classification system." Port-
>   land, Oregon: Health Services Research Center, Kaiser
>   Foundation Hospitals, mimeo.
>   1971   "A disease classification system for the analysis of medical
>   care utilization, with a note on symptom classification."
>   Health Services Research 6 (Fall): 235–250.

Kalimo, Esko
>   1969   "Determinants of medical care utilization." Helsinki, Fin-
>   land: National Pensions Institute, Research Institute for So-
>   cial Security.

Katz, Sidney, et al.
>   1969   "Chronic disease classification in evaluation of medical care
>   programs." Medical Care 7 (March/April): 139–143.

Lancaster, Kelvin J.
>   1966   "A new approach to consumer theory." Journal of Political
>   Economy 75 (April): 132–157.

Leveson, Irving
>   1972   "Access to medical care: The Queensbridge experiment."
>   Inquiry 9 (June): 61–68.

Lilienfeld, A. M. *and* A. J. Gifford (eds.)
 1966   Chronic Diseases and Public Health. Baltimore: Johns
         Hopkins University Press.
Michael, Robert T. *and* Gary S. Becker
 In press "On the new theory of consumer behavior." Swedish Journal
         of Economics.
Muth, Richard
 1966   "Household production and consumer demand functions."
         Econometrica 34 (July): 699–708.
National Center for Health Statistics
 1969   "Marital status and living arrangements before admission to
         nursing and personal care homes, United States, May–June
         1964." Public Health Service Publication No. 1000, Series
         12, No. 12, May.
 1970   "Limitation of activity and mobility due to chronic condi-
         tions, United States, July 1965–June 1966." Public Health
         Service Publication No. 1000, Series 10, No. 45.
 1971   "Chronic conditions and limitations of activity and mobili-
         ty, United States, July 1965–June 1967." Public Health
         Service Publication No. 1000, Series 10, No. 61, January.
Newhouse, Joseph P. *and* Charles E. Phelps
 1973   "Price and income elasticities for medical care services."
         Paper presented at the International Economic Association
         Conference on Economics of Health and Medical Care, To-
         kyo, Japan.
Pauly, Mark V.
 1971   Medical Care at Public Expense: A Study in Applied Wel-
         fare Economics. New York: Praeger.
Phelps, Charles E.
 1973   "The demand for health insurance: A theoretical and em-
         pirical investigation." Unpublished dissertation, University
         of Chicago, Chicago, Illinois.
Phelps, Charles E. *and* Joseph P. Newhouse.
 1973   Coinsurance and the Demand for Medical Services. Santa
         Monica: The RAND Corporation, R-964-OEO.
Richardson, William C.
 1970   "Measuring the urban poor's use of physicians' services in
         response to illness episodes." Medical Care 8 (March/April):
         132–142.

1971 Ambulatory Use of Physicians' Services in Response to Illness Episodes in a Low-Income Neighborhood. Chicago: Center for Health Administration Studies, University of Chicago.

Tagliacozzo, Daisy M., et al.
1972 "Influencing the chronically ill: The role of prescriptions in premature terminations of outpatient care." Medical Care 11 (January/February): 21–29.

Twaddle, Andrew C.
1968 "Aging, population growth and chronic illness: A projection, United States, 1960–1985." Journal of Chronic Disease 21: 417–422.

Tyroler, Herman A.
1969 "The classification of disease." In Greenlick, M. R. (ed.), Conceptual Issues in the Analysis of Medical Care Utilization Behavior. Washington, D.C.: National Center for Health Services Research and Development.

United States Department of Commerce, Bureau of the Census
1972 Statistical Abstract of the United States 1972. Washington, D.C.: Government Printing Office.

Consumer
Incentives for
Rehabilitative
and Restorative Services

JAMES E. BILLINGS
AND MARIE-PAULE DONSIMONI

Definitions of Health Terms

The World Health Organization (1969) has developed the
following definitions:

Comprehensive rehabilitation: As applied to disability,
the combined and coordinated use of medical, social,
educational, and vocational measures for training or re-
training the individual to his highest possible level of
functional ability.

Medical rehabilitation: The process of medical care aim-
ing at developing the functional and psychological abilities of the individual, and, if necessary, his compensato-
ry mechanisms, to enable him to attain self-dependence
and lead an active life.

Social rehabilitation: That part of the rehabilitation process aimed at the integration or re-integration of a disabled person into society by helping him to adjust to the
demands of family, community, and occupation, while

reducing any economic and social burdens that may
impede the total rehabilitation process.

Vocational rehabilitation: The provision of vocational services, such as vocational guidance, vocational training,
and selective placement, designed to enable a disabled
person to secure and retain suitable employment.

Handicapped person: A person whose physical or mental
well-being, or both, is temporarily or permanently im-
paired, whether congenitally or through age, illness, or
accident, with the result that his self-dependence,
schooling, or employment is impeded.

Impairment: A permanent or transitory pathological condition resulting in a diminution of functions.

Disability: The reduction of functional ability to lead a
productive daily life. It is the result not only of mental
and/or physical impairment but also of the individual's
adjustment to the condition.

Incentives for selecting, completing, and maintaining rehabilitation
and restorative health services are discussed in this paper. Rehabilitation and restorative services in this context refer to post-acute
services that are intended to improve physical functioning or to otherwise enhance adjustment to a disability. Although a clinical distinction may be made between rehabilitative and restorative services, they will be referred to here simply as rehabilitation.

Incentives for seeking rehabilitation appear at the opposite end
of a continuum from those seeking emergency services. Rehabilitation is comparatively elective; it is not required to maintain life; its
timing may be planned and, when paid for by the consumer, it may
take a large part of his budget. Hence, one would expect the demand for rehabilitation services to be elastic; that is, the decision to
use them would be expected to be sensitively determined by price.
The demand relation, however, is too complex to assume a priori a
high elasticity.

Several factors cause complexity in predicting demand. They include the ambivalent attitude of private insurers, uncertainties in
payoffs for those with certain types of disabilities, the seemingly

rather poor economic return to geriatric patients, problems in geographical availability of services, the fact that family physicians and relatives often select the program, and the somewhat abrupt separation between programs particularly between medical and vocational rehabilitation.

This paper will discuss incentives for rehabilitation in three stages of care—before commencing rehabilitation (usually immediately after discharge from the acute stage), during the active rehabilitation process, and after discharge. This separation is useful because the incentives, and the persons to whom they should be directed, differ between these stages. That is, before commencing rehabilitation the physician and family are the key figures in selection, often in cooperation with a social caseworker; during the process, the patient is the key figure; and after discharge, the role of the family again becomes important. The focus of the incentives for rehabilitation, namely, the disabled population, will be defined before discussing types of incentives.

The Disabled Population

To determine the need for rehabilitation services or, in other words, to identify the disabled population who may benefit from the services, two surveys were used. The first, the Public Health Survey (National Center for Health Statistics, 1969a), is disease-oriented and estimates chronic conditions. The second, the Social Security Survey (Allan, 1972; Haber, 1968; 1969; 1972; Treitel, 1970; Cinsky, 1968), covers disabled adults of working age in terms of degrees of impairment for major activities. Both surveys sample households, excluding individuals living in institutions. The exclusion of the institutionalized population tends to understate the disabled population. Moreover, the surveys are somewhat dated because highway accidents and Vietnam war casualties have increased the disabled population since their publication. The surveys are in the process of being updated, however.

Degree of Disability

In the Public Health Survey, the population having chronic conditions is divided into four categories:

1. those who have no limitation in activity,
2. those who have limitation but not in major activity,
3. those who have limitation in amount or kind of major activity, and
4. those unable to carry on major activity, where a major activity refers to ability to work, keep house, or engage in school activities.

In the Social Security Survey, the disabled population is divided into three groups based on their ability to work:

1. the severely disabled, or those who are unable to work regularly or to work at all,
2. the occupationally disabled, or those who are able to work but unable to do the same work as before the onset of the disability, or unable to work full-time, and
3. those with a secondary work limitation, or those who can work full-time, regularly and with the same hours as before the disability started but who have limitations in other activities.

The data of these two surveys are not homogeneous because the concept of major activity is more extensive than the concept of work activity. For example, a handicapped woman who has some limitation in major activity might not have worked before her handicap. For purposes of the Social Security Survey she would be in category number three, whereas she would be classified in category number four of the Public Health Survey.

At least twelve percent of the population, or 22.5 million persons, had some kind of limitation in their activity in 1963–1965 (see Table 1), and about seventeen percent of those of working age, or 17.8 million, were disabled in 1966 (see Table 2). On the

TABLE 1   Persons with One or More Chronic Conditions

	Number in Millions	%
Total population (all ages)	187.1	100.0
Population with one or more chronic conditions	108.1	57.9
With no limitation in activity	63.1	33.7
With limitation in activity	22.5	12.1
With limitation, but not in major activity[a]	6.1	3.3
With limitation in amount or kind of major activity[a]	12.3	6.6
Unable to carry on any major activity[a]	4.1	2.2

Source: National Center for Health Statistics (1969[a]).

[a] Ability to work, keep house, engage in school or preschool activities.

TABLE 2   Persons with Long-Term Disability

	Number in Millions	%
Total population (aged 18–64)	103.0	100.0
Total disabled population	35.5	33.8
Total with work limitations	17.8	17.2
Severely disabled	6.1	5.9
With occupational disability	5.0	4.3
With secondary work limitations	6.6	6.4

Source: Haber (1968).

basis of those percentages, it is estimated that 25.8 million Americans are disabled or limited in their ability to work or both in 1973.

The distinction by degree of disability is useful as a proxy for predicting need for rehabilitation services. Although, patients with a severe disability and those with a minor disability may benefit so slightly that rehabilitation would not be recommended in view of the resource input needed for the rehabilitative process.

Age

Two types of age are considered: The age of the disabled when surveyed, and at the onset of the disability.

The burden of disability is heavier for the elderly; thirty percent of the disabled are over age sixty-five, representing forty-nine percent of their age group, while five percent of the disabled are under the age of seventeen, representing two percent of their age group (see Table 3). Part of the reason of this correlation between age

TABLE 3   Age of the Disabled

Age	Survey	Number in Millions	Distribution in Percentages	Percentage of their Age Group
All ages	ª	27.6	100	—
Under 17	P.H.S.	1.4	5	2
18–44	S.S.S.	6.6	24	10
45–54	S.S.S.	5.1	18	23
55–64	S.S.S.	6.1	22	36
Over age 65	P.H.S.	8.4	30	49

Source: For P.H.S.., National Center for Health Statistics (1969: 19, Table 2); for S.S.S., Haber (1968: 5, Table 1).

ª By combining the P.H.S. and the S.S. surveys, the disabled population reaches the level of 27.6 million persons instead of the amount in Table 1 and Table 2.

and disability is the accumulation of the impairment; that is, once a disability is incurred it is often permanent, and cumulative disability conditions are added over the individual's lifetime.

As the age of onset of disability increases, the mode of the levels of disability changes from "secondary work limitation" to "severely disabled" (see Table 4). This may be an indication that the

TABLE 4   Age of the Working-Age Population at Onset of Disability by Severity of Disability

AGE AT ONSET OF DISABILITY	ALL THE DISABLED	SEVERITY OF DISABILITY		
		Severe	Occupational	Secondary Work Limitation
Total	100%	100%	100%	100%
18	15.3	13.9	9.5	21.0
18–24	11.0	6.4	14.1	12.9
25–34	16.9	16.6	17.9	16.9
35–44	21.9	23.7	24.7	18.1
45–54	20.9	22.9	22.9	17.4
55–64	11.4	15.6	9.0	9.6
Not reported	2.6	0.3	1.8	4.8
Median age	37	40	38	33

Source: Allan (1972: 5, Table 1).

younger the patient, the better the ability to adapt to impairment and therefore to find an occupation that suits one's disability. It is assumed that the disability does not appreciably interfere with education and on-the-job-training. Obviously, the handicapped elderly will find it more difficult to continue the same work or to find a new job.

Race

There are more disabled nonwhites than their relative proportion of the population. In effect, twenty-two percent of the severely disabled are nonwhite, while they only represent eleven percent of the sample population in the Social Security Survey (Allan, 1972). Race, per se, has nothing to do with disability; however, it is an indicator for conditions that lead to a higher risk of disability: higher exposure to poor living and working conditions, greater likelihood of participation in wars, and so on.

Income

Income of the disabled population is estimated in the 1966 Social Security Survey and in the unpublished data from the National Health Interview Survey (NCHS, 1969b). The estimates, of course, are only for income after disability. In other words, we may have the impact of disability upon income more than the impact of income upon disability. But, at least, the employment characteristics of the disabled can be examined in the 1966 Social Security Survey. In 1966 the unemployment rate was 3.7 percent for the working-age population and 7.6 percent for the disabled population, with a rate of 15 percent for the severely disabled. Among men who had been working before onset, about three-fourths were still working at the time of the survey. The income category of the disabled that seems most affected by disability is the unmarried population, especially women with severe limitations. They had, in effect, a median family income of $824 for 1965, while the married women with secondary work limitations had a family income of $7,381 (Allan, 1972: 6, table D).

Individual Values

In the Social Security Survey, three questions were asked of the disabled concerning their interest for rehabilitation: (1) have you received rehabilitation services in the past? (2) have you tried to get rehabilitation services? and (3) are you currently interested in receiving rehabilitation services?

The data show (Treitel, 1970) that twelve percent of the disabled population of working age received some services; in other words, 2.1 million out of 17.8 million disabled received rehabilitation services. One-third or about 700,000 of the 2.1 million received services in 1965, of whom 120,000 received services in a vocational rehabilitation center.

Table 5 shows that the proportion receiving rehabilitation services is higher for severely disabled persons than for those who have

TABLE 5   Receipt of Services in the Past and Interest in Rehabilitation by Severity of Disability

RECEIVED OR INTERESTED IN SERVICES	ALL THE DISABLED		SEVERITY OF DISABILITY					
			Severe		Occupational		Secondary Work Limitation	
	Number in Million	%	*Number in Million*	%	*Number in Million*	%	*Number in Million*	%
Received services	0.8	13	0.6	13	0.8	10	2.1	12
Interested in services	a	18	a	16	a	10	a	15

Source: Treitel (1970: 16–17, Tables 1 and 2).
a Not available

secondary work limitations. The difference also appears for those interested in obtaining services: eighteen percent of the severely disabled are interested in receiving services, compared with ten percent of those who have secondary work limitations. Consequently, it appears that attitudes toward rehabilitation are not positive. Chronic diseases are often considered to be fatal, especially in rural areas or among those with little education. In rural areas the rehabilitation agency has done some studies of attitudinal barriers (Simmons, 1970). The findings show that, in general, people in those areas resign themselves to their situation and do not think it possible to improve. There is also a communications problem when the counselors visit them to explain the impact of rehabilitation.

Services Which Decrease Disability

The utilization of rehabilitation services is related to the incidence of disability across the nation. In turn, the incidence of disablity may be sensitive to the presence of economic conditions, including incentives across the health care stages from prevention to rehabilitation.

When there are several alternatives to reaching an objective, an economic optimum is characterized by no alternative having a higher return relative to expenditures than any alternative which is taken. For example, when an equal reduction in disability is expected per dollar expended on a campaign to wear seat belts as on a program to rehabilitate spinal cord injuries, then the expenditures are appropriately balanced. Otherwise, the expenditure with the higher return should be encouraged.

For the purpose of analyzing consumer incentives for rehabilitation services, incentives concern not only ways of increasing the demand of rehabilitation services but also ways of reducing the need of those services. By reducing the need, we mean that the root of the problem of disability has to be eradicated.

For prevention services that lessen the number of future disabled, refer to Bauer's paper presented at this conference (1973). There are other types of programs that can lessen the numbers of the disabled. Knowing their characteristics by geographical distribution and socioeconomic factors, one can try to improve their status.

The next section will focus on the process of entering the rehabilitation programs which reduces or develops adjustment to a disability.

Procedures to Enter the System

Before presenting incentives for entering the rehabilitation programs, it is useful to justify them. A few studies on the costs and benefits of rehabilitation are summarized below.

Costs and Benefits of Rehabilitation

The first comprehensive analysis of costs and benefits of vocational rehabilitation services was by Conley (1965) who studied the costs and benefits of vocational rehabilitation. He found that an impairment produces a loss of potential productivity; consequently it directly lessens the gross national product. He also concluded that an impairment generally requires the assistance of an individual at home who thereby cannot produce in other sectors.

In a later report, Conley (1969) measured the costs and benefits of vocational rehabilitation programs, using the medical expenditures involved by the program as costs and income resulting from the program as benefits. Income is measured by the difference between income after and before contact with vocational agencies. This flow of income is then discountned at two different rates—four and eight percent. In his estimates, Conley studied the impact of factors such as age, race, and level of education. He took the different socioeconomic characteristics of the disabled without cross-tabulations and found that lower costs to those with expected lower benefits resulted in approximately equal ratios of benefits over costs for "low" and "high" productivity groups. "From all this we were led to the unorthodox conclusion that from the standpoint of an efficient allocation of resources it may be as desirable to assist the uneducated, the middle-aged, the severely disabled, the nonwhite, the unmarried, and other low productivity groups (sic) as their more vocationally successful counterparts" (Conley, 1969:251).

Bellante (1972) reassessed the costs and benefits of vocational rehabilitation. He took a cross tabulation of the socioeconomic characteristics of the disabled—taking simultaneously age, race, level of education, sex, and disability as explanatory variables. His findings are that the return on investment are the highest for those who are young and have a low degree of disability. The returns indicated by Bellante vary from one to thirty.

Some preliminary work on costs and benefits of medical rehabilitation was done by Billings and Wass de Czege (1972). In working with data from an unpublished National Health Interview Survey and with data from the Texas Institute for Rehabilitation and Research, they found that medical rehabilitation benefits exceed costs for age groups eighteen to forty-four and forty-five to sixty-four. The economic return in terms of medical bills saved and incomes to rehabilitation for ages sixty-five and over appears slightly under costs.

Assuming, then, that the rehabilitation of disabled individuals is worthwhile for the society, the next sections discuss barriers to entering the system.

Cost and Coverage of Services

Rehabilitative services are relatively expensive because they occur for a long period of time, because they require the services be entirely completed and be followed by a maintenance program, in order to be effective.

The actual costs of services for severely disabled patients undergoing an intensive inpatient program are relatively high. The Texas Institute for Rehabilitation and Research, Baylor's Research and Training Center, reports costs for patients enrolled between 1959 and 1968 (de Wever, 1968). Of those, the average cost per patient ranged from $3,195 for those age sixty-one and over to $6,002 for those age nineteen to thirty-five. The average cost for those under age nineteen was $3,982. Cost ranged well above these averages, however; maximums were reported as: $35,999 among those age sixty-one and over, $23,289 for the age group thirty-six to sixty, $46,598 for the age group nineteen to thirty-five, and $63,506 for those under age nineteen. Average costs for the Sister Kenny Institute in Minneapolis were $6,962 for paraplegia, $9,104 for quadriplegia, $3,825 for rheumetoid arthritis, and $2,846 for hemiplegia. Maintenance costs are not included in the figures. Extended care facilities offer rehabilitation services in a less intensive program in terms of expensive types of health manpower. One extended care facility in Minneapolis claims that costs in their center run about half of those for comprehensive chronic hospitals. Physical rehabilitation is also available in both ambulatory and home care setting; these costs vary extensively as, of course, do the severity of disabilities.

Rehabilitative services can be paid for by the individual, by the provider itself, or by some third party. Payment by a third party is the most common form of payment, and therefore will be briefly discussed. There are three types of third-party payments for rehabilitative services: the private insurance company, Medicaid, and the vocational rehabilitation program. The latter is a program at the federal level—$550 million for 1972–1973—that covers all the expenditures of the patient. Anyone can apply, and there is a team from the program which decides if the potential client may or may not benefit from vocational rehabilitation.

Medicaid coverage is the same for rehabilitation as for any other medical service. In other words, if, at the state level, money is available and a physician decides that a patient needs rehabilitation services, those services are typically covered by Medicaid.

The private insurance company from the point of view of the rehabilitation centers that have been surveyed is more inclined to cover the services than is Medicaid. This needs clarification in terms of the percentage of services covered by one type or another of insurance.

Actually there is no mechanism for cooperative purchase of the third parties. In terms of efficiency and cost this division of the insurance system is costly. Should cooperative purchases by third parties be possible, their purchase would be more likely to occur.

One example will help clarify this statement: Patient One has a spinal cord injury and receives assistance partly from workmen's compensation and partly from Medicaid, which contains both state and federal funds. Patient Two suffers from loss of sight and receives both medical and income-loss payments from his own but separate insurance policies. In both cases, if the third party indemnifiers could agree on a way of sharing the purchase, the services are more likely to be provided.

A recent publication of the Department of Health, Education, and Welfare (Copeland, 1969) found that "cooperative purchase-of-service agreements or other kinds of third-party agreements, made possible by the 1967 and 1968 Amendments to the Social Security and Vocational Rehabilitation Acts, can thus double or even quadruple the rehabilitation services purchased." The report also found that "the incentives to service expansion which are built into current law are also very strong financial incentives to cooperation between agencies whose work—even with less funds—may have been overlapping or may have ignored great areas of need for rehabilitation services."

It is occasionally alleged in the health delivery literature that the tort process of compensation may influence a patient's utilization of rehabilitation in timing if not in kind. Awards for compensating damages for liability, such as automobile accidents and medical malpractice, are based upon economic losses, which include lost income and medical bills. Hence, any program that intends to reduce such losses would reduce th expected amount of the award. It is argued that this factor tends to delay commencing a rehabilitation program.

The point deserves serious empiricial investigation. It is conceivable that a few would attach their hopes for damages to the uncertain awards. The tort system, however, and the related plaintiff strategies are complex and largely unexplored and are certainly not possible to predict. Little is known of the extent and adequacy of health coverage for the disabled population.

The most extensive survey of coverage was the 1966 Social Security Survey of the Disabled, which found that "less than two-thirds of the disabled population age eighteen to sixty-four had health insurance coverage in 1966" (Cinksy, 1968:1). Also noted was the small variation in coverage by severity of disability. At the time of the survey, it was found that for men about half the coverage was obtained through the consumer's past or present employment, and about half from individually purchased policies. Similar findings were evident for women, except that the insurance coverage from employment was usually from the husband's employment. The 1966 survey predated any significant impact by Medicaid, which has increased financial assistance for rehabilitation.

In the previous sections the focus was on the impact of cost and coverage among the consumption of rehabilitative services; the subsequent paragraphs will focus on the information on and the knowledge of rehabilitation services. For this purpose the referral and outreach processes are identified and then suggestions to improve these processes are provided.

Referral Process

The key to selecting the rehabilitation program is the referral. The referrer is usually a person other than the patient. The physician who is responsible for the patient during the acute stage of care is most likely to make the referral. Incentives in referring from the acute stage to the rehabilitation stage act on the physician's attitude to his loss of professional control, and perhaps income from a patient, and toward a procedure which is qualitatively different from traditional surgery or drug prescribing.

Several studies have found that physicians are often unaware of and reluctant to refer to rehabilitation programs. In one study, Wylie (1969) found that "physicians have been slow to accept as a legitimate activity the rehabilitation of their stroke patients." The study examined the characteristics of referring and nonreferring physicians in Baltimore from 1956 to 1964. The physicians who, according to epidemiological estimates, should have seen between nine and twenty-seven new stroke patients during that time make the referrals shown in Table 6. A more receptive attitude about re-

TABLE 6   Extent of Referral of Stroke Patients by 294 General Practitioners, 1956–1964

Extent of Referral	Number of General Practitioners	Number of Stroke Referrals
Total	294	321
Making no referral	159	0
Referred 1 or more patients	135	321
Referred 1 patient	54	54
Referred 2 patients	41	82
Referred 3 patients	17	51
Referred 4 or more patients	23	134

Source: Wylie (1969: 552).

ferrals has been developing over time (Table 7), and this evidence also indicates a greater acceptance on the part of younger physicians (Table 8).

The hesitancy to refer for rehabilitation is contrasted by Wylie (1969) to the usual willingness to try a new drug:

TABLE 7   Time Trends in Referrals by General Practitioners and by Other Sources

Referrals and Admissions	Total	1956	1957	1958	1959	1960	1961	1962	1963	1964
Referred by general practitioners	321	4	21	30	20	36	45	56	54	55
Percentage admitted	61.5	25.0	47.6	53.3	60.0	66.7	66.7	67.9	50.0	69.1
Referred by other sources	1,932	69	127	151	186	260	264	311	319	265
Percentage admitted	52.8	47.8	33.1	51.7	53.8	58.1	50.1	55.6	57.1	51.3

Source: Wylie (1969: 552).

**TABLE 8 Years Between Physician's Graduation and 1956
by Number of Referrals**

		YEARS SINCE GRADUATION		
	Total	Less than 21	21–35	More than 35
All general practitioners	294	144	106	44
Referring general practitioners	135	71	51	13
Percentage referring	45.9	49.3	48.1	29.5

Source: Wylie (1969: 553).

1. Rehabilitation is not subject to advertising companies in the way that drugs are.

2. Rehabilitation is not a dramatic recovery process.

3. Rehabilitation often involves a loss of control by the primary physician, unlike drugs which fit well into the patient-physician relationship.

4. Rehabilitation has not become well established in the medical culture, again in contrast to drugs.

Consequently, important differences cause rehabilitation to be adopted more slowly than using a new drug (Wylie, 1968:553).

The medical profession's lack of interest in rehabilitation is indicated by the fact that during the period 1972 through mid 1973 only two articles were devoted to rehabilitation in the *American Medical News* and the *Hospital Tribune,* which are the two medical newspapers with the largest circulation.

The attitudes of physicians toward rehabilitation found in Wylie's results concurred with two surveys. In 1959, a sample of two hundred physicians of all specialities in the Harris County Medical Society (Texas) revealed that one in three had never heard of the vocational rehabilitation program, that only one in five had ever referred a patient to a rehabilitation agency (Conley, 1965:158–159). Similarly, in 1966, for the University of Minnesota Medical School, ninety-eight percent of the sophomores and seventy-five percent of the juniors had never heard of rehabilitation and forty-four percent of a sample of physicians in the Twin Cities did not know what a physiatrist was or could not define the difference between physiatrists and physical therapists (Athelstan, 1973).

But the physician is not the only referral source for rehabilitation service. Disabled patients can self refer, or be referred by friends, by schools or by public agencies to rehabilitation agencies. As can be seen in Table 9, thirty percent of the referrals are made by the medical profession, twenty-three percent are due to the initiative of the clients or one of their friends.

Outreach

The practice of outreach consists of going outside the institutions providing rehabilitation services to find potential clients. Out-

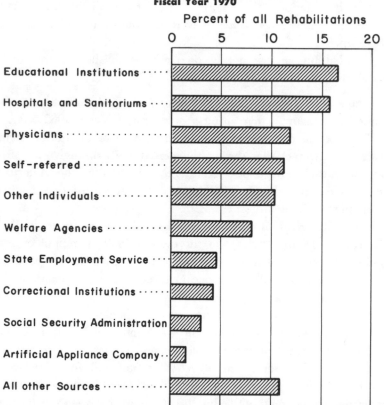

TABLE 9   Source of Referral of Persons Rehabilitated by State Vocational Rehabilitation Agencies, Fiscal Year 1970

Source: Social and Rehabilitation Service (1972: 7, Figure G).

reach can take place through information-producing activities directed to the public and to the medical profesion. For outreach through dissemination of information directed to the public, only the vocational rehabilitation centers provide a structured program. The centers use counselors who visit the disabled, presenting the benefits of rehabilitation. Several studies have been made by the counselors to determine how they could improve their methods (Simmons, 1970). Counselors seem to have an incentive to choose subjects whose situations will be easily improved, since their results are measured in terms of effectively rehabilitated people.

For outreach by information to the medical profession, it is necessary first to gain recognition of the existence of rehabilitation as a medical specialty, and second to impart knowledge of rehabilitation.

An incentive to consider is subsidizing the specialty in medical schools to enhance its recognition. A 1966 survey (Athelstan, 1968) found that only fifty-seven out of eighty-four medical schools were providing physical medicine and rehabilitation training under physiatrists. (A physiatrist is defined as a physician who specializes in physical medicine and rehabilitation.) As the number of physiatrists is approximately the same as it was twenty years ago (eight hundred physiatrists in 1972), the Commission on Education in Physical Medicine and Rehabilitation (1968) recommends that medical students be required to know of these services and how to use them. A subsidy to educational programs would be important, but it would affect only the flow of new physicians, not the stock of existing physicians. For the latter, continual information would serve as an incentive to refer to rehabilitation services. For the incentive to be effective, physicians should know the nature of the improvement that is possible for patients.

Incentives to Improve the Referral Process and the Outreach

Informing the Public. One of the most common ways of informing the public of the existence of a service is to advertise it on television or radio. A distinction should be made between national campaigns for specific conditions and advertising for special institutions.

A national campaign is designed to educate the public to the possibilities of rehabilitation and to overcome the misconception that chronic conditions represent unchanging outcomes. The public should be made aware that chronic conditions and disability can get worse without rehabilitation or better with rehabilitation. For that purpose the National Advertising Council has made films and posters available since 1969.

The purpose of advertising the services of a special rehabilitation institution is to increase the number of persons who will use the rehabilitation services. Several methods can be used, and they are described briefly, using as an example the Sister Kenny Institute in Minneapolis. The first method is promotion by means of public service announcements on television and radio. This is estimated to attract an additional dozen patients from the average flow of clients; then admissions return to their previous level. The second method is to educate the people through discussions and panels. The outcomes of these programs are difficult to measure in terms of clients. The Sister Kenny Institute uses a member of its public service personnel staff to present talks and lead discussions in clubs and other organizations. During the discussions, an attempt is made to introduce the concepts of rehabilitation, of chronic diseases, and of disability. Most of the time the audience is familiar with physical therapy, poliomyelitis, and strokes, but is not aware of techniques available for the rehabilitation of stroke patients and of other available services.

Informing the Medical Profession. The most common method of educational outreach is through brochures. But physicians receive large amounts of literature, and much of it ends up in the wastebasket. Therefore, the rehabilitation centers have decided to visit physicians in their office. In the Midwest, two methods are commonly used.

The first method, practiced by the staffs of the University of Minnesota Hospital and Sister Kenny Institute, consists of having one staff physiatrist who regularly visits small hospitals and physicians' offices in rural areas and talks with the physicians about several cases of chronic disease or disability that have occurred in those areas. The method has been used for three years, and there is now a small group of physicians throughout Minnesota who are linked to the University Hospital Rehabilitation Service and the Sister Kenny Institute.

The second method, practiced by the Sister Kenny Institute, used professionals (occasionally a physician, but generally a marketing specialist) who visit health care physicians' offices throughout the state as a part of the Institute's marketing services. Since the system has been in existence only six months it is not yet possible to evaluate the outcome.

The information systems can expect to create a flow of patients coming to the rehabilitation institutions. The second method might be more efficient in terms of staff utilization and cost effectiveness. But because some of the information is provided by a nonmedical individual, there might be some referrals whose disabilities could have been adequately cared for at the local level. The education of physicians by one of their peers may enable the local physicians to provide the needed rehabilitation care in their community, which allows the patients to remain in their local areas.

Informing the Patients At Their Request. Finally a service that might have incentive effects on utilization would be to advise patients on the location of the rehabilitation institutions, the services provided, eligibility, and cost.

A center providing such information would also have the task of lessening the problems of administrative split in responsibilities between medical and vocational rehabilitation. At the federal level, both forms of rehabilitation are under the Department of Health, Education, and Welfare; at the state level, medical rehabilitation activities are administered by the welfare department and vocational rehabilitation is administered by the education department.

The last type of information that can be given to the patients is to inform them of the different jobs that would be available after rehabilitation and to show the eventual income that would result. The public could be shown, for example, the increased earnings resulting from the efforts of vocational rehabilitation centers where the results are spectacular and known.

The Rehabilitation Process

Once a disabled person has been admitted to an institution providing medical or vocational rehabilitation, he remains there as an inpatient for a time period dependent upon the severity of the disability, quality of the care, attitude of the patient, and philosophy of the team rendering the services. The services that can be provided are classified below.

Rehabilitation Services

The evaluation process includes medical, social, and vocational services. It is fundamental to rehabilitation, because it usually is the first contact between the disabled person and the therapists. To be efficient, evaluation must be comprehensive. It must also be provided with great delicacy to avoid any emotional disturbances for the patient. Medical examination includes a muscle examination—for each muscle the degree of strength, coordination, and range of movement of the joints are determined. The medical examination also consists of evaluating patient-functioning during daily activities, such as self-care (hygiene, eating, dressing), standing up and sitting down, climbing and traveling, and using appliances (artificial limbs, wheelchair, crutches).

In planning an appropriate rehabilitation program during this process, it is necessary to know the demographic characteristics of the patient's family, conditions of living, and the physical environment of the patient's home, in order to adapt the disabled person to his environment. A psychological evaluation of the patient, determining his attitude toward disability and his relationship with his relatives and his companions at work, is also important as the patient goes through several psychological phases as rehabilitation progresses. The assistance of counselors is usually required during these phases.

The vocational examination process consists of taking into account the physical and intellectual future and actual abilities of the patient, in order to determine the kind of training he should have.

Accordingly, it is necessary that the patient correctly understand the improvement which is possible through rehabilitation in order to accept the training program.

Care may include physical medicine and physical therapy. Physical medicine includes thermal therapy, using infrared radiation, hydrotherapy, whirlpool therapy, and contrast-baths. Through the physical medicine services, the patient learns how to get in and out of a wheelchair, exercises on parallel bars, elementary ambulation with and without assistance, and how to go up and down stairs. Teaching the activities of daily living includes that of adapting to orthotics and developing new methods for homemaking skills.

In general, the services are provided by physical therapists, occupational therapists, or nurses under the supervision of a physician. In such a physical rehabilitation program, the physiatrist provides medical expertise and also functions as the team leader. But services can also be provided without the presence of physicians if the paramedical manpower is sufficiently trained.

Vocational rehabilitation is the penultimate step in the rehabilitation process. It provides skills to the disabled that will enable him to again be a productive member of society. Vocational agencies provide the most comprehensive services, which include general academic training and specialized skills such as lip reading and braille. Special training may also include technical training. Generally it consists of personal and vocational adjustment in which the disabled person is taught how to adjust to a particular situation hindering his rehabilitation potential through, for example, work conditioning, developing work tolerance and training in the use of artificial limbs.

Role of the Patient

The patient is the key participant in the rehabilitation process. One's disability will act not only on physical potential, but on social and psychological activities as well. Consequently, the patient's attitudes toward rehabilitation must be managed before rehabilitation will be effective.

Our society places value on physical appearance as important to social acceptance. An individual who acknowledges that he has a permanent physical impairment will have to value himself in spite of physical handicaps. In such cases the family plays an important role in helping the patient build up his self-esteem.

The disabled commonly suffer more psychologically than physically from their disability; they feel inferiority, shame, depression, and frustration; their relatives feel pity and sorrow. Several studies have been made concerning the psychological stages of the disabled. Rigoni (MacDermott, 1973) analyzed patients with spinal cord injury in four stages. The first is the shock phase, soon after injury, when the patient is generally mentally paralyzed as well as physically paralyzed. Acute care is provided and the rehabilitation team generally does not have access to him in this phase. The shock phase is short and may last only a couple of days, while the subsequent phases may last for months and even years.

The second or denial phase is when the patient retreats into himself as a defense mechanism and will not comprehend that his physical self is seriously or permanently changed. It is a period when the patient has unrealistic hopes, and thinks that the physicians will provide care enabling him to recover completely.

Next follows the acknowledgement phase, when the person is absorbing the new realities about himself and may realize in his mind: "I am paralyzed, I shall never walk again." He may in effect go into mourning. During that period, reality becomes clear to the patient, and he has to accept it piece by piece. It is a phase in which severe, even suicidal, depression may occur. The patient may be questioning his worth to himself and to his family.

When the patient begins to perceive that the realities of the rehabilitation program can be helpful to him, as he becomes cooperatively involved with the therapy, and is increasingly able to think about manipulating the environment to meet his needs, the adaptive phase sets in. In this last phase the patient decides to cope with his impairment and to adapt himself to his environment.

Incentives During Rehabilitation

During the shock phase it is impossible to contact the disabled. That is one reason why the "defensive retreat" and the "acknowledgement" phases can last too long. One way of lessening the importance of the denial phase would be to have contact between the rehabilitation team and the patient while he is receiving intensive care. Since during this phase the patient generally is still under care at the hospital, information concerning the patient should immediately go to the rehabilitation service. This would tend to give the patient a smoother transition to a rehabilitation program.

Once the evaluation process has been completed—generally some time between the shock phase and the denial phase—the patient is under care in the rehabilitation center. At that moment it is necessary to gradually present to him the reality of his situation, informing him of the progress which he can realistically expect to achieve. For certain patients that can be a fruitful period as new possibilities of adapting are opened. The patients, for example, who do not know the rehabilitation possibilities might develop new hopes when new goals are presented to them during the initial discussion. At that time it will be better to indicate small immediate goals to the patient rather than to describe long-term possibilities. The patient can thus progressively experience self-rewards every time a goal is reached. Otherwise the goal might seem to be too far into the future and can even become a disincentive in light of day-to-day rehabilitation frustrations.

For some patients, arrival in a rehabilitation center might be a totally depressing experience. In effect, a patient may arrive thinking that through physical medicine he will recover his full function and, for example, be able to walk normally after the conclusion of the rehabilitation program. If the evaluation determines that it will be impossible to walk without the help of devices, the patient may enter the phase of acknowledgement where one wonders about self-worth. During this period of grief and loss the patient needs considerable support, and the counselor's intervention will be required to make the patient accept the situation and to provide motivation to proceed. For example, for the patient who expects to be able to walk without help, which is not possible, it is necessary to make him accept progressively that life in a wheelchair can be worthwhile. For that process where the patient must revise his self-concept, the attitude of the hospital staff and of the family must help the patient by:

(1) enlarging the scope of values; the disability must be viewed as only part of a person's life and many other things are important and

(2) subordinating physical orientation as a value; other qualities of the patient must be outlined, such as intelligence, perseverance, and moral standing (MacDermott, 1973).

The extent of the disability's effects may be minimized by determining the many situations in life that are not affected. Sometimes it gives the patient more self-confidence to demonstrate that he is not unique, and that others in equally as bad physical condition are coping with the problem. When the patient is not making the progress that the staff expects from him, it may be helpful to use as an example a person with similar handicap who is reaching the goals.

Another incentive used during the rehabilitation process is presenting success stories. Movies can be shown to rehabilitants, and discussed in light of their own possibilities. Another effective means of motivation is to provide biographies of disabled persons who have successfully coped with their disability.

When the patient has recovered his self-confidence, incentives like discussing vocational plans and how to live in the community are used. Vocational programs must be of high quality for the patient's family to consider them worthwhile. In the rehabilitation of children, rehabilitation must be combined with good learning situations.

Followup Process

The last step in rehabilitation is a program for maintaining the results which have been achieved during the more intensive rehabilitation process. The maintenance process consists of the followup of the patient after discharge, and a program which retains the level of independence that had been achieved at the time of discharge. The rehabilitation institutions have difficulties in maintenance programs, however, because of their lack of manpower to adequately followup on a patient.

Because a disabled person who is physically handicapped usually has emotional side-effects, he needs support. When he is inside the medical institution, he is confronted only with other disabled persons and the medical staff, all of whom understand his limitation. When he again enters society he will be confronted with the realities of those not experiencing a disability. The family, for example, might interact with the rehabilitant as before the rehabilitation process. Consequently, a disabled person whose goal for a month has been to try to open a door will be frustrated when one of his relatives opens the door for him.

Incentives can be provided to lessen the risk of dissipating the effects of rehabilitation. The family can be taught their roles in maintenance through a detailed program. Generally rehabilitation centers give that instruction, but not in a followup program. Unless the family is able to appreciate the benefits of a maintenance program, followup may not be encouraged. As an example, consider a mentally retarded young girl who has been taught how to eat by herself. She requires a rehabilitation process that has lasted six months in an institution. Then a program of progressive exercises is taught to the family. But the program requires that a certain amount of family time be spent with the child. It is probable that the family will think that the return is not worth their time and that it is preferable to feed her as they did before her hospitaliaztion.

To minimize this problem of maintenance, two incentives can be given: First, a social worker or a paramedical person providing home care, or a counselor who often visits the family may remind them of the long-term benefits resulting from maintenance instruction. Second, the medical staff may talk with teachers at school, and with employers and work companions of the disabled, who must learn how to act with the disabled person, treat him as normal, and avoid feelings of pity.

Availability of medical services on an outpatient basis is important. There must be capable persons in the rehabilitation centers ready to answer the questions of the disabled person, either about physical or psychological problems. It is necessary to have a regular followup of the patient's physical condition because severe complications might otherwise occur and their cost can be high. A patient with a spinal cord injury, for example, might incur complications as pressure sores occur. While the medical rehabilitation cost of a spinal cord injury averages sixteen thousand dollars, medical care to heal a pressure sore costs twenty thousand dollars. To avoid such cost, incentives can be provided through information to the third-party payer that explains the risks due to lack of followup.

The last barrier for recovering complete social activity for a disabled person who has been rehabilitated is the physical environment. The problem, however, is not directly an incentive for rehabilitants. An important incentive for those being rehabilitated is to show that society does recognize those with ambulatory problems. This could be demonstrated through architectural modification in public buildings and streets, where major problems for the disabled occur. Ramps for wheelchairs, grab bars to aid in transfers, wide doorways and elevators are all to be considered for the benefit of the handicapped.

Summary

In this paper we have attempted to determine the scope of rehabilitation services, and the setting relevant to commencing, completing, and maintaining the services. The settings for service are described in order to suggest incentives which will alter utilization as policymakers consider this to be beneficial.

But we are cognizant that this approach is not sufficient. Further research is necessary to determine the magnitude of unmet need, barriers to expected services and returns from rehabilitation alternatives, and ultimately to suggest where programs may be most effective per dollar expended.

Unmet rehabilitation needs and barriers to services could be determined by means of followup and even statistically structured household samples. These samples could emphasize the conditions underlying the need for rehabilitation. Needs would be related to a number of socioeconomic and medical characteristics. The surveys of disability are dated and do not adequately differentiate measures of long-term health status from short-term episodes requiring care.

An updating is, however, already underway. In addition, the results of alternative services should be recorded, specific to the socioeconomic and medical characteristics of the patient. This information would serve as a data base for forecasting the expected results of care for each patient and for evaluating the actual results. In this sense, the survey may effectively become a useful input into the Professional Standards Review Organization System and into various utilization review programs.

References

Allan, K.
  1972 "General characteristics of the disabled population." Survey of Disability: 1966, Report #19. Washington, D.C.: Social Security Administration, Office of Research and Statistics.
Athelstan, G. T.
  1968 Bulletin #9. Minneapolis: Commission on Education in Physical Medicine and Rehabilitation.
  1973 Personal communication.
Bauer, K. G.
  1973 "Adverting the self-inflicted nemeses (sins) from dangerous driving, smoking, and drinking." Paper presented before the Milbank Round Table on Consumer Incentives for Health Care, June 8–9, 1973, Washington, D.C.
Bellante, D. M.
  1972 "A multivariate analysis of a vocational rehabilitation program." Journal of Human Resources 7 (Spring): 226–241.
Berkowitz, M. *and* W. Johnson
  1970 "Towards an economics of disability: The magnitude and structure of transfer and medical costs." Journal of Human Resources 5 (Summer): 271–297.
Bernstein, L.
  1966 "Economic and geriatric rehabilitation." Geriatrics 21 (July): 199–204.
Billings, J. E. *and* M. Wass de Czege
  1972 "Benefits derived from physical rehabilitation." Paper presented before the Operations Research Society of America, April 27.

Brooks, R. G.
  1969   "Cost benefit analysis of patients treated at rheumatism
            center." Annals of Rheumatical Disease 28: 655–661.
Chapelain, Maria Therese
  1971   "L'etude R.C.B. perinatalite." Rationalisation des Choix
            Budgetaires (Mars): 7–23.
Cinsky, M. E.
  1968   "Health insurance coverage of the disabled." Survey of Dis-
            ability: 1966, Report #4. Washington, D.C.: Social Secu-
            rity Administration, Office of Research and Statistics.
Commission on Education in Physical Medicine and Rehabilitation
  1968   "Rehabilitation medicine in American medical colleges.
            Recommendations for teaching programs," Bulletin #8.
            Minneapolis: Commission on Education in Physical Medi-
            cine and Rehabilitation.
Conley, R. W.
  1965   The Economics of Vocational Rehabilitation. Baltimore:
            Johns Hopkins University Press.
  1969   "A benefit cost analysis of the vocational rehabilitation pro-
            gram." Journal of Human Resources 4 (Spring): 226–252.
Copeland, W. C.
  1969   "Financing rehabilitation services." Report prepared for the
            National Citizens Conference on Rehabilitation of the Dis-
            abled and the Disadvantaged. Washington, D.C.: Social and
            Rehabilitation Service.
Haber, Lawrence D.
  1967   "Identifying the disabled: Concepts and methods in the
            measurement of disability." Survey of Disability: 1966, Re-
            port #1. Washington, D.C.: Social Security Administra-
            tion, Office of Research and Statistics.
  1968a   "Disability, Work, and Income Maintenance: Prevalence
            of Disability, 1966." Survey of Disability: 1966, Report
            #2. Washington, D.C.: Social Security Administration,
            Office of Research and Statistics.
  1968b   "The effect of age and disability on access to public income
            maintenance programs." Survey of Disability: 1966, Report
            #3. Washington, D.C.: Social Security Administration,
            Office of Research and Statistics.
  1969   "The disabled beneficiary. A comparison of factors related
            to benefit entitlement." Survey of Disability: 1966, Report

#7. Washington, D.C.: Social Security Administration, Office of Research and Statistics.

Iverson, I. *and* C. Thompson
 1967 The Griffis Study: Decision Models in Disability Determination and Rehabilitation Assessment. Minneapolis: American Rehabilitation Foundation.

Kelman, H. R.
 1964 "Evaluation of rehabilitation for the long term ill and disabled patient: Some persistent research problems." Journal of Chronic Diseases 17: 631–639.

Klarman, H. E.
 1964 "Economic impact of heart disease." Pp. 693–707, Vol. 2, in National Conference on Cardiovascular Disease, Second, The Heart and Circulation. Washington, D.C.: Federation of American Societies for Experimental Biology.

MacDermott, P.
 1973 "Occupational therapy and the self concept of the spinal cord injury." Unpublished paper. Bowney, California: Rancho Los Amigos.

Minnesota Department of Health
 1972 Minnesota Hospitals Fiscal Year 1970–1971. St. Paul: Minnesota State Welfare.

National Center for Health Statistics
 1969a "Chronic conditions causing activity limitations, July 1963–June 1965," Series 10 #51, February.
 1969b "The Sullivan report." Unpublished paper.

Rusalem, H. *and* R. Baxt
 1969 "Delivering rehabilitation services." Report prepared for the National Citizens Conference for the disabled and the disadvantaged. Washington, D.C.: Social and Rehabilitation Service.

Rusk, H. A.
 1971 Rehabilitation Medicine. St. Louis: The C. V. Mosby Co.

Silberstein, J., I. Margulec, Y. Elliahu, E. Gasper, A. Hovneh, E. Hubbert, C. Dinkerfield, E. Gottlieb, *and* R. Kossowsky
 1964 "Costs of non-rehabilitation in Israel." Journal of Chronic Diseases 17: 991–1018.

Simmons, Raymond H.
 1970 "Vocational rehabilitation of the disabled and disadvan-

taged in a rural setting." Washington, D.C.: Social and Rehabilitation Service.

Social and Rehabilitation Service

1961   People Power: A report of the Conference on Rehabilita-
            tion of the Disabled and the Disadvantaged, June 24–27.
            Washington, D.C.: Government Printing Office.

1972   Characteristics of Clients Rehabilitated in Fiscal Years
            1966–1970: A Federal-State Vocational Rehabilitation Pro-
            gram." Washington, D.C.: Government Printing Office.

Spencer, W.A, Josse deWever, N. Hott, J. Howell, J. Mallernee, *and*
     E. Grefe

1968   Actual Costs and Sources of Funds for Rehabilitating 1,003
            Physically Disabled Patients at the Texas Institute for Re-
            habilitation and Research During Nine and ½ years,
            1959–1968. Houston, Texas: Texas Institute for Rehabilita-
            tion and Research.

Spindler, Arthur

1969   "Social and rehabilitation services: A challenge to opera-
            tions research." Paper prepared for the Social and Rehabili-
            tation Service, Department of Health, Education, and Wel-
            fare, December 30.

Thurz, D.

1969   "Consumer involvement in rehabilitation." Paper prepared
            for the National Citizens Conference on Rehabilitation of
            the Disabled and the Disadvantaged. Washington, D.C.:
            Social and Rehabilitation Service.

Treitel, R.

1970   "Rehabilitation of the disabled.: Survey of Disability:
            1966, Report #12. Washington, D.C.: Social Security Ad-
            ministration, Office of Research and Statistics.

World Health Organization

1969   Technical Report No. 419. Geneva: World Health Organi-
            zation.

Wylie, C. M.

1968   "Early rehabilitation promises greater improvement to
            stroke patients." Journal of the American Hospital Associa-
            tion 42 (July 16): 100–104.

1969   "Clues to stroke rehabilitation referral among family physi-
            cians." Journal of American Geriatrics Society 17:
            549–554.

Terminal
Illness and Incentives for
Health Care Use

SELMA J. MUSHKIN
ASSISTED BY ALLAN DiSCUILLO

Summary

A large share of the nation's hospital resources goes for the care of the terminally ill. This writer estimates that share at about four billion or more than twenty percent of all nonpsychiatric hospital and nursing-home expenditures (other than outlays in federal hospitals).

The fragmentary research that exists suggests that services for terminal illness are technical medical team responses to illnesses that cannot be cured. And the resulting heroic efforts of the health professionals are reinforced by family decisions made out of fear, guilt, and love.

The resources spent paradoxically do not contribute to the well-being of the patient. On the contrary, for the dying the period of deterioration and loss of dignity of being is prolonged.

An incremental upping of price for the patient and his family will not significantly reduce use. What is required is a reassessment of ethical and legal principles, along with a restructuring of institutions that are contributing to anguish and suffering while diverting health resources that could be used to prevent disease or effect cures.

Two questions regarding services for the dying stand out as we consider incentives for consumer use of health care. First, does the present pattern of health care for the dying affect the responsiveness of expenditures to price of care, or does the magnitude of services to the dying have only a negligible impact on overall averages or quantities? The second question centers on whether the incentive structure of care gives those whose time of living is running short a choice between a faster death, and one more in keeping with human dignity, or whether the advances in the science of medicine are to maintain life by artificial methods without maintaining living.

The two questions are compelling for very different reasons. The first question cautions that special circumstances and considerations may be affecting particular outcomes of, for example, price incentives or coinsurance. The particular mechanisms being considered for restricting care may be far less effective than optional methods might be. And, thus, the first question comes to be linked to the second. Should religious, ethical, and legal practices of the past be continued without a searching re-examination of their application to care for the dying, when modern medical technology is used? Or should these practices be questioned so that the consumer can make a choice based on more information about chances of length of life, chances of and extent of pain, loss of consciousness, costs and the related financial burden on families, and so forth with differing methods of treatment.

Toward a Definition

Before discussing the first question, it is important to clarify the meaning of the terms "dying" and "terminal illness" as they are used here in considering consumer incentives for use of health care.

The terms are used interchangeably. And, in doing so, emphasis is given to the restricted way in which terminal illness is viewed in this paper. An alternative definition might be formulated in which the chance of continuing living is small but death within a short period is not a certainty. The economics of such a change in condition for choice works differently but with the same consequences. Health care that may alter the facts of death within a short period is not included, nor is the broad range of primary or secondary preventive measures that might have altered the course of the terminal condition.

A terminal disease is defined as one that results in death; those who have a terminal disease and have restrictions in normal activity are considered dying for the purposes here. Beyond that simple formulation there is no set, rigid definition. This paper will regard terminal illness as one in which the patient has been given a short time to live (not longer than two years) and has had restrictions placed on his normal living activities because of the illness. The cancer victim, for example, who will die three months from now and has been forced to leave his job would be considered a "terminal" case according to the above definition, but the person who will collapse of a fatal heart attack next month during a weekly golf match does not fit into the definition. Death must be the prognosis; normal activity must be restricted before death.

In arriving at this definition for purposes of asking about the effect of terminal illness on health-care use, alternative formulations were tried. Is it more functional to define terminal by disease category? One option, thus, is to define terminal diseases. Are there types of diseases that universally carry with them the prognosis of a short period of life and restrictions of activity? The brief skirmish with medical literature and expert consultants underscores the fact that terminal periods of "dying" vary by disease, and that periods of illness for the same disease vary widely from person to person. For different individuals the same disease may have varying impacts, depending in general on age, physical vigor, the extent of multiple disablements, state of mind, and so forth. Terminal periods for two persons suffering from the same type of cancer may vary, for example, five years or more. In ischemic heart disease, one victim may survive for up to ten years following the onset of symptoms, while another patient may collapse fatally soon after the initial attack. Thus, averages are deceptive in describing terminal illness.

A second option is to define "terminal" backward from the date of death. Those who died had a terminal illness, and the fixing of an arbitrary limit on time before death is a method of defining "terminal." For statistical purposes, that approach to a formulation is the rule. In the data from the National Center for Health Statistics (NCHS), for example, terminal hospital is defined as "use within a 12 month period before death" (NCHS, 1971). Similarly, a definition of "terminal" for health insurance purposes would require the arbitrary fixing of a period prior to the date of death as the "period of terminal illness." Such a time limit for health expenditures incurred as terminal expenses results in the counting of expenses unrelated to the death, but any other course would lead to much debate and ambiguity. It would be most difficult to isolate expenditures attributable solely to a terminal illness and restricted specifically to the cause of the death. Just a simple statement of the question brings to mind the automobile accident victim who had a chronic heart condition. If death results, what is the cause of death —automobile accident or chronic heart condition? What health expenses are to be counted as terminal?

Physicians are reluctant to discuss the duration of a patient's illness in length of days, months, or years and prefer instead to refer to it in terms of stages: an initial stage where care and treatment are necessary, a second phase where there is no recognizable hope of a cure but the patient is still able to function, and a final care period in which the patient is debilitated.

The divisions we have given are far from satisfactory. For most purposes, such as those concerned directly with clinical care, the major operative facts are the unfavorable prognosis and the response of the patient, the family, and also the provider of care to the prognosis. But here we are asking a very different order of questions; we are asking not about clinical facts but about behavior patterns of groups of persons. And we are asking in concept, not case by case, about the meaning that utilization of health care has for individual and family well-being. What motivates the use of a specific care in terminal illness? Is the pricing mechanism operating against inelastic demand for services, or are services for the dying price elastic? And, we ask, to what extent is the care of terminal illness consuming the limited health resources that are available?

Demand for Services for the Dying

Research, such as that by Scitovsky and Snyder (1972) and Phelps and Newhouse (1972), suggests that coinsurance reduces use of health services. Is the response observed partly, at least, a consequence of terminal illness? Does higher price restrict the use and volume of terminal care and thus contribute to the research findings on coinsurance? It seems reasonable to expect that, in the care of the dying, higher prices could reduce total health expenditures. This hypothesis is reinforced by the fact that the lowered expenditures could by definition alter the outcome little, if at all.

The information on expenditures for the dying is incomplete and several years old. But the information that is available does not support the notion of a highly elastic demand for care for the dying, at least with respect to hospital care. On the contrary, the information available, mostly on use of hospitals and extended-care facilities, indicates that use is related more to psychological and sociological responses of patients, families, and providers of care than to the economics of the price system.

Essentially, we have very little quantified information about the behavior that governs the demand for health services for terminal illness. When children are dying, we assume that adult guardians make important sets of decisions about health-care use. They do so with all the anguish that loss of a child brings. Parenthetically, the cause of death has some bearing; the average age of death for most children is under one year of age and most of those deaths are caused by congenital malformations. Half or more of the deaths of those under age one take place within the first four weeks of life.

For young children under school age, and increasingly as the age advances into young adulthood, deaths from accidents become a larger and larger share of all deaths at each age group. Accidental death leaves little room, at least initially, for choice of types of care.

The further hypothesis is advanced here that, in the event of accident, the margin of decision about health care is very narrow for the patient or family. Decisions are governed by the nature of the medical response to the emergency condition that confronts the practitioner. Many accidents clearly end in death, with little use of health resources. In fact, in the NCHS (1971) study of adult decedents, only thirty percent of the accidental deaths involved patient hospital-care costs. But for those who incur costs the expenditures run high—averaging an estimated $1,500 per case at 1973 prices. It is reported from the Children's Hospital (1973) in Washington, D.C., that the most expensive of their accident cases are burn cases.

It is not only care of children that calls for family decision. Certainly for many older patients, and six out of every ten deaths are among persons aged sixty-five or over, the patient's children become part of the decision structure. And no recital of relevant facts about decisions of health care for the dying would be complete without awareness of the pain and loneliness for husbands or wives of the dying, and the complex factors that combine to exacerbate their tensions in deciding about health care for the spouse.

Thus the consumers of health care are the patient and his family, with (a) parents deciding for young children, (b) grown children often deciding for their parents, (c) one spouse deciding for the other, (d) the patient making a decision alone, or (e) the patient and other relatives or friends deciding. All the potential consumer decisions are strongly affected by the advice of the physician and the medical decisions taken by the professional staff in the hospital.

Expenditures

Two primary national sources of data on expenditures of the dying are available, and each has its own special characteristics and limitations.

Medicare data are reported for the years 1967 and 1968 to

show expenditures reimbursed under the program for institutional care in the year of death. The data separately report Medicare reimbursements for hospital and other institutional care and also supplementary medical benefits (Rice, 1973).

The second source is the 1964–1965 survey by Monroe Sirken made for NCHS (1971) on decedents and is addressed to the question of a statistical correction for deaths of household interview data. In the National Health survey, data are collected for a twelve-month period from living persons, thus relating hospitalizations and hospital stays only to those who survive. Specifically, the estimates of hospital utilization derived from the survey exclude the hospitalization and deaths of persons who died during the twelve-month period before the interviewing week.

Two earlier reports had dealt with adjustments of surveys for deaths. One reported that if care were received by decedents aged sixty-five and over, as reported on household surveys, such care would increase the total days of hospital use by all persons by approximately one-fourth (Falk and Brewster, 1952). Siegel, Belloc, and Hesse (1957) estimated in a San Jose study that adjustments for use of hospital care by the dying would increase hospital admissions by six percent and hospital days by ten percent. For persons aged sixty-five and over, the adjustments increased both rate of admission and rate of days in the hospital by approximately one-third.

These data, while addressed to a different problem—namely, that of adjusting for the probability that data (when collected for a twelve-month period) omit decedents and thereby understate hospital utilization rates—can be used to measure the relative share of hospital care attributable to decedents.

The NCHS survey shows that the 1.2 million persons who died after receiving short-term hospital care in the twelve-month period preceding death received on the average 25 days of care (1971). Decedents accounted for an annual total of 79 million days in hospitals and institutions during the last year of life. Stays for those who are dying are far in excess of the average length of stay for all patients (National Center for Health Statistics, 1970). On the average, decedents had 44 days of hospital or institutional care. Short-term hospital care for terminal cases averaged 25 days, a figure that contrasts with an average of 8.4 days for all patients. Short-term stays of the dying accounted for about twelve percent of all days of short-term hospital use (National Vital Statistics Branch, 1972).

The second source of data provides information on expenditures. Medicare statistics for the years 1967 and 1968 show that twenty-two percent of the reimbursements were for illnesses that ended in death in the year the expenditure was incurred. The figure is a minimum that does not reflect the expenses incurred in the calendar year before death and would not include expenditures, for example, even for December of the preceeding year for those who died in January.

Medicare reimbursements amounting to $1 billion were made in 1968 for hospital and extended-care facility services for the aged dying. That sum represents about one-fourth of all Medicare hospital costs. In accord with the statute, however, reimbursements represent—on the average—only eighty percent of the total in-hospital care bills for all Medicare claims. When adjusted to account for the reimbursement ratio, the $1.0 billion claims paid for the dying would amount to at least $1.2 billion. Further adjustment to take account of the definitional problems—namely, the counting of expenditures for only those who died during the calendar year, or again the counting, for example, of only January's expenditures for the patient who died in the first month of the calendar year—suggests a doubling of that amount, or $2.4 billion. The doubling assumes that the reporting of reimbursements for those who died during the year of the Medicare payment represents an average one-half year of hospital expense. Such an assumption may lead to some overestimating, but the extent is not large. Of the 1968 aggregate outlays of $18.7 billion by nonfederal hospitals and institutions (including skilled nursing homes but excluding psychiatric hospitals), the aged who were dying thus accounted for $2.4 billion of those outlays, or thirteen percent. When to that percentage is added an allowance for hospital care for persons under age sixty-five who died in that year, the share of hospitalization attributable to the dying becomes more than twenty percent.

An additional approach to estimating the aggregate shares is possible using NCHS (1971) data available on hospital costs for the dying, or costs of hospitalized illness by disease category. The data for 1964–1965 were inflated to a 1968 level by the hospital price component of the Bureau of Labor Statistics index. Averages so adjusted were applied to the most recent data (for 1971) on deaths by cause. An estimated expenditure for hospitalized illness in excess of $1.5 billion was thus computed, a figure representing about fifteen percent of private consumer expenditures for hospital care.

Medicare data indicated hospital reimbursements were $1,244 per person who died, in contrast to $861 per person alive at the end of the year. Program reimbursements, for physicians' services as well as hospital care, for persons who died during the year averaged about double the reimbursements for persons alive at the end of the year.

The shortcomings of existing data are many. Costs counted are mostly hospital costs and exclude, for example, many other costs such as nursing care and home health aid and nursing home expenditures. The data show that terminal illness claims a significant share of all hospital resources. And the use of hospital resources varies by nature of illness and cause of death and by age. The NCHS (1971) survey showed that about seventy-five percent of all adult decedents incurred hospital or institutional expenses in the twelve-month period preceding death. About seventy-eight percent of the decedents with an annual income of two thousand dollars or less received care in hospitals or other institutions, while the rate for decedents in other income classes ranged from sixty-eight percent to seventy-one percent. Use of hospital and institutional care and expenses for such care appear to be more nearly a function of the cause of death than of other factors. Expenses for hospital and institutional care were reported in the NCHS survey for fewer than a third of the accident cases, about half of the suicides, about two-thirds of the heart disease cases, and more than ninety percent of the deaths from malignant neoplasm.

The median hospital bill for decedents was $691 in 1964–1965. In 1968 prices that would be about $1,050, and in 1973 prices it

would be about $1,865. The median hospital bill for the live patient
in 1964–1965 was $259. That is slightly more than 35¢ for every
$1 spent for the dying. The averages obscure the large bills incurred
by upwards of one-third of the terminal cases. It is possible to estimate roughly an average amount of hospital expenses by finding the
median costs of each illness and, once again, applying a medical-
care price inflator to arrive at current 1973 prices. What is significant about the figures is the large concentration of expenses at the
upper expense intervals, thus re-emphasizing the cost of terminal
disease.

High dying costs are characteristic of each income group.
Though there is some proportionality in increased costs of hospital
care as family income rises, even at the lowest income levels
($2,000 and under) more than one-third of the decedents who re-
ceived care in 1965 were reported to have had bills of $1,000 or
more. In 1973 prices, they would have bills of $2,400 or more.

Institutional expenses appear to have less than unitary income
elasticity, ranging from 0.3 percent to 0.7 percent per one-percent
rise in income. Costs tend to rise as patient income rises but by less
than the rate of income increase. For instance, 51.4 percent of decedents with an income of $2,000 or less incurred expenses of
$500 or more; the increase is to only 60 percent at the middle-in-
come levels ($2,000–$6,999) and to 68 percent at the highest income bracket ($7,000 and over). (The figures are in 1965 prices.)

In 1965 more than eighty percent of the institutional residents
—those in hospitals and nursing homes—had incomes of two thousand dollars a year or less. Of all residents, forty-seven percent had
hospital bills of one thousand dollars or more in the twelve-month
period prior to death. Thus, high medical bills are not restricted to
higher income groups alone, although, among all groups, the highest income class reported (seven thousand dollars and over) had, as
would be expected, the greatest proportion of hospital bills of one
thousand dollars or more—almost one out of every two hospital
bills.

The effect of noneconomic factors on medical-care use is suggested by the NCHS (1971) survey's finding that the amount of the

bill for persons with care in medical institutions is universally proportional to the age at death, with expenses diminishing as age increases. Although a higher proportion of older decedents received personal care than did younger decedents, expenses for those who had care were lower for older than for younger decedents. For about one in every two decedents aged twenty-five to forty-four, bills of one thousand dollars or more were reported in 1964–1965. The comparable proportion was 38.3 percent for those aged sixty-five and over. Part of the difference may be attributed to the nature of the medical condition affecting the younger and older patients. But at the younger ages more expensive measures may be taken to save the life of a person. And for many older persons, and increasingly as they age, the patient is likely to receive medical care in lower-cost nursing institutions

Perhaps the hardest hit is the age group forty-five to sixty-four, which is second in number of terminal cases only to group aged sixty-five and over. It has the highest proportion of deaths from cancer and cirrhosis, the two most expensive diseases for hospital treatment, but is denied the medical and hospital benefits of Medicare available to the older group. Thus, this age group is caught with high expenses and relatively less access to third-party payments. In 1973 prices, $2,400 or more in hospital and institutional expenses would be incurred for about four out of every ten decedents aged forty-five to sixty-four.

Toward a Definition of Incentives

We have little hard data and scant research on which to draw scientific generalizations about the determinants of care for the dying. Research scholars in most disciplines have until recently ignored this part of the contract of man with his society. The mysticism of dying and death has stood in the way. Perhaps the darkness of knowledge about death itself has enveloped the termination of life.

Such studies as have been reported direct their attention largely to clinical aspects; that is, to support of decisions in adjustment from life to death, and the need for development of health personnel schooled in methods of providing such clinical assistance (Kubler-Ross, 1969).

Here we address a different problem—motivation to use health care by individuals and families and the determinants and procedures at the various decision levels. What incentives are now at work? How may they be altered to provide more choice, and how may one get the information required for choice? At the start it may be useful to summarize the research that has been done and to formulate, at least approximately, the basic set of choices and the underlying issues.

State Of the Art In Brief

Economic research assumes that avoidance of premature death is a strong motivating force. The quantification that has been done centers on the value of human life, and that value is largely based on estimates of earning power lost to the economy by premature death. Death for those in retirement as non-earners tends to be disregarded. Weisbrod (1961b), Fein (1958), Klarman (1965), and this writer (Mushkin, 1962) have contributed to formulating the idea of health as an investment in people and, accordingly, to counting the value of lives saved in terms of earnings. Vickrey (1963) and others have noted that society places great value on the lives of identifiable single individuals, as witnessed by the large resources that go into attempts to rescue miners who are trapped or the child who has fallen in an unused pit or well. Valuation of life is not restricted to measurements of health program effects. Many economic projects—whether airways, highways, or housing design —involve decisions about cost of added protection (i.e., life-saving) (Reynolds, 1956). Schelling's (1968) work is of special interest in that he distinguishes between the life and the livelihood to the family and the loss to other members of the economy—the taxpayers, insurance policyholders, and kin. What is it worth to the individual to reduce the statistical probability of death? asks Schelling. And he writes,

As an economist I have to keep reminding myself that consumer sovereignty is not just a metaphor. . . . Welfare economics establishes the convenience of consumer sovereignty and compatibility with economic efficiency. . . . And it includes the inalienable right of the consumer to make his own mistakes. . . . The fact that they (the patients) may not do it well, or may not quite know what they are doing as they make the decision, may not bother them and need not disenfranchise them in the exercise of consumer and taxpayer sovereignty (p. 128).

Sociological studies on the dying cover a wider range of medical-service determinants. In the Parsonian paradigm, the sick are expected to seek competent health care and to want to get well (Parsons, 1964, 1963). The terminally sick person does not fit that pattern, as Lipman and Sterne (1969) have indicated. Petroni (1969) reviews the perceptions of the legitimacy of the sick role and concludes that illness seems to have the opposite effect. Values of personal self-reliance and independence are strong. Apple's (1960) findings—that the interferences with one's usual activities are the single most important condition associated with illness—become an essential component of the definition of terminal illness. The feedback effects that the place of health care have on mortality are reported by Dael Wolfle (1970). In the year following the death of one member of a family the death rate among close relatives is found to be twice as high when the primary death occurred in a hospital or nursing home than when it occurred at home.

Fear as a deterrent to use of health care is the subject of a number of studies, including that of Ketcham (1972) and Wakefield (1962). Kubler-Ross (1969) in her highly acclaimed study of two hundred terminal cases describes five stages of dying—from disbelief to anger to acceptance—that are characteristic of most dying patients; she counsels against current practices determining medical services. Ramsey's (1972) the *Patient as Person* emphasizes in a more general way the ethical considerations of patient and physician relationships, and the loss of professionalism felt by the physician in the face of the dying patient. Wald (1971), in her study of nurses' care of the dying, reports in a similar vein.

The advancing pace at which extraordinary means, such as artificial respirators, are being used in services to terminal patients has created a new set of issues about standards for determining human death. Many persons are reported now to be maintained in a sort of twilight state by the use of machines that do the work of lungs or heart while they are completely unconscious. Death itself has come to be redefined. Capron and Kass (1972) address themselves to the question of criteria for determining death in the light of medicine's increasing ability to maintain signs of life aritficially. Their review article summarizes discussions on death and dying of the Institute of Society, Ethics, and the Life Sciences and proposes a set of criteria on death. But they conclude by noting that the proposal leaves for future resolution the even more difficult problems concerning the conditions and procedures under which a decision may be reached to cease treating a terminal patient who does not meet the criteria of the proposed definition of death.

Formulation of Choices

Individuals who have a terminal illness go through phases in the process of transition from dying to death that involve, among other things, changes in the opportunity costs of time and in the cost of medical care. Such data as are available suggest a decreasing cost of medical care with the passage of time. The lower costs, with extended days of care, are averages that obscure the costs in the last stages of heroic efforts when the patient approaches a state of coma. Costs of services per day tend to decline as stays are extended in hospitalized and institutionalized illnesses. The decline is shown in Fig. 1 by the curve *IH;* the subsequent increase is shown by *HD.*

For those dying but yet able to function, the value of time would tend to grow greater as the availability of time diminishes (shown by the line *RS* in Fig. 1.) Underlying the opportunity cost of time for the dying is not only the preciousness of the remaining

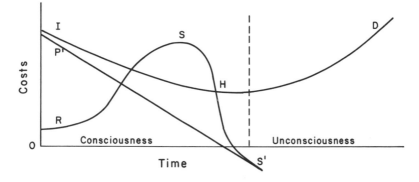

Figure 1. *Transition from Dying to Death*

days but also the capacity to function, the extent of pain, the hazard of a long drawn-out illness that exhausts not only physical ability to function but the financial capacity for independence, the diminution of personal dignity, and the burden of preparing for death (including such decisions as dividing the estate). When the individual grows physically weaker the value of time diminishes even as his time grows short (if other factors remain unchanged). The opportunity costs in value of time are illustrated in the diagram as lines *R'S'*. If one were to extend time further and to assume that the individual has reached a state of functional incapacity or coma, then time for the dying would seem to have no or even negative value. Perhaps almost simultaneously, the efforts of family and providers of care to maintain life push up the per diem costs.

There is a risk keenly felt by some, less keenly by others, of the uncertainties about the length of the period of dying and the chance of not being able to function independently. At the same time there is the worry of being increasingly without the financial means to provide care. The future is heavily discounted, and for any opportunity cost the discount rate is high; however, the planning of decision takes place for the dying against a background of great uncertainty about the length of continued living, the extent and acceleration of pain, the continued need for services, and the ability to finance those services. (It is assumed here that the fact of dying is not altered by decisions taken but simply that the length of the terminal period is affected by the decisions.)

Time requires choices of reduction in pain or of maintenance of the dignity of mental activity.

Painkillers may reduce the "hurt" for a time, but they also often involve a loss of mental agility. There is some trade-off between loss of pain and willingness to forego some amount of dignity. Perhaps those who have been most vital in the days before illness strikes view the process of transition to death as involving the greatest sacrifice, and the loss in dignity the highest loss.

It may be that the focal point in terminal treatment is the question of decisions about palliative treatment. Palliative care is intended to relieve pain caused by a fatal disease and to help the patient overcome the anxieties usually associated with terminal illness. It is given at a point when further curative care is limited and there is little chance of patient survival.

In discussing palliative treatment, Dr. William Lirette et al. (1969) comment that a number of suitable methods are available to the physician in terminal cases when cure is beyond his capabilities. Palliative treatment is essentially pain-relieving, and it raises the question of choice—how to insure maximum pain-relieving protection with the least loss of human dignity. Lirette has been among the advocates of reducing morphine usage as a palliative measure and substituting X-ray therapy for cancer patients. At the same time he sharply presents the issue of determining criteria for the minimum pain maximum dignity scheme, notably among patients for whom the only possible means of a relatively painless death is the use of seemingly inhumane drugs and treatments. It is at this point that the question of palliative care often becomes one of euthanasia. Medical literature rarely discusses by whom that decision is to be made, and on what information it is to be based.

Schelling (1968), as an economist, approaches the topic of pain and death and asks where boundaries exist and what the criteria for judgment are. He writes:

> Death is indeed different from most consumer events and its avoidance different from most commodities. There is no

sense in being insensitive about something that entails grief, anxiety, frustration, and mystery, as well as economic deprivation. But people have been dying for as long as they have been living; where life and death are concerned we are all consumers. We nearly all want our lives extended and are probably willing to pay for it. It is worth-while to remind ourselves that the people whose lives may be saved should have something to say about the value of the enterprise and that we analysts, however detached, are not immortal ourselves (p. 128).

A range of critical questions on choice originates deep in legal and religious sanctions against suicide and euthanasia. And those sanctions date back to a time when little was known about diseases and their causes. Precise classification of diseases was initiated as late as 1836 with the Annual Register of that year. The effect was to place on the medical profession for the first time the responsibility for describing the patient's condition before death. Taboos about the dying seem more appropriate to the ages of darkness in medical knowledge than to today.

Determinants of Decisions

What factors lead to the strange decision resulting in large medical bills (and substantial use of health resources) for those who attach little or negative value to time (or continued life) and whose preferences may run counter to the decisions taken?

Among the factors discussed here sequentially and briefly are:

(1) the impersonality of team medical care;

(2) the perverse effect of curative ·medicine on coping with dying;

(3) the lack of physician-family relationship and ties;

(4) the withholding of information from the patient about the nature of the disease, optional treatment methods, and probable effects; and

(5) the tragedy and guilt of families involved in death and the hope of "cures."

Impersonality of team medical care. At present about two out of every three deaths occur in hospitals or institutions where medical care is provided impersonally by teams of nurses, aides, and physicians. All are strangers who have no ties to the patient. Only thirty years earlier the percentage of deaths in institutions was half as large (National Vital Statistics Branch, 1972). Personal involvement in a patient's life is in fact frowned on by some because involvement may create barriers in making professional choices. But the impersonal nature of the care has the effect of prolonging care. Physician, nurse, and other medical team members apply those medical skills they have learned in the heroic effort to maintain life, without assessing the overall consequences for the patient of continued existence without capacity to function. And that reaction is reinforced by recent experience with malpractice suits and threats of such suits.

Perverse effect of curative medicine on coping with dying. The craftsmanship of medicine added to the sayings of Hippocrates gives the medical staffs a mode of coping with the processes of dying. That mode, when practitioners face a defeat for their curative skill, is to give more and more care. But "all that can professionally be done is being done" may be more a salve for the staff than for the patient. It is that incentive to professional action that raises the costs of direct care for the dying and makes for a negative value of time to the dying. Medical care can become a scientific weapon for the prolongation of agony.

Bailey (1965) emphasizes the orientation of the medical profession toward curative services. Moreover, when confronted with the lack of prospect of a cure, professional knowledge drops away and, as some sociological studies suggest, the health professional becomes a layman with lay reactions.

Studies within the medical profession show the reactions of physicians to care of terminal patients. Brodsky (1969), for one, describes the difficulties in recruiting physicians to study and provide care for the terminal cancer patient. The excessive use of sedatives and pain relievers is the usual response made by physicians treating terminal cancer patients. And a survey by Schoenberg et al. (1972)

finds that sixty-two percent of all medical school respondents are dissatisfied with teaching efforts to prepare medical students for care of the dying.

Lack of physician-family relationship and ties. Today the family physician is a rarity in our major cities, and those who practice as general practitioners in rural areas are fast leaving those areas. Decisions, therefore, about care of the dying are now made in isolation from family needs and by practitioners who are strangers. Many assume that in years past the physician silently, in the interests of patient and family, prescribed in the light of those interests. But selectivity in medical approaches becomes less possible with current medical organization. In the course of the move away from general practice and toward medical specialties, furthermore, medical care is fragmented both for family and for the patient. And it makes the decision on medical services more nearly a market decision, subject, however, to all the lack of financial constraints that originate in third-party payments and to potential overuse of services as professional safeguards.

So far away has the medical profession moved from personal care of the patient that new reforms are being proposed to meet the psychiatric need of terminal patients as they are dying. Treatment is suggested by Fink and Oaks (1970) for regression, depression, and denial. Psychological therapy during the initial stages of terminal treatment is emphasized. Kubler-Ross' (1969) important work is directed to achieve counseling for the dying in the expectation of higher quality care.

Withholding of information from the patient. Adult patients make some decisions about their own care, but they do so in an atmosphere of uncertainty, lack of information, false information, fear, and anguish. For the dying person, the decisions are thus clouded even if his mind is clear. A number of physicians report that they make a practice of not informing patients of terminal illness because of the effect such knowledge has on the patient's well-being. Others take an opposite position and insist that disclosure is important to the patient's welfare.

Tragedy and guilt of involved families. Families are called on to contribute to decisions about care of the dying when deep concern, guilt, and hope of reversing the odds all contribute to the actions taken on medical care. The consequences are likely to be demand for care without immediate regard to price if there is a probability of life. And even when the outcome is certain, the added days of life, particularly for the child who is ill, result in much inpouring of services in the hope that somehow life will be prolonged.

The family decisions often are made without certain knowledge of financial cost or drains. Even the billing procedures of hospitals are such that the patient and his family have little information about resources and treatment costs at the time of decision.

New Facts, Old Traditions, and the Agenda for the Future

The factors that lead to extensive and intensive use of health services for the dying, without regard to price or income, are compounded to create much inflexibility in use and, from the perspective of some patients or families, undue lengthening of life.

Not too long ago death was a familiar part of family living. "Death in the family," however, has by virtue of many changes—social, economic, and medical—become a more rare and a less familiar experience in the family. The lack of experience with the price of dying adds to use of medical services. Among other things, the conquest of infectious diseases has altered family experience with death. The natural effect of the conquest of the contagious diseases is lower mortality rates in the younger ages and higher death rates from heart diseases, cancer, and diseases of the kidney, the more costly diseases in any case.

And natural forces no longer are the sole determinant of who shall die and how long the process of dying shall be. Death that was once an unambiguous certainty has become a highly differentiated phenomenon requiring standards and criteria on the several psychological processes of "living."

However, advances in medical knowledge contribute greatly to

an understanding of the consequences of various medical treatments. Those advances also provide to physicians and patients additional information that can serve as criteria for making decisions
about trade-offs between pain and capacity to function and between pain and length of continued life. They serve the physician in
the selection of patients for optional courses of medical treatment.
Choice of care by the consumer becomes more essential and more
feasible.

Important in examining the choices is the fact that major advances against some killers of an earlier day now give to the patient
access to death in a way that has been unfamiliar. The simple non-
turning on of a battery or the pulling out of an electric plug means
death. The capacity to control the means to death makes for a different kind of choice about dying and a different locus of choice for
those who incur the kinds of illness for which medical science has
now provided ready access to "means" to death.

The new facts in combination—improved mortality, scientific
advances, as well as the ever increasing costs of care—create a very
different climate within which to examine the question of consumer
behavior with respect to use of medical services by the dying and
their families.

Important at present is discussion of old prohibitions and new
facts about:

(1) using death-dealing pain killers;
(2) ceasing treatment that prolongs a patient's life or hinders
his death; and
(3) withholding treatment altogether.

The third method, withholding treatment, has received most
of the consideration both because of its economic consequences and
because of the ethical conflicts attached to it. Joseph Fletcher
(1960), writing in *Harpers* during the period of initial experimentation with the renal dialysis machines, said:

Death control, like birth control, is a matter of human dignity and without it persons become puppets. To perceive this is

to grasp the essential . . . notion—widespread in medical cir-
cles—that life as such is the greatest good. This type of reasoning seduces its victims into being more loyal to the physical
spark of mere biological life than to the personal values of self-
possession and human integrity (p. 143).

The withholding of medical treatment from the terminally ill
has received more than literary treatment. Moore's (1965) critique
begins with the hypothetical situation of a patient about to die saying to his doctor, "I am old and I am dying of cancer. I may get
pneumonia first. Don't give me antibiotics. I'd rather die of pneumonia than of cancer." The law, says Moore, is unclear; throughout
his critique he chastises both the legal and the medical professions
for what he calls continued unclarity in coming to grips with situations such as those described above.

In recent years, however, an attempt has been made to clear up
the uncertainties about the methods and types of choice. Lister
(1969) is among the more recent to provide some clarity on euthanasia. He states that the "need for inquiry into euthanasia and
the question of omission of treatment is obvious. Medicine has become a victim of runaway technology which leaves a gap between
technical know-how and human values. We have to recognize this
and establish a set of values appropriate to our times" (p. 1203).

Research Tasks Ahead

No sets of problems beg for the transformation of institutions as
much as the transition from life to death. Understanding of the
means for prolonging life has been enlarged, but the institutional
structure and social fabric have failed to respond. What is intended
as a harnessing of human capacity for living has turned into the introduction of gadgetry that imperils the very integrity and dignity of
persons who are terminally ill and that threatens the financial security of their families. The past two years or so have witnessed a
deep concern about institutional change commensurate with the
new technology of medicine.

Without a change in institutional structure the outlook for a number of terminal patients is a continuing life without living: a condition that, combined with loss of personal dignity and of independence of person, plus financial strain, begs for new approaches. Further prolongation of life without prolongation of the individual's capacity to function is a condition that cannot long continue.

The past record of human achievements calls for an unfolding of access to death in dignity. The questions that require scrutiny if we are to devise better means to that access are many. They include, for example:

—Under what conditions and circumstances should treatment be ended or access to death be provided?
—How shall the decisions be made about the existence of those conditions and circumstances?
—Who should decide to end treatment when the specified standards are met?
—How shall the application of the standards be reviewed and enforced?

Living wills are proposed by some as a means. When may such wills be valid? Application of criteria on vital decisions of life is not untried. Transplants and equipment for renal dialysis are in short supply: rationing is required and the use of rationing raises sharply the issue of standards on care determining who should live and who should die. Criteria on use of curative therapies are now made explicit, and are administered by committees of hospital staffs and lay members. As a consequence, experience is being accumulated on application of criteria to the awesome question of human life.

Age, responsibilities, general condition, and financial means are among criteria that have been used in determining the rationing of scarce medical treatments. Consideration of the immediate family is one criterion, and the family's willingness to pay the expenses is another. Religion is still a third. Some criteria reflect the interests of society and the ability of the practitioners to provide treatment. In general, the rationing methods or criteria emphasize the impersonal relationships betweeen providers and the dying.

A notable example of forced selection among patients occurred in the middle and late 1960s, with the initial patient use of the kidney hemodialysis units. The framework of the decision-making process and the specific criteria used by the committee in selecting the first five patients for dialysis in Swedish Hospital, Seattle, involved the determination of standards for admission to the program and application of those standards. Among the criteria used were job status, family size, "moral" status, and economic worth—both present and potential—of the prospective patients (Alexander, 1962).

Patient selection models are in need of review, with consideration of additional variables on which to base accurate and objective judgments. The potential patient's desire to live longer and the possible resultant trade-offs between rigorous treatment and financial strain and a longer life demand further elaboration.

Providing access to curtailment of treatment and access of the patient to death poses far easier questions than those involved in transplants and renal dialysis. The newer therapies require the asking: Who should die, and who should live, and who should decide? It is paradoxical that, despite the fact that providing access to a dignified death for those dying would appear to be a less complex question than rationing life-giving transplants, it faces a much larger barrier in the form of ancient traditions. Religious tenets, law, and professional ethics all stand in the way. What strategies should be followed in gaining a re-examination of ancient tenets?

While the patient's access to termination of care and to means of death is the primary issue requiring new institutional arrangements, other questions also require extensive new research.

What types of new health services would patients and their families buy to take the place of the family practitioner of an earlier epoch? New approaches are suggested, including training and use of full-time psychologists for those with terminal illness. The problems most difficult for the attending physician to deal with are patient regression, denial, and depression which, if deep enough, requires counseling, both for the patient's ability to cope with the final terminal stages and for the general morale of attending staff and family.

Counseling has in some cases, it is reported, reduced unnecessary patient costs and eliminated the repetition and often duplication of tests performed on terminal patients to determine the exact spread of the disease. And a patient's frank discussion of pain has saved staff members from conducting still other tests, thus reducing the patient's costs.

Use of new health practitioners in terminal illness care opens new questions on the locus of professional decision. McKegney and Lange (1971) differ from other writers in that they state that the decision-making process should at all times rest upon the physicians and not the psychiatrists, who are often out of reach for most patients. Communications with the patients have often been found to be a benefit in renal treatment. The McKegney-Lange study is, in part, supported by Abrams' (1969) contention that better communications are needed between the medical team and patients.

Herter (1972), more so than Elizabeth Kubler-Ross (1969) or Alfred Ketcham (1972), advocates talking openly to the patient about his condition. His approach is straightforward; the patient, says Herter, who participates in the treatment process is better equipped to approach the terminal period, and in fact may be especially helpful in providing doctors and surgeons with suggestions for palliative services. Moreover, when a patient has received exact information on the nature of his illness, the attending staff has been more at ease with him and surrounding patients. Herter has found the decision-making process facilitated when patients have been told how serious their disease is, and he has urged other surgeons' approval of a "frank talk" with terminal patients.

Despite the increasing application of the principles of social medicine, care of the dying indigent patient has received altogether too little attention. In the studies that have been conducted a radical shift in program orientation is indicated as necessary to meet the additional demands made upon attending staff. Such demands are not unexpected because the limited intelligence and financial situation of many indigent patients produce extremely poor relations. Ritan and Lewis (1966) found that the increased depression and suicidal wishes of indigent patients are often a factor in tense relations with attending staff members. Since few staff members volunteer for indigent care, attending staff for those wards must be appointed, and such appointment becomes another source of strained relations. What kind of training would overcome such strains?

Hard information on the costs of terminal illness is needed that is specifically addressed to the costs of prolonging life beyond living, with analysis of the personnel resources involved and optional uses of such resources. What is the impact of large bills on patients and their families? Does higher price reduce care? For what kinds of medical care?

The agenda for research is long and cuts across many disciplines—but the locus of choice and the information for choice are among the major items.

> The ancestral ethic which prolongs the degradation and tortures of dying by delaying death—whether for the old, the sick unto death or the unborn—on the ground that life must be prolonged, is one of the cruelest sanctions of the inhumanity of man to man. The command it imposes on the aged, or on any whose living is a miserable dying in a dehumanization of loneliness and pain, is the ultimate immorality. An authentically moral "Society" would let such freely choose, enable them to choose, and help them to achieve their choice. For some it will be to live dying to the dehumanized end. For others it will be to die living as the consummation of the human end (Kalen, 1972:21).

References

Abrams, H. S.
    1969   "Psychiatry, the treatment of chronic renal failure and prolongation of life." American Journal of Psychiatry 18: 50–57.
Ad Hoc Task Force on Cardiac Replacement
    1969   Cardiac Replacement, Medical, Ethical, Psychological and Economic Implications. Washington, D.C.: Government Printing Office.

Alexander, James
1969 "Exercise and coronary heart disease." Cardio-Vascular Research Center Bulletin 8: 2–8.
Alexander, Shana
1962 "They decide who lives, who dies." Life 52 (November 9): 102–109.
Anthony, Sylvia
1940 The Child's discovery of Death. New York: Basic Books.
Apple, Dorrian
1960 "How laymen define illness." Journal of Health and Human Behavior 1 (Summer): 219–225.
Arrow, K.
1963 "Uncertainty and the welfare economics of medical care." American Economic Review 53 (December): 941–974.
1968 "The economics of moral hazard: Further comment." American Economic Review 58 (June): 537–539.
Bailey, Richard
1965 "Economic and social costs of death." Pp. 75–94 in Klarman, H. E. (ed.), Economics of Health. New York: Columbia University Press.
Beard, Howard
1958 A New Approach to the Conquest of Cancer, Rheumatic and Heart Diseases. New York: Pagent Press.
Bhatt, Usha
1963 Socioeconomic Problems of Cancer Patients. Bombay: Indian Cancer Society.
Brodsky, Isadore
1969 Death and the Cancer Patient. New York: Grune and Stratton.
Capron, A. M. *and* T. R. Kass
1972 "A statutory definition of the standards for determining human death." University of Pennsylvania Law Review 121: 87–118.
Cartwright, Ann, Lisbeth Hockey, *and* John L. Anderson
1973 Life Before Death. Boston: Routledge and Kegan Paul.
Children's Hospital
1973 Personal Communication, May.
Church of England
1965 Decisions About Life and Death. London: Westminister Press.

Cotter, Sister Zita Marie
    1971   "Institutional care of the terminally ill." Hospital Progress
             52, 6 (June): 42–48.
Falk, I. S. *and* A. W. Brewster
    1952   "Hospitalization insurance and hospital utilization among
             aged persons." Social Security Bulletin 15 (March): 3–13.
    1957   "Hospitalization insurance and hospital planning: Adjust-
             ments for decedents missed." Public Health Reports 72
             (November): 989–997.
Fein, Rashi
    1958   Economics of Mental Health: A Report to the Staff Direc-
             tor. New York: Basic Books.
Fink, Paul *and* W. Oaks
    1970   Psychiatry and the Internist. New York: Grune and Strat-
             ton.
Fletcher, Joseph
    1960   "The patient's right to die." Harpers 221, 1325 (October):
             121–160.
Fox, Renee C.
    1970   "A sociological perspective on organ transplantation and
             hemodialysis." Annals of the New York Academy of Sci-
             ence 69: 406–427.
Franksson, Curt (ed.)
    1968   Kidney Transplantation. Stockholm: Almqvist and Wiksell.
Glaser, B. G.
    1966   "The social loss of aged, dying patients." Gerontologist 6
             (June): 67–80.
Glaser, B. G. *and* A. L. Strauss
    1965   Awareness of Death. Chicago: Aldine Publishing Compa-
             ny.
Group Health Insurance of New York
    1971   Health Care Issues of the 60's. New York: Metropolitan
             Life Insurance.
Hedinger, Frederic
    1966   Social Role of Blue Cross, Health Care Series No. 2. Wash-
             ington, D.C.: Government Printing Office.
Herter, Frederick
    1972   A Surgeon Looks At Terminal Illness. New York: Colum-
             bia University Press.

Institute of Medicine of Chicago
1950   Terminal Care for Cancer Patients. Chicago: Institute of Medicine of Chicago, April.

Kaje, M., D. McDade, *and* C. Comty
1968   An Appraisal of Equipment for Hemodialysis in the Home. New York: Basic Books.

Kalen, Horace
1972   "Philosophy, aging and the aged." Journal of Value Inquiry 6, 1 (Winter): 1–21.

Kantrowitz, Adrian
1964   "Implantable cardiac pacemakers." Annals of the New York Academy of Science 3: 1049–1067.

Ketcham, Alfred
1972   A Surgeon's Approach to a Patient with Advanced Cancer. New York: Columbia University Press.

Kidney Disease Program Analysis
1967   A Report to the Surgeon General. Washington, D.C.: Government Printing Office.

Klarman, Herbert E.
1965   Economics of Health. New York: Columbia University Press.

Kelgerman, Martin
1972   A Radiotherapist's View of Management of the Cancer Patient. New York: Columbia University Press.

Kubler-Ross, Elizabeth
1969   On Death and Dying. New York: Macmillan Company.

Lawson, Herbert
1963   "Kidney machines save doomed patients lives but raise ethical issue." Wall Street Journal 162, 38 (August 22): 1–3.

Liberman, Aaron
1966   Options in Medicare, Health Care Series No. 6. Washington, D.C.: Government Printing Office.

Lipman, Aaron *and* Richard S. Sterne
1969   Aging in the United States. New York: Grune and Stratton.

Lirette, William, R. L. Palmer, J. D. Ibarra, Jr., P. M. Kroening, *and* Richard K. Gaines
1969   "Management of patients with terminal cancer." Postgraduate Medicine 46 (December): 145–149.

Lister, J.
  1969   "Voluntary euthanasia." New England Journal of Medicine
          281, 22: 1203–1210.
Lowenthal, David T., M. C. Gelfand, Thomas Rakowksi, W. A. Briggs,
  W. J. Cirksena, Larry Siegel, *and* J. H. Knepshield
  1972   Who Needs Dialysis: A Closer Look at the Dialysis Candi-
          date. Bethesda, Maryland: Walter Reed Hospital, Metro-
          politan Washington Renal Dialysis Center.
Marshall, A. W.
  1965   Cost-Benefit Analysis in Health. Santa Monica, California:
          RAND Corporation, December.
McKegney, F. P. *and* Paul Lange
  1971   "The decision to no longer live on chronic hemodialysis."
          American Journal of Psychiatry 128, 3 (September):
          267–275.
Merrill, John
  1965   Treatment of Renal Failure. New York: Grune and Strat-
          ton.
Moore, E. Garth
  1965   Some Legal Aspects of One's Duty to the Sick. London:
          Westminister Press.
Morison, Robert S.
  1973   "Dying." Scientific American 229, 3 (September): 54–75.
Mushkin, Selma J.
  1962   "Health as an investment." Journal of Political Economy
          70, 5 (October): 129–157.
National Center for Health Statistics
  1970   "Inpatient utilization of short-stay hospitals by diagnosis:
          United States—1965." Washington, D. C.: Government
          Printing Office.
  1971   "Expenses for hospital and institutional care during the last
          year of life for adults who died in 1964 or 1965." Washing-
          ton, D.C.: Government Printing Office.
National Health and Medical Research Council of Australia
  1970   The Family of the Dying Patient. Sidney, Australia: Na-
          tional Health and Medical Research Council of Australia.
National League for Nursing
  1969   Health Care Needs: Basis for Change. New York: National
          League for Nursing.

National Vital Statistics Branch
>   1972   "Care in hospitals and institutions during the last year of
>   life: United States, 1962–1965 deaths." Unpublished data.

Natterson, J. M. *and* A. G. Knudsen
>   1960   "Observations concerning fear of death in fatally ill chil-
>   dren and their mothers.: Psychosomatic Medicine 22, 6:
>   456–465.

Nealon, Thomas
>   1965   Management of Patients with Cancer. Philadelphia: Saun-
>   ders Company.

Parsons, Talcott
>   1963   "Social change and medical organization in the United
>   States: A sociological perspective." The Annals of the
>   American Academy of Political and Social Science 346
>   (March): 21–33.
>   1964   "Definition of health and illness in the light of American
>   values and social structure." Pp. 257–291 in Social Struc-
>   ture and Personality. Glencoe, New York: The Free Press.

Pearson, Leonard (ed.)
>   1969   Death and Dying: Current Issues in the Treatment of the
>   Dying Person. Cleveland: The Press of the Case Western
>   Reserve University.

Petroni, Frank A.
>   1969   "The influence of age, sex and chronicity of perceived legit-
>   imacy to the sick role." Sociology and Social Research
>   53:2.

Phelps, C. E. *and* J. P. Newhouse
>   1972   "Effect of coinsurance: A multivariate analysis." Social Se-
>   curity Bulletin 35 (June): 20–28.

President's Commission on Heart Disease, Cancer and Stroke
>   1965   Report of the President's Commission on Heart Disease,
>   Cancer and Stroke. Washington, D.C.: Government Print-
>   ing Office, February.

Ramsey, Paul
>   1972   Patient as Person: Exploration in Medical Ethics. New Ha-
>   ven: Yale University Press.

Reich, Francois
>   1963   Clearance Tests in Clinical Medicine. Springfield, Ill.:
>   Charles C. Thomas.

Reynolds, D. J.
    1956   "The cost of road accidents." Journal of the Royal Statistical Society 119: 393–408.
Rice, Dorothy
    1962   Cardiac Vascular Diseases and Cancer. Washington, D.C.: Government Printing Office.
    1966   Estimating the Costs of Illness, Health Care Series No. 6. Washington, D.C.: Government Printing Office.
    1973   Personal Communication, April.
Ritan, J. W. *and* Harvey Lewis
    1966   "Repeated dialysis in indigent patients." Annals of Internal Medicine 64 (February): 284–292.
Schelling, T. C.
    1968   "The life you save may be your own." Pp. 127–158 in Case, Samuel (ed.), Problems in Public Expenditure Analysis. Washington, D.C.: Brookings Institution.
Schoeck, Helmut (ed.)
    1962   Financing Medical Care: An Appraisal of Foreign Programs. Caldwell, Idaho: Caxton Printers.
Schoenberg, Bernard, A. Carr, David Peretz, *and* Austin Keitcher
    1972   Psychosocial Aspects of Terminal Care. New York: Columbia University Press.
Schreiner, George *and* John Maher
    1965   "Hemodialysis for chronic renal failure, medical, moral, ethical and socioeconomic problems." Annals of Internal Medicine 113, 3: 551–557.
Schwartz, Jerome
    1968   Medical Plans and Health Care. Springfield, Ill.: Charles C. Thomas.
Scitovsky, Anne *and* Nelda Snyder
    1972   "Effect of coinsurance on use of physician services." Social Security Bulletin 35 (June): 3–19.
Siegel, B. M., N. B. Belloc, *and* F. E. Hesse
    1957   "Household surveys for hospital planning: Adjustments for decedents missed." Public Health Reports 72 (November): 989–997.
Starzl, Thomas
    1964   Experience in Renal Transplantation. Philadelphia: Saunders Company.

Sunderman, F. W. *and* F. W. Sunderman, Jr.
   1970   Applied Seminar in the Laboratory Diagnosis of Kidney
           Diseases. St. Louis, Mo.: W. H. Green.
U.S. Department of Health, Education, and Welfare
   1970   Facts of Life and Death. Washington, D.C.: Government
           Printing Office.
Vernon, Glenn M.
   1970   Sociology of Death: An Analysis of Death-Related Behav-
           ior. New York: Roland Press Company.
Vickrey, William
   1963   Personal communication prior to the publication of Robert
           Dorfman's Measuring Benefits of Government Investments.
           Washington, D.C.: Brookings Institution, 1963.
Wakefield, John
   1962   Cancer and Public Education. London: Cambridge Publish-
           ing Company.
Wald, Florence S.
   1971   A Nurse's Study of Care of the Dying Patient. Washington,
           D.C.: Government Printing Office.
Weisbrod, Burton A.
   1961a   Economics of Mental Health. Philadelphia: University of
           Pennsylvania Press.
   1961b   Economics of Public Health: Measuring the Economic
           Impact of Diseases. Philadelphia: University of Pennsyl-
           vania Press.
Welford, A. T. (ed.)
   1967   Decision Making and Age. New York: Grune and Stratton.
Welford, A. T. *and* James E. Birren (eds.)
   1969   Decision Making and Age, Conference on Decision Making
           and Age. Basel, New York: S. Karger.
White, Kerr L.
   1973   "Life and death and medicine." Scientific American 229, 3
           (September): 22–33.
Wipple, H. E. (ed.)
   1964   "Discussion of cardiac pacemakers." Annals of the New
           York Academy of Science 3: 955–1005.
Wolfle, Dael
   1970   "Dying with dignity." Science 168 (June 19): 1403.

Worchester, A.
  1961   Care of the Aged, Dying and Dead, 2nd ed. Springfield, Ill.: Charles C. Thomas.
Zohlman, Lenore
  1970   Cardiac Rehabilitation. New York: Grune and Stratton.
Zoll, Paul, F. Howard, *and* Arthur Linenthal
  1964   "Implanting cardiac pacemakers." Annals of the New York Academy of Science 3 (June): 1068–1074.

Socioeconomic Incentives in Consumer Use

Economic

Aspects of

Consumer Use*

MARK V. PAULY

The task of explaining the economic factors affecting the use of medical care would, in principle, be equivalent to the task of explaining all the economic influences in the medical-care market. To explain or predict use, one must know everything that determines what people will demand and everything that determines what providers will supply. Only satisfied demand and utilized supply result in actual use.

This paper does not take on the prodigious task of explaining everything but attempts instead the possibly more manageable task of summarizing and commenting on what we know and do not know about economic influences on the demand for medical care. In theory, whatever the difficulty in practice, the separation of knowns and unknowns is feasible for most consumer purchases. When we ask about demand we want to know what other factors affect the quantity the consumer would demand at a particular price. We also want to know how he changes the quantity he demands when prices change but the other factors do not. Then his use is that quantity at which, given a particular price, he demands exactly the same quantity that suppliers are willing to supply.

But with medical care the separate specification of demand influences is much more difficult, for two reasons. First, the price that

* The author benefited in writing this paper from the helpful comments of David Salkever, Jon Joyce, and Joseph Newhouse.

is relevant to determining an individual's use, the marginal user price, is not taken by him as given, as it would be in a competitive market, nor is it even a datum to be manipulated unconstrainedly, as in a monopsony. Instead, the consumer can vary the user price he pays by purchasing customary forms of insurance. But, one way or another, he pays for price cuts in his insurance premium. Thus the user price is not parametric, nor is it necessarily equal to the price producers receive. To explain demand for care, then, one must also explain demand for insurance, for it is the latter that determines the user price.

The second difficulty arises because there is reason to suspect that the supplier can manipulate demand relationship. In the more typical economic model of an undifferentiated good, the only way a provider of a good can increase the amount that people are willing to buy from him is by lowering the price. When goods are differentiated, it may be worthwhile for a provider to advertise, though advertising is costly and not always effective. It is also an influence not well incorporated into economic theory.

But it is alleged that availability of medical care—unfilled hospital beds, physicians seeing fewer patients than they would like—affects the quantity of care a person is willing to pay for. It has that effect not because price falls, but because the physician, in his role as advisor to the patient on the usefulness of care, can almost costlessly shift the patient's willingness to pay for care, perhaps within rather wide limits. For purposes of explaining demand, we must therefore know something about the extent of persuasion or advocacy by physicians. That means that, in a very critical sense, consumers' demand for care may not be independent of physicians' willingness to provide care. So in what follows insurance and supply must be discussed to explain demand.

Taxonomy of Economic Influences

To classify economic influences on the use of medical care, it will be helpful to begin with the paradigm of consumer choice that the economist employs in analyzing the demand for other goods and services. The paradigm does more than indicate which are important independent variables; it also indicates, for some of them, the direction of their effect. One purpose of this paper will be to examine the extent to which studies of empirical reality seem to fit the "economic man" paradigm.

In a sentence, the economist's model is one of an individual who maximizes his utility subject to a budget constraint. That constraint equates his money income to his expenditures on all goods, and those expenditures in turn are the products of multiplying quantity by price. The model implies that there are four main influences on demand for any good:

(1) things that determine the "shape of the utility function," called "tastes," and are assumed to be given,

(2) money income,

(3) the price of the good, and

(4) the prices of closely related goods, either substitutes or complements.

More sophisticated versions of the model differ in several ways. First, they recognize that income is more than just money income; in addition to a money-budget constraint, a person may face a time-budget constraint. Second, and similarly, not all prices are money prices—some services have time prices and inconvenience prices, which affect demand. Third, it is sometimes useful to view the household itself not as a final consumer but as a producer whose inputs are purchased goods, services, and time of household members and whose outputs are useful characteristics. In the case of medical care, for example, one useful characteristic may be "health," and medical care may be but one input into its production. Fourth, if a good adds to an individual's ability over time to earn income, in a human capital sense, the utility of the good is the present value of the extra income it permits a person to earn.

But these extensions are fully consistent with, though they are improvements upon, the simpler model described earlier. Consequently, in what follows, influences will be characterized as having predicted effects on use that are "price-like," "income-like," "taste-like," and so on.

Are there any peculiar characteristics of medical care that do not fit in this framework? One characteristic is uncertainty—uncertainty about the incidence of illness. In the case of medical care as in other contexts, the response of the risk-averse consumer is to purchase insurance. In its purest form, insurance affects only the money-income constraint, in effect transferring income from one possible state of the world to another. The insurance premium reduces income in no-loss states, but insurance benefit payments raise income in states that are insured against. Unfortunately for simplicity of analysis, typical medical insurance does more than transfer income. It also reduces the user price of some kinds of care. The implication of these remarks is that neither money income nor the price of the good is parametric when the consumer can choose his insurance coverage.

A second problem is that "tastes" for medical care may not be fixed. The most striking illustration is in the incidence of illness. One's "taste" for an appendectomy will vary, depending on whether or not he has abdominal pain. The problem could be handled with an ad hoc rule relating "tastes" to illness, or by defining health as the output and illness as a random reduction in the stock or flow of health. A second serious analytical problem is that consumers may be persuaded by physicians or by others to like or dislike various kinds of medical care. Unless such changes can be predicted, the explanatory power of the economic theory of demand is much reduced. To the extent that physicians are economically motivated, it may be possible to predict the effect of their advice on tastes.

Finally, the market for medical care may be such that demands are not fully satisfied. Then the pattern of use may be affected little, if at all, by demand elements and may simply reflect the curious behavior of suppliers.

In the following pages each of the influences on demand—income, prices, and tastes—will be examined, with comment on the normative implications of the findings for "appropriate" incentives to seek. An area of considerable importance, and one that is as yet relatively sparsely investigated, is that of interaction effects (the point has recently been made most strongly by David Salkever, of Johns Hopkins University). At question here is not the influence of prices when income, tastes, and illness incidence are held constant, but rather how responses to price changes vary with different incomes or tastes or illness states.

We might also wish to ask whether income affects use differently at high user prices than it does at low ones. So after indicating what we know and need to know about the direct effects on use, we shall consider interaction effects as well. Perhaps the omission of interaction effects, in most empiricial work, is the result of the multivariate regression analysis customarily used by economists; that analysis typically picks up the independent effect of one variable with the others held constant, but in doing so gives no information on interaction effects.

Effect of Income on Demand

A proper definition of income would distinguish between transitory and permanent income, with the latter being a measure of the true wealth constraint implied by theory.

Even if it were possible to measure permanent income, there are additional reasons why the "pure" effect of income on demand for medical care is difficult to estimate. The incidence of illness itself may be related to income (positively or negatively), and the existence of illness surely affects income. To get a pure income effect, we would have to determine the effect of income on use for given states of health, and that effect should be separated from any effect of income on health status. In principle, some of those separations can be made by using the concept of time. Income presumably affects health not instantaneously, but with a lag (as yet not too well known). Thus, two individuals with the same present income but with unequal income in the past should differ in their use of care. Illness may, of course, have the effect of reducing permanent income more or less immediately.

Pure Effect of Income

Why should we expect income to have an effect on use for a given condition? There are two reasons, but they point in opposite directions. First, there may be a time cost whose value varies directly with income, since the opportunity cost of time would be roughly proportional to income. Opportunity cost would, however, be even more appropriately measured by the wage rate, but no study has looked at the effect severity of illness has on the response of use for persons with different wage rates. Second, as income increases, persons have more to spend. One of the goods on which they spend more could be medical care. The only goods for which use actually declines with income are those goods for which higher priced substitutes exist, e.g., steak and hamburger. There does not seem to be a higher priced substitute for medical care in general, although the use of some kinds of care—clinics, physician—substitutes—may decline with income.

Relatively few studies have used data on state of health or illness as well as income. In one study, Richardson (1970) showed that income did indeed affect use, and in the expected way; the poor tended to use less care for a given state of health. A second study by him gave less conclusive results but looked at the effect of income with only seriousness of illness held constant, and did not control for other variables (Richardson, 1971). A study by Andersen, Anderson, and Smedby (1968) also indicated that income did affect use, and more strongly in the United States, where user prices are mostly positive, than in Sweden. Unfortunately, the only indicator of health used in the study was whether a person had a symptom; the seriousness of the symptom was not considered.

Surprisingly, there seems to be no large-scale, definitive data on the use of hospitals by individuals with given symptoms that would shed light on the effects of income. While there have been some studies of the variation of use with income by diagnosis, the severity of illness for a given diagnosis has not been considered, perhaps because of the difficulty of getting an independent measure of severity. An unpublished study in Rhode Island indicates that, for some kinds of illness, low income is likely to lead to more frequent hospitalization (e.g., for pneumonia and bronchitis) because desirable home-care alternatives are less readily available (see Scott, 1973). Moreover, the effect of income on care is obscured in simple cross-tabular analysis by the positive relationship between income and insurance coverage.

When medical condition is not included as a control variable, the effect of income on use becomes twofold. It affects both health and use.

Effect of Income on Health

There are at least four separate ways in which income might affect health, where health is defined as a stock that accumulates or depreciates over time. First, and most obviously, if income positively affects the use of medical care in each time period, and if additional medical care adds to the stock of health, rich people will be healthier. Second, other goods whose consumption increases with income—good housing, good food—may improve health. Third, still other goods may not affect health directly but may improve the efficiency by which health is produced; education is the prime example, although in theory it could also be considered as an input, like entrepreneurial capacity in the theory of the firm. Finally, other goods whose consumption increases with income may reduce the health stock at any point in time—goods such as rich food or liquor or even habits, such as reduced physical exercise.

Michael Grossman's recent work (1972) and that of his colleagues at the National Bureau of Economic Research, has shed light on the relationship between income and health (see, also, Auster et al., 1972; Silver, 1972). Surprisingly, Grossman's work indicates that income in itself does not affect the stock of health and that it affects the flow of health services negatively. What does affect both measures in the appropriate way is not total income but the wage rate, which is positively and significantly related to health.

Grossman interprets that finding in the context of an investment model. Since the wage is the "cost" of workdays lost, the higher the wage the fewer workdays a person will want to lose. Consequently, he will choose a larger stock of health and the flow of healthy days from that stock. Of course, wage income and total income are likely to be correlated, since the bulk of most peoples' income is from wages. But Grossman says that in his data "these variables are not so highly correlated that the results are dominated by multicollinearity." When wages are left out of the equation, income is positively related to health.

What do these results suggest about behavior patterns? Grossman's answer is that the negative relationship between income and health may be due to the fact that higher income induces people to buy more "bads" as well as "goods" and that the former dominate. He interprets the results as indicating that health is not mainly wanted as a consumption good but as an investment good.

Taken literally, Grossman's results indicate that transfers of income (e.g., family assistance to the poor) that do not depend on work effort or that reduce the net wage rate will worsen health. Extra income allows people to buy things that are bad for them, at least those who are in the labor force, are white, and who have a record of not using sick time.

Grossman's results have two alternative explanations. The first is that those persons who have large nonwage components of income —the self-employed, moonlighters, etc.—may be in situations tending to affect their health adversely. The second is that a work-loss day provides leisure time. If leisure is a normal good, an individual will buy more of it as his income rises. Hence work-loss days will rise as income rises for a given "price" of a lost day of work. The rise occurs even if a work-loss day does not represent perfect leisure, in the sense that some illness is needed as a psychological excuse for staying home from work.

Grossman did not estimate the effect of income on the demand for medical care with health status held constant. Instead, he estimated an equation in which use of medical care was regressed on income, wage rates, age, sex, and family size. Note that no price variable was included. Here the wage rate is not significant, nor is education. Income has a significant positive effect, as it does in the "health demand" equations if the wage rate is left out. Insignificance of the wage rate probably stems from its two conflicting effects: A higher wage rate makes health more valuable and so induces a person to buy more care, but it raises the time cost of care, which tends to reduce use.

When Grossman estimates a "production function" for health, medical care has the right sign, it does contribute to health. But its significance is sensitive to the measure of health and to the particular set of variables excluded or included.

Measuring "Total Effect" of Income on Use

The permanent income elasticity of demand was the subject of an estimation attempt by Andersen and Benham (1970). Theory suggests that permanent income elasticity should be greater than transitory income elasticity, and their results confirm the theory. When a measure of quality is included, income elasticity of demand for physicians' services is 0.17 (i.e., a 10-percent increase in income increases use by 1.7 percent, but it is not significantly different from zero). When quality is excluded, the measure for income elasticity is 0.24.

In a study by Morris Silver (1972), the medical expenses of only currently employed persons are studied. The limitation should reduce some of the income-health relationship, since persons in very ill health (because of previously low income, for example) would not be included. Paradoxically, Silver found a high income easticity of demand in the range 1.2 to 2.0 for care as a whole, with lowest values for hospital and physician expenditures and highest values for dental expenditures. When Silver includes the earnings rate as well as income (though in his data the two valuables are highly correlated), income elasticity drops to the lower portion of the range. But because of data limitations, Silver was unable to separate out the effect of insurance, and insurance tends to be positively related to income.

Richard Rosett and L. F. Huang (1973) also estimated income elasticities that differ by income classes. They obtained measures for insured households ranging from 0.25 for those with incomes of four thousand dollars a year to 0.45 for those with ten thousand dollars a year. Feldstein (1971a) has estimated an income elasticity of demand for hospital bed-days of 0.54, using cross-section, state-aggregated data.

The results of the studies suggest that a good guess, if we had to pick a single number, would be an income elasticity of 0.5 or a little less. Note, however, that this is a "combined" or "total" income elasticity. If income does affect health status adversely (either in it-self or as a proxy for wages), these measures overstate the pure or instantaneous effect of income on demand for care.

What we do not know is how the interactions occur. Theory would predict, for example, that the effect of income on use would decline as the user price declined. At the zero price extreme, people with the same utility functions would be likely to use about the same amount of care. Only Rosett estimated a "cross effect" term, which was positive and significant, suggesting the opposite. On the other hand, a study by K. Roghman and his associates (1971) indi-cated that differences in use remained even after people received Medicaid, indicating that full-coverage insurance did not remove all differences in use. Likewise, Andersen, Anderson, and Smedby (1968) found that income was more important in the United States, where the population is not fully insured, than in Sweden, where it is close to being fully insured. Another interaction effect is that of income and seriousness of illness. Richardson (1971) found, as we might expect, that the less serious the illness, the stronger the effects of income (and other economic influences).

Future Research

We are still ignorant about the relationship between income and the use of medical care. It appears that, as Paul Feldstein (1966) conjectured in 1965, the use of medical care does increase with in-come. Yet we are woefully ignorant of the pure effect of income on health, and Grossman's work is one of the few studies indicating that it may be wages, not income, that governs the relationship. There must be a more serious look at the effect of income on health, of medical care on health, and of income on use, given health status. What is clear, however, is that income transfers would affect the incentives people have to use health services.

The most important policy implications of findings about the disincentive effect of low income on use of care relates to some national health insurance proposals. One possible rationale for government interference in the financing of care is that some subsidization of care for the poor is necessary to make sure that the poor get what people in general regard as appropriate or needed care. To deal with presumably less use by the poor, several plans (Pauly, 1971b; Feldstein, 1971b) suggest arrangements in which reductions in user price via increased insurance coverage are used to offset the inability of the poor to afford care. The plans are appropriate only if lower income in fact leads to less use, and the subsidy depends in part on the extent to which use varies with income. The subsidy also depends on the responsiveness of use to price cuts. If there is no relationship between income and use, or if it is only a weak relationship, there would by that argument be no or almost no rationale for subsidization.

Tastes as a Determinant of Use of Care

The interest here is in those determinants of taste that are capable of direct economic interpretation. In this sense, they are taste-like variables, rather than the pure residual influences that the economist usually calls "tastes."

Education

Why should education affect the use of medical care? First, it may make consumers more aware of the utility and limitations of health care. The direction its effect will have on use is therefore unpredictable, since ignorance can lead to either too little or too much care. Second, education may enhance the value to the consumer of health. If he believes that care affects health, it may increase his use of care. If adjustment is made for wages, the only effect would be on consumption. Finally, as Grossman has suggested, education may enhance the "efficiency" with which the family produces health. Here its effect could be negative; education could make the family so efficient in producing health that it would use less medical care.

In most empirical studies, education and income are highly correlated, and education is perhaps better correlated with permanent income than with present income. When the wage rate was included, Grossman found that education had little effect on use. It is safe to say that we still do not know much about the pure effect of education on use.

Family Size and Composition

An individual's use of care will be affected by the kind of family of which he is a member. Although that influence is included here as a demographic determinant of "tastes," recent research suggests that in its economic influence it resembles both income and prices. If the family is viewed as a production unit that produces useful attributes employing goods as inputs, it does so constrained by the total amount of resources it has available. Those resources are obviously total family money income (and indeed family income rather than individual income or even family income per capita has customarily been employed in use or demand studies), but they also include the total amount of time available to the family and the total amount of human capital (e.g., education) available to the family as a whole. Similarly, the "price" of a unit of a family member's time in producing care for himself or others will vary with the alternative uses of his time.

The critical empirical question is whether alternative family configurations involve budget and price effects, and demand effects too, that will influence an individual's use, as suggested by a considerable amount of casual and less casual empirical evidence. Individuals who live alone, for example, use more care than others. That is doubtless because, in two-person families, one individual can produce care for the other that would otherwise have to be sought from the formal medical-care system. Other family characteristics, involving which person in the family is ill, whether the wife works and at what wages, and so on, are also relevant.

Recent economic research has begun to emphasize the "economics of the family," but relatively little has been done in health care. (The only research of which the author is aware is some yet unpublished work by Jon Joyce of Wesleyan University.) Even descriptive empirical work in the area might be very useful and have important policy implications. To give one example: There is a fair amount of evidence that hospital stays can often be shortened without adverse medical consequences and that many procedures can be done on an outpatient basis. Since such steps reduce costs incurred within the system, it is natural that many people consider desirable those arrangements that appear to produce these results, such as health maintenance organizations (HMO's). Yet in reckoning the true social cost of care, it is clear that the extra implicit costs imposed on the household must be considered. What does the household lose by virtue of the fact that it must produce care? Home care is desirable only if it "costs" less than institutional care. In the empirical studies of the advantages and disadvantages of reimbursement arrangements that reduce use, the offsetting cost imposed on the household is rarely considered.

Price and Price-Like Incentives

The economist naturally thinks of price as an incentive to encourage or discourage use. In a normative sense, the "wrong" price may provide an incentive to use too much or too little of a good. Conversely, given a definition of what constitutes appropriate use and given enough information, it is possible, at least theoretically, to design a price system that will induce individuals to choose that level of use.

While the role of price as an incentive has sometimes been recognized by noneconomist specialists in health care, there appears to be a curious sort of schizophrenic conventional wisdom in much of the policy-oriented work. Thus it is sometimes maintained that positive prices are likely to be bad because they discourage needed care, and at the same time there is an unwillingness to believe price has much effect on decisions to seek care. Recent research by economists and others has, however, increased our knowledge of the potential magnitude of price effects and has also provided some analysis of the appropriate use of prices. In both cases, research has served mainly to suggest that there are many more unanswered questions.

Why Price Might Affect Use

Price can affect use in two ways: First and most obvious is in the individual consumer's decision whether to seek care. If additional care has a positive cost to him, he will seek care only as long as he values the care he receives more than the other goods and services he might have purchased. The second way is in the effect the price paid by the consumer may have on the physician's decision about how much and what kind of care to render. The physician, acting properly in his role as proxy decisionmaker for the consumer, may decide that some kinds of beneficial care are not worth their cost to the consumer. Or a physician's orders for care may meet resistance from consumers who must pay the user price and acquiescence from those whose insurance pays the price. Even if the physician does not know the net or user price paid by a particular patient, he may adjust his behavior to an average level of the price that prevails among all his patients.

All this discussion is frankly speculative, since we know little about the precise way in which price affects the physician-patient decision nexus. In large part, our lack of knowledge is the result of a more basic ignorance about the way in which physician prices are set and the extent to which nonphysician charges affect the price the physician can get. We do not know, for example, whether a scheme in which physicians, rather than patients, were billed for hospital services would affect use and total cost to the consumer.

Concepts of Price

The true concept of the price that affects demand is broader than that of simple transfers of money. Obviously, what is relevant to a consumer's use of care is not the price charged for the services but the price he has to pay for them, the "user price." The higher the price charged or the greater his insurance coverage, the higher will be his premiums, but the effect of higher premiums in reducing spendable income will be spread over all his purchases and affect his purchases of medical care only slightly.

Prices can be paid in ways other than money. For many types of medical care price is the sacrifice of time, either in getting care or in traveling to a source of care, and psychological and physical pain and discomfort may be more important than money price. (Since medical insurance does not usually provide pain and suffering benefits, use is likely to be less than infinite even at a zero money price.) The cost of time is the value that time would have had in its next best use. Here again, we know relatively little about the effect of time on use, although Grossman's result of a zero wage elasticity of demand for care is suggestive, and there is currently some research being done on the effect of time costs on use.

Finally, a change in the price of a good affects more than just the demand for that good; it affects the demand for closely related goods. In the most extreme case, competition can be defined as an infinitely great cross-elasticity of demand between the price charged by one seller for a given good and the quantity demanded from another seller for the same good. Thus, the price charged by one physician or hospital might affect the demand for other physician or hospital services, and the user price in the outpatient department might affect the use of care in physicians' offices.

Effect of User Charges on Use

Common sense suggests that the more "discretionary" the type of care, the greater the effect of user charges. It is probably lack of data that accounts for the fact that most documentation of the effect of user charges is on inpatient hospital care, probably the most non-discretionary sort of care. In addition, many studies have looked at the effects that represent combinations of incentives to consumer (user charges), incentives to physicians and hospital administrators (reimbursement mechanisms), and organizational form (solo practice, multi-specialty group). As a result, it is hard to isolate the effect of charges on demand.

The difficulty is particularly marked in a series of studies begun in the mid-1950s and continued up to the present. The earlier studies have been summarized by Klarman (1965) and Donabedian (1969). Their main message was (with some exceptions) that prepaid group practices had lower levels of hospital utilization and lower inplan costs than did insurance plans that provided mainly fee-for-service coverage for inhospital procedures.

But only rarely was it possible to tell whether observed differences in utilization were the result of the way physicians were paid, the price incentives facing consumers, the mode of organization, or the characteristics of plan members. In some of the studies, plan members were matched to reduce the last problem, that of self-selection.

A more recent study of the same sort done at the University of California at Los Angeles has not been published, but some of the results were the subject of a statement by the study director before a congressional committee (Roemer, 1972). Extensive data on use and demographic characteristics were obtained on three types of plan (two examples of each): commercial indemnity, Blue Cross service benefit, and prepaid group practice. Group practices had the lowest hospital admissions, but the indemnity plan was a close second. The Blue Cross plans had the greatest use. The smallness of the gap between indemnity plans and prepaid group practice was attributed to the fact that indemnity plans covered better risks. Length of stay is, however, much lower in the group-practice plans, so that total hospital bed-days are much lower there. Ambulatory-care use is least for the commercial plans and greatest for the Blue Cross plans. Unfortunately, these gross findings have not yet been subject to multivariate analysis, so that their main cause is not known. And since only four noncomprehensive plans were studied, there will be at most only four possible values for user price.

Whatever the studies may tell us about the advantages of one particular plan over another, they do not provide answers to the general question of incentives. In addition to failing to separate effects, they are plagued by "small number" problems of two sorts. First, at best they compare half a dozen plans, surely a small sample. Second, they provide relatively few differential observations on alternative user prices. Consequently, some recent economic analyses have departed from the case-study approach in order to use larger or more diverse bodies of data.

Earlier work had indicated that higher levels of insurance coverage tended to be associated with greater expenditures in, and presumably greater use of, medical care. A recent, more sophisticated study by Martin Feldstein (1971a) used state-aggregated hospital admissions and mean stay as measures of use. Constructing a measure of user price by multiplying the gross price by an "average" measure of coverage for that state, he found that use was indeed responsive to coverage. An instrumental variable technique, not too clearly described, was used to avoid simultaneity problems.

Feldstein estimated that price elasticity of demand for hospital bed-days was about 0.67, with elasticity being somewhat greater for mean stay and less for admissions. All three are substantial elasticities and suggest that reduction from the present twenty percent to ten percent in the fraction of care costs would increase hospital expenditures by one-third. A somewhat similar estimate by Davis and Russell (1972), using similar data but a slightly different measure of insurance coverage and ordinary-least-squares regression analysis, estimated own-elasticity of demand to be 0.32 to 0.46.

A recent study by Richard Rosett and L. F. Huang (1973) used observations on coverage and total medical expenditures for individual spending units. Some ingenious methods of estimation were necessary to get around deficiencies in the data. Nevertheless, their estimates of elasticity range from 0.35 at a twenty percent copayment to 1.50 at an eighty percent copayment. Their figures suggest that, for example, going to zero copayment under a national health insurance plan from the present one-third level could as much as double expenditures.

Some other recent work, of a case-study nature, provides estimates of elasticity of demand for physicians' services (Scitovsky and Snyder, 1972; Phelps and Newhouse, 1972b). The work studied the effect of introducing a twenty-five percent copayment for physicians' services in one prepaid comprehensive group practice for employees of Stanford University. Imposition of the copayment reduced usage about twenty-five percent. The arc elasticity, using average price as a base, is calculated to be 0.14. A similar study of the introduction of a forty-one percent copayment in Saskatchewan indicated an arc elasticity of 0.13, although it is unclear whether this "use" elasticity is uncontaminated by supply as well as demand responses (Phelps and Newhouse, 1972a).

For the Stanford study, it is clear that results need not be comparable to what they would be in a more typical setting. Presumably there would already have been an incentive in that plan for physicians to keep physician use low (especially since hospital services were not obtained within the plan). Consequently, the possibilities for further reduction in use would have been limited. For the other studies, the low elasticities are a little more difficult to explain, although fixed prices might contribute to the Saskatchewan results. The results may also indicate rationing behavior by physicians, as Feldstein (1970) has suggested.

Finally, although one might have expected physician visits to be more price sensitive, the published results are certainly possible. Moreover, if the demand curve is linear rather than constant-elasticity, low levels of elasticity at low absolute prices are to be expected.

Can anything be said about the direction of bias in the Feldstein-Rosett-Huang-Davis-Russell estimates? The most serious aggregation problem arises because researchers have used an average rather than a marginal measure of insurance coverage. Since a typical policy will contain a deductible, the average fraction covered will ordinarily fall short of the marginal fraction covered. Thus, when a person with no insurance is compared with a person who has positive but relatively low average coverage but high marginal coverage, any increase in use will be attributed to the relatively slight increase in average coverage rather than to the large increase in marginal coverage. Consequently, estimates of the effect of coverage on use will be biased upwards.

The argument is correct as far as it goes, but it does not go far enough. An offsetting bias arises if it is true that marginal coverage is likely to remain high over a wide range of expenses. The change in marginal user price over such a range will be low or zero, while the change in average user price will be relatively greater. The change in expense associated with that change in average coinsurance will in fact reflect the zero or slight change in marginal coinsurance, and so a measure of the effect of coinsurance on use will be biased downward. The direction of bias in the estimate of the overall effect of coverage on use will depend on the strengths of the two effects, and there is no reason to suppose that the resulting bias will be necessarily upward.

A similar criticism is made in a paper by Newhouse and Phelps (1973); the results of Rosett-Huang's study are also properly criticized in it for omitting (because of data deficiencies) employer-financed coverage, leading to a large group of low-estimated coverage, low-estimated expenditure observations.

Insurance Effects

Another kind of omitted criticism is related to a problem endemic in all the studies of use so far completed. Results may be biased because the adjustment to user price caused by insurance is not exogenous. If individuals can choose their level of insurance coverage, potential expenditures and potential effects of coverage on use would affect the amount of coverage they buy. Even when obvious demographic characteristics are used to match populations, the fact that one individual chooses one form of coverage and another chooses a different form is evidence that they are not identical individuals. As long as insurance may affect use, the differences in individuals may likewise affect use.

There are no published studies that directly consider the simultaneity problem. Feldstein uses an instrumental variables approach rather than ordinary least squares, but it is not possible to tell whether the set of exogenous variables used to determine the instruments is the appropriate set. Attempts are presently being made, both at the RAND Corporation and elsewhere, to tackle the problem. It may be useful to consider the issues involved.

The endogenous nature of insurance can induce two sorts of bias into estimates of the effect of coverage on use. The biases arise from the problems of adverse selection and moral hazard.

Adverse selection occurs when premiums are not tailored to the expected losses of individuals. If, for example, all pay the same premium but have different expected losses (and hence different actuarially fair premiums), those for whom the premium charged is low in relation to what would be actuarially fair (the bad risks) will tend to choose high coverage, and those for whom the premium is high (good risks) will tend to choose low coverage. Coverage will then be related to losses, but the causal relationship runs from losses to coverage, not the other way around.

Adverse selection is less likely to raise estimation problems when geographically aggregated data are used. It arises when individuals have expected losses that differ from the average expected loss on which premiums are based. If a Blue Cross plan in a state is to break even, it must charge premiums that, on the average, cover its costs. If higher incomes increase medical-care expenses but premiums do not vary with income, and if other things (including risk aversion) are equal, higher income families would demand more insurance. But those are families with incomes higher than that of the average family on whose experience premiums are based, not necessarily families with higher absolute income. Families with high relative incomes may buy more insurance, but families with low relative incomes will buy less. The effect of income on insurance depends on the strength of the effects of each group's changes. This statement implies that one of Feldstein's reasons for attributing a possible positive effect to income in an insurance-demand equation was misleading (see Feldstein, 1973). So long as premiums are "experience rated" for a group, that group's average expenditure need not be affected by adverse selection. But unaggregated data, such as those used by Rosett and Huang, may give estimates that are biased upward.

Moral hazard will also affect the quantity of insurance bought. Families may differ in their responsiveness to user price changes. If so, families most responsive to price incentives will tend to purchase little insurance, because the "welfare cost" to them of such insurance will be relatively great. And families who do restrain use will purchase more extensive coverage (see Cummins, 1973). The differences would be accentuated if the marginal price of insurance reflected differential moral hazard, something that is plausible for experience-rated groups. If differential moral hazard does affect insurance choice, empirical estimates of the effect of additional coverage on overall use that ignore differential moral hazard will be biased downward. Families with little insurance are only those who, if given more coverage, would have much greater use than those who now have relatively extensive coverage.

In summary, it is fairly easy to come up with a number of reasons why existing estimates of the effect of insurance on use may be biased. Unfortunately, since even a guess at the direction of bias appears to be impossible, it seems appropriate to conclude only that prices do affect use.

Prices and Substitutes

Though a number of attempts have been made to relate the change in user price of a type of medical care to its use, there have been few empirical attempts to see whether changes in price can produce substitution between different types of care. It has always been an article of faith (or perhaps logic) that comprehensive coverage would reduce inpatient hospital use by reducing the user price of outpatient care to at least the level of inpatient care. (Indeed, the own-elasticity effects on outpatient care of such coverage changes have generally been ignored in policy-oriented discussion.)

That faith is confirmed in the study by Davis and Russell. Use of outpatient services is indeed affected by the price of inpatient care, with a cross-elasticity of 0.85 to 1.45. Outpatient care is also sensitive (elasticity = 1) to its own price. Since outpatient services are often very similar to the services a physician provides in his office, the numbers are also suggestive about own and cross-elasticities of demand for physician care.

There have been almost no estimates of the effect on use of prices charged for close substitutes, such as hospitals or physicians providing the same care. Although ostensibly similar hospitals may have very different charges, they do not necessarily have different user prices. A study by Newhouse (1970) in which he claimed that there was little competition between physicians was shown to be seriously flawed (Frech and Ginsburg, 1972). Lack of data on individual physician charges has prevented a direct approach to the problem. Yet if we are to determine if schemes that propose making the patient aware of differential hospital or physician charges are to be useful, we need to know more about the individual hospital or physician-level response of use to price.

Price as a Rationing Device

As noted above, there is now strong empirical evidence that user price is a feasible device for affecting use. The critical policy question is whether the device is desirable. It is commonplace to remark that, while price may discourage excess use, it may also inhibit needed care. But to make any sense out of the remark, we need a definition of "excess" and "needed."

There are at least three alternative notions of desirable levels of care: (1) medical necessity; (2) personal preferences; and (3) private and social benefits.

The notion of medical necessity as a method of specifying appropriate use is probably what most people have in mind. But it may not even be a feasible norm. It is clearly impossible to set up standards for appropriate treatment that apply to every individual case. Physical illnesses, patient personalities, and physician attitudes are too diverse. The most that could be expected is to set up standards for samples of identifiable diagnoses. While the appropriate length of stay for an appendectomy may vary, depending on the situation, the average length of stay (among a physician's patients, in a hospital) could be examined for conformance with a norm. Probably that is what the emerging professional standards review organizations will try to do, though it is not clear that sufficient agreement on proper care will be obtained.

Even if a consistent definition of medical necessity is possible, there still remains the question of whether it is a proper definition of appropriate levels of care. There are reasons to believe that it may not be. Within the scope of health per se, it is unlikely that what medical men are able to agree upon will correspond to that allocation which maximizes health. With limited resources, maximization of health implies care should be used only up to the point at which the health benefit (expected benefit, in an uncertain situation) from that care equals the benefit the same resources would produce if used for health elsewhere. In other words, care that may do an individual some good ought in some circumstances not to be given.

It is doubtful that the judgment of medical men will reflect that kind of thinking about trade-offs and cost, for their training is not usually in such terms. And if it is recognized that people have goals other than health, the appropriate question becomes the even more difficult one of whether extra medical care in a given situation provides as much benefit to the individual as would the same resources used for housing, for education, or even for entertainment. In summary, whether or not medical necessity in fact gets elevated to the status of a policy norm, there are important reasons to believe that it is not an appropriate norm.

A second kind of norm assumes that individual choices should determine the level of care. A rational individual will, of course, consult physicians and other experts to determine the possible benefits from care, but ultimately he will make a choice on whether to take care (or take a physician's advice about taking care) by considering both the costs and benefits to himself. Given such a norm, any reduction in user price caused by insurance is positively pernicious. It is likely to push price below cost and hence will induce the individual to use care which, as far as he is concerned, is worth less to him than its cost. Of course, he will have to pay the cost in the premium, so he is worse off with a reduction in user price than he would have been if his decision on use had reflected the full cost—that is, the full value of the alternative uses of his resources.

The dead-weight welfare cost of health insurance may, of course, be a necessary evil, in the sense that the individual may be willing to pay it in order to get coverage of risky expenditures, but the individual would still be better off if some way could be found to provide the same protection without reducing the user price. Indemnities of various sorts would be preferable to service benefits, and service benefits with some copayments would often be preferable to full coverage.

If an individual bought insurance at prices reflecting its cost, he would buy coverage up to the point at which additional risk-reduction benefits exactly offset additional welfare cost. In fact, various tax incentives are likely to induce the individual to buy too much insurance (Feldstein and Allison, 1972).

The thought here is that, by reducing insurance coverage, individuals are faced with a positive user charge, and the reduction in overuse may more than compensate for increased exposure to risk. The latter point should not be overemphasized, since much of present "first dollar" coverage does not cover very risky situations. But there is some additional risk of expense associated with reductions in coverage. Is there no way "to have the cake and eat it too," to retain both appropriate price incentives and coverage of risk?

There is another form of insurance, used extensively outside the medical-care area, that does preserve incentives. It is indemnity insurance, insurance that as far as possible makes the insurance benefit depend not on expense, which is manipulable by the insured, but on the occurrence of a loss-producing event. To take a concrete example, a pure indemnity insurance would pay a fixed amount if tonsillitis occurred, regardless of the amount of care sought. The user price would be unaffected by such an insurance payment. Indemnities have, of course, sometimes been used in medical expenses cases, mostly for physicians' fees, but their importance is diminishing. Pure indemnities may not be feasible because of the practical impossibility of determining "medical condition" with sufficient accuracy. But some forms of indemnity modified to preserve both price incentives and risk coverage may still represent improvement over customary forms of insurance. The author has discussed such forms of indemnity coverage elsewhere (Pauly, 1971a); on a priori grounds it appears that, for many medical-care situations, indemnity coverage would be both feasible and desirable.

One legitimate objection to the analysis of user charges, and to calculations that make them benefit measures, is that they assume that individuals' choices are in fact made with "appropriate" information (which is not necessarily complete information if information is costly). One rather cavalier though correct answer is that, if information is deficient because of monopoly restrictions on supply or competition, then the appropriate remedy is more information on the benefits of care. A more useful response for the purposes of this discussion is that, even if individuals had appropriate information, (a) there is no reason to suppose they would buy the quantities of care they are induced to buy by existing or proposed insurances and (b) in an ideal situation, user prices should still be as close to true factor opportunity cost as possible. In other words, prices might still be appropriate incentives. Indeed, if it were possible to determine what individuals would buy if fully informed of benefits and costs, it might be better to structure insurance so that user prices induce persons who are less than fully informed to buy the same quantities. Such user prices might be above as well as below market prices. In summary, given this view of appropriate norms, prices are not only desirable as incentives, they are probably essential.

The third norm recognizes that society, in the sense of other people, may be concerned about the level of care an individual receives. Medical care may well be one of those goods whose consumption generates a kind of "external benefit" and not only in cases of contagious disease. Altruistic or humanitarian motivation may make individuals willing to pay something for care for others when that care would relieve perceived suffering (Pauly, 1971b).

Not all care would generate such benefits, since there may certainly be cases in which an individual buys enough care on his own so that others would perceive no benefit from additional care. But for those individuals who, if faced with the full user price, would buy what others regard as too little care, some device to increase use would be desirable. One device would be to reduce user charges by providing or subsidizing an "insurance" that gives more coverage (lower user prices) than any amount of insurance the individual buys on his own. Since empirical studies of the effect of income on demand indicate that the poor will use less care, the rationale given above suggests that relatively extensive coverage should be provided to the very poor, and then the extent of coverage should decline with income.

Individuals' willingness to pay for the care of others is reflected via the political process. While the expert adviser cannot tell the politician-representative what portion of his constituents' incomes should be spent on subsidizing health care, possible "reasonable" norms and their costs could be suggested. It would be useful to know, for instance, the cost of a scheme of price cuts needed to bring the poor up to the median level of use for various illnesses. Information would also be useful on the consequences of price cuts on use for different kinds of individuals, different kinds of care, and different types of illnesses. Or it might be worthwhile to consider a kind of "original position" approach, in which individuals are thought of as asking themselves what kind of public medical care subsidy, if any, they would wish to see if they were completely ignorant of what was to be their status, income, or position in life.

For different kinds of care, we have already seen that in general the measured response to price changes differs. What is perhaps more important to know is how the use of various kinds of care responds to price incentives for different kinds of illnesses. Almost all the studies by economists, and many of those by others, have failed to look at the relationship of price response to price incentives for different kinds of illness.

The only exception in the former group is in the study of the Stanford group practice by Scitovsky and Snyder (1972). They find some suggestion that a greater share of use reduction occurred in "minor complaints." They also find a decline in physical examinations (by 18.7 percent), which fell short of the overall decline in use (25 percent), but for some groups was in excess of the average decline. For male nonprofessionals the increase in user price cut physical examinations in half (from an already low base). Though one need not agree with their judgment that this was probably a reduction in "needed" care (since they have no standard of need), such information is clearly useful for those who must make policy decisions. Of course, Scitovsky and Snyder were only looking at a price change over one range, for one type of care, and for the grossest illness categories. More detailed study, and a method of summarizing results, would clearly be desirable.

Whatever the level of information obtained, it will never be possible to design a system of prices that guarantees that every person will use the right amount of care. Ostensibly identical people may respond in different ways to the same price, and some of the factors that affect use (level of education, family size) might themselves be distorted if user price varied with them. At any price, therefore, there will be some underuse and some overuse. As user price is reduced from any level, overuse will decrease as underuse increases. A balance will have to be sought, and it is surely possible that underuse might be regarded as worse than overuse. But it is unlikely that balance will be achieved in a system in which everyone is faced with a zero user price for every type of care. And even if the money price of care were zero, the time, distance, and inconvenience costs would still be positive.

One final comment should be made on the relationship between changes in user prices and severity of illness. It has sometimes been suggested that severity of illness and response to changes in user price might be related in a nontautological way. Zola (1964) suggested, for example, that the extent to which illness interferes with activities might be a better measure of that severity which is related to use than type of symptom.

The relevant point here is that an economic approach may also be useful in generating hypotheses about interrelationships between illness characteristics, user, charges, and use or demand. To take the simplest case, consider the "investment" approach suggested by

Grossman, in which care is desirable only as it influences the stock of health and health is desirable only as it affects the ability to earn income. At any user price, care will be used for any illness up to the point at which the increment in earnings expected from the use of that care equals its user price. The expected increment in earnings can, crudely, be considered as the product of the effect that care has on illness and the effect that an illness change has on the ability to earn income. Only the latter second effect, the effect of illness on function, seems to correspond to Zola's measure of severity.

Now let the user price rise. By how much will care be reduced? It will be reduced relatively less for those kinds of illnesses for which an increase in illness severely limits activities and for which a small reduction in care use greatly increases the likelihood or severity of illness. Conversely, care will be reduced relatively more for those kinds of illness in which the marginal illness effect on income and the marginal care productivity of illness are low. Note that absolute severity of illness alone does not predict response; the marginal effect of illness on functioning and the marginal effect of care on illness must also be known. In principle, both concepts can be defined and measured empirically. A useful classification of illness might be based on this sort of analysis.

Supply Effects on Demand

Up to this point the author has tried to avoid discussing the effects on use of supply responses. But even though it was intended to discuss only demand effects on use, such a separation is not possible in any discussion of medical care. The reason is that there are strong theoretical and empirical grounds for believing that supply response affects demand directly, in addition to whatever other effects it may have on price or rationing or other determinants of use. The quantity of care people are willing to take at various prices may be affected by the incentives facing suppliers of care.

The theoretical reason is that people are sometimes unsure about the effects of medical care and tend to buy advice about how much care to use from the same persons or firms who supply that care. Especially if competition is not strong, it is possible that suppliers may be able to "shift" demand. One piece of empirical evidence to that effect is the substantial difference in use sometimes detected between prepaid group practice, where the incentive is to supply little care, and fee-for-service medicine, where the incentive is to supply as much care as yields the provider additional real income. Although some of the difference is undoubtedly due to selfselection in that the people who choose to belong to a prepaid group would have demanded a bundle similar to the bundle supplied, probably not all of it can be explained away. A second kind of empirical evidence, a little less substantial, is Feldstein's (1971a) finding that hospital beds, numbers of general patients, and numbers of specialists affect hospital use. The results are less substantial because the relationship could also reflect supply response to omitted demand parameters.

At the present time we know little about the extent to which suppliers can affect demand. It seems reasonable to conjecture that there are upper and lower bounds. Few people could be persuaded to have surgery for a cold or to take aspirin as a cure for a lacerated finger. It seems reasonable to suppose that the limits vary for the different kinds of illness or symptoms that individuals experience. It also seems reasonable to suppose that, within this range, incentives faced by providers will determine how much they shift or try to shift demand. Finally, one suspects that the effect of physician persuasion or other supply influences on an individual's demand should differ depending on the information he has; if more education really leads to more efficient production, for instance, it is likely that the demand of better educated people should be less influenced by supply influences. But other than these speculations and the gross empirical evidence mentioned above, there is little that we know.

Conclusion

In this essay I have discussed a number of economic or economically interpretable influences on use, but I have given the most stress to and spent the most space on the influence of user price. This emphasis is proper, since economics is, in a sense, about the influences price exerts on individuals' behavior. The general message is that, in medical care especially, price is not likely to be a "pure" incentive. Its interaction with other determinants of use, almost all of which are subject to economic interpretation, is an area in which both public policy and intellectual curiosity suggest that we should try to find out much more than we now know.

References

Andersen, R. J., O. W. Anderson, *and* B. Smedby
    1968   "Perception of and response to symptons of illness in Sweden and the United States." Medical Care 6: 18–30.
Andersen, R. J. *and* L. K. Benham
    1970   "Factors affecting the relationship between family income and medical care consumption." Pp. 73–95 in Klarman, H. M. (ed.), Empirical Studies in Health Economics. Baltimore: Johns Hopkins University Press.
Auster, Richard A., I. J. Leveson *and* D. K. Sarachek
    1972   "The production of health, and exploratory study." Pp. 135–160 in Fuchs, V. R. (ed.), Essays in the Economics of Health and Medical Care. New York: Columbia University Press.
Cummins, J. M.
    1973   Cost Overruns in Defense Contracting. Ph.D. dissertation, Northwestern University, Evanston, Illinois.
Davis, Karen A. *and* Lucille B. Russell
    1972   "Substitution of hospital outpatient for inpatient care." Review of Economics and Statistics 54 (May): 108–120.
Donabedian, Avedis B.
    1969   "An evaluation of prepaid group practice." Inquiry 6 (September): 3–27.
Feldstein, M. S.
    1970   "The rising price of physicians' services." Review of Economics and Statistics 52 (May): 121–133.
    1971a   "Hospital cost inflation: A study in nonprofit price dy-

namics." American Economic Review 61 (December): 853–872.

1971b "A new approach to national health insurance." Public Interest 23 (Spring): 93–105.

1973 "The welfare loss of excess health insurance." Journal of Political Economy 81 (March/April): 251–280.

Feldstein, M. S. *and* E. E. Allison

1972 "Tax subsidies of private health insurance: Distribution, revenue loss, and effects." Boston: Harvard Institute of Economic Research, Discussion Paper No. 237.

Feldstein, P. J.

1966 "Research on the demand for health services." Milbank Memorial Fund Quarterly 44 (July): 128–165.

Frech, H. E. *and* P. B. Ginsburg

1972 "Comment." Southern Economic Journal 38 (April): 573–577.

Grossman, M. J.

1972 The Demand for Health: A Theoretical and Empirical Analysis. New York: Columbia University Press.

Klarman, Herbert E.

1965 "Effects of prepaid group practice on hospital use." Public Health Reports 78 (November): 955–965.

Newhouse, J. P.

1970 "A model of physician pricing." Southern Economic Journal 37 (October): 174–183.

Newhouse, J. P. *and* C. E. Phelps

1973 "On having your cake and eating it too: A review of estimated effects of insurance on the demand for medical care." Preliminary draft. Santa Monica: The RAND Corporation, October.

Pauly, Mark V.

1971a "Indemnity insurance for health service efficiency." Journal of Economics and Business 32 (Fall): 53–59.

1971b Medical Care of Public Expense. New York: Praeger Publisers, Inc.

1972 An Analysis of Alternative National Health Insurance Proposals. Washington, D.C.: American Enterprise Institute.

Phelps, C. E. *and* J. P. Newhouse

1972a Coinsurance and the Demand for Medical Care. Santa Monica: The RAND Corporation, R-964-OEO/NCHSRD.

1972b   "Effects of coinsurance: Amultivariateanalysis."SocialSe-
         curity Bulletin 35 (June): 20–28.
Richardson, William C.
    1970   "Measuring the urban poor's use of physicians' services in
            response to illness episodes." Medical Care 8: 132–142.
    1971   Ambulatory Use of Physicians' Services in Response to Ill-
            ness Episodes in a Low-Income Neighborhood. Chicago:
            University of Chicago, Center for Health Administration
            Studies.
Roemer, Milton I.
    1972   Testimony before the House Committee on Ways and
            Means, June.
Roghman, K. J. et al.
    1971   "Anticipated and actual effects of Medicaid on the care pat-
            tern of children." Unpublished paper.
Rosett, R. M. *and* L. Huang
    1973   "The effect of health insurance on the demand for medical
            care." Journal of Political Economy 81 (March/April):
            281–305.
Scitovsky, Anne A. *and* Nelda M. Snyder
    1972   "Effect of coinsurance on the use of physician services."
            Social Security Bulletin 35 (June): 3–19.
Scott, H. D.
    1973   "Uses of hospital discharge data for community planning
            and quality assessment." Providence Evening Bulletin
            (April 5).
Silver, Morris
    1972   "An economic analysis of variations in medical expenses
            and work-loss rates." Pp. 97–118 in Fuchs, V. R. (ed.), Es-
            says in the Economics of Health and Medical Care. New
            York: Columbia University.
Zola, I.
    1964   "Illness behavior and the working class: Implications and
            recommendations." Pp. 76–94 in Shostak, A. *and* W. Gom-
            berg (eds.), Blue Collar World. Englewood Cliffs: Pren-
            tice-Hall.

Social-Psychological Factors Affecting Health Service Utilization

JOHB B. MCKINLAY
AND DIANA B. DUTTON

Perception of Need for Care

In studying the determinants of utilization of health services, researchers have generally reported what may seem to be an obvious conclusion: that need for care—an illness condition of some sort—is the primary cause of the decision to seek medical care (Andersen, 1968; Mechanic, 1969; Bice, 1971; Richardson, 1970). Yet the simplicity of the notion is deceptive.

What the "need" is—what factors are associated with the perception of medical need, how they are distributed among different population groups, and how they affect decision-making in the seeking of care are questions which do not have simple answers. Suchman (1965b) describes the decision to seek medical care as a progression of stages, beginning with the recognition of symptoms, leading to the definition of oneself as ill, followed by a possible decision to seek medical care. Each stage occurs within and is shaped by an aggregate context of social, cultural, economic, and situational circumstances, as well as an individual context of particular psychological attitudes and beliefs. In this paper we will discuss some of the social-psychological factors that bear on various stages in the decision to seek medical care.

Factors Influencing the Perception of Health and Recognition of Symptoms

A review of the literature does much to undermine the notion of "objective" illness. It is now apparent that illness is in large part "a matter of social definition which varyingly reflects cultural and individual differences in orientation toward the biological organism" (Twaddle, 1969:106). Most simply, illness is a subjective reaction to a physical state (Hochbaum, 1958; Kirscht, 1971), but it is the subjective reaction, and not the physical state, which is the measure of a person's "illness."

Investigators have noted the wide variety in popular conceptions of illness and symptoms (Lerner, 1969; Zola, 1966; Apple, 1960; Baumann, 1961; Robinson, 1971). Zola (1966) refers to the many factors that contribute to the shaping of definitions of health and illness and also to the sensitizing of people to certain physiological symptoms that are perceived as symptoms of illness or are accepted as the normal order of things. He suggests, for example, that if the symptom is very prevalent or if it is closely congruent with dominant or major value-orientations of the culture, then it is unlikely to be perceived as a sign of something wrong. Andersen et al. (1968) suggest that variation in the reporting of symptoms is related to demographic differences, in addition to cultural and societal differences in the interpretation of symptoms as disease. Even within a single culture, diseases are perceived in many ways. Content analysis of peoples' beliefs and perceptions about various diseases has revealed systematic differences among people with varying social, economic, and demographic characteristics (Jenkins, 1966).

Even what people mean by "good health" seems to vary. Analyzing responses to open-ended questions on perceptions of health and good physical condition, Baumann (1961) found three distinct orientations in the way "good health" was defined: (1) a general feeling of well-being; (2) the absence of general or specific illness symptoms; and (3) the ability to perform normal social roles. The symptom-oriented response was slightly more prevalent among more highly educated individuals, and the general-feeling orientation was more prevalent among those with less education. The third orientation, however, performance of social roles, was evenly distributed among all social classes.

Many studies have found that interference with the ability to perform normal social roles is the most common way for people to define a physical condition as "illness" or a physical sign as an "illness symptom" (Apple, 1960; diCicco and Apple, 1958). Furthermore, there are reported class differences in the use of inability to perform normal social roles as a criterion of self-defined "sickness." Gordon (1966), for example, gave a group of respondents twelve different descriptions of ill health and asked if each should be called sickness. Unfavorable prognosis was the most common factor considered to indicate sickness and did not seem to vary by social class.

Inability to work was found to be a more important determinant of what was viewed as sickness for upper income persons than for those with lower incomes. Thus, the more highly valued the activities of the "well role," the more likely that interference with them through adoption of the "sick role" is resisted (Twaddle, 1969; Zola, 1964; Robinson, 1971). Correspondingly, when the well role is unsatisfactory for some reason or when the individual feels a sense of failure in fulfilling that role, the sick role can provide a refuge from the well role (Twaddle, 1969; Cole and LeJeune, 1972). Illness can thus be used to legitimize a sense of failure to fulfill socially prescribed roles.

The point to be stressed is that adoption of the sick role, since it represents a rejection of well-role activities, will be very much affected by what those activities are and what valuation is placed on them. As Twaddle (1969:114) puts it, "Parsons suggested that exemption from normal activities depends on the severity of the illness, [but] it seems equally true that the respondents' assessment of severity depends on exemption from normal roles."

Factors Influencing the Differential Experience
of Illness Symptoms

It is not only the ways in which health and disease are perceived
that are influenced by cultural and social characteristics but also apparently the *actual experiencing* of physiological symptoms. Wide
divergencies between people's perceptions of their own diseases and
the clinical diagnoses have been noted (Richardson, 1970; Zola,
1964; Kirscht, 1971; Maddox, 1964; Suchman et al., 1958; Friedsam and Martin, 1963). Two studies comparing physicians' evaluations with respondents' evaluations of their own health found that
roughly forty percent did not agree.

There are clearly many factors related to the distortion of people's perceptions of their own health; unfortunately most of them
are unknown. Kasl and Cobb (1966:256) discuss the effects of age
and sex on the perception of symptoms, concluding that "men and
older subjects are more optimistic about their health than women
and younger subjects [although] one study found no age or sex differences." They go on to say that the conclusions are based on
tendencies to underrate or overrate health conditions, and "since
under-reporting varies with the nature of symptoms and since many
symptoms are age or sex-related, or both, more refined analyses
than are presently available need to be made."

In a comparison of matched groups of men and women, Hinkle
et al. (1960) found significant differences in both the nature and
number of illnesses reported by both groups. The women reported
more illnesses that, although minor, were perceived as disabling,
while the men were diagnosed as actually having more serious illnesses. Hinkle et al. (1960:1335) attributed the differences in perception of illness severity to "culturally and socially determined attitudes."

In addition to age and sex, other factors that have been found
to be associated with differential response to disease symptoms are
such social characteristics as religion, marital status, and living situation (Hessler et al., 1971)—and cultural differences among ethnic groups. Zborowski (1958) reported that ethnic values affect
the reactions to physical pain—the "meaning" attached to it and

the emotional content in its expression. Croog (1961) noted that in a group of army inductees, Jews at all education levels reported the greatest number of symptoms, reflecting greater concern with or sensitivity to illness symptoms.

Zola (1966) also reported that there are ethnic differences in reaction to symptoms. In a study of 196 hospital patients of Italian Catholic, Irish Catholic, and Anglo-Saxon Protestant backgrounds, he found that even with the same diagnosed disorder there were differences among those ethnic groups in the ways symptoms are perceived and experienced. The Irish tended to deny that they experienced pain in connection with their illness and typically described their problem in terms of specific dysfunctions while the Italians more often spoke of a diffuse difficulty, sometimes spreading and generalizing complaints into the area of interpersonal behavior.

Stress

Research on the relationship between psychological stress, physiological symptoms, and behavioral response has identified at least three potential roles for stress: (1) Severe or prolonged stress actually causes physiological illness. (2) Stress heightens symptom sensitivity, producing an increased awareness of illness symptoms that might otherwise have been ignored. (3) Stress increases the likelihood that some corrective action will be taken in response to a perceived symptom of illness—e.g., professional medical care will be sought. In fact, the evidence in support of all three roles is convincing. Stress has been reported to be associated, apparently physiologically, with the onset of a number of chronic diseases (see Sparer, 1956; Conference of the Society . . . , 1959; Travis, 1961; Holmes et al., 1951; Rahe, 1964), although it is not clear in some studies that new physiological symptoms have been distinguished from heightened sensitivity to symptoms already existing (Kasl and Cobb, 1966). For our purposes, it will not be important to distinguish the actual physiological effects of stress from its effects in heightening sensitivity, as both result in the perception of increased illness.

There is ample evidence that stress does increase the likelihood of perceiving illness, whether through increased mental or physical susceptibility. In a study of about 7,000 mothers in California, Berkman (1969) found that the stress resulting from being a spouseless mother was significantly related to the frequency of self-reported chronic conditions and functional disabilities, controlling for a number of other associated economic, environmental, and personality stresses. Similarly, Mechanic (1964) found that mothers under temporary psychological stress tended to report more illness symptomatology for both themselves and their children. In a study of 194 Underwater Demolition Team trainees, measures of stressful life changes were found to be significantly correlated with the development of severe illness (Rahe et al., 1972). Even the degree of "consonance" with respect to cultural and social characteristics among residents in a housing project was found to be related to the amount of physical and mental stress experienced (Hessler et al., 1971). Mechanic and Volkhart (1961) and Stoeckle et al. (1963) have reviewed a number of studies concerning the role of psychological stress that support the correlation between stress and increased prevalence, or at least awareness, of illness.

A close relationship between psychological stress and physiological disorders is also indicated in studies suggesting that certain individuals are particularly susceptible to both forms of distress. The work of Engel (1967) on "pain prone" individuals and a study by Fabrega and colleagues (1969) on the medical and behavioral features of low-income medical "problem patients" are illustrative of that relationship. The latter study found that patients identified as "problem patients" by a panel of doctors, according to such criteria as emotionalism, lack of cooperation, and vagueness in communication, were more likely to rate themselves as more physically "sick" than other patients (although their actual hospitalization rates were comparable) and were also more likely to introduce social problems into the medical consultation.

Finally, there is evidence that it may be not only difficult in practice to distinguish between the first two roles posited for stress, but that actually they may be interrelated. In other words, stress may first result in heightened (or imagined) sensitivities to illness symptoms but may then take a real physiological toll of health status. A study by Rosengren (1964) of two hundred maternity patients of various social classes concluded that lower class women and also women with class-inconsistent cultural values, role conflict, and recent social mobility tended to regard themselves as more "sick" during pregnancy than did women of middle or upper-middle class status. In fact, it turned out that those women who believed themselves to be sicker actually did have more difficult pregnancies. Though poorer general health status and lower quality care may have been partly responsible, it seems likely that the women's attitudes also affected their physiological states (McKinlay, 1972b).

Another example of the interaction between psychological and physiological states comes from a study by Epstein et al. (1957) of a homogeneous group of clothing workers in New York City. Rates of manifest arteriosclerosis were found to be twice as high among Jewish men as among Italian men and were associated with such factors as serum cholesterol levels, blood pressure, and body weight among the Italians but not among the Jewish men. Although real physiological differences existed, it is not clear whether their origins were physiological and psychological. The tendency of different ethnic groups to have different psychological reactions to physiological symptoms may result in real differences in physical symptom patterns.

In the context of influencing the concept of stress, the perception of physiological symptoms and utilization decisions is characterized by anxiety, discomfort, and emotional tension (Janis, 1958). Although the effects, in terms of increased sensitivity to physiological symptoms, of many forms of stress seem to be similar, sources of stress are numerous and varied. They include major changes in life situation (Rahe et al., 1972), overcrowding, inconsistency or ambiguity in tasks or roles, changes in customary activities (McGrath, 1970), low status (Meile and Haese, 1969), status inconsistency (Jackson, 1962; Jackson and Burke, 1965), social or marital incompatibility (Hochstim, 1968), and socio-environmental (Coe et al., 1969; Hochstim, 1968).

Two sources of stress that have been studied in detail are status inconsistency and lower class status. The findings suggestst that both are (independently) associated with higher than average stress symptoms. The degree of "status integration" is seemingly related to patterns of chronic illness in a number of empirical tests although alternative explanations of the relationship are possible (Dodge and Martin, 1970). Jackson and Burke (1965) found that the number and seriousness of stress symptoms experienced are related to the number and type of status inconsistencies as measured by occupation, education, and racial ethnic group.

An index of "psychophysiological disorder," based on twenty-two questions concerning both physical and mental disorders, has been used to study the relationship between mental stress, physical disorders, and social class. Crandell and Dohrenwend (1967) conclude from responses to those questions that "there is a distinct tendency on the part of lower-class groups to express psychological distress in physiological terms."

Meile (1972) claims, however, that this tendency represents not only a transference between psychological and physiological symptoms but the additional presence for lower class groups of real psychological burdens. Controlling for sex and education, he concludes that "structural variables may not only affect the type of expression of psychological disorder, but they may in fact be 'causally' linked to the presence or absence of the disorder."

Meile and Haese (1969) investigated the relationship between status inconsistency and status itself and found that lower class status, as measured by an average of socioeconomic status indicators, is more closely associated with mental and physical stress symptoms than is status inconsistency. They suggest that, as in the Crandell and Dohrenwend (1967) study, the association may be due to the presence of greater real sources of stress for the poor.

Additional evidence that lower class status is associated with greater experience of stress comes from studies contrasting the stress experiences of people living in poverty areas to those of people comparable in other respects but living in better-off neighborhoods. Two such studies concluded that the conditions of the poverty neighborhood itself constitute a source of stress for residents that is related to greater than average experience of illness, injury, and psychological disruption (Coe et al., 1969; Hochstim, 1968).

Salience of Health

A matter of some debate has been the question of possible differences in the "salience" of health and illness to different social groups. In particular, there has been a continuing argument about whether persons categorized as lower social class were more or less "concerned" about their health and its maintenance than are others. Koos launched the argument in 1954 by reporting that health is more salient to the upper classes, that lower class persons are more likely to "put up" with a variety of symptoms and not to seek medical care for them. It is important to note that this is not a single but a double claim, which deals with both the attitudinal as well as the behavioral response of persons to symptoms of illness. In fact, the claims should be evaluated separately, as different factors may influence each. Thus, one claim may be true and not the other. We shall first examine evidence regarding differences in the salience of health as measured by attitudes concerning health and illness.

Zborowski (1958) reported that more highly educated persons appear to be more conscious of their health and more aware of pain as a symptom of disease. That reaction is interpreted, however, as differential response to illness fostered by education and socialization rather than as an internal attitudinal difference. In the same year, in the field of mental health, Hollingshead and Redlich (1958) purported to document the relationship between social class and tolerance of symptoms of ill health. More recent evidence, however, clearly challenges the view that lower socioeconomic groups are less concerned about health or more tolerant of symptoms of ill health. Suchman (1965a) found little difference among socioeconomic groups in the interpretation of symptoms as indicating illness or in the amount of concern expressed about symptoms. Mc-Broom (1970) found no evidence that lower status persons tend to overreact to or overreport symptoms of illness, and little relation between socioeconomic status and perceived illness level. Mechanic

(1969) concluded on the basis of available research that there is little evidence of significant differences in response to pain and discomfort among various socioeconomic groups.

There is in fact some evidence that lower class persons *are more concerned* than upper class persons about their health. Crandell and Dohrenwend's findings concerning the tendency of lower class persons to translate psychological distress into physiological form suggest that the physical health of the body is of enough concern to them to serve as a vehicle for the expression of both mental and physical ills. Kadushin (1967) cites several studies, based on responses to check-listed items measuring concern with health or anxiety about physical symptoms, which suggest that lower class persons are more likely than upper class persons to worry about their health (Bradburn and Caplovitz, 1965; Crandell and Dohrenwend, 1967). These studies are particularly convincing since they avoid the pitfall of open-ended responses to questions that tend to elicit fewer responses from lower class persons, regardless of the questions being asked. As noted earlier, Rosengren (1964) found in his study of maternity patients that lower class women tended to regard themselves as more "sick" during pregnancy than women of middle and upper classes.

The suspicion may arise that the apparently greater concern of the poor for their health may be primarily because their health is worse. It is certainly true that the impact of illness is more burdensome for the poor, and it may be that past experiences, either personal or those of friends, have heightened the fear of repeated illness and have thus increased their concern about their health status. But it does not seem to be greater prevalence of present illness that accounts for their greater concern. Data from the National Health Survey suggest that, given comparable states of health, the poor are more concerned about their health. Self-administered medical history questionnaires given to a sample of adults were compared with the results of their medical examinations for hypertension and heart disease, and it was found that, at the lower income and lower educational levels, the self-reported disease prevalences were slightly exaggerated (National Center for Health Statistics, 1967). That is, lower income individuals tended to perceive themselves as sicker than they actually were as measured by clinical examination.

Use of Health Services

Since the perception and experiencing of illness symptoms affect a person's response to those symptoms, and since one possible response is the decision to seek medical care, all the factors discussed thus far bear at least indirectly on the decision to seek medical care. They affect the symptom-response (what might be termed the "pre-patient" or "pre-action") phase of the utilization-decision process. But many of them bear directly on utilization decisions as well. Stress seems to play a role both in increasing symptom sensitivity and in increasing the likelihood that the individual will seek professional medical care (Stoeckle et al., 1963). And it has been shown that seeking care is usually preceded by defining oneself as "ill" (Antonovsky, 1972). The connection between perceptions of illness and the decision to seek care is as tenuous, however, as the subjectivity of the notion of illness might suggest. Among a group of people who all perceived themselves as ill, it was found that the number or severity of illness symptoms was not significantly related to whether or not care had been sought (Ludwig and Gibson, 1969). Instead, situational factors and faith in the medical-care system were found to be most closely related to whether or not a doctor had been consulted.

In the same way that the perception and experiencing of symptoms are influenced by both external factors (social, cultural, economic, etc.) and internal (psychological) factors, so the subsequent decision to seek medical care, given certain perceived symptoms, is influenced by those factors. The role of external factors in influencing use of services is especially important. Many studies have shown that the availability, acceptability, and financial accessibility of services are critical factors in accounting for much variation in utilization behavior. In addition, the effects of demographic, social, and cultural factors have been found to be related to patterns of utilization (McKinlay, 1972a).

Tendency to Use Services

Little effort appears to have been made to distinguish the effects of psychological factors on the *decision* to seek care from their effects on the *perception* of symptoms, and this could be fruitfully pursued in future research. What work has been reported in the area has been primarily concerned with the measurement and/or explanation of a psychological state of "readiness" or "tendency" to use services. Typically, respondents have been asked if they would seek care if they noticed a given symptom of illness; their responses are then combined into an index, which is viewed as measuring the tendency or readiness to seek care. Some studies have treated the concept as an exogenous variable—a characteristic of people that is taken as given and is used in helping to predict utilization. More interesting are studies that have attempted to determine the characteristics to which such a tendency might be related and why.

The concept of readiness to initiate physician care was first employed by Koos in 1956 in the form of a collection of responses to the question of whether a doctor should be consulted for each of a list of common illness symptoms. In a subsequent study Hochbaum (1958) presented a model that specified three components of the state of psychological readiness to initiate care, especially preventive care—perceived seriousness of the disease, perceived vulnerability to the disease, and perceived efficacy of medical treatment. He contended that it was the presence of these beliefs that accounted for observed use patterns. Evidence has accumulated to support his claim, at least for discretionary use (preventive or patient-initiated therapeutic visits).

While Hochbaum's particular model dealt with psychological factors relevant to initiating the use of preventive services, most other studies of the tendency to use services have focused on psychological factors influencing use of therapeutic services, usually in response to the recognition of some sign of illness. Zola (1964) designates five "triggers" that may precipitate the decision to seek care. They are, briefly, interpersonal crisis, interference with valued social activity, sanctioning by others, threat to major activity, and nature and familiarity of symptoms. All are viewed as influencing both the perception of and the response to symptoms. Mechanic and Volkhart (1961), in contrast, emphasize that perception and response should be treated separately. They find that stress (in Zola's terms, interpersonal crisis) is related primarily to symptom sensitivity and perception, while a different psychological process —which they term "tendency to adopt the sick role"—which is a summary index based on the merged responses to several general symptom questions, and is thought to intervene between the perception of need for care and actual use of services.

Other findings on the role of "tendency to use services" have been somewhat mixed. Bice (1971) found that a measure of tendency to use services was important in explaining the use of preventive services but not in explaining any of his measures of symptomatic or therapeutic use. This is consistent with the original focus of the readiness concept in explaining use of preventive services. Kalimo (1969) and Antonovsky (1972) reported that measures of tendency to use physicians' services are positively correlated with total (preventive and therapeutic) utilization. In Andersen's model (1968) of families' use of health services, an index of "attitude toward physician use" was found to have only a slight positive relation to a measure of total physician use.

That the various findings differ somewhat is not surprising in view of the variation in the different tendency measures. Bice (1971) and Antonovsky (1972), for example, based their tendency measures on questions concerning psychosocial needs and problems (difficulty in getting along with other people, status, coping with failure, etc.), Kalimo's index (1969) was based on the perceived benefits and barriers to the use of medical services, and Andersen merged responses to questions about seeking physician's care for a number of physical symptoms of illness. The approaches taken by Hochbaum (1958) and Zola (1964) in their analyses of the psychological factors associated with readiness to seek care illustrates an even more fundamental difference in method. It is clear that there is no consensus on what psychological factors are involved in the tendency to use services or even on the best way to approach the formulation or measurement of such a concept.

Investigators have also been concerned with the relationship between some measure of tendency to use services and social class. To the extent that this psychological tendency is unevenly distributed among various social classes, it might account for use patterns that otherwise might be attributed to other characteristics of the groups. Koos (1954) and Rosenstock (1969) found, based on responses to check lists of medical danger signals, that persons classified as of upper socioeconomic status seemed more inclined to seek medical care for a given set of symptoms. Similarly, Hetherington and Hopkins (1969) reported that respondents of higher occupational status were more likely to judge that a list of symptoms warranted seeking medical care. The inclination to seek care was also related to a number of other social and demographic characteristics.

Other studies have failed to find a significant relationship between tendency to use services and social class (Feldman, 1966). Bice's (1971) measure of tendency to consult a doctor for a psychosocial problem was not related to either economic class or to education. Apple (1960) found that, in a sample of mostly middle class respondents, there was little variation in responses to a list of somatic symptoms by age, sex, occupation, or education, but the reason may have been the rather restricted range of educational and occupational groups included in the study.

In a study of the utilization behavior of older adults, Battistella (1968a) found that persons of lower socioeconomic status seemed to be more, rather than less, inclined to seek care in the presence of illness symptoms; they reported having delayed less than persons of upper status after they had recognized symptoms of disease. Battistella suggests that one explanation may be that the sick role offers lower status persons relief from the anxieties and strains of their normal social roles. No attempt, however, was made to determine if symptoms were recognized at comparable stages of seriousness by the two groups—a major weakness of the study that makes the findings somewhat inconclusive. On a larger scale, Andersen and colleagues (1968) found that social and economic factors seemed to account at least in part for international differences in utilization rates, although not for differences in the perception of symptoms.

It is difficult to draw a coherent picture from these widely different studies and the varied findings concerning the concept of tendency to use services. To some extent, variability is inherent in the nature of the phenomenon. Steele and McBroom warn that "health behavior"—use of preventive health services—is a multidimensional concept. Use of different types of preventive services varies among different groups and is differentially affected by various socioeconomic and situational characteristics (Steele and McBroom, 1972). Thus, one might expect that attempts to study psychological factors related to inclination or readiness to use different services would produce diverse results.

But much of the variety in the studies and findings results from inconsistencies in conceptualization and measurement and from further inconsistencies in the study contexts in which the concept is tested. One inconsistency is the type of utilization behavior the tendency measure is supposed to predict. Battistella (1968a) makes the important point that the appropriate measure of utilization in studying the role of psychological readiness or tendency to use services is the initial visit per illness episode, since the patient has maximum control over the decision to make the initial visit and much less control over the number and frequency of all subsequent visits. Thus, it is not surprising that studies find little if any relationship between tendency measures and total utilization frequencies; yet that is the relationship most frequently tested.

Perhaps the most fundamental weakness of research in the area is its failure to place the tendency concept in its proper context—as one of many factors affecting, or likely to affect, utilization. Battistella (1968b) has again correctly pointed out that whatever has been measured by the various indices of "subjective inclination to use health services" is relatively insignificant in relation to other factors affecting use, such as the accessibility and availability of physicians' services. Though there may in fact be real differences in such subjective tendencies, in general their effects have not been measured above and beyond the effects of other factors that are known to affect utilization patterns, such as availability of care, cultural and ethnic preferences, and age and sex effects. Characteristic of most studies is the analysis of single associations between measures of tendency and actual use or measures of socioeconomic status; the interrelation between even tendency, use, and social class is rarely examined. Bice's study (1971) is one exception. As a result, the effects of differences in subjective tendencies are probably largely lost among or at least confounded by the more predominant influences of all the other factors affecting use decisions, the effects of which are not controlled. A similar criticism is relevant to much of the work on the role of other psychological factors in utilization decisions, although it seems to be somewhat less critical to the analysis of factors affecting the symptom-response (pre-action) phase of the utilization decision-making process.

To some extent, the simultaneous interdependence of variables is rarely examined because to do so requires a fairly large data base that is often unavailable. But it also seems that the importance of the interdependencies has not been sufficiently appreciated, and the forms of multivariate analyses that would allow both an examination of and compensation for interrelations have only begun to be exploited. Advances in methodology may herald new substantive findings, or at least allow old disputes about the relative effects of variables that have been traditionally analyzed on a one-to-one basis to be laid to rest.

Influence of Stigma and the Labeling Process

A number of conditions and/or states are regarded, at least in Western societies, as stigmatizing those who possess them. Notable examples are alcoholism, venereal disease, mental illness, the menopause, obesity, drug dependence, and an unwanted pregnancy. One would suspect a priori that the possession of some stigmatizing characteristic may, in various ways, influence the use of services. Despite the fairly widespread recognition of its influence, however, stigma has received scant attention in this particular context. Little empirical research has been conducted on its nature, but there is a body of more theoretical social-psychological literature that does explore the dimensions of the question. Some of this work as it may relate to utilization behavior is considered below.

The most insightful work on the concept of stigma appears in the writings of Erving Goffman (1959) who began with an interest in "impression management." For him "impression management" denotes the efforts that people make to create and sustain desired images about themselves and thus to control the conduct of others, especially their responsive treatment, by controlling the types of information they receive. More recently, Goffman (1961) has focused specifically on the behavior of people with a stigma or "undesired differentness," and he identifies three main types: (1) physical disfigurement; (2) aberrations of character and/or personality; and (3) social categorizations, such as race, nationality, and religion. In short, "an individual who might have been received easily in ordinary social intercourse possesses a trait that can obtrude itself upon attention and turn those of us whom he meets away from him, breaking the claim that his other attributes have on us." Goffman argues that the type of impression management involved is largely a function of whether the stigma is visible or invisible, known about or not. If it is visible (e.g., facial deformities, polio paralysis), the person is *discredited,* knows or assumes that others are aware of the differentness, and the primary interactional task is the *management of tension.* If it is not immediately visible (e.g., an unwanted pregnancy, alcoholism, or the menopause) the person is only *discreditable* and his or her primary interactional task is the *management of information* about the condition.

From such a perspective, it is clear that the subjective meanings of their "undesirable differentness" for the stigmatized are of central importance. For those with some *permanent* stigma, a viable self-identity must be sustained; for the individual *acquiring* a stigmatized condition or entering a stigmatized state, a new self-identity must be created. They are no longer what they had presumed themselves to be and must devote considerable attention to achieving what is vaguely termed "acceptance" by the normal person. Goffman (1959, 1961, 1963), among others, describes at some length the protective or defensive strategies that constitute the impression-management repertoire of the stigmatized. Such tactics as "passing," "covering," and working out "lines" and "codes" of conduct help the "undesirably different" to cope with their discrediting or discreditable attribute and protect them from mortifying situations.

It seems that the stigmatized are involved in a tortuous dilemma of self-contradiction. They are clearly denied *real* acceptance in most social encounters, but they also, perhaps more importantly, act in such a way as to confirm the negative evaluation of their condition or state and remain stigmatized in their own eyes. The paradox of the situation is that, no matter how vast their repertoire of impression-management strategies or how successfully those strategies are deployed to manage tension or informaton, the stigmatized remain wedded to the same identity norms as normal persons—the very norms that disqualify them. Consequently, they are both *other-* and *self*-stigmatized.

One important influence of stigma on the utilization of health care relates to the involved person's *self-identity* and probably exerts an early influence in his help-seeking. Denial of the presence of some stigmatized condition (for example, conditions of a cosmetic nature like skin blemishes) may be viewed as an attempt to protect or delay some change in a person's own self-concept. Such denial is facilitated by the development of counterideologies or of self-rationalizations that the condition is, among other things, unimportant; that others' evaluations are misinformed; or that the condition is only temporary and will pass with time (Voysey, 1972a, b; Davis, 1961; Garfinkel, 1967; Glaser and Strauss, 1965). The self-rationalizations and the reluctance to alter behavior can be viewed as protective of those affected, or their significant others.

The alterations in behavior and ideology associated with self-identity should be distinguished from other behavior that relates to alterations in *social identity* (how *other* people and agencies react once disclosure occurs). Since many health and welfare agencies appear to shape the nature of a person's social identity through the isolation and confirmation of stigmatizing conditions, various types of utilization behavior (especially the delay and misuse of certain services) may be viewed as attempts to retain, for as long as possible, control of social identity.

Goffman (1963) has described a situation in which certain individuals are obliged to share some of the discredit of the stigmatized person to whom they are related. The relationship through the social structure leads the wider society to treat both the stigmatized person and his relations, in some respects, as one (Birnbaum, 1970). In such a situation the stigma flows from the initially discredited to his affiliates.

One can conceive of situations where stigma can initially reside in both mandated officials (e.g., the social worker, the policeman, the psychiatrist) and service organizations (abortion clinics, detoxification centers, welfare departments, and, perhaps, emergency rooms) and discredit those clients with whom they have contact. The stigma then flows *from the already discredited official or agency* to clients with whom they interact. It can of course be argued that the services—disease clinics, for example—receive a courtesy stigma because they interact with individuals and groups who are *already* stigmatized. The precise direction and sequence are, however, somewhat irrelevant as far as understanding utilization behavior is concerned, partly depending on the origins of particular organizations and the typical problems that they handled at their inception. Health and welfare facilities often have a reputation that precedes their current client membership, a prevailing ideology concerning their activities and clients and an existing set of typifications and degradation procedures that are learned by new personnel—all perpetuated by the agency and generally existing before current clients became members.

In addition, the stigma incurred by a multiservice health or welfare agency from one group of clients may be passed on to other clients with different problems or conditions who use the same agency. In Great Britain, for example, the agency that distributes unemployment benefits is also responsible for the employment services; to locate a new job a person has to risk the stigma of being labeled unemployed. If there is any doubt concerning whether or not health and welfare agencies are stigmatized, we can look at the almost perennial attempts that they make to change their public image by changing their name.

So far we have explored the possible importance of stigma in the decision to utilize a service and the possible utility of the concept in understanding utilization behavior in relation to specific agencies. The underuse or misuse of services can be viewed as an attempt to *avoid the application of a "label"* as a result of the recognition by others of some stigma. There is now a voluminous literature on the process by which professionals and organizations have a mandate to apply labels to behavior or conditions and the long-term consequences labeling often has for the perpetuation of the so-called "problem." The labeling perspective (often loosely termed the symbolic interaction, interactionist or societal reaction approach) has assumed prominence within sociology and social psychology and offers a valuable conceptualization of the development of deviant or illness careers that apparently become permanent.

In essence, labeling theory focuses on the ways "primary deviants" become "secondary deviants" and stresses the importance of the impact of societal reaction on the afflicted person rather than his individual characteristics. Primary illness or deviance may arise from many sources. The extent and nature of any societal reaction to an illness condition or stigma are functions of its visibility, the power vested in the social position of the afflcted person, and the normative parameters or tolerance for deviance and/or illness that exist within the community. Primary illness (heavy drinking, "idiosyncratic" behavior, etc.) that is visible and exceeds the community tolerance level may bring the actors to the attention of mandated labelers, such as psychiatrists, clinical psychologists, social workers, the police, and various "helping" organizations.

If the mandated agencies see fit to "officially" classify the actor as a type of ill person (or deviant), a labeling process is hypothesized to occur that eventuates in (1) a change in the person's self-identity and (2) a change in his social identitity among significant others as well as in the wider community. Behavior that results from the revised identities is termed "secondary deviance." According to the labeling theorists, secondary deviance is substantially similar to the original primary deviance but has as its source the actor's revised self-identity, as well as the revised social identity he has in the community. We have already described how stigma may be related to both aspects of identity.

Previous research and theoretical literature have concentrated on the negative results of labeling, particularly in cases of mental illness, in terms of delayed help seeking and selective health-service utilization. Several writers have noted that the labeling process might in some cases have a positive effect on future behavior. Fear of stigma or of the application of some derogatory label may also serve to increase utilization or to terminate "at risk" behavior, depending on the nature and severity of the stigma involved, the contextual situation in which it presents itself and the availability of services. The labeling of certain conditions may pressure deviants to conform to group norms, relinquish earlier stigmatized life styles (promiscuity, obesity, alcoholism, etc.), and perhaps even reverse behavior in an attempt to delabel or relabel themselves.

It is clear from the preceding discussion that there is considerable uncertainty over whether and how stigma influences utilization behavior. Empirical investigations will do much to expand our knowledge of the various effects of labeling, and such research may show that its nature and force are a function of, among other things, the type of stigma, the social position of the stigmatized, whether the labeled person is a primary or secondary deviant, who the mandated labeler is, which organizations support the label, and whether the labeled behavior has ceased.

There is clear evidence that communities label and exclude through institutionalization a disproportionate number of "cultural marginals"—people classified as of lower social status and those more isolated from stable group ties who do not possess the power to resist (Gibbs, 1962; Leiffer, 1966–67; Linsky, 1970). Such differential labeling and exclusion by mandated professionals and organizations can be viewed as a form of social control and, given the increasing tendency towards the medicalization of everything (Zola, 1972) and the general permanence of labels, should be viewed with considerable alarm.

From such a perspective, underutilization becomes not a social problem to which resources are directed in order to eliminate it but, rather, healthy behavior to perhaps be encouraged. This notion, of course, questions the decision rule guarding the behavior of professionals operating with a medical model of illness; namely, when in doubt, diagnose, label, and treat—all in the interest of prevention. The labeling theorists, aware of the process described above, argue for the application of the converse decision rule; namely, when in doubt deny, in the interest of preventing the stabilization and exclusion of individuals for what may turn out to be only a transitory, unremarkable episode (Scheff, 1964; Scheff and Sundstrom, 1970).

Alienation

For several decades now social scientists—working mainly within a political context—have been concerned with the development and consequences of what is loosely termed the "mass society." The theory of mass society holds that the destruction of the old community has separated the individual from binding social ties and that his isolation produces a sense of powerlessness that can be both personally devastating and destructive of the democratic processes. The theory consists of an historically oriented account of contemporary social structure, a set of statements about the present and emerging alienating effects of that structure, and derived predictions about some possible behavioral consequences. It is clear that there is still debate over the mass-society thesis and the plausibility of some of its assumptions and implications. Some subscribe to the view that, far from functioning as mediating forces allowing individual expression and control, complex organizations are simply agencies for further alienation. C. Wright Mills espoused this view when he wrote:

> [that voluntary organizations] have lost their grip on the individual. As more people are drawn into the political arena, these associations become mass in scale, and as the power of the individual becomes more dependent upon such mass associations, they are less accessible to the individual's influence (1956:307).

While the debate on the mass-society thesis proceeds, some evidence has emerged that lends support to the view that membership in a work-based organization is associated with a relatively strong sense of control over events and that the greater powerlessness of the unorganized worker is not simply a function of his socioeconomic status. Although findings of this study appear relatively conclusive, attention is drawn to the obvious problem of causal imputation. Does participation in various kinds of complex organizations reduce alienation, or do only the nonalienated participate in organizations, whose essential purpose is to exercise control over certain spheres of life? If the former interpretation is correct, then it becomes clear that the estrangement of the poor from formal organizations (underutilization) can be regarded as a serious disadvantage and that the trend toward increasing bureaucratization—not only in health and welfare but also in the economic, occupational, and educational spheres—must result in further systematic exclusion and alienation of those in poverty from the main stream of social life. These statements are perhaps a little extreme, but their plausibility is often argued by social and political theorists. Their viability, of course, depends partly on the plausibility of the mass society thesis and as yet, in our view, insufficient empirical evidence has been gathered with which to make a judgment.

There is an impressive body of evidence showing that the nature and extent of involvement in society (measured by participation in voluntary associations) are closely related to socioeconomic status; the lower one's social class, the less likely one is to belong to various types of organizations (Curtis, 1959; Babchuck and Edwards, 1965; Babchuck and Booth, 1969). Although voluntary association memberships showed a small but noteworthy overall increase between the mid-1950s and the early 1960s, involving particularly blacks and thus reducing previous subgroup differences, strong socioeconomic differentials still remain (Hyman and Wright, 1971). Such findings are manifestly important when the problem of the underutilization of health services is being considered, since they show that behavior to be not idiosyncratically specific to health but consistent with behavior in a number of related spheres of social life (e.g., education, leisure, religion, economics, politics). Such a perspective allows us to note several shortcomings of a purely social-psychological approach. First, it enables us to see how the emergence of particular behaviors may be realistic adjustments to one's social position and diminished life chances. Second, it facilitates the inference of so-called "pathologic" behavior in related spheres of life other than health. If certain individuals, groups, or social categories cling to certain health beliefs and action, it may be not only because they are traditional and familiar but also because they are linked to other important elements of their subculture. To effect a change in one area of a subcultural system (say, increased utilization of health services) may result in unanticipated changes in other areas in awkward dislocations (Paul, 1958).

Estrangement from major social organizations and the consequences for individual functioning have, of course, received considerable attention from social scientists over the past several decades. The concept that best captures the phenomenon that has been discussed and that also has been developed to a point of operational utility is "alienation." This concept has, of course, engaged the attention of thinkers since the time of Hegel (1955) and Marx (1963) (Fromm, 1955; Durkheim, 1933; Seeman, 1959; Nisbet, 1966; Blauner, 1964); and today is widespread. It has been usefully applied to the study of, among other things, educational achievement, ghetto life, work, reformatories, the behavior of interns, voting behavior, and public opinion on fluoridation. On the few occasions when it has been applied to utilization behavior, it has yielded promising results. Alienation has recently been challenged, however, on the grounds that it is the popular catchword of our age and is becoming a device to rationalize service inactivity (Feuer, 1963; Lee, 1972).

An early study by Seeman and Evans (1961, 1962) explored the relevance of alienation to health behavior with particular reference to hospital settings. They clearly demonstrated, in a group matched for background characteristics, that patients who felt more powerless were less able to learn about their disease (tuberculosis). They argue that it is a "sense of personal control which makes knowledge concerning one's affairs motivationally relevant" and conclude that an aspect of alienation (powerlessness) "serves as the hypothetical intervening variable between the individual's social circumstances (i.e., his social structural place) and his social learning."

A more recent investigation by Morris and his colleagues (1966a) related two components of alienation (powerlessness and social isolation) to well-child supervision. They found in a study of 246 black and white mothers of low socioeconomic status with ten-month old children, that the more powerless and socially isolated had received less preventive care for their children. Moreover, mothers who were more powerless were less in agreement with the statements of professionals about the purposes and potentialities of well-child supervision.

Another often neglected study analyzed the relationship between alienation as measured with Dean's (1961) alienation scale and polio immunization participation (Gray et al., 1967; Moody and Gray, 1972). The results are consistent with earlier studies and show that highly alienated mothers had their children immunized less frequently than did mothers showing less alienation and that the relationship held regardless of the subjects' socioeconomic status, age, education, and friends' expectations. We believe that the notion of alienation has been developed to a point of operational utility where it could, if systematically employed, contribute to the explanation of utilization behavior.

What Goes on Between Consumers and Health-Care Agencies

The preceding discussion of the various influences of alienation knowledge, perception, symptom recognition, stigma, stress, and satisfaction summarizes only a sample of the central issues in the social-psychological literature on utilization behavior that has appeared in the last few decades. We believe it fairly accurately reflects the predominant emphasis of past work—concern with important factors in the process of seeking care. In other words, attention has been principally directed at variables that exert some influence up to the point of utilizing some service, and not at what goes on between all those involved when a service organization is actually being utilized. In the light of recent developments in organization theory, it is clear that what goes on between clients and agencies may be as highly related to utilization behavior as the personal characteristics that so many have previously highlighted.

A growing body of knowledge of organizational structure and processes, as well as developments in theories of organizations, has made us aware that organizational factors encourage officials to develop particular orientations towards clients, with the result that service to them is measurably affected (Adams and McDonald, 1968; Janowitz and Delany, 1957–58; Blau, 1960–61; Walsh and Elling, 1968; Ben-David, 1958; Wilensky, 1964). In particular, it has been proposed that, in order to maintain itself, client-centered bureaucracy tends to neglect those in greatest need of its services —those the organization was, in fact, primarily established to assist —or who present difficult problems (Sjoberg et al., 1963; Zald, 1965; Cloward and Epstein, 1965; Beck, 1967; Scott, 1967; Levin and Taube, 1970; Lindenberg, 1958; Bredemeier, 1964; Hunt et al., 1958; Hollingshead and Redlich, 1958; Clark, 1960; Fisher, 1969). In a recent paper, Levin and Taube (1970) argue that, given client-centered bureaucracy's investment in its own success, it has little reason to accommodate itself to the orientation of those whom it perceives as impairing its capacity to achieve that success. It is clear that services to clients from lower socioeconomic categories are nearly always found to be limited by organizational factors (Miller, 1964; McKinlay, 1968; Walsh and Eling, 1968; Cloward and Epstein, 1965; Scott, 1967).

Numerous studies investigating certain aspects of lower working-class life have suggested that members of that particular social category do not have the requisite expertise for performing effectively in various types of bureaucratic settings. Summaries of these and other studies, not directly related to utilization, are available (Boum and Rossi, 1969; Rosenblatt and Suchman, 1964a, 1964b; Jefferys, 1957; Osofsky, 1968; Zola, 1964; Shostak and Gomberg, 1964; Gans, 1962; Cohen and Hodges, 1962; Miller, 1964; Young and Willmott, 1960; Schatzman and Strauss, 1955; Hausknecht, 1964; Bernstein, 1959, 1967).

Through increasing knowledge of working-class behavior and experience with ill-fated health and welfare programs, intervention studies, eradication programs, etc.—principally with the poor—the difficulties of changing the knowledge, attitudes, and practice of any group in relation to health, illness, and other social problems have been recognized. Workers have commented on the ever-widening gap between modern medical care, as it is being increasingly provided, and certain groups of the population who continue to cling to what are regarded as traditional beliefs. Consequently, recognition has been increasingly given to the need for services themselves to be tailored to meet the particular needs of clients. It is perhaps noteworthy that the suggestion has almost always followed recognition of the failure of some initial attempt to change knowledge, attitudes, and practice.

Another factor, related to those already discussed but worthy of separate consideration, concerns our knowledge of the systematic uniqueness of the values, beliefs, definitions of situations, and life styles of the poor. Far from being random and idiosyncratic, their knowledge, attitudes, and practice can be viewed as responses that are consistent with, and understandable in relation to, problems associated directly with their social structural position. More than any other, the notion that has fathered that particular view is the concept of a "subculture" or a "culture of poverty," which—like many other concepts currently in vogue—is not without its ideological, analytical, and empirical limitations (Jaffe and Polgar, 1968). Despite its limitations, the concept has focused attention on the fact that behavior from this perspective appears to be patterned and systematically interrelated rather than idiosyncratic.

Recognition of the interrelatedness has led to the view that attempts to change aspects of lower working-class life, without also alleviating or altering the social structural problems to which certain types of behavior are adjustments, may do more harm than good. We have already alluded to the suggestion by Schneiderman (1965) that the underutilization of certain types of services by various subgroups of society may, in some senses, be regarded as healthy behavior. It is suggested that the general factors outlined here helped promote a concentration on organizational and client-agency interaction factors in the use of services and reoriented efforts away from the personal pathologies of underutilizers.

Social scientists studying formal organizations have produced considerable evidence suggesting that not all subgroups of society have an equal facility with and the requisite expertise for performing effectively in various types of formal organizational situations. As yet, however, only a relatively small amount of the material has been employed in the study of services—their organization, provision, and rates of utilization. It is now clear that the middle class have a considerable advantage over the poor in the field of medical care and social welfare as long as services are presented in an almost exclusively bureaucratic fashion. Some of the reasons that experts have given for their relatively advantaged position are listed below.

(a) The basic assumptions underlying the structure of health services (rationality, future orientation, etc.) are often reported as being consonant with the values and life styles of the middle class.

(b) Professional health-care personnel are generally middle class in origin and thus there is minimal status sensitivity during an encounter between them and middle class recipients, and they are best able to understand middle class problems.

(c) Middle class socialization patterns provide individuals with a role repertoire that enables them easily to adopt the role of listener, understand and tolerate the object orientation of officials, and maintain considerable role distance during an encounter.

(d) Socialization, combined with middle class educational advantages, provides a general middle class facility with form-filling and fosters the ability to verbalize feelings, attitudes, and need.

(e) Middle class education and socialization also fosters greater receptivity to health-education campaigns, which, it is often claimed, tend to be biased in their favor.

Health and welfare services then, it is claimed, tend to be based on a middle class rationale, require middle class knowledge and sophistication, generally recruit staff from the middle class, and to many, are open only in middle class hours!

The nature of the interaction between clients and agencies probably varies among different types of organizations (for voluntary organizations, for example, and for universities and churches), as well as among comparable organizations that appear to undertake different activities (a prison, compared with a hospital for the criminally insane). Not only have there been few discussions of the interaction of clients with officials and organizations, but the methodology for such studies remains inadequately developed, although some work in the area is now underway.

Particularly promising is the work of Danet and her colleagues, who have attempted to isolate and describe the attempts by external participants (clients) to influence bureaucratic decisions in their favor (Katz and Danet, 1966). They focus on the kinds of reasons or "persuasive appeals" that clients offer to substantiate their requests to officials in formal organizations, and they identify five sets of organizational circumstances in which "persuasive appeals" may occur.

They are, first, appeals to reciprocity, in both positive and negative forms (inducements and threats). This type of appeal takes the form: "if you grant the request, I will reward you," or, "if you don't, I will deprive you." Second, there are appeals based on pure persuasion as in "you will reward yourself." Third, there are appeals to altruism—"if you grant the request, you will reward me." All three persuasive strategies appeal to someone's profit, while depending on some aspect of the personal exchange relationship of the two parties involved, and compliance is, in principle, voluntary.

The two remaining types of appeals listed are normative in character, and compliance is supposedly obligatory. Danet distinguishes between appeals to the norm of reciprocity and appeals to impersonal norms. While appeals to simple reciprocity say, "I will reward you" (future tense), appeals to the norm of reciprocity say, "you owe it to me now because I have rewarded you in the past." Although the latter type of appeal also involves an exchange relationship between the parties, compliance is presumably experienced as obligatory. In the case of appeals to impersonal norms, which is the fifth basic type of persuasive appeal, compliance is also obligatory but independent of past interaction or any personal acquaintance between the two parties. ("You owe it to me because some abstract principle you have internalized obliges you to do so.")

In one study, Katz and Danet (1966) investigate the relation-

ship between the background characteristics of clients and variations in their use of the different types of appeals, as well as the relationship between different appeals and different organizations.
Four hypothetical situations, in which a client seeks services from
an official, were presented to a heterogeneous sample of Israeli
army reservists. The men were all asked to state what they thought
should be said in each case, in order to get the official to grant the
request. The authors were particularly interested in the variability
of persuasive appeals, and in whether some clients discriminated
more than others in what they said to different organizations, as
well as in whether certain organizations were distinguishably similar
or different judging from the variability in types of appeals addressed to them.

The arguments or persuasive appeals suggested by the reservists
were found to vary with both their personal background and the
type of organization involved. In general, it seems from the evidence presented that the nature of the organization did influence
the types of persuasive appeals of clients in trying to get what they
wanted. It is perhaps noteworthy that the content of the appeals appeared to be influenced more by the normative basis on which the
organization rested (the prime beneficiary whom it was serving)
than on the client's ability to offer his resources in exchange for the
services offered by the organization.

In a subsequent report Danet (1971), employing a promising
methodological technique, examined the patterns of variation in the
language of persuasive appeals to the Israeli customs authorities.
Persuasive appeals were chosen as the focus of the study on the
grounds that they would reflect client orientations to bureaucracy. It
was found that there were no appeals to reciprocity or attempts at
pure persuasion. The clients neither offered inducements, nor did
they threaten customs officials. Moreover, of the three basic types
of appeal that were common, appeals to impersonal norms ("the
customs owes me rights") were least frequent.

It was found that only fifteen percent of all appeals were to normative obligations, compared with twenty-three percent to the norm
of reciprocity and a high forty-one percent to altruism. The propor-

tion of appeals to altruism is perhaps an indication of the weakness of external clients in that particular organizational situation. Since appeals to impersonal norms were low, it was suggested that the clients lacked both bargaining power, which would be best expressed by appeals to impersonal norms. Danet further suggests that even in a powerful commonweal organization, the properly socialized client feels equal to the official before the law in some ultimate sense, while those less socialized define themselves as more subservient and make their appeals in a style that the socialized would regard as degrading and perhaps obsequious.

Some recent attempts have been made to study the strategies designed to gain or maintain personal power, using the techniques of laboratory experimentation. Jones (1964), perhaps more than any other, has developed a promising approach to what he terms "strategic behaviors." He notes that all interpersonal relationships involve some mutual dependence and that each party to a social interchange has potential influence over cetain rewards available to and costs incurred by some other. If the dependence of one on the other are not only mutual but approximately equal, then there is a balance of power in which each can either enforce a minimal set of rewards through his capacity to act or fail to enact the responses sought by the other. When the power in a two-person relationship is asymmetrical, Jones suggests that a repertoire of strategic alternatives is open to the dependent person that guarantees him a certain minimum of rewards but does so at the expense of confirming or strengthening the power asymmetry that defines his dependence.

An example suggested is compliance—the use of overt obedience to avoid punishment and secure available rewards. Other strategies, however, may be effective in modifying the asymmetry itself so that the dependent person's power is in the long run increased. Ingratiation is regarded by Jones as power-enhancing or dependence-reducing. He suggests that, by making himself attractive, the more dependent person reduces the value of his own sanctioning responses and at the same time makes it more difficult for the powerful person to apply the full range of sanctions that were initially part of his repertory.

In our view then, much can be gained in the understanding of health-service utilization by looking at the interaction between clients and agencies, and we have noted some promising beginnings. A concern with such issues will complement much of the work to which earlier sections of this paper are devoted and consequently lead to a more complete picture of the use of services.

Lacking the requisite expertise in and feeling estranged from bureaucratic settings, the lower class often opts for a more person-oriented, individualistic type of medical care. Studies have pointed to the tendency of people of low socioeconomic status to choose the more personal, continuous, and noncoercive care of local general practitioners, corner drugstores, and semiprofessionals. It is plausible to regard a closely knit lay referral system as a direct reaction against increasingly formal and confusing health services. That reaction, of course, while functioning to insulate the lower class from impersonalization and frustration, further widens and reinforces their alienation from the very care to which they are entitled.

Current trends suggest, however, that the days of even the insulative reaction patterns are numbered. For various reasons, lower class persons will probably find it increasingly difficult to retain the traditional, simple, and essentially individualistic medical-care arrangements to which they are accustomed.

The rationalization of services can be seen in both the trend toward group practice and the interest in the development of health centers. Can that mean that even the traditionally inviolable doctor-patient relationship is being eroded—is eventually to be replaced? The rationalization of pharmaceutical services and the establishment of clinics are events that will likely exacerbate lower class alienation. Bureaucratization in the field of health and welfare is, of course, not developing in a vacuum. It is occurring alongside and is probably being reinforced by a more general trend toward impersonality in the political, occupational, educational, and economic spheres.

Suggestions aimed at minimizing lower class frustration with bureaucratic settings have been presented during the past few years. Some researchers, apparently assuming the sanctity of bureaucracy,

have suggested that special programs should be established to educate the lower class in the skills and knowledge required for effective functioning in a formally organized society. Such campaigns,
however, appear to require the establishment of more and more bureaucracy. The problems arising out of bureaucracy are, if you like,
to be solved by bureaucracy. Researchers and administrators sel-
dom consider the possibility of different and more effective forms
of organization.

Few attempts have been made to study the doctor-patient relationship in a variety of organizational settings. Research so far has
largely concerned itself only with doctor-patient communication in
outpatient departments and health clinics. Almost without exception the studies report a breakdown of communication with lower
class patients. How does the doctor-patient relationship vary in different settings? Why is the traditional surgery situation for general
practitioners often thought to be conducive to good communication? How do outpatient departments, child health and welfare,
family planning, and antenatal clinics inhibit personal relationships?
These questions have yet to be answered. It is possible that comparative studies of situational influences on the doctor-patient relationship may uncover techniques for enhancing such individuality and
for reducing the confusion that members of some subgroups experience in formal organizations.

Clearly a more flexible, innovative, and even daringly experimental approach to medical-care organization and delivery is urgently needed. We also need more than a simple variation on the
bureaucratic theme. Fresh attempts must be made to devise entirely
new forms of delivery that take account of and overcome many of
the problems outlined in the preceding sections. Perhaps we are
seeing the beginning of a more innovative approach with the development of such phenomena as storefront clinics, outreach programs, crisis intervention units, and hotlines. At the same time
there appears to be some emphasis on broadening the scope of traditional health personnel to include paraprofessionals, indigenous
workers, and other entirely new categories of personnel. There is a
suggestion that such services are more understandable and cultural-

ly acceptable to the poor in particular because they are more akin to their own life styles.

Some commentators may suggest that the proposed more innovative approach, by taking account of particular needs, involves the provision of special facilities for "different" groups. On the surface that may seem to involve a radical departure from traditional health-service philosophy—namely, relinquishing the principle of universality. One can, however, after highlighting the social class differentials in utilization under the present unitary bureaucratic structure, maintain that greater selectivity in provision may result in greater universality in use.

Some Doubts about "Patient Satisfaction"

In recent years attention has been devoted to the influence of patient satisfaction on utilization behavior. It is assumed that people expressing satisfaction with some type or aspect of medical care will be more likely to utilize medical facilities, follow regimens, comply with advice, etc. Such an assumption appears unwarranted since researchers have pointed out that few studies have been able to establish any sort of correlation between expressed attitudes and subsequent behavior (Festinger, 1964; Kegeles, 1967). Despite this and other known limitations, such studies, for a variety of questionable reasons, continue to engage the attention of medical-care researchers.

There is, of course, a range of different techniques for measuring attitudes and satisfaction. Some researchers make vigorous efforts to measure satisfaction in an objective and structured fashion (Hulka et al., 1971). Others, adopting less structured approaches, have listed several major factors associated with patient satisfaction (waiting time, time spent with the physician, ease of communication, exactness of diagnosis, etc.) and have requested responses regarding satisfaction or dissatisfaction with each of them. Another approach is simply to ask respondents what they like or dislike most about utilizing a particular health facility; a more recent, imaginative technique is to offer subjects several hypothetical situations or short vignettes and require them to state feelings and attitudes.

Many researchers employ some combination of structured and unstructured techniques. Subjects may, for example, be interviewed about their expectations before utilizing a service; then, by content analysis of the recorded happenings, an effort is made to determine the influence of expectations on satisfaction (Francis et al., 1969; Reader et al., 1967; Deisher et al., 1965).

When reviewing the plethora of studies of patient satisfaction and considering the wide variation in methods employed, we note a surprising consistency in findings. The expressed satisfaction with physicians and medical care is phenomenally high for all social categories and, where there is variation, it presented as varying levels of positive attitudes rather than as really negative sentiment. One of the very lowest levels of satisfaction appears to be the seventy-six percent reported in a study of doctor-patient communication (Francis et al., 1969), but the usual figure is around the ninety-eight percent found in a study of mothers' opinions of their pediatric care (Deisher et al., 1965).

The high expressions of satisfaction found in many studies may be a function of who sponsors the research, the subject content of the inquiry (nearly always associated with pediatrics), and where the interviews are conducted. It has often been reported that respondents tend to reply in a stereotyped, socially acceptable manner, and hesitations are often noted. One group of researchers concedes that those conducting the survey had some feeling that the respondents were generally reluctant to express any dissatisfactions they might have had because of the nature of the doctor-patient relationship (Deisher et al., 1965).

With such constraints, it is surprising that researchers continue to elicit responses through interviews and/or written questionnaires at the very place that respondents are expected to comment on and even continue to utilize. Respondents in several earlier investigations of patient attitudes and satisfactions clearly reported positively (and therefore produce the phenomenally high rates of satisfaction) for fear of possible recriminations. A comparable situation in criminology would be a study by prison guards of the satisfaction of long-term prisoners with the treatment received from the guards.

Information concerning satisfaction with care elicited from respondents when they are not actually utilizing a facility may also show a higher degree of satisfaction. When not actually receiving a service, respondents may tend to overlook matters that trouble them when they are using it; satisfaction is expressed rather with its availability. The person making only occasional visits to health facilities can tolerate irritations or inefficiencies that may accompany such infrequent visits without becoming dissatisfied with the system of care. Or the costs of potentially dissatisfying aspects of care may, for the patient, be outweighed by the long-term benefits of the treatment. Kosa and his colleagues (1967) noted that the "errors of recall are not simple functions of forgetfulness but tend to follow a complex, psychologically motivated selectivity." They felt that a person "when furnishing information, feels impelled to apply a selective censorship, separating the reportable events and suppressing the others."

Some of the most insightful work on attitudes and beliefs associated with medical care comes from Kegeles, who has expressed open skepticism with earlier work and has advanced several ideas worthy of serious attention. He writes:

> . . . as to attitude surveys as means of gathering information, people will generally answer questions posed them by interviewers in surveys. This will happen whether they have ever thought of the question or not. There seems to be a growing body of data which indicates that such expressed attitudes have no functional significance unless they fit into the cognitive organization of the person (Kegeles, 1967:921).

Kegeles points out that Converse (1963) has already labeled such statements "non-attitudes"—which seemingly bear no relationship to the behavior of the persons or to anything else and argues that, "without demonstration that such attitudes have relevance for behavior, they provide merely interesting and perhaps useful hypotheses for further testing." Kegeles also suggests that there are few indications of the persistence or reality of the beliefs and attitudes studied and that the best prediction of subsequent behavior is previous behavior.

These criticisms of attitude and satisfaction studies are clearly not exhaustive but relate principally to utilization behavior. Many other researchers have considered a number of the more technical methodological problems with attitude studies per se. Certain questionable ideological factors appear to perpetuate those studies, despite their dubious status on other methodological grounds.

Studies of patient satisfaction often appear to be value-laden and biased in their allocation of responsibility for dissatisfaction. When almost everyone, according to researchers, is satisfied with his medical care, it becomes easy to allocate culpability to some seemingly negligible minority, especially since it has been repeatedly claimed that dissatisfaction is more often present among the aged, the less educated, and lower socioeconomic groups. Hulka and her colleagues (1971) in a recent paper claim that the "use of the medical care system and knowledge of how to use it, as evidenced by having a regular doctor and hospital insurance, are associated with increased total satisfaction." What appears to be implied in such a statement is that those people unfortunate enough not to have a regular doctor or health insurance do not know how to use the system correctly and have brought upon themselves any dissatisfaction they might experience. The same implication is present in some of the work of Suchman, who suggests that if an individual maintains an informed, objective, professional, and independent approach to illness and health care, then he will be likely to express satisfaction with it.

Such research appears to justify the status quo and provides a rationale for either inactivity or lack of progress. According to this view, it is not that the service is inequitable or inefficient but that the nature and characteristics of the recipients obstruct effective delivery and undermine purposeful social policy. It follows that such a perspective and the findings of the studies which it employs, tend to support the existence of demonstrably ineffective programs. Accompanying the federal and private funding in the health field has been the formal or informal requirement that service agencies who receive funds must occasionally justify their continuance. Evaluation studies, with patient satisfaction as a principal component, have been conducted as one of their primary aims

For some time behavioral scientists (especially sociologists and psychologists), who have been interested in utilization behavior, have ascribed culpability for underutilization (or overutilization) to particular individuals or groups—usually the poor—employing such labels as distrustful, disreputable, irresponsible, alienated, parochial, dissatisfied, etc. By adopting such a perspective, we have attempted to deemphasize social structural or organizational determinants of utilization and have disproportionately highlighted the characterological features of clients. We believe that social scientists, among others, guided in part by the availability of funds, have acted as midwives during the birth of much of the present day punitive welfare legislation. While most of them have not actually designed and administered the legislation, they have, through certain findings and concepts, facilitated its delivery. Coser (1969) has noted that researchers espouse a status quo ideology and fail to consider the unanticipated consequences of their liberal theorizing. We have already alluded to studies, mainly in the area of deviance, which show how the process of labeling an offender, and making him conscious of himself as a deviant may evoke the very behavior that is thought to be undesirable (Becker, 1963; Kitsuse, 1964; Scheff, 1966; Lemert, 1951). It surely must be time for researchers to reappraise the effects of their involvement and their perennial invention of new words and concepts. Becker (1967), for example, has described how officials develop ways both of denying the institution's failure to perform as it should and of explaining those failures that cannot be hidden. He also reminds us that researchers who favor officialdom are almost always spared the accusation of bias. Perhaps we should, along with Becker, consider whose side we are on, the various consequences of our research involvements, and the extent to which we are prepared to comply in the coverup of the real sources of dissatisfaction.

There is one outstanding issue that relates to the extent to which so-called patient satisfaction (leaving aside all its methodological and ideological questionability) should be an ingredient in the evaluation of the quality of medical care. We do not deprecate the importance of lay consumer attitudes, nor do we believe that they must be confined to such relatively minor aspects of care as working time, tone and manner of the physician, and clinic surroundings. We must, however, be mindful of the many limitations of attitudinal research and the real possibility that consumers may be misguidedly satisfied with what is actually medical care of poor quality or dissatisfied with what is actually care of good quality.

References

Adams, P. L. *and* N. F. McDonald
  1968   "The clinical cooling out of poor people." American Journal of Orthopsychiatry 38 (April): 457–463.

Andersen, R.
  1968   A Behavioral Model of Families' Use of Health Services. Chicago: University of Chicago, Center for Health Administration Studies.

Andersen, R., O. W. Anderson, *and* B. Smedby
  1968   "Perceptions of and response to symptoms of illness in Sweden and the United States." Medical Care 6: 18–30.

Andersen, R., L. M. Gunter, *and* E. Kennedy
  1963   "Evaluations of clinical, cultural and psychosomatic influences in the teaching and management of diabetic patients." American Journal of Medical Science 76:682–690.

Antonovsky, A.
  1972   "A model to explain visits to the doctor: With special reference to the case of Israel." Journal of Health and Human Behavior 13 (December): 446–454.

Apple, D.
  1960   "How laymen define illness." Journal of Health and Human Behavior 1 (Fall): 219–225.

Babchuck, N. *and* A. Booth
  1969   "Voluntary association membership: A longitudinal analysis." American Social Review 34 (February): 31–45.

Babchuck, N. *and* A. Edwards
  1965   "Voluntary associations and the integration hypothesis." Sociological Inquiry 35 (Spring): 149–162.

Battistella, R. M.
    1968a   "Factors associated with delay in the initiation of physi-
             cians' care among late adulthood persons." American
             Journal of Public Health 61 (July): 1348–1361.
    1968b   "Limitations in use of the concept of psychological readi-
             ness to initiate health care." Medical Care 6: 308–319.

Baumann, B. O.
    1961   "Diversities in conceptions of health and physical fitness."
             Journal of Health and Human Behavior 2: 39–46.

Beck, B.
    1967   "Welfare as a moral category." Social Problems 14 (Win-
             ter): 258–277.

Becker, H.
    1963   Outsiders: Studies in the Sociology of Deviance. New
             York: The Free Press.
    1967   "Whose side are we on?" Social Problems 14 (Winter):
             239–247.

Ben-David, J.
    1958   "The professional role of the physician in bureaucratized
             medicine." Human Relations 11 (August): 255–274.

Bergner, L. *and* A. Yerby
    1968   "Low income and barriers to use of health services." New
             England Journal of Medicine 278 (10): 541–546.

Berkman, P.
    1969   "Spouseless motherhood, psychological stress and physical
             morbidity." Journal of Health and Social Behavior 10 (4):
             323–334.

Bernstein, B.
    1959   "A public language: Some sociological implications of a
             linguistic form." British Journal of Sociology 10 (Decem-
             ber): 311–326.
    1967   "Social class and linquistic development." Pp. 288–314 in
             Halsey, A. H., J. Floud, *and* C. A. Anderson (eds.), Edu-
             cation, Economy and Society. New York: The Free Press.

Bice, T. W.
    1971   Medical Care for the Disadvantaged. Baltimore: Johns
             Hopkins University, Department of Medical Care and Hos-
             pitals.

Birnbaum, A.
  1970   "On managing and courtesy stigma." Journal of Health and
          Social Behavior 11 (June): 196–206.
Blau, P. M.
  1969-61 "Orientation towards clients in a public welfare agency."
          Administration Science Quarterly 5: 341–361.
Blauner, R.
  1964   Alienation and Freedom. Chicago: University of Chicago
          Press.
Blum, Z. D. *and* H. Rossi
  1969   "Social class research and images of the poor: A biblio-
          graphic review." Pp. 343–397 in Moynihan, D. P. (ed.),
          On Understanding Poverty. New York: Basic Books.
Bradburn, N. H. *and* D. Caplovitz
  1965   Reports on Happiness. Chicago: Aldine Publishing Co.
Bredemeier, H. C.
  1964   "The socially handicapped and the agencies: A market
          analysis." Pp. 205–235 in Riessman, F., J. Cohen, *and* A.
          Pearl (eds.), Mental Health of the Poor. New York: The
          Free Press.
Clark, B.
  1960   "The 'cooling out' function in higher education." American
          Journal of Sociology 65 (May): 569–576.
Cloward, R. *and* I. Epstein
  1965   "Private social welfare's disengagement from the poor. The
          case of family adjustment agencies." Pp. 623–644 in Zald,
          M. N. (ed.), Social Welfare Institutions. New York: John
          Wiley and Sons.
Coe, R. M., J. M. Goering, *and* M. Cummins
  1969   Health Status of Low Income Families in an Urban Area.
          Final Report for the Bi-State Regional Medical Program.
          St. Louis: Medical Care Research Center.
Cohen, A. K. *and* H. M. Hodges
  1962   "Characteristics of the lower blue-collar class." Social Prob-
          lems 10 (Spring): 303–335.
Cole, S. *and* R. Lejeune
  1972   "Illness and the legitimation of failure." American Socio-
          logical Review 37 (June): 347–356.

Conference of the Society for Psychosomatic Research, Royal College of
Physicians
1959   The Nature of Stress Disorder. Springfield, Ill.: C. C.
        Thomas.
Converse, P.
1963   Attitudes and Non-Attitudes; Continuation of a Dialogue.
        Washington, D.C.: International Congress of Psychiatry.
Coser, L. A.
1969   "Some unanticipated conservative consequences of liberal
        theorizing." Social Problems 16 (Winter): 263–272.
Crandell, D. L. *and* B. P. Dohrenwend
1967   "Some relations among psychiatric symptoms, organic ill-
        ness and social class." American Journal of Psychiatry 123:
        1527–1538.
Croog, S. H.
1961   "Ethnic origins, educational level and responses to a health
        questionnaire." Human Organization 10 (Summer):
        65–69.
Cumming, J. *and* E. Cumming
1965   "On the stigma of mental illness." Community Mental
        Health Journal 1: 135–143.
Curtis, R. F.
1959   "Occupational mobility and membership in formal volun-
        tary associations: A note on research." American Sociologi-
        cal Review 34 (December): 846–848.
Danet, B.
1971   "The language of persuasion in bureaucracy: 'Modern' and
        'traditional' appeals to the Israel customs authorities."
        American Sociological Review 36 (October): 847–859.
Davis, F.
1961   "Deviance disavowal: The management of strained interac-
        tion by the visibly handicapped." Social Problems 9
        (June): 120–132.
Dean, D. G.
1961   "Alienation: Its meaning and measurement." American So-
        ciological Review 26 (October): 753–758.
Deasey, L. E.
1956   "Socio-economic status and participation in the poliomylitis
        vaccine trial." American Sociological Review 21 (April):
        185.

Deisher, R. W., et al.
  1965   "Mothers' opinions of their pediatric care." Pediatrics 35
           (January): 82–90.
diCicco, L. *and* D. Apple
  1958   "Health needs and opinions of older adults." Public Health
           Reports 73: 479–481.
Dodge, D. *and* W. T. Martin
  1970   Social Stress and Chronic Illness: Mortality Patterns in In-
           dustrial Society. Notre Dame, Indiana: University of Notre
           Dame Press.
Durkheim, E.
  1933   Suicide. Glencoe, Illinois: The Free Press.
Engel, C. L.
  1967   "Psychogenic pain." Journal of Occupational Medicine 3:
           249–257.
Epstein, F. H., E. P. Boas, *and* R. Simpson
  1957   "The epidemiology of arteriosclerosis among a random
           sample of clothing workers of different ethnic origins in
           New York City: I and II." Journal of Chronic Diseases 5:
           300–341.
Fabrega, H., R. Moore, *and* J. Strawn
  1969   "Low income, medical problem patients: Some medical and
           behavioral features." Journal of Health and Social Behavior
           10 (4): 334–343.
Feldman, J. J.
  1966   The Dissemination of Health Information. Chicago: Aldine
           Publishing Co.
Festinger, L.
  1964   "Behavioral support for opinion change." Public Opinion
           Quarterly 28 (Fall): 404–417.
Feuer, L.
  1963   "What is alienation? The career of a concept." New Politics
           1 (Spring): 116–134.
Fisher, B. M.
  1969   "Claims and credibility: A discussion of occupational iden-
           tity and the agent-client relationship." Social Problems 16
           (Spring): 423–433.
Francis, V., B. M. Korsch, *and* M. Morris
  1969   "Gaps in doctor-patient communication: Patients' responses

to medical advice." New England Journal of Medicine 280: 535–540.

Friedsam, H. J. *and* H. W. Martin
1963   "A comparison of self and physicians' health ratings in an older population." Journal of Health and Human Behavior 4: 179–183.

Fromm, E.
1955   The Sane Society. New York: Rinehart and Company.

Gans, H. J.
1962   The Urban Villagers. New York: The Free Press.

Garfinkel, H.
1967   Studies in Ethnomethodology. Engelwood Cliffs: Prentice-Hall.

Gibbs, J. P.
1962   "Rates of mental hospitalization: A study of societal reaction to deviant behavior." American Sociological Review 27 (December): 782–792.

Glaser, B. G. *and* A. L. Strauss
1965   Awareness of Dying. Chicago: Aldine Publishing Co.

Goffman, E.
1959   The Presentation of Self in Everyday Life. New York: Doubleday.
1961   Asylums. Chicago: Aldine Publishing Co.
1963   Stigma. Engelwood Cliffs: Prentice-Hall.

Gordon, G.
1966   Role Theory and Illness: A Sociological Perspective. New Haven, Conn.: College and University Press.

Gray, R. M., J. P. Kesler, *and* P. M. Moody
1967   "Alienation and immunization participation." Rocky Mountain Social Science Journal 4 (April): 161–168.

Hausknecht, M.
1964   "The blue-collar joiner." Pp. 402–431 in Shostak, A. B. *and* W. Gomberg (eds.), Blue Collar World. Englewood Cliffs: Prentice-Hall.

Hegel, G. F. W.
1955   The Phenomenology of Mind, 2nd ed., rev. New York: Macmillan and Co.

Hessler, R. M., P. Kubish, P. Kong Ming New, P. L. Ellison, *and* F. H. Taylor

1971 "Demographic context, social interaction and perceived health status: Excedrin headache #1." Journal of Health and Social Behavior 12 (3): 191–199.

Hetherington, R. W. *and* C. E. Hopkins
1969 "Symptom sensitivity: Its social and cultural correlates." Health Services Research 4 (1): 63–75.

Hinkle, L., R. Redmont, N. Plummer, *and* H. Wolff
1960 "An examination of the relation between symptoms, disability and serious illness in two homogeneous groups of men and women." American Journal of Public Health 50: 1327–1336.

Hochbaum, G. M.
1958 Public Participation in Medical Screening Programs: A Socio-Psychological Study. Washington, D. C.: Government Printing Office.

Hochstim, J. R.
1968 "Poverty area under the microscope." American Journal of Public Health 58 (10): 1815–1827.

Hollingshead, A. B. *and* F. C. Redlich
1958 Social Class and Mental Illness. New York: John Wiley and Sons.

Holmes, T. H.
1951 "Psychosocial and psychophysiological studies of tuberculosis." Psychosomatic Medicine 19: 134–143.

Hulka, B., S. Thompson, J. Cassel, *and* S. Zyzanski
1971 "Satisfaction with medical care in a low-income population." Journal of Chronic Disease 24: 661–673.

Hunt, R. G., O. Gurrslin, *and* J. L. Roach
1958 "Social status and psychiatric service in a child guidance clinic." American Sociological Review 23 (February): 81–83.

Hyman, H. *and* C. R. Wright
1971 "Trends in voluntary association memberships of American adults: Replication based on secondary analysis of national sample surveys." American Sociological Review 36 (April): 191–206.

Jackson, E. F.
1962 "Status inconsistency and symptoms of stress." American Sociological Review 27 (August): 469–480.

Jackson, E. F. *and* Peter J. Burke
   1965   "Status and symptoms of stress: Additive and Interaction
             effects." American Sociological Review 30 (August):
             556–564.
Jaffe, F. S. *and* S. Polgar
   1968   "Family planning and public policy: Is the 'culture of pov-
             erty' the new cop-out?" Journal of Marriage and the Fami-
             ly 30 (May): 228–235.
Janis, I. L.
   1958   Psychological Stress. New York: John Wiley and Sons.
Janowitz, M. *and* W. Delany
   1957–58   "The bureaucrat and the public: A study of informa-
             tional perspectives." Administrative Science Quarterly
             2: 141–162.
Jeffreys, M.
   1957   "Social class and health promotion." The Health Education
             Journal 15 (May): 109–117.
Jenkins, C. D.
   1966   "The semantic differential for health: A Technique for
             measuring beliefs about diseases." Public Health Reports 81
             (6): 549–558.
Jones, E. E.
   1964   Ingratiation. New York: Appleton-Century-Crofts.
Kadushin, C.
   1967   "Social class and ill health: The need for further research.
             A reply to Antonovsky." Sociological Inquiry 37: 323–332.
Kalimo, E.
   1969   Determinants of Medical Care Utilization. Helsinki: Re-
             search Institute for Social Services, National Pensions Insti-
             tute.
Kasl, S. *and* S. Cobb
   1966   "Health behavior and sick role behavior." Archives of En-
             vironmental Health 2: 246–266.
Katz, E. *and* B. Danet
   1966   "Petitions and persuasive appeals: A study of official-client
             relations." American Sociological Review 31 (December):
             811–822.
Kegeles, S. S.
   1967   "Attitudes and behavior of the public regarding cervical cy-

tology: Current findings and new directions for research."
Journal of Chronic Diseases 20 (December): 911–922.

Kegeles, S. S., J. P. Kirscht, D. P. Haefner, *and* I. M. Rosenstock
1965   "Survey of beliefs about cancer detection and taking pap-
anicoloau tests." Public Health Reports 80: 815–824.

Kirscht, J. P.
1971   "Social and psychological problems of surveys on health
and illness." Social Science and Medicine 5: 519–526.

Kirscht, J. P., D. P. Haefner, S. S. Kegeles, *and* I. M. Rosenstock
1966   "A national study of health beliefs." Journal of Health and
Human Behavior 7: 248–254.

Kitsuse, J.
1962   "Societal relations to deviant behavior: Problems of theory
and method." Social Problems 9 (Winter): 247–256.

Koos, E. L.
1954   The Health of Regionville: What the People Thought and
Did About It. New York: Columbia University Press.

Kosa, J., J. J. Alpert, *and* R. J Haggerty
1967   "On the reliability of family health information: A comparative study of mothers' reports on illness and related behavior." Social Science Medicine 1 (July): 165–181.

Kutner, B. *and* G. Gordon
1961   "Seeking care for cancer." Journal of Health and Human
Behavior 2: 128–145.

Lee, A. M.
1972   "An obituary for 'alienation.'" Social Problems 20 (Summer): 121–127.

Leiffer, R.
1966–67 "Involuntary psychiatric hospitalization and social control." International Journal of Social Psychiatry 13:
53–58.

Lemert, E. M.
1951   Social Pathology. New York: McGraw-Hill.

Lerner, M.
1969   "Social differences in physical health." Pp. 69–112 in Kosa,
J., A. Antonovsky, *and* I. Zola (eds.), Poverty and Health.
Cambridge: Harvard University Press.

Leventhal, H., I. M. Rosenstock, *and* G. M. Hochbaum
1960   The Impact of Asian Influenza on Coming Life: A Study

in Five Cities. Washington, D. C.: Government Printing
Office.

Levin, J. *and* G. Taube
    1970   "Bureaucracy and the socially handicapped: A study of
lower-status tenants in public housing." Sociology and
Social Research 54 (February): 209–219.

Lindenberg, R. E.
    1958   "Hard to reach: Client or casework agency." Social Work 3
(October): 23–29.

Linsky, A. S.
    1970   "Who shall be excluded: The influence of personal attrib-
utes in community reaction to the mentally ill." Social
Psychiatry 5: 166–171.

Ludwig, E. *and* G. Gibson
    1969   "Self perception of sickness and the seeking of medical
care." Journal of Health and Social Behavior 10: 125–133.

Maddox, G. L.
    1964   "Self-assessment of Health Status: A longitudinal study of
selected elderly subjects." Journal of Chronic Diseases
17: 449–460.

Marx, K.
    1963   Early Writings. London: C. A. Watts and Co.

McBroom, W. H.
    1970   "Illness, illness behavior and socio-economic status." Jour-
nal of Health and Social Behavior 11 (December):
319–326.

McGrath, J. E. (ed.)
    1970   Social and Psychological Factors in Stress. New York:
Holt, Rinehart and Winston, Inc.

McKinlay, J. B.
    1968   "Better maternity care for whom. . . ?" Medical Officer
3147 (November 15): 275–276.

    1972a   "Some approaches and problems in the study of the use of
services: An overview." Journal of Health and Social Behavior 13 (June): 115–152.

    1972b   "The sick role—illness and pregnancy." Social Science
and Medicine 6: 561–572.

Mechanic, D.
    1964   "The influence of mothers on their children's attitudes and
behavior." Pediatrics 33: 444–453.

1969   "Illness and cure." Pp. 191–214 in Kosa, J., A. Antonovsky, *and* I. Zola (eds.), Poverty and Health. Cambridge: Harvard University Press.

Mechanic, D. *and* E. H. Volkhart
1961   "Stress, illness, behavior, and the sick role." American Sociological Review 26: 51–58.

Meile, Richard L.
1972   "The 22-item index of psychophysiological disorder: Psychological or organic symptoms?" Social Science Medicine 6: 125–135.

Meile, R. J. *and* P. N. Haese
1969   "Social status, status incongruence and symptoms of stress." Journal of Health and Social Behavior 10 (3): 237–244.

Miller, S. M.
1964   "The American lower classes: A typological approach." Sociology and Social Research 48 (Spring): 1–22.

Mills, C. W.
1956   The Power Elite. New York: Oxford University Press.

Moody, P. M. *and* R. M. Gray
1972   "Social class, social integration, and the use of preventive health services." Pp. 250–261 in Jaco, E. G. (ed.), Patients, Physicians and Illness. New York: The Free Press.

Morris, N., M. H. Hatch, *and* S. S. Chipman
1966a   "Alienation as a deterrent to well-child supervision." American Journal of Public Health 56 (November): 187–192.
1966b   "Deterrents to well-child supervision." American Journal of Public Health 56 (August): 1232–1241.

National Center for Health Statistics
1967   Three Views of Hypertension and Heart Disease. Washington, D.C.: Government Printing Office.

Nisbet, R. A.
1966   The Sociological Tradition. New York: Basic Books.

Osofsky, H. J.
1968   "After office hours: Some social psychological issues improving obstetric care for the poor." Obstetrics and Gynaecology 31 (March): 437–443.

Paul, B.
1958   "The role of beliefs and customs of sanitation programs." American Journal of Public Health 48 (November): 1502–1506.

Pratt, L.
  1971   "The relationship of SES to health." American Journal of
          Public Health 61: 281–291.
Rahe, R. H.
  1964   "Social stress and illness onset." Journal of Psychosomatic
          Research 8: 35–44.
Rahe, R. H., R. J. Biersner, D. H. Ryman, *and* R. J. Arthur
  1972   "Psychosocial predictors of illness behavior and failure in
          stressful training." Journal of Health and Social Behavior 3
          (December): 393–397.
Reader, G. G., L. Pratt, *and* M. C. Mudd
  1967   "What patients expect from their doctors." Modern Hospi-
          tal 89 (July): 88–94.
Richardson, W. C.
  1970   "Measuring the urban poor's use of physician services in re-
          sponse to illness episodes.' Medical Care 8: 132–142.
Robinson, D.
  1971   The Process of Becoming Ill. London: Routledge and Ke-
          gan Paul.
Rosenblatt, D. A. *and* E. A. Suchman
  1964a   "Blue-collar attitudes and information toward health and
          illness." Pp. 324–333 in Shostak, A. B. *and* W. Gomberg
          (eds.), Blue Collar World. Englewood Cliffs, N.J.: Pren-
          tice-Hall.
  1964b   "The underutilization of medical care services by blue col-
          larites." Pp. 341–349 in Shostak, A. B. *and* W. Gomberg
          (eds.), Blue Collar World. Englewood Cliffs, N.J.: Pren-
          tice-Hall.
Rosengren, W. R.
  1964   "Social class and becoming ill." Pp. 362–370 in Shostak, A.
          B. *and* W. Gomberg (eds.), Blue Collar World. Englewood
          Cliffs, N.J.: Prentice-Hall.
Rosenstock, I. M.
  1966   "Why people use health services." Milbank Memorial Fund
          Quarterly 44 (3, Part 2): 94–127.
  1969   "Prevention of illness and maintenance of health." Pp.
          168–190 in Kosa, J., A. Antonovsky *and* I. Zola (eds.),
          Poverty and Health. Cambridge: Harvard University Press.
Rosenstock, I. M., D. P. Haefner, S. S. Kegeles, *and* J. P. Kirscht
  1966   "Public knowledge, opinion and action concerning three

public health issues: Radioactive fallout, insect and plant sprays and fatty foods." Journal of Health and Human Behavior 7 (2): 91–98.

Samora, J., L. Saunders, *and* R. F. Larson
    1961   "Medical vocabulary knowledge among hospital patients." Journal of Health and Human Behavior 2: 83–92.

Schatzman, L. *and* A. Strauss
    1955   "Social class and modes of communication." American Journal of Sociology 60 (January): 329–338.

Scheff, T. J.
    1964   "Preferred errors in diagnosis." Medical Care 2 (July/September): 166–172.

    1966   "Typification in the diagnostic practices of rehabilitation agencies." Pp. 139–147 in Sussman, M. B. (ed.), Sociology and Rehabilitation. Washington, D.C.: American Sociological Association.

Scheff, T. J. *and* E. Sundstrom
    1970   "The stability of deviant behavior over time: A reassessment." Journal of Health and Social Behavior 11: 37–43.

Schneiderman, L.
    1965   "Social class, diagnosis and treatment." American Journal of Orthopsychiatry 35 (January): 99–105.

Schonfeld, J. et al.
    1963   "Medical attitudes and practices of parents toward a mass tubercular testing program." American Journal of Public Health 53: 14–18.

Scott, R. A.
    1967   "The selection of clients by social welfare agencies: The case of the blind." Social Problems 14 (Winter): 248–257.

Seeman, M.
    1959   "On the meaning of alienation." American Sociological Review 24 (December): 783–791.

Seeman, M. *and* J. W. Evans
    1961   "Stratification and hospital care I: The Performance of the medical intern." American Sociological Review 26 (February): 67–80.

    1962   "Alienation and learning in a hospital setting." American Sociological Review 27 (December): 772–782.

Shostak, A. B. *and* W. Gomberg (eds.)
    1964   Blue Collar World. Englewood Cliffs, N.J.: Prentice-Hall.

Sjoberg, G., R. A. Bryner, *and* B. Farris
   1963   "Bureaucracy and the lower class." Sociology and Social
            Research 50 (April): 325–337.
Sparer, P. (ed.)
   1956   Personality, Stress and Tuberculosis. New York: Interna-
            tional University Press.
Steele, J. L. *and* W. H. McBroom
   1972   "Conceptual and empirical dimensions of health behavior."
            Journal of Health and Social Behavior 13 (December):
            382–392.
Stoeckle, J. D., I. K. Zola, *and* G. E. Davidson
   1963   "On going to see the doctor, the contributions of the patient
            to the decision to seek medical aid: A selected review."
            Journal of Chronic Diseases 16: 975–989.
Suchman, E. A.
   1964   "Sociological variations among ethnic groups." American
            Journal of Sociology 70: 319–331.
   1965a   "Social factors in medical deprivation." American Journal
            of Public Health 55 (11): 1725–1733.
   1965b   "Stages of illness and medical care." Journal of Health
            and Human Behavior 6: 114–128.
Suchman, E. A., B. S. Phillips, *and* G. F. Streib
   1958   "An analysis of the validity of health questionaires." So-
            cial Forces 36: 223–232.
Taglacozzo, D. M. *and* I. Taglacozzo
   1970   "Knowledge of illness as a predictor of patient behavior.'
            Journal of Chronic Diseases 22: 765–775.
Travis, G.
   1961   Chronic Disease and Disability. Berkeley: University of
            California Press.
Twaddle, A. C.
   1969   "Decisions and sick role variations: An exploration." Jour-
            nal of Health and Social Behavior 10 (2): 105–115.
Voysey, M.
   1972a   "Impression management by parents with disabled chil-
            dren." Journal of Health and Social Behavior 13
            (March): 80–89.
   1972b   "Official agents and the legitimation of suffering." The So-
            ciological Review 20 (November): 533–551.

Walsh, J. L. *and* R. H. Elling
   1968   "Professionalism and the poor: Structural effects and pro-
             fessional behavior." Journal of Health and Social Behavior
             9 (March): 16–28.
Watts, D.
   1966   "Factors related to the acceptance of modern medicine."
             American Journal of Public Health 56 (8): 1205–1212.
Wilensky, H. L.
   1964   "The professionalization of everyone?" American Journal
             of Sociology 70 (September): 137–158.
Williams, T. F. et al.
   1965   "The clinical picture of diabetic control, studied in four set-
             tings." Paper presented before the Association of Public
             Health Administrators Meeting, Chicago, Illinois.
Young, M. *and* P. Willmott
   1960   Family and Class in a London Suburb. London: Routledge
             and Kegan Paul.
Zald, M. N. (ed.)
   1965   Social Welfare Institutions. New York: John Wiley and
             Sons.
Zborowski, M.
   1958   "Cultural components in response to pain." Pp. 256–268 in
             Jaco, F. G. (ed.), Patients, Physicians, and Illness. Glen-
             coe, Illinois: The Free Press.
Zola, I. K.
   1963a   "Problems of communication, doctors, and patient care:
             The interplay of patient, physician, and clinic organiza-
             tion." Journal of Medical Education 38: 829–838.
   1963b   "Socio-cultural factors in the seeking of medical aid: A
             progress report." Trans-Cultural Psychiatric Research
             14:62–65.
   1964   "Illness behavior of the working class: Implications and rec-
             ommendations." Pp. 350–361 in Shostak, A. B. *and* W.
             Gomberg (eds.), Blue Collar World. Englewood Cliffs:
             Prentice-Hall.
   1966   "Culture and symptoms—an analysis of patients' presenting
             complaints." American Sociological Review 31: 615–630.
   1972   "Medicine as an institution of social control." The Sociolog-
             ical Review 20: 487–504.

The

Satisfaction Continuum

in Health Care: Consumer

and Provider Preferences*

MARIAN OSTERWEIS RIVKIN
AND PATRICIA J. BUSH

In designing health-care systems, many questions that relate to satisfactions must be answered. Given a choice, what do people prefer? Are consumer and provider preferences in conflict? Without firsthand experience with alternatives, is it worthwhile to ask about preferences? Will people accept changes? How widespread is the current dissatisfaction with medical care? Should we worry about dissatisfaction? Although the medical care system is criticized for a variety of reasons, are people, in fact, rejecting the current system and/or the innovations? This paper will review what is presently known about these questions on both the consumer and provider sides.

One output of the incentive-disincentive structure in health care is the satisfaction or dissatisfaction of those involved in that system. If consumers of health services are dissatisfied they may render

* The authors are grateful for the assistance of Thomas W. Bice in conceptualizing the problem and to Mary S. Albert for her suggestions.

those services less effective, either by neglecting to seek care when needed or by refusing to comply with the prescribed course of treatment. If providers are dissatisfied with the organization of practice they may give less or poorer quality of care.

Measuring satisfaction is in vogue. Many requests for proposals on the evaluation of health services from the government ask specifically about consumer and provider satisfactions. However, relatively little work has been done in this area (when compared with utilization, for example); methodology is weak, and we know much less about providers than we do about consumers. The set of attitudes that we refer to as satisfactions lies on a continuum and is the output of interactions between a person and a system or between two persons.

There are considerable problems in measuring satisfaction. While observable behavior is objective (and, therefore, frequently preferable to questionnaires), those studies in which satisfaction and dissatisfaction are indicated by use or nonuse of services are too limited. We suggest a continuum, rather than a dichotomy, ranging from preference through satisfaction or acceptance through dissatisfaction to rejection.

1. To *prefer* a condition implies knowledge of alternatives. While a person may accept an arrangement, given a choice, he may actually prefer another.

2. To be *satisfied* with or to accept a condition means to be contented with it.

3. To be *dissatisfied* implies some discontentment, usually having a specific cause and often temporary.

4. To *reject* is to refuse.

Each point on the continuum is, of course, affected by the values, beliefs, and expectations people bring to any particular situation and by the interactions that occur in that situation.

In examining the current incentive-disincentive structure and in designing changes in the health-delivery system, every point on the satisfaction continuum is important.

Unfortunately, none of the methods used to measure satisfaction is without considerable problems. If we ask those who are not in a particular situation, we are usually asking the uninformed; if we ask those who are in the situation, we are asking the self-selected; if we ask those who have been in the situation, we are asking those who may be reinterpreting their history in the light of new knowledge. Nor are we cheered by knowing that attitudinal reports are not likely to predict future behavior, or that what people report they think is best is not necessarily what they report they prefer (LaPiere, 1934; Scholton et al., 1966; Feldman, 1966; Colombotos, 1968).

Furthermore, theories of cognitive dissonance have taught us that there is a tendency for people to try to achieve consonance between their behavior, their attitudes, and their surroundings. Therefore, if we ask, for example, a patient or physician in a health maintenance organization (HMO) if he is satisfied with that organization, we should not be surprised to hear "yes." We can theorize about the disadvantages of bureaucratic medicine, but once an individual (either consumer or provider) has chosen to participate in that bureaucracy, for him to express major dissatisfaction would upset his cognitive consonance.

Thus, presumably the degree of satisfaction results from a comparison between what is wanted and what is, i.e., a preference-reality comparison. When preferences are not well articulated, which may be the case in health care where clear alternatives usually do not exist, people tend to fall in the middle of the continuum. However, it is possible for consumers or providers to have one position on the satisfaction continuum with respect to the health system, but quite another with respect to the particular organization, its parts or personnel, that has been organized to implement the system. Furthermore, satisfactions may be fluid, depending on such factors as severity of illness or availability of alternatives that affect consumer-provider interaction.

The Consumer's View

Many people seem to be complaining about a general crisis in medical care and about the inadequacies of the present system.

Some of the complaints reflect the well-known "pendulum effect," which has yet to reach its equilibrium point. For example, twenty or thirty years ago there were few specialists. Now there are many specialists, but not enough generalists. Today the public looks back wistfully to the days of the family general practitioner and decries fragmentation and lack of continuity in medical care.

Other, and more serious, changes in the public's expectations reflect the mood and philosophy of the nation as a whole. The 1960s brought the civil rights movement and Moynihan's (1969) "maximum feasible participation." The 1960s also introduced the idea that health is a right, not a privilege. If health is a right, then it is legitimate for consumers to complain about present inadequacies and to demand minimal health care for everyone that is accessible and affordable. If health is a right, the government should take some responsibility for controlling the costs and quality of health care. And if there are to be changes, the consumer expects to be part of the decision-making process, in both the planning and delivery of services (Andersen et al., 1971; Glasser, 1972; Mechanic, 1972; Strickland, 1972).

The results of two recent nationwide surveys (Andersen et al., 1971; Strickland, 1972) indicate that there is indeed a widespread belief that we are in "crisis" but that dissatisfactions with specific aspects of medical care are much more restricted. Furthermore, it appears that the perception of crisis and the desire for change are not inconsistent with the public's pervasive confidence in its ability to get good medical care as needed.

Andersen and his colleagues (1971) found that, overall, three-fourths of the 3,232 households in their national survey believed there was a crisis in health care and that ninety-six percent of the nonwhite, nonpoor people over age sixty-five believed there was such a crisis. The figures are astounding. Yet when asked about specific components of six presumably critical aspects of care (quality, cost, accessibility, courtesy, adequacy of information given by physicians, and coordination of care), people voiced widespread dissatisfaction about only two: cost (thirty-eight percent) and accessibility (thirty-eight percent thought waiting times were too long, forty-three percent thought medical care was not readily available at night and on weekends). Dissatisfaction with other aspects of care was expressed by fewer than twenty percent of those surveyed.

Strickland (1972) found that although "changes in the health care system are desired by most (sixty-one percent) and anticipated by all," eighty-four percent of the public think they can get good medical care. Thus, seemingly contradictory feelings are generalized in the population, cutting across all socio-demographic lines. Those who were most likely to have high confidence in their ability to get good care (those with high education and income, the white, and the young) were also the most likely to desire change and to perceive the "crisis." The crucial problems were thought to be a shortage of physicians and various aspects of cost. Again, results were fairly consistent across all groups with a few notable exceptions: the oldest and least educated felt that physicians' refusal to make house calls was the most crucial problem, and the youngest claimed that poor living conditions were the chief problem. The public's first priority in restructuring the system is to increase the accessibility of care.

Patients, Their Doctors, and the Treatment Process

Physicians are often quoted as saying that laymen, because they lack clinical knowledge, are in no position to evaluate the medical care they receive. Alpert et al. (1970), Leonard et al. (1967), and Freidson (1961) found that patients tend to assume technical competence on the part of medical practitioners and are most concerned with physicians' interest—their willingness to talk and to answer questions and their ability to convey to the patient a sense of personal worth. Patients want doctors to show concern and to communicate effectively about medical problems. When asked specifically about competence, consumers emphasize the need for good equipment and facilities and reliance on tests and specialists for diagnosis; they are more satisfied if physicians try to actively intervene in illness. Often patients relate the time spent by the physician to his competence (Freidson, 1961).

Alpert et al. (1970) found that some of the common dissatisfactions with organizational characteristics, such as waiting time, could be modified by good doctor-patient relationships. And Freidson (1961) found that interest and sympathy shown by receptionists, aides, and nurses can mediate between doctors and patients. Thus, it appears that if at least some of the staff take an active interest in patients, dissatisfaction with the doctor-patient interactions can be allayed and dissatisfaction with organizational shortcomings can, in turn, be overcome.

Why is a satisfactory doctor-patient relationship so important? Many studies have shown that dissatisfaction with or distrust in doctor-patient relationships can affect treatment outcomes (Alpert et al., 1970; Leonard et al., 1967; Pratt et al., 1957; Davis, 1966, 1968a, b; Francis et al., 1969; Vuori et al., 1972).

In his review of compliance behavior, Davis (1966) found that an average of one-third of the patients in a variety of clinical circumstances fail to comply with doctors' orders. Women, the less educated, and older people are less likely to follow orders (Davis, 1968b). Charney (1972) reported that in several specific instances, such as orders to stop smoking and orders for diabetic treatment and rheumatic fever prophylaxis, social class factors were not important. He postulated that "as factors within the patient-doctor relationship or the disease itself increase in importance—where the patient is likely to be treated as an *individual* rather than as a *group member*—social class factors diminish in importance."

Several empirical studies show that gaps in doctor-patient communication affect compliance. Good communication requires that physicians deal with the "whole patient"—psychological and social, as well as medical. Lack of feedback from doctors or tension in the relationship leads to noncompliance. Francis et al. (1969) found in their study of eight hundred outpatient visits to Childrens' Hospital of Los Angeles that mothers expected and wanted to learn the cause and nature of their children's illness. When their expectation was met, mothers were satisfied and were more apt to comply with followup instructions than they otherwise would be. The study found that neither socioeconomic status (income and education) nor ethnic background was significantly related to compliant behavior. Friendliness of the doctor and high satisfaction due to expectations having been met in the interaction were significantly related to compliance. Seriousness of the illness as perceived by the mother, complexity of instructions, and practical circumstances also had a significant influence on compliance, regardless of satisfaction.

Vuori et al. (1972) found that, for hospitalized patients, expressive factors of physicians were most important for the doctor-patient relationship, while outpatients were more concerned about instrumental behavior of their physicians (e.g., thoroughness of examination and establishment of a diagnosis).

Leonard et al. (1967) and Pratt et al. (1957) found that nurses and other staff could alter the physician's effect by listening to patients and giving them explanations. With more thorough explanations, even from someone other than the physician, patients were more likely to accept the doctor's diagnosis and treatment and to comply. Thus, it seems that there is a causal connection between staff-patient interaction and the quality of care as measured by the outcome of treatment. That outcome (cure, improvement, stability, etc.) frequently depends on compliance with the treatment regimen, which in turn depends on satisfaction with the interaction.

Although some studies caution against placing too much emphasis on satisfaction (Charney, 1972; Mechanic, 1972), arguing that patients do not know enough to judge appropriately, we argue that if satisfaction influences the treatment process, if only because of a placebo effect, it is important (Bush, in press). If consumers or providers perform less well because they are dissatisfied with a situation, their perception—however idiosyncratic or inappropriately determined—becomes important to the system's overall functioning. And we believe that the success or failure of any system depends ultimately on client and provider satisfaction with that system.

Solutions to the Crisis in Theory and Practice

How would consumers prefer to see the health-care system restructured? How have consumers reacted to limited innovations in the organization of health care, especially to use of paramedical personnel and to HMOs?

In the two recent national surveys cited earlier (Andersen et al., 1971; Strickland, 1972), consumers were asked about proposed solutions to the crisis. In the Andersen study, opinions were asked about extension of Medicare, national health insurance, physician payment, and delegation of tasks to nonphysicians. High-income whites over age sixty-five were most resistant to extending Medicare. Thirty-four percent of those surveyed thought it should cover all people who could not afford their own health insurance, and eighteen percent said Medicare should extend to the entire population. Eighty-one percent of low-income, working-age blacks favored extension.

Although seventy-seven percent favored national health insurance in general, a significant number of respondents foresaw problems, including interference with physicians' decisions on treatment, too much government regulation, overutilization of medical care, and longer waits to see doctors. Fifty percent of those surveyed thought that fee-for-service encouraged better care, thirty-eight percent said payment did not affect service, and only twelve percent said physicians should be salaried.

Strickland (1972) also found that education, age, and professional and economic status affected consumer priorities. There was, however, broad agreement on the federal role in health policy. Forty-six percent said the government should have primary responsibility for national health insurance; forty percent said the federal role should be to administer a national program. Clearly, according to those surveyed, the government should not take over the health system but should bear the responsibility for holding down costs. Great confidence was expressed in the ability of the American Medical Association (AMA) to develop new federal health legislation (seventy-four percent of those surveyed), but little confidence was expressed in labor unions (except by households of union members). Eighty-two percent thought that local physicians and citizens should determine how to spend the money. The public exhibited great faith in consumer participation in planning, a view not shared by physicians.

Little difference was found by age, race, or income concerning task delegation to physician assistants (PAs), but there was great variation in the tasks people were willing to have delegated. Eighty-seven percent said PAs could perform the preliminaries of medical examinations, sixty-seven percent said they could handle follow-up care, fifty-four percent said they could provide normal prenatal and well-baby care, and only thirty-three percent said they would trust PAs to do triage. These findings are more enthusiastic than Rivkin and Sehnert's (1973) findings among women of childbearing age: ninety-eight percent thought physicians should be relieved of some of their duties, but only four percent thought PAs should handle prenatal care. Litman (1972) found similar responses in rural Iowa and Minnesota. Sixty-six percent said they would accept a PA if his services were sanctioned by their own family doctor. Most thought routine histories and physicals, simple emergencies, normal postnatal care, and immunizations could be delegated, but seventy-one percent would be unwilling for a midwife to handle normal deliveries even when supervised by a physician, and sixty-six percent opposed delegating screening and triage to nonphysicians.

Empirical evidence suggests that factors leading to acceptance of new manpower vary according to geographic location, type of practice, medical problem, and socio-demographic characteristics of patients. Use of physician assistants and nurse practitioners is less common in urban areas than in rural areas, where it is widely accepted because of the shortage of physicians (Adamson, 1971).

In private practice, acceptance of new personnel depends largely on the physician. If he informs his patients, explains the need, and is enthusiastic, acceptance tends to be high (Silver, 1969; Fairweather and Kifolo, 1972; Litman, 1972). It appears that in prepaid group practice, in contrast, people can be successfully introduced to new manpower in a much more impersonal way, perhaps because the consumers are more attuned to innovation.

The Kaiser-Portland HMO introduced nurse midwives simply by referring patients to them when they called for appointments with doctors. Ninety-one percent of those referred accepted appointments; broken appointment rates were only one percent higher than they were for physicians, and the return rate was high. Preliminary data indicate that acceptance depends more on the nature of the medical problem than on patient characteristics.

Thus, it appears that what people think they are willing to accept, and why, may underestimate what they actually will accept when faced with a real situation.

Consumer Acceptance of Prepaid Group Practice

As we have seen, people are most concerned about the accessibility and cost of medical care. One of the best ways to solve those problems, according to many experts, is to establish prepaid group practices. Although the idea is not new, there has been a recent surge of interest in that form of health-service delivery, and a number of articles have appeared concerning public acceptance of prepaid group practice, now often referred to as HMOs. In this section, we will not attempt a comprehensive review of HMOs but will merely outline the key findings concerning public choice, acceptance, and satisfaction with that type of organization.

What makes people, given the choice of traditional health insurance and prepaid group practice, enroll in HMOs? Financial security and comprehensive coverage emerge as the primary reasons for enrollment (Bashshur et al., 1967; Donabedian, 1969; Metzner et al., 1972; Weinerman, 1964). Preference for group practice decreases with age, is directly related to the presence of young children, is strongest for the middle-income groups and is stronger among blacks than whites (Metzner et al., 1972). The data suggest that, at least to some extent, those people who feel most vulnerable choose HMOs over traditional insurance. There are, however, a few anomalies in the findings, particularly those concerning young, single people who normally use services less than older, married people with children, who tend to be very much in favor of group practice.

According to Donabedian (1969), the principal disincentive in choosing to enroll in HMOs is free choice of physician and the preexistence of a relationship with a physician. Thus, he claims: "To some extent consumer acceptance of prepaid group practice plans is an expression of the absence of a prior patient-physician relationship or of a breakdown in such relationships."

Once they have chosen an insurance plan, most people are satisfied with their choice, despite enormous differences in coverage and organization (Donabedian, 1969; Bashshur et al., 1967; Freidson and Feldman, 1959). This finding is similar to that we discussed earlier—namely, that most people are satisfied with their own physicians. In neither case does the general satisfaction preclude dissatisfaction with specific aspects of the relationship or of the plans.

Once a person enrolls in a prepaid group-practice plan, what happens to satisfaction? Bashshur et al. (1967), in their study of five hundred union workers enrolled in the Community Health Association in Detroit, hypothesized that:

1. Satisfaction would increase over time.

2. Increased satisfaction would be related to increased dissatisfaction with specifics.

3. The major factor in both of the above would be utilization.

In general, their hypotheses were confirmed. The authors found that the general level of satisfaction did increase over time. Single people were the least satisfied (they also used few services), while families with children had the highest increase in satisfaction. Satisfaction was related to socio-demographic variables in the following ways: Blacks were more satisfied than whites, family income was negatively related to satisfaction, white Catholics started out the most skeptical and ended up the most satisfied. Job seniority, knowledge about the plan, and time with the company were directly related to satisfaction. Wife's use of the plan was an important determinant of satisfaction, and conversely her use of outside services was related to dissatisfaction.

Utilization was also related to complaints, as predicted. Complaints tended to be specific and were related to general interest in and familiarity with the plan, rather than to overall dissatisfaction or rejection. Criticism centered around specific inconveniences of the services. Income and education were directly related to number of complaints: Blacks had fewer complaints than whites, and greater family use of services was associated with the greater number of complaints.

Thus, as we found earlier with respect to physicians, familiarity does not breed contempt; it breeds commitment and a feeling of freedom to voice specific complaints. HMOs are likely to encourage consumer participation. Often they have emerged because of consumer pressure, especially from labor unions in the Midwest and Far West. Several studies report that consumer participation in planning and delivery leads to satisfaction and, that conversely, lack of participation leads to dissatisfaction. When channels exist for their participation, members work to increase the efficiency of services and use of facilities. Given the formal right to complain, people do express dissatisfaction about specific organizational inadequacies, but they also work hard to correct those deficiencies (Schwartz, 1965, 1968; Sussman et al., 1967).

Thus, the data suggest that consumer dissatisfaction does not necessarily, or even usually, mean rejection of the total system. It is more often an indication of commitment to that system and a desire to make it better.

The Provider's View

Although interest in provider satisfactions has accompanied changes in health-care systems, few attempts have been made to measure physician satisfactions, or to measure the satisfactions of providers other than physicians. Regardless of the structure of the nation's health-care system, physicians will continue to occupy the central role. They control not only their own working conditions, but those of ancillary health professionals as well (Mechanic, 1972). Thus, the training, skill, and commitment of physicians are essential to the success of any health plan.

Physicians' satisfactions may be measured in terms of autonomy, status, and rewards. Clearly the three variables are interrelated; the degree of autonomy determines the place of a profession on a status hierarchy, and rewards normally depend on status. Other variables, such as intellectual stimulation, quality of care, and doctor-patient relationships may be indicators of satisfaction in particular work organizations.

Physicians and the State

It is useful conceptually, when attempting to assess the effect of a change on the satisfactions of physicians, to determine whether the change affects the position of medicine as an institution in the society with respect to autonomy, status, and rewards, or whether the change affects the particular organization in which the day-to-day work of medicine takes place.

We suggest that organizational changes at the state level (e.g., Medicare, Medicaid, national health insurance) cannot affect the autonomy and status of medicine as a profession or membership in the profession. The reason is that the state cannot change the source of the profession's powers, which derive from the universal threat of illness, helplessness, and uncertainty. Thus, federal changes in health-care organization do not succeed or fail because they threaten the autonomy or status of the profession but because they are disconsonant with values that are commonly held in the society (Colombotos, 1969; Strickland, 1972).

The threat of a boycott against Medicare failed because its goal supported the belief or value that adequate medical care is a right rather than a privilege (Colombotos, 1969). Its implementation not only did little to disrupt the organization of practice but had a salutary effect on the income of providers. Colombotos (1969) also found, in a telephone panel study of physicians in New York State, that before the enactment of Medicare legislation, thirty-eight percent of the sampled physicians were in favor of the hospitalization provision. Ten months after passage, however, the number in favor increased to seventy percent, and six months after implementation it was eighty-one percent. Six months after passage, ninety-three percent said they intended to treat Medicare patients.

In contrast, Medicaid has not received the support of the profession. In spite of the fact that Medicaid legislation is in conformity with the value that medical care is a right, a majority of physicians have continued to oppose the program. Their opposition is in line with Elling (1971) who argues that there are certain organizational forms that do not fit the cultural beliefs and values of a society. Colombotos states that there are beliefs about the poor in society which conflict with the premise that medical care is a right. These beliefs spring from racism and a lack of personal identification with the poor. Furthermore, Medicaid has a greater impact than Medicare on particular organizations of practice in that it affects one class of patients, provides most types of service, and establishes criteria in cost and quality.

Reorganizations in health care at the national level have never threatened the total income reward to the profession. Nor has resistance come because of the source of the reward, but because of effects on particular organizations of practice.

The Strickland (1972) survey of consumers and providers that assessed areas of agreement on perceived needs and solutions in health care found that physicians share the common belief that change is needed and that they accept federal involvement. While not ascribing to health-crisis theories, they recognize serious problems in areas of cost, physician shortage, malpractice suits, unnecessary hospitalization, and inadequate health insurance. Fifty-one percent favor national health insurance. They agree with consumers that health insurance should have a deductible portion which further explains the reason for Colombotos' finding that Medicaid does not fit the cultural beliefs of a society. Consumers also agree in general with suggestions that financial barriers for consumers should be lowered but are skeptical of any basic alterations in the organization of medical practice.

The major disagreement between physicians and the public is over who shall administer a national health insurance program. The Medicaid and Medicare experience, as well as responses to Strickland's questionnaire, suggests that physicians would readily accept a national program run by the federal government but that they have little confidence in consumer participation.

Mechanic (1972) found that fifty-two to eighty percent of primary-care physicians support community centers, such as those established by the Office of Economic Opportunity. From thirty-eight to fifty-seven percent support the concept of federal financing, such as Medicaid, while thirty-two to fifty-four percent support the concept of national health insurance. Physicians in group practice support federal intervention more strongly. That physicians accept changes in payment schemes is supported by an American Medical Association survey (USDHEW, 1972) of 4,500 members and 3,000 nonmembers. Thirty percent of the members and forty-seven percent of the nonmembers responded that they preferred prepaid capitation fees over fee-for-service practice. More than fifty percent of senior medical students, interns, residents, faculty, and full-time hospital staff supported such a change in traditional methods of payment.

In the United States, where the profession has no large homogeneous groups with respect to organization of practice, organizations that represent medicine are not as likely to muster substantial numbers to resist change as they are in Great Britain, where physicians divide clearly into hospital-based salaried specialists and community-based general practitioners. Nor are arguments between the state and the physicians likely to concern the relative deprivation of rewards as they are in Great Britain (Mechanic and Faich, 1970). In contrast, the organization of physicians in the United States is characterized by: fragmentation of types of practice; departure of physicians from traditional general practitioner roles; increases in group practices and specialization; extension of hospital privileges to general practitioners; dependence on facilities and equipment providing techncial support; opportunities for physicians to work in research organizations; and differential conceptions of responsibility among medical subgroups (Mechanic, 1972; Loftus, 1971).

Physicians and the Organization of Practice

A step in predicting how change in the organization of practice may affect performance is to find the correlates of physician satisfaction. A next step is to attempt to assess the effect a proposed change will have on those satisfactions, keeping in mind that they may be assessed in terms of autonomy, status, and rewards.

Indicators of autonomy are freedom from supervision, freedom to be innovative, and freedom to communicate freely with patients, colleagues, or allied professionals in the patients' behalf. Freedom from supervision involves regulating working time, managing patients independently, and assuming responsibility (Calahan et al., 1957; Freidson, 1970; Engel, 1969; Phillips, 1964).

Attitudinal orientations that reflect the physicians' value system and affect the status of physicians in their work organizations are intellectual values, such as desire to learn, to do research, to receive stimulation from colleagues (Calahan et al., 1957; Phillips, 1964; Sussman et al., 1967); to provide high quality care (Calahan et al., 1957; Engel, 1969; Freidson, 1970; Sussman et al., 1967); and to have a close personal relationship with patients (Calahan et al., 1957; Engel, 1969; Freidson, 1970; Sussman et al., 1967).

Rewards are best considered in terms of money or substitutes for money, such as time (either total time spent in performance of work or time per patient), or in terms of sanctions from colleagues, patients, or self.

If there is a value in a profession for rewarding members who work in areas of administration and organization, satisfactions are earned from colleague approval or self-reward. Evidence suggests, however, that organizational and administrative abilities in medicine have not been rewarded, that medical students are initially selected who express little interest in jobs where they might have to rely on the experience of others, and that this attitude is further reinforced in medical training (Coker et al., 1966). Rather, physicians are self-selected and rewarded for independent and technological problem-solving (Fuchs, 1968).

Many recent and proposed changes in the organization of day-to-day practice are in the direction of increased bureaucratization (Neighborhood Health Centers, Health Maintenance Organizations, Professional Standards Review Organizations, Experimental Medical Care Review Organizations), which may decrease autonomy and perhaps status and rewards. We need to know which aspects of physician satisfaction are likely to be affected by group practice.

Autonomy. Freidson and Rhea (1964) suggest that as far as group practice involves constraints of cooperation among and coordination of varied services, autonomy may be *most significant* to physicians' satisfaction in group practice. Banta and Fox (1972) in their investigation of a neighborhood health center found that, despite a stated commitment to egalitarianism among health teams, high motivation was not sufficient to overcome considerable role strain. The strain was felt to result from the blurring of boundaries of responsibility, role overlap, unclear goals, and inability to overcome traditional deference patterns.

If quality of care is affected by loss of autonomy as Engel (1969) suggests, it would be detrimental if bureaucratization were to reduce responsibility, communication, and innovation. Engel suggests also that organizations do not necessarily interfere with autonomy. She found that physicians associated with moderately bureaucratic settings, as opposed to those in a nonbureaucratic setting, were likely to perceive themselves as autonomous. There may thus be an optimal level of bureaucratization with respect to professional autonomy. Perceived autonomy may be relative in the most structured and vertical of organizations. In a military organization the degree of perceived autonomy was found to be related to the physician's opinion of his superior officer (Bentley, 1973).

The negative value usually associated with administration may compensate for perceived loss in autonomy. A physician joining a group practice does not have the problems of setting up and managing associated with "hanging out his shingle." Additional information indicates that values relating to giving service may outweigh loss of autonomy (Baily, 1970). Calahan and his colleagues (1957) also suggest that the values of helping and serving and having a close personal relationship are relatively more important than some loss of autonomy.

Status. Mechanic (1972) reports that only a small minority of his sample in prepaid group practice expressed dissatisfaction with community status and esteem. McElrath (1958), however, reports that some physicians believe association with group practice lowers status in the eyes of colleagues.

Evidence suggests that the organization of work may not affect status with respect to colleagues as much as the status conferred within the status hierarchy of specialties. A general practitioner, for example, is likely to rank below a brain surgeon within the profession of medicine, whether he works in an institution or private practice. The question is, to what extent do peers in a particular specialty assign status according to organization of work?

Rewards. Rewards, as well as autonomy and status, may be affected by the organization of work. Rewards may be viewed as income or its substitutes, time, self- or colleague sanctions, intellectual stimulation, quality of care, and doctor-patient relationships:

(1) Income: Unlike their British counterparts, only a small minority of primary practitioners in this country express dissatisfaction with income (Mechanic, 1972). There is some evidence that group practice affects satisfaction with income. Those physicians in the largest group (fifty-one or more colleagues) are least likely to express high satisfaction, but there is no clear pattern with respect to dissatisfaction. Lowest satisfaction was expressed in groups with six to twenty colleagues. Both Ross (1969) and Prybil (1970) found money foremost among factors motivating a shift to other forms of practice.

(2) Time: Both the amount of leisure time available and the amount of time spent with each patient are valued by physicians, and within limits may serve as a substitute for income. Faich (1969) reports that the bulk of research before 1968 suggests that professionals require reasonable time investments if they are not to be dissatisfied with their positions. There is evidence that weighs in favor of prepaid group practice as far as total work time and its complement, leisure time, are concerned (Cartwright, 1967; Mechanic, 1972). Four time measures used by Mechanic found fewer doctors worked fewer hours in groups than in other forms of practice. The tendency was particularly strong among physicians in

groups of fifty-one or more colleagues, but it is also evident in groups of twenty-one to fifty. Doctors in the latter group expressed highest satisfaction and reported greatest opportunities for leisure time. Of those in groups of fifty-one or more, fifty percent were very satisfied with total time spent in practice, compared with twenty-eight percent in groups of six to ten.

In group practices, where there is an income incentive to increase productivity, and in practices where physicians are paid by a capitation fee, physicians express concern over work pressures that interfere with the time available for each patient. They see high patient loads as a threat to quality of care and the doctor-patient relationship (Faich, 1969; Mechanic, 1972; Sussman et al., 1967; Cartwright, 1967). Where physicians are salaried they may be allowed fewer patients as a compensation for lower salary (Bentley, 1973). Fee-for-service practitioners are assumed to be less concerned with patient loads because they have greater control over the number of patients and the time spent per patient, and therefore over income.

(3) Intellectual stimulation: Sussman et al. (1967) found a high correlation between stimulating professional contacts, new learning opportunities, challenging problems, and staff morale. Freidson and Rhea's study (1964) is supportive. More than seventy percent of their sample felt that group practice had been responsible for their keeping up with the latest medical advances, and fifty-six percent reported an increase in intellectual stimulation.

(4) Quality of care: Physicians place a high value on being able to provide care of high quality. In this area, technical capacities, physical facilities, and ancillary personnel are relevant. The inaccessibility of equipment and consequent inability to apply new techniques were a major source of dissatisfaction among general practitioners in Great Britain during the 1965 threatened strike (Faich, 1969). In Caplan and Sussman's (1966) outpatient department study, physical facilities were rated as the second most important variable affecting satisfaction.

Though relief from paperwork is valued, the situation with respect to new categories of personnel, such as physician assistants and nurse practitioners or midwives, is unclear. Faich (1969) found no relationship between practicing with other physicians or physician assistants and satisfactions with professional situations. Having other ancillary assistance in one's practice and use of an appointment system were also unrelated to satisfaction. Diagnostic facilities were, however, positively correlated with satisfaction.

Many of the new work categories of personnel may be as role extenders involved in additional services (Bailey, 1970) instead of physician substitutes. Thus, they relate to consumers' satisfactions more than physicians' satisfactions. In response to a questionnaire, Coye and Hansen (1969) found, that of those physicians who responded, forty-one percent said they would use a physician assistant, but in general assistants would not be used for the tasks for which they are being trained.

Acceptance of ancillary personnel, however, may be related to specialty. The American Academy of Pediatrics is the only group representing organized medicine that has acknowledged a need for nurse assistants and expressed willingness to work collaboratively with ancillary personnel (Adamson, 1971).

Mechanic and Faich (1970) have suggested that modifications of work organizations might bring advantages in terms of more efficient operations, economies of scale, and better use of ancillary help, but they caution that dissatisfactions flow from these modifications. Interrelationships among staff produce strains; persons with diverse training, experience, and opinions must try to coordinate with others. In addition, there are differences in authority and status that create tension and stress (Sussman et al., 1967).

(5) Doctor-patient relationships: Physician satisfaction with practices depends upon the extent to which the physician-patient relationship fulfills certain valued expectations. A number of factors such as time spent per patient and work setting effect the relationship.

In a complex organization it may be difficult for the physician to provide psychological support and establish rapport. That such concern may be meaningful to frequently or chronically ill patients only is suggested by Wolfe and Badgley (1972), who found that seventy percent of the population use none or less than one-half hour of a physician's time per year. Nevertheless, the psychological variable of physician-patient rapport is frequently cited as important to physicians, and it needs to be incorporated within organizational practice to meet concepts of high quality practice (Engel, 1969). A work setting where the patient sees the same physician on each visit has been found in one study to be the most highly ranked variable for staff morale because it supports beliefs about continuity of care (Sussman et al., 1967). Thus, physician and patient have similar expectations concerning their interaction, and it is important for the satisfaction of each that their expectations are realized.

Summary and Conclusions

Patient and provider satisfaction in health care and its organization depends on an interrelated set of factors. For the patient, the key variables to examine are cost, accessibility, quality, interpersonal relationships, and system characteristics. For the provider the variables are different. They include autonomy, status, rewards, and interpersonal relationships. Preferences, satisfaction, and acceptability to the patient are likely to vary with sociodemographic characteristics, while provider preference, satisfaction, and acceptability are more likely to vary with specialty and current practice setting. For both consumers and providers their position on the satisfaction continuum depends on the expectations they bring to particular situations.

Patients and physicians are in basic agreement about many aspects of health care. Both perceive serious inadequacies in the current system, primarily because of high costs and suboptimal accessibility of care. Both accept the fact that there are likely to be major changes in medical-care delivery and agree that the federal government must take responsibility for correcting current inadequacies. Providers and consumers disagree about some of the specifics—whether the government should administer national health insurance, what should be the composition of local planning groups, and so on.

We have compared prepaid group practices to other forms of practice because, although not particularly new, that form of organization is becoming widespread, because it is advocated by many as "the solution to today's crisis," and because it allows us to see just how flexible people are.

It appears that consumers and providers who are involved with HMOs are generally satisfied, a fact that in and of itself is of little importance, since the tendency to cognitive consonance leads people to be satisfied with what they have chosen to do. More importantly, it seems that consumers and providers accept trade-offs for many aspects of satisfaction as long as certain critical elements are kept intact. Specifically, for consumers, complete coverage, controlled costs, and access to the total range of services are worth some organizational inconvenience and perhaps some loss in the doctor-patient relationship. Dissatisfaction with system arrangements (such as waiting time) can be rectified by good doctor-patient interaction, and, to some extent, other staff can compensate for inadequacies in doctor-patient communication. Thus, it appears that for patients the first priority is to have someone who will show interest and concern, who will take time to listen and to explain.

For providers, prepaid group practice may result in some loss of status vis-a-vis colleagues and some loss of autonomy because of the increased bureaucracy, but the rewards in terms of free time, intellectual stimulation, and access to the complete range of facilities are valued trade-offs. What must not be jeopardized, according to providers, are freedom to treat patients as they see fit and time to develop good doctor-patient relationships. Thus, the priorities of patients and doctors are in no way divergent.

In conclusion, there is strong evidence indicating that doctors and patients are in essential agreement about what is critical to good medical care and its organization. Once in a situation, both can compromise their expectations, but they must be educated about the details of any particular arrangement. Most importantly, dissatisfaction tends to be focused on specific aspects of a system and does not usually indicate rejection of that system. On the contrary, it appears that to voice complaints may be to commit oneself to working to change a situation in the hope of making it better, thereby reaffirming a basic acceptance and satisfaction.

What we do not know are the limits to adaptabilities: How much can medical care be restructured without its rejection? We also have little comparative data from similar types of practice organizations that allow us to determine specifically how organization affects satisfaction.

References

Adamson, T. E.
   1971   "Critical issues in the use of physician associates and assist-
              ants." American Journal of Public Health 61: 1765–1779.
Alpert, J. J., J. Kosa, R. Haggerty, L. Robertson, *and* M. Heagarty
   1970   "Attitudes and satisfactions of low income families receiv-
              ing comprehensive pediatric care." American Journal of
              Public Health 60: 499–506.
Alport, G. W.
   1954   The Nature of Prejudice. Cambridge: Addison-Wesley.
Andersen, R. J., J. Kravits, *and* O. W. Anderson
   1971   "The public's view of the crisis in medical care: An impe-
              tus for changing delivery systems?" Economic and Business
              Bulletin 24 (Fall): 44–52.
Bailey, R. M.
   1970   "Philosophy, faith, fact and fiction in the production of
              medical services." Inquiry 7: 37–53.
Banta, H. D. *and* R. C. Fox
   1972   "Role strains of a health care team in a poverty communi-
              ty." Social Science and Medicine 6: 697–722.
Bashshur, R., C. A. Metzner, *and* A. B. Worden
   1967   "Consumer satisfaction with group practice, the CHA
              case." American Journal of Public Health 57 (November):
              1991–1999.
Bentley, J.
   1973   Personal Communication.
Burns, T. *and* G. N. Stalker
   1968   The Management of Innovation. London: Tavistock Press.

Bush, P. J.
   in press "The placebo effect." Journal of the American Pharmaceutical Association.
Calahan, D., P. Collete, *and* N. Helman
   1957   "Career interests and expectations of U.S. medical stu-
           dents." Journal of Medical Education 32 (8): 557–563.
Caplan, E. *and* M. Sussman
   1966   "Rank order of important variables for patient and staff
           satisfaction with outpatient service." Journal of Health and
           Human Behavior 7: 133–137.
Cartwright, A.
   1965   "General practice in 1963: The conditions, contents and
           satisfactions." Medical Care 3: 69–87.
   1967   Patients and Their Doctors: A Study of General Practice.
           New York: Atherton Press.
   1970   The Developing Role of the General Practitioner in Family
           Planning. London: Routledge and Kegan Paul.
Charney, E.
   1972   "Patient-doctor communication: Implications for the clini-
           cian." Unpublished paper.
Coker, R. E., B. G. Greenberg, K. W. Back, T. G. Donnelly, F. S. Mc-
   Connell, N. Miller, and J. Kosa
   1966   "The University of North Carolina study of public health
           physicians." Milbank Memorial Fund Quarterly 44 (2, Part
           1): 149–155.
Colombotos, J.
   1968   "Physicians' attitudes toward medicare." Medical Care 6:
           320–331.
   1969   "Physicians and medicare: A before-after study of the ef-
           fect of legislation on attitudes." American Sociological Re-
           view 34: 318–334.
Coye, R. *and* M. Hansen
   1969   "The medical assistant: A survey of physicians' expecta-
           tions." Journal of the American Medical Association 209:
           529–533.
Davis, M. S.
   1966   "Variations in patients' compliance with doctors' advice:
           Analysis of congruence between survey responses and re-
           sults of empirical observations." Journal of Medical Educa-
           tion 41: 1037.

1968a   "Physiological, psychological and demographic factors in patients' compliance with doctors' orders." Medical Care 6 (2): 115–122.

1968b   "Variations in patients' compliance with doctors' advice: An empirical analysis of patterns of communication." American Journal of Public Health 58: 274–288.

Donabedian, A.
1969   "An evaluation of prepaid group practice." Inquiry 6 (3): 3–27.

Elling, R. N.
1971   "Health planning in international perspective." Medical Care 9: 214–234.

Engel, G. V.
1969   "The effect of bureaucracy on the professional autonomy of the physician." Journal of Health and Social Behavior 10 (March): 30–41.

Faich, R. G.
1969   "Social and structural factors affecting work satisfaction: A case study of general practitioners in the English National Health Service.: Ph.D. dissertation, University of Wisconsin, Madison, Wisconsin.

Fairweather, J. L. *and* A. Kifolo
1972   "Improvement of patient care in a solo OB-GYN practice by using an RN physician's assistant." American Journal of Public Health 62: 361–363.

Feldman, J. J.
1966   The Dissemination of Health Information. Chicago: Aldine Publishing Company.

Francis, V., B. M. Korsch, *and* M. J. Morris
1969   "Gaps in doctor-patient communication: Patients' responses to medical advice." New England Journal of Medicine 280: 535–540.

Freidson, E.
1959   "Specialties without roots: The utilization of new services." Human Organization 18: 112–116.

1961   Patients' Views of Medical Practice. New York: Russell Sage Foundation.

1970   Profession of Medicine. New York: Dodd Mead and Company.

Freidson, E. *and* J. Feldman
1959   Public Attitudes Toward Health Insurance. Chicago: Health Information Foundation, Research Series No. 5.

Freidson, E. *and* J. H. Manu
1971   "Organizational dimensions of large-scale group medical practice." American Journal of Public Health 61: 786–795.

Freidson, E. *and* B. Rhea
1964   "Physicians in large medical groups." Journal of Chronic Diseases 17: 827–836.

Fuchs, V.
1968   "The growing demand for medical care." New England Journal of Medicine 297: 190–195.

Garfield, S. E.
1970   "The delivery of medical care." Scientific American 222: 15–23.

Gish, O.
1970   "Britain and America: Brain drains and brain gains." Social Science and Medicine 3: 397–400.

Glasser, M. H.
1972   "Consumer expectations of health services." Pp. 29–38 in Corey, L., S. Saltman, and M. Epstein (eds.), Medicine in a Changing Society, St. Louis: C. V. Mosby Company.

Health Insurance Plan of New York
1970   HIP Statistical Report: 1968–1969. New York: Health Insurance Plan of New York, Division of Research and Statistics.

Kissick, W. L.
1968   "Health manpower in transition." Milbank Memorial Fund Quarterly 46 (1, Part 2): 53–90.

LaPiere, R. T.
1934   "Attitudes vs. Actions." Social Forces 3: 230–237.

Leonard, R. C., J. K. Skipper, *and* P. Woolridge
1967   "Small sample field experiences for evaluating patient care." Health Services Research 2: 46–60.

Litman, T. J.
1972   "Public perceptions of the physicians assistant—a survey of the attitudes and opinions of rural Iowa and Minnesota residents." American Journal of Public Health 62: 343–346.

Loftus, G. T.
    1971   "Differential conceptions of physician responsibility among medical subgroups." Journal of Medical Education 46: 290–298.

McElrath, D. C.
    1958   "Prepaid group medical practice: A comparative analysis of organizations and perspectives." Ph.D. dissertation, Yale University, New Haven, Connecticut.

Mechanic, D.
    1972   Public Expectations and Health Care: Essays on the Changing Organization of Health Services. New York: Wiley-Interscience.

Mechanic, D. *and* R. Faich
    1970   "Doctors in revolt: The crese in the English National Health Service." Medical Care 8: 442–455.

Merton, R. K., G. Reader, *and* P. L. Kendall (eds.)
    The Student Physician. Cambridge: Harvard University Press.

Metzner, C. A., R. L. Bashsur, *and* G. W. Shannon
    1972   "Differential public acceptance of group medical practice." Medical Care 10 (4): 279–288.

Moynihan, D. P.
    1969   Maximum Feasible Misunderstanding. New York: The Free Press.

National Center for Health Statistics
    1970   "Current estimates from the Health Interview Survey." Public Health Service Series 10 (60). Washington, D.C.: Government Printing Office.

Phillips. B.
    1964   "Expected value deprivation and occupational preference." Sociometry 27: 151–160.

Pope, C. R.
    1971   "Determinants of medical care utilization: Members' use of and attitudes toward Kaiser Physicians." Paper presented before the Health Services Research Conference, December 10–11, 1971, University of Chicago, Chicago, Illinois.

Pratt, L., A. Seligmann, *and* G. Reader
    1957   "Physicians views on the level of medical information among patients." American Journal of Public Health 47: (August) 1277–1283.

Prybil, L.
1970   Physicians in Large, Multi-Specialty Groups: An Investiga-
        tion of Selected Characteristics, Career Patterns and Opin-
        ions. Ph.D. dissertation, University of Iowa, Iowa City,
        Iowa.

Record, J. C. *and* H. R. Cohen
1972   "The introduction of midwifery in a prepaid group prac-
        tice." American Journal of Public Health 62 (3): 354–360.

Reeder, L. G.
1972   "The patient-client as a consumer: Some observations on
        the changing professional-client relationship." Journal of
        Health and Social Behavior 13: 406–413.

Ross, A., Jr.
1969   "A report on physician terminators in group practice."
        Medical Groups Management 16: 15–21.

Rivkin, M. O. *and* K. W. Sehnert
1973   "Consumer knowledge and preference." Unpublished pap-
        er.

Saward, E. J., J. Blank, *and* M. Greenlick
1968   "Documentation of twenty years of operation and growth
        of a prepaid group practice." Medical Care 6: 239–244.

Scholton, J. E., R. Rubin, *and* C. E. Lewis
1966   "Medical care and medical students." Journal of the Ameri-
        can Medical Association 197: 333-338.

Schwartz, J. L.
1965   "Consumer sponsorship and physician sponsorship of group
        practice health plans: Some similarities and differences."
        American Journal of Public Health 55: 94–99.

1968   "Medical Plans and Health Care, Consumer Participation
        in Policy-Making with a Special Section on Medicare.
        Springfield, Illinois: Charles C. Thomas.

Silver, H. K.
1969   "The pediatric nurse practitioner and the child health asso-
        ciate: New types of health professional in education and
        the health related professions." Annals of the New York
        Academy of Sciences 166: 927–933.

Strickland, S. P.
1972   U.S. Health Care: What's Wrong and What's Right. Wash-
        ington, D.C.: Potomac Associates.

Sussman, M. B., E. K. Caplan, M. R. Hang, *and* M. R. Stern
  1967   The Walking Patient: A Study of Outpatient Care. Cleveland: Western Reserve University Press.
U.S. Department of Health, Education, and Welfare
  1972   "Questions physicians are asking about HMO's and the answers." Washington, D.C.: Government Printing Office.
Vuori, H., T. Aaku, E. Aine, R. Erkko, *and* R. Johnson
  1972   "Doctor-patient relationship in the light of patients' experiences." Social Science and Medicine 6: 723–730.
Weinerman, E. R.
  1964   "Patients' perceptions of group medical care." American Journal of Public Health 54: 880–889.
Wolfe, S. *and* R. F. Badgley
  1972   "The family doctor." The Milbank Memorial Fund Quarterly 50 (2 Part 2): 1–203.

Impact of

Cost-Sharing on Consumer

Use of Health Services[1]

CHARLES P. HALL, JR.

Perhaps the most impressive fact about the various incentives—more typically, disincentives—that have been devised to influence the use and distribution of health-care services is the degree of ignorance that still prevails about their impact. Though much attention has been directed toward the subject in several nations and in a variety of public and private settings, there is a paucity of data that belies the plethora of strongly held convictions about the relative merits of various approaches.

For purposes of this paper, the primary focus will be on the

[1] This paper is based largely on the results of the study, "The effects of cost-sharing in the Medicaid program," which was conducted jointly by Temple University and the University of Pennsylvania, under support received from the Social and Rehabilitation Service of the U.S. Department of Health, Education, and Welfare, Contract No. 18-P-56651/3-01 (Hall, 1971; 1972). The author was project director, and he is indebted to his coinvestigators, who did much of the research. Several unpublished reports generated by the study will be referred to, including: Beck (1972), Chester (1972), Dolfman (1972), Zelten (1972), and Zelten et al. (1972). In addition, a 20-page annotated bibliography on cost sharing and several memos and interim reports were developed. Other investigators involved in the study include Dr. Jerry S. Rosenbloom and Dr. William H. Wandel.

more common economic incentives that have been invoked to control or alter the distribution and/or the cost of health-care services to consumers. Typically, they include at least the following cost-sharing arrangements:

(1) deductibles,
(2) coinsurance or percentage participation,
(3) copayment, and
(4) maximum limits on benefits (external and internal).

Equally important, of course, is the package of health benefits that is covered under any specific health or health insurance plan, since uncovered services require full payment by the consumer—the ultimate "deductible." Special attention will be directed to the impact those controls have on the poor.

Since there is clearly an almost infinite number of possible combinations of coverages and controls, the suspicion is strong that "gamesmanship," as practiced by both patient and practitioner, may tend to subvert or pervert the intent of many efforts to influence the distribution of care.

The purpose of this paper, then, will be to digest current knowledge and attitudes about distributional incentives in the health-care field, to recommend areas where additional research might be fruitful, and, if possible, to suggest alternative approaches that may have merit.

Definitions and Objectives of Cost-Sharing

As used in this paper, deductibles refer to provisions in health insurance schemes that call for a defined financial outlay by the insured before his eligibility for insured benefits is established. Though normally applied to front-end costs, they are sometimes used as a "corridor" requirement between basic and major medical benefits. Deductibles vary widely in size and may be differentiated by type of service. Typically, they apply broadly on a calendar-year or benefit-period basis, and once satisfied they are not repeated unless another independent episode ensues.

Coinsurance or percentage participation provisions are commonplace in major medical or comprehensive health insurance programs. They simply require the insured to pay a stated percentage —usually twenty to twenty-five percent—of all covered charges; frequently, a deductible must first have been satisfied.

Copayment provisions may be viewed as deductibles levied on a unit-of-service basis or as a coinsurance stated in dollar terms rather than percentage points. In effect, there is a flat charge per unit of service—e.g., office visit or prescription. Typically, copayment charges are not large.

In some instances the distinction between deductible and copayment is purely semantic, with commercial insurers tending to use the former term and the "Blues"—Blue Cross and Blue Shield—tending to prefer copayment.

There are at least two widely recognized objectives of cost-sharing and they are closely related. One is to lower the cost (in terms of premiums) for a given health insurance program. A second objective is to reduce or eliminate unnecessary utilization. To the extent that utilization is influenced, of course, there is an even further tendency to lower costs. A less widely recognized function of a deductible is to eliminate many trivial losses that are not technically covered under a specific plan. By eliminating the claim altogether, the deductible helps solve the public relations problem of explaining to the insured that a given loss is not provided for in the policy.[2]

The deductible is commonplace in many lines of insurance. Generally, in addition to the advantages described above, it is justified on the grounds that it makes insurance serve its "true" function —to deal with the serious or catastrophic loss—rather than to "waste" premiums on the disproportionately high administrative costs of handling a multitude of small, budgetable claims. Coinsurance is also a reflection on insurers' constant concern with "moral hazard." Insurers want the insured to retain a continued financial stake in getting well in order to minimize the risk of malingering.

[2] Virtually every article dealing with cost-sharing identifies two major objectives. One of the earliest, and the only one to recognize this last point is Williams (1953). See also Dickerson (1959) and Pollack (1957).

As will be shown, empirical evidence demonstrating the success of these cost-sharing techniques in fulfilling their objectives is difficult to find.

Philosophical Issue

Aside from the question of which incentives have greater merit in a given situation, the fundamental philosophical issue of whether any economic barriers to the use of health-care services are appropriate often gives rise to a degree of emotionalism that produces more heat than light. That reaction is particularly noticeable when the issue is discussed in the context of programs designed to cover the entire population or specifically designated low-income groups. Paradoxically, empirical data are especially sparse with reference to the poor, so that most arguments are based on a priori logic that seems reasonable to advocates of a particular point of view but that carries little weight with opponents.

Too frequently, the differences are pictured in black and white or "good guy" versus "bad guy" terms. Thus, insurance companies and economists, both of whom are naturally and of necessity concerned with dollar costs, are often characterized as being inhumane or insensitive to problems of the poor and the elderly when they express reservations about the feasibility of all-encompassing promises to deliver unlimited health services without providing any point-of-service economic controls. The mere suggestion that deductible, coinsurance, or copayment provisions ought to be considered is often greeted with something close to contempt and the comment by health-care workers that, "We save lives, not dollars."

Nevertheless, if there is any truth in the frequently stated claim that most Americans want more health care than they are willing to pay for, it is clear that optimum allocation of available economic resources will maximize our life-saving capacity. In addition, all societies, whether overtly or covertly, do establish priorities in the allocation of scarce resources. To date, health care in the United States does not seem to have acquired the degree of popular or political support necessary to command the top spot in a list of priorities.

Historical Perspective

There can be little doubt that the historical development of the health-care delivery system and private health insurance in this country has had a significant impact on attitudes toward various cost-sharing mechanisms. Unlike most other western nations, the United States has neither the tradition of a national health service nor a national health insurance system. For the most part, health has been viewed as an individual responsibility.

Since the late 1940s, health insurance has also been a major issue in collective bargaining and thus of concern to employers and unions. Indeed, in 1970 group health insurance accounted for over eighty-two percent of the benefit payments made by insurance companies (Source Book for Health Insurance Data, 1972: 30). Thus, it is hardly surprising that heavy emphasis has been put on various measures to control costs, particularly in light of the rapid increases in health-care costs in recent years. The suspicion that employees and insurers both lack adequate built-in incentives to control costs is inescapable, especially where the employer is paying the full premium (noncontributory plans) and the insurance package is experience rated. More surprising, perhaps, is the fact that insurers seem never to have attempted to measure the real impact of various cost-sharing mechanisms on utilization patterns. And employers, who, for the most part, have borne the financial burden, never insisted on having that information.

In the tough, pragmatic arena of wage-package negotiations, even fractions of pennies per hour often loom as major obstacles to labor peace. Therefore, although labor leaders frequently say that they prefer to have economic barriers to access to health care removed, when faced with bargaining decisions they have often been forced to compromise. In other words, they must and do establish priorities. Sometimes the priorities are reflected in the illnesses or services to be covered; in part, they are seen through specific cost-sharing provisions or dollar limits on allowable benefits. But always, they are influenced by economic considerations, even though other factors are also present. For an excellent analysis of this process, see Munts (1967: Chapter 16).

Implicit in the American history of health insurance, then, has been the fact that it has evolved largely as a mechanism available to employed (and generally healthy) workers and their dependents. In that situation an assumption of some ability to pay for health services was appropriate and economic controls resulting from conscious bargaining choices may not have been unreasonable. But in its first venture into a national health insurance program, Medicare, the government retained exactly the same kinds of economic controls that had been used in private insurance—despite the fact that the beneficiaries are mostly unemployed and poorer and in less robust health than those covered by private insurance. In any case, neither private health insurance nor a government insurance program has yet adequately dealt with the health-care needs of the poor in this country, though Medicaid, a welfare mechanism, has been a significant development.

England, of course, has its National Health Service, and most other Western European nations have long-established national health insurance programs. With the exception of the Netherlands, all make some use of cost-sharing techniques. The charges tend, however, to be smaller than those found in the U.S., and usually special exemptions or monetary refunds are available for designated groups, including the poor. The more moderate cost-sharing undoubtedly reflects the social concern inherent in compulsory national programs. Yet even in those presumably more liberal plans, fairly extensive cost-sharing continues to exist, and it is justified on the same general grounds as in the United States (Chester, 1972).

Impact of Cost-Sharing—An Overview

In view of the widespread international use of such techniques as deductibles, coinsurances, and copayments and the consistency of their stated roles, it is surprising to discover that there is scanty documentation of their effects. The lack of data was first reported as early as 1966. Little has happened since then to change the state of knowledge.

The most apparent conclusion to be drawn from this investigation is that the effect of coinsurance and deductible provisions in health insurance contracts on the utilization of health-care services and facilities is extremely difficult to quantify. There is considerable evidence which supports the intuitive conclusion that these provisions do act as a brake on utilization, yet there are sufficient examples of no or negative correlation to cast a lingering doubt as to the exact role which they play. There is little doubt that at very high levels a very important braking effect would be manifest, but short of this, the "threshold" concept of Weisbrod and Feisler might well apply. It is also apparent that the breadth of the underlying coverage and the range of applicability of the deductible and percentage participation provisions are important. In many cases they tend merely to shift the pattern of utilization—sometimes from less expensive (out-patient) to more expensive (in-patient) forms of treatment—rather than reduce utilization.

Because of the variety of deductible provisions in use and the seemingly infinite number of other variables which influence the utilization of health services—many of them uncontrollable —very little useful data are currently available (Hall, 1966: 262).

In a progress report on "The Effects of Cost-Sharing in the Medicaid Program" (Hall et al., 1971), the following findings of an extensive literature search were reported:

(1) There has been very little research conducted to date which focuses on the question of the impact of cost-sharing on any population.
(2) Nothing has been done in the area of establishing the effect of cost-sharing on health services utilization by the poor or near-poor.

(3) There is no general agreement on whether cost-sharing provisions have as their primary goal the reduction of unneces-
ary utilization or the reduction of program costs (i.e., insured
costs).

(4) Deductibles and coinsurance provisions should not be considered as having the same type of impact.

(5) The hard data contained in existing studies and the conclusions reached are not unqualified and are frequently in conflict with each other.

(6) Most studies have suffered from poor design.

These and other findings were explored in considerably more
detail in a later paper prepared as part of the same study. Zelten
(1972:1) states:

> First, there is disagreement concerning the primary purpose
> of cost-sharing, especially the deductible provision. Second, the
> limited research performed contains little stratification. Existing
> studies typically measure the effects of cost-sharing on an entire
> group with scant attention paid to income level, occupation,
> sex, age or any other possibly important factor. Third, many of
> the studies have been carelessly designed, necessitating . . . con-
> siderable skepticism in interpreting results. Further, many of the
> studies have been conducted by persons who obviously began
> their research with the thought in mind of demonstrating what
> they felt was true in the project's inception.

One more recent study does contain significant stratification,
but it deals only with the effect of coinsurance on the use of physician services (Scitovsky and Snyder, 1972).

Available evidence suggests that other nations also have based
decisions regarding cost-sharing largely on intuitive assumptions
rather than hard data. Chester (1972: 4–5) notes that "The broad
pattern of demand for drugs and their costs to the National Health
Service seems to have been little affected by the imposition of prescription charges. . . . Little research has been conducted on the
effect of drug charges on the use made by patients." He also notes that
in West Germany, "Research studies and controlled experiments

about the effect of cost-sharing and charges on the behavior of patients have not been made. Most statements which can be found in the press and in other publications are based nearly always on assumptions" (p. 18). Similar findings were reported elsewhere.

To summarize, what little data are available on the impact of cost-sharing on utilization and cost of health services are inconclusive. Further, they have been gathered almost exclusively from working, middle class insured persons and their dependents. In most cases, the nature of the investigation made it impossible to isolate the influence of the cost-sharing provisions from that of other program changes. Insurers, employers, and unions have all been derelict in not making efforts to document the impact of the provisions, though their reasons are understandable. Not only has each group had fairly strong preconceived convictions, but they have, as a result of experience rating under most group health insurance plans, focused their attention largely on overall retentions and net premiums rather than on more specific points, such as the impact of deductibles or disease-specific utilization rates for various covered services.

Effects of Cost-Sharing in Medicaid

At the outset of the study it was agreed that there was little reason to expect that even the limited data then available on cost-sharing would be reliable in the case of a poor population. It was felt that a whole different set of responses might emanate both from the poor who need health-care services and from the providers. At the same time, it was recognized that social and political dissatisfaction with the health-care system was generating considerable pressure for legislative remedies. To forestall potentially irreversible legislative or administrative action based on either incorrect or inadequate data, it was clear that prompt action was necessary.

Conference

A small group of experts was invited to a conference in Washington, D.C., on October 22, 1971, to help the project team to (a) identify specific researchable topics of high priority, at least some of which would have a short-run payoff potential and (b) discuss research design/strategy to carry out the studies. Conferees were provided in advance with ten "Position Statements" (Appendix 1), a list of "Potential Areas of Investigation" (Appendix 2), and an annotated bibliography of the existing literature, all prepared by the project team.

The conference produced few surprises. Most of those attending were strongly opposed to the concept of cost-sharing in a medical program designed primarily to serve the poor and near poor. It was noted, for example, that there is considerable evidence suggesting that the poor currently underutilize rather than overutilize health services—an inference derived from such available health indicators as infant mortality rates, life-expectancy projections, and the incidence of certain diseases. In most instances, the statistics indicate a clear relationship to economic status, though the major causal factor in the apparent underutilization has yet to be convincingly demonstrated. The cause may be economic. It may also be ignorance of the availability and benefits of health care, or it may be a combination of these and other factors. Whatever the cause, in the face of statistics it is easy to question the morality of a program that injects an additional financial barrier between the poor patient and his receipt of care. Most of the conferees agreed with the proposition that:

> It is imperative to remember, however, that the goal of these provisions [deductible, coinsurance] is not to limit utilization *per se*, but to eliminate *unnecessary* utilization. This is a concept which is difficult if not impossible to define, and in the interests of the overall health and well-being of the nation, large scale attempts to limit the demand for health services should be made only after careful consideration has been given to all potential consequences (emphasis added) (Hall, 1966: 262).

Nevertheless, it must be recognized that, both politically and economically, it would be difficult to enact any major health legislation in this country today without some sort of cost control built in

—especially after the experience under Medicare and Medicaid during the past few years. In this respect, we seem to differ little from the British.

> Whatever both parties may proclaim when in opposition has had, therefore, little relevance to their decisions when they form the government. Thus, a member of the Labour Party may volubly attack charges as a regressive tax on the poor during the election campaign, but his enthusiasm as a Labour Minister of Health for similar action will quickly evaporate when facing the dilemma of increasing costs and shortages! After all the [monies] obtained from charges represent nearly 50% of all capital expenditures on new hospitals and health facilities!
>
> Equally, Conservatives have for long at party gatherings advocated additional charges, hoping to reduce taxation and prevent abuse. . . . The professional advisors of the government, the permanent Civil Service, has seemingly successfully pointed out that the revenue which could be expected from such new charges would be quite disporportionate to the costs of the machinery which would have to be created for their collection, apart from the resentment by the electorate. . . . (Chester, 1972: 11–12).

The objective, clearly, is to make both patients and physicians more responsible in their demands for services without at the same time inhibiting the needy from seeking care.

Thus, while most of the conferees objected to cost-sharing for the poor, they also recognized that the administration seemed to be leaning toward some such mechanism as part of any national legislation (e.g., the family health insurance plan). Under existing Medicaid law, cost-sharing is severely limited. The administration, however, seems to favor permitting such provisions for noncash welfare recipients (the medically indigent) and may even be willing to accept some cost-sharing for cash welfare recipients, as long as the cost-sharing applies only to "optional services" under Medicaid.

In fact, personnel from the U.S. Department of Health, Education, and Welfare (USDHEW) attending the conference reported increasing pressure on the agency to permit waivers for experimentation with various cost-sharing devices in a number of state Medicaid programs. The motive is a desire to curtail the program's rapidly rising expenditures. Only California had been granted a waiver at the time of the conference, and it was being challenged in the courts. (The challenge was subsequently rejected.) Other requests were already on hand, and more were expected. In addition, H.R. 1, pending at the time of the conference, encompassed a variety of cost-sharing arrangements.

In reviewing the "Potential Areas of Investigation," it was somewhat frustrating to find that many of the areas thought to be of greatest importance were believed unlikely to produce short-run results because of difficulties relating to experimental design.

The group considered of primary importance the questions relating to the impact of copayment provisions (items 6–9, Appendix 2). The choice was attributable to the belief that copayment was the most likely form of cost-sharing to become a reality.

Deductibles (items 1–5, Appendix 2) were generally ranked as the next most important area to be studied, though most of the participants were skeptical as to whether or not provisions of that type would actually be implemented—both for economic and political reasons. Practically, a deductible of any magnitude would add to administrative costs because of the recordkeeping necessary if more than one visit were required to satisfy the deductible. Politically, a deductible would probably be less popular than a modest copayment, although, with the economy continuing to stumble along, it may be that some sort of catastrophic protection plan with substantial deductibles—even for the poor—may be all we can expect as a national health insurance program in the short run. In the short run, though, it was felt that the only research result possible might be an answer to the question, "What would be the impact of a uniform deductible on program costs?"

All present believed it would be useful to study both short- and long-term effects of deductibles and copayment provisions on utilization, program costs, and health status of the population, but no suggestions were forthcoming on how best to measure them. The question of health status was particularly troublesome, since any attempt to measure accurately the impact that cost controls would have in that area would require long-term study under strictly controlled conditions.

Aside from the more obvious research problems such a study would create, the legal, moral, and ethical questions seem enormous. Witness, for example, the recent furor over the conduct of the long-term syphilis study in the South. We are not willing to treat human subjects as we do an experimental rat colony! Nevertheless, efforts continue to measure the impact of cost-sharing (see Trowbridge, 1972).

The next most important questions (items 17–20, Appendix 2 —especially items 17 and 19) were also thought to have little chance of payoff. Though generally ranked relatively low in importance, measurement of the physicians' (or other providers') attitude toward the ordering of services, program participation, and charges for services were thought to have a good chance for short-term payoff.

Another area of investigation, not on the original list, emerged from the conference—measurement of the administrative costs associated with cost-sharing. Does a particular provision generate a sufficient cost benefit ratio to make the activity worthwhile? Or might increased administrative costs largely cancel the effect of any reductions in utilization?

Finally, investigation of what techniques other than cost-sharing might achieve similar objectives was thought to be worthwhile.

The Physician and Cost-Sharing

Most previous studies have attempted to evaluate the impact of cost-sharing on the insured/patient. But what of the provider? Surely, there is abundant evidence that, among insured populations, the "service follows the dollar." It is widely recognized that physicians sometimes hospitalize patients for services that could be provided on an outpatient basis, simply because the applicable insurance policy does not cover outpatient services except after a sizable deduction. If that pattern exists for middle class insured persons who, in most cases, could well afford to pay whatever deductible exists, how much more prevalent might it be if the provider had the added concern that the poor patient would be unable to pay him the difference between the full charge and the allowable insurance reimbursement? Thus, if cost-sharing applies unequally to different medical services, it may have a greater impact on provider behavior than on patient behavior.

As noted earlier, proponents of cost-sharing generally claim that it will reduce unnecessary utilization, lower program costs, or both. But program costs may be reduced without lowering utilization.

> Physicians could choose not to bill patients the cost-sharing amount, thereby experiencing a reduction in their private practice incomes, assuming they do not simultaneously increase their customary fees. This would have the effect of reducing program costs but not as a result of reduced utilization (Zelten et al., 1972: 2).

To determine how physicians would react to cost-sharing imposed on poor patients, the same study suggested that the provider of services might "deflect the impact of the cost-sharing provision(s) imposed." What alternatives are open to the physician serving a poor patient under a program that imposes a two-dollar copayment for each office visit? According to Zelten and associates, he could:

(1) conform to the provision by leaving his customary fee unchanged and bill the patient the $2.00 called for by the provision;

(2) raise his fees slightly (less than $2.00) to make up for the possibility of not collecting the $2.00 from all those patients billed the copayment amount;

(3) forget about billing the patient and raise his customary fee by $2.00; or

(4) forget about billing the patient and not raise his fees, thereby incurring a reduction in income to the extent of the foregone copayments.

The physician could change his billing practices in numerous other ways as well. He could raise his fees for patients not affected by the cost-sharing provisions while leaving his fees unchanged for others (pp. 3–4).

Obviously, the results in terms of utilization will vary with the physician's response. Another alternative—independent of the billing process—would be the physician's refusal to serve patients affected by the cost-sharing, which would aggravate an already serious supply problem.

Evidence does exist that physicians have responded in that fashion. In Saskatchewan, for example, the introduction of copayment led to a marked decline in "regional examinations" in comparison with "complete examinations." Absence of a corresponding increase in laboratory charges, however, suggests that the data reflect a change in billing rather than in service (Beck, 1972: 13). Chester (1972) hints at a similar result with reference to prescription charges in England:

> British experience shows that patients and in particular, physicians, must be expected to adjust their actions so as to minimise the impact of these charges. Whatever the immediate effect of their imposition may be, it seems that long-term repercussions will probably be neutralised (p. 11).

In speaking with Medicaid officials in New York State, it was suggested that low allowances for Medicaid office visits coupled with an eighty-percent coinsurance provision for the medically indigent had had a dual impact. First, some physicians withdrew their services from the poor. Second, others simply refused to see the patients in their private practice (four dollars allowed for an office visit, with an eighty-percent coinsurance provision), and referred them instead to a nearby outpatient clinic that would provide similar services but that, as an institution, would be reimbursed through Medicaid at cost—easily several times the allowable payment for an office visit.

It is clear, then, that the attitude of the provider is an important variable to be considered in predicting the impact of any cost-sharing provision relating to the poor. For that reason, physicians in Philadelphia County were surveyed to determine how they would be likely to react to the imposition of cost-sharing for the poor. The physicians were classified by type of practice (specialty), percent of patient load classified as poor, physician's income level, and other potentially important characteristics. Several types of cost-sharing provisions were also hypothesized. The major conclusions are as follows:

1. If cost sharing provisions are introduced into the Medicaid program about one-half of the physicians in Philadelphia County delivering primary care can be expected to cooperate with the provision.

2. The poor patients in the study area face restricted accessibility to health care insofar as 23 percent of the respondents indicated they were accepting no new patients covered under welfare programs.

3. Osteopaths deliver a great deal of primary care to welfare patients and they tend to react to cost-sharing considerably differently than M.D.'s. From the standpoint of what policymakers would favor as physician reaction, D.O.'s digress more than M.D.'s.

4. For reasons enumerated in the study, the deductible type of cost-sharing provision would likely elicit the most physician cooperation while coinsurance would elicit the least.

5. There does not appear to be a significant relationship between the way physicians react to cost-sharing and either medical specialty or level of private practice income.

6. Physicians with a high percent of their patient load on welfare will react to cost-sharing differently than a physician with a low percentage of poor patients. One-half of the D.O.'s with over 25 percent of their patient load on welfare would react to cost-sharing by raising fees and foregoing the billing of patients. Many M.D.'s would also react in this manner.

. . . [T]he introduction of cost-sharing into the Medicaid program will not simply be a matter of exacting a dollar sum from each program eligible as he receives care . . . important side-effects are likely to occur . . . policymakers [should] give careful thought to the type and amount of cost-sharing to be used, the manner in which it should be applied, and how it should be administered, if, indeed one should be used at all (Zelten et al., 1972:36–37).

Even allowing for the fact that people often do not act as they say they will, the results of the study provide some important insights into the way providers will react.

Other results of that study cited 61.2 percent of the responding physicians as agreeing with the statement that "cost-sharing may reduce unnecessary but not necessary utilization;" in addition, 53.1 percent of the respondents felt that "patients subject to a deductible will over-utilize once the deductible is met." Interestingly, only 49.1 percent of the respondents disagreed with the statement that "physicians will increase services under cost-sharing to maintain their level of income." Almost 23 percent had no opinion on that statement (Zelten et al., 1972:33–35).

Hospital Utilization

In one sense, Dolfman (1972) reports the introduction of Medicaid was the same as the removal of a deductible in its effect on hospital utilization in Philadelphia. With the advent of Medicare and Medicaid, large numbers of the elderly and the poor suddenly obtained a choice in seeking institutional health care. Before 1966, Philadelphia General Hospital was the only hospital in the city providing free care. If that were all that happened, he says, "it could be argued that Medicaid and Medicare have been successful in 'opening up' the hospital system to all segments of our population" (p. 8).

Preliminary investigations of available data, however, particularly with reference to death rates among the elderly, suggested to him the following hypothesis:

Changes in utilization practices by low income and elderly patients was due to the fact that these patients were captured by institutions in search of additional revenue (p. 8).

Though still tentative and currently being pursued in greater depth, the initial findings of the Dolfman (1972) study, if they hold up under further testing, could have far-reaching policy implications:

> As financial burdens increase, hospitals are seeking new sources of revenue. It appears that certain institutions have made an attempt to admit and treat low income and/or elderly patients in the attempt to increase their revenues. . . . With Medicaid and Medicare reimbursing hospitals for the full cost of in-house treatment . . . certain hospitals can relieve some of their financial pressures by regularly admitting these patients . . . there may be increased pressures to "capture" low income patients (pp. 10–11).

Not only, Dolfman adds, would this result call for intensified controls—perhaps in the form of tighter utilization review—but it could also generate a financial crisis for our large municipal hospitals, thus creating a potentially serious disruption to our existing health care system.

Physicians' Services and the Poor

Thanks to the sophistication of the computer records for the public medical care insurance program in the Province of Saskatchewan, Beck (1972) has been able to isolate the impact of various cost-sharing provisions on the poor. As he notes:

> There is little reason to doubt that as the price of medical care is increased through the imposition of copayment the quantity of service taken will decline. The major issue confronting policymakers is, however, the effect on the distribution or provision of services to selected population groups. The desire to ensure access to medical services for population groups who by inference may "need" health care was the primary reason for introducing public medical care insurance. If copayment provisions affect such groups by unduly restricting their access to service the benefits of the public medical care program may be lost (p. 1).

Saskatchewan has experimented with copayment under the medical insurance program. In the absence of a statutory definition of "poor" families, Beck (1972) arbitrarily set an annual income of five thousand dollars as his measure. He then set about trying to measure the impact of changes in cost-sharing during the first year after its imposition. He did not then attempt to measure the lasting effect of copayment, but that is being pursued under a separate grant. Impact on different components of care is considered.

Beck (1972) establishes a multiple-variable model incorporating a variety of economic and demographic variables. His is probably the most comprehensive effort to date to directly measure the impact of cost-sharing per se on the poor. Nevertheless, the model used does impose a number of restrictions on the analysis. His data were taken from a random sampling of Saskatchewan families drawn for each of the years 1963–1968. A subsample was then taken to include only families with incomes under five thousand dollars (p. 6).

He was able to show that the introduction of a $1.50 copayment per office visit and a $2.00 charge for home, emergency, or hospital outpatient visits in 1968 reduced total utilization of physician's services in the province by an estimated six to seven percent. During the same period, services to "poor" families declined about twelve percent. He adds, however, that "if a definition of the 'poor' were used which includes age and family size as well as income, the impact of co-payment will be found to be even greater. An analysis of family utilization by age of the head and family size, but not considering income, revealed that reductions in use of services of up to twenty-four percent occurred among aged and large families" (Beck, 1972: 9–10).

The data further show that the impact is greater on general practitioner (first contact) services than on specialist services. While both "patient elective" and "physician elective" services declined, the latter did so by a lesser amount. And he adds that, "It is, of course, not possible to infer whether the reduction in these services represents a decline in 'abuse' through over-servicing and over-utilization" (Beck, 1972: 10–13). This last unanswered question, unfortunately, is the one for which an answer is most needed. Indeed, it may simply not be possible to get a definitive answer. It is of interest to note that the one United States study that did have reasonably sound experimental control as well as a fairly reliable proxy for income stratification found that the impact of coinsurance fell more heavily on the lower income (though not "poor") group (Scitovsky and Snyder, 1972: 16).

The European Experience

As noted previously, virtually no effort has been made to either impose or measure the effect of cost-sharing on the poor in Western Europe. Chester (1972) makes the point that, in the application of various cost-sharing provisions—and they are widely used —the poor have almost always been provided special treatment. In France, however, everyone is subject to the same "ticket moderateur" (copayments) under the health insurance program, but the poor may "apply for help through public assistance in case of hardship" (Chester, 1972: 24).

Further:

The Committee of Ministers of the Council of Europe has recently been considering means to achieve a reduction of costs for health care within the Member States of the Council. Among these recommendations the Council considered in particular the problem of whether and how far patients should participate in cost-sharing. It accepted in principle that patients should be made to bear a share of the costs. It laid down, however, that this should be done only if such contributions were being kept small and should not be applicable:
a) In the case of an illness creating large expenses such as would be the case in a major operation and long term diseases.
b) For low income groups.
c) If there is no danger of abuse, as for example in pregnancy (Chester, 1972: 31).

His survey cites further from a convention adopted by the International Labour Conference in June 1969:

If legislation accepts the principle that the insured has to participate in bearing a part of the costs, such a participation has to be calculated in such a way that hardship is avoided and that the effectiveness of the medical and social protection is not infringed (p. 31).

Finally, Chester quotes Milton Roemer:

. . . [T]he ultimate justification of cost-sharing in a social security scheme is a matter of political ideology. . . . [I]t is a method of keeping social insurance premiums or general taxes lower than they would otherwise be. It is a principle of greater individual, as against social, responsibility that is being implemented. There may well be sound reasons for striking a balance . . . in the operation of a medical care scheme. . . . In the long term, however, cost-sharing is probably a less desirable method of raising money than the classical devices of social insurance or general revenues. If economies must be achieved in a medical care scheme, then these ought ideally to be through implementation of the pattern of medical care organisation which is inherently most economical (p. 32).

Administrative Costs

Though it initially appeared promising, an attempt to measure the administrative costs of implementing various cost-sharing mechanisms ended in frustration. Neither commercial insurers, the "Blues," nor the Social Security Administration (under Medicare) was able to provide any breakdown of costs involved in keeping track of cumulative deductibles. For the other cost-sharing techniques discussed, no identifiable costs exist. In coinsurance, the adjuster simply must push a different key on an office calculator. In the case of copayments, the cost of administration automatically shifts to the middleman—the provider. As we have seen, the physician has several options available to him.

As to the deductible, most professional insurance people contacted felt that no significant costs were involved. In fact, since most claim costs are "contact costs," a deductible may actually

serve to reduce administrative costs by reducing the number of contacts. That is probably true in commercial insurance groups, where
there is a middleman—the employer—to screen claims and/or explain coverage to the insured. Whether or not it would be true with
a poverty group—lacking the employer middleman and probably
lacking full understanding of the coverage—is problematic. Substantial costs might be incurred here simply in corresponding with
claimants to explain why coverage is not available. (For a further
discussion, see Hall et al., 1972).

Future Research

As a followup to this study, the author is currently directing another, which is designed to measure the effect of optional services
in the Medicaid program, also sponsored by the Social and Rehabilitation Service, USDHEW, Contract No. 18P-56701/3-01. The
initial investigation is directed toward ascertaining what medical
services are actually used by Medicaid elgibles under different program benefits, where and from whom the services are received, and
how they are paid for. By selecting four locations with diverse optional services (Atlanta, Georgia; Little Rock, Arkansas; Oklahoma City, Oklahoma; Trenton, New Jersey), it is hoped that patterns can be discerned that may be causally linked to the presence
or absence of certain optional services. Presumably, it should be
possible to get some inkling of the degree to which some services
can be substituted for others, as well as an indication of the impact
of cost-sharing—since failure by a state Medicaid program to provide a given optional service amounts to a one hundred percent deductible for that service. The heart of the study will consist of one
thousand personal interviews in each of the four locations. Samples
will be drawn on a proportional random basis based on certain demographic and aid-category criteria. The study will be limited to
cash welfare recipients in the programs of Office of Administration
on Aging, Aid to Families with Dependent Children, and Aid to the
Permanently and Totally Disabled.

Additional studies are also underway or contemplated for the
future. In one, under the waiver granted by the Social and Rehabili-

tation Service, the Medicaid program in California (Medi-Cal) is attempting to measure the effectiveness of the device.

Beck, Scitovsky and Snyder, and others have all indicated that additional studies are planned with their basic data. Further exploration of provider-directed cost-sharing may also be in order.

Summary

Slowly, it may be possible to piece together additional parts of the puzzle of cost-sharing. More likely, perhaps, it will never be possible, because of ethical constraints on experimental design, to satisfactorily determine whether the alleged negative effects—in terms of discouraging desirable treatment—may outweigh the alleged economic benefits. Even the relatively short-run economic benefits have not been clearly established in all cases. British experience with prescription drugs, for example, suggests that a deductible may actually increase program costs by encouraging physicians to prescribe larger amounts, thus possibly leading to extra costs and waste (Chester, 1972).

There is, of course, substantial evidence in the literature that even under the best of circumstances a variety of cost-sharing arrangements would be needed to fulfill normal objectives, since the impact varies significantly by type of service.

But the dilemma still remains. If set too low, an economic constraint may be so trivial that it does not have the intended effect on utilization or cost; in fact, a slight constraint may have the perverse effect of encouraging some people to take advantage of it by seeking unnecessary care. If set very high, it will be clearly burdensome to all, thus constituting a real barrier to access to medical care. Finally, if set at a moderate level, it would be easily borne by the wealthy, thus not affecting their use of health services; at the same time it would continue to represent a significant barrier for the poor, thus perpetuating and accentuating the politically and socially abhorrent situation of two levels of care.

In the final analysis, then, it may be that the "political ideology" referred to by Roemer will govern. Certainly, the concept of cost-sharing is so universally accepted as a part of both public and private health insurance plans that no realist can expect it to disappear in the foreseeable future. But other mechanisms may emerge. The Dutch, for instance, provide restorative dental treatment free, conditional upon regular half-yearly examinations (Chester, 1972). Can other preventive care be so identified and mandated? Perhaps. So, too, prior authorization, utilization review, and professional review may develop into effective, yet noninhibiting, controls.

But it is still important to remember that no panaceas are in sight. Glaser (1970) points out that

> [A] great deal more than free availability seems necessary to induce insured persons to use preventive services. . . . Apathy is at least as important as financial barriers in determining the use of preventive services (p. 183).

And again he says:

> Capitation cannot reorient styles of medical practice, but it can support traditional practices. . . . If medical care and medical education traditionally emphasize therapy, more than a capitation system is necessary to instill a preventive viewpoint (p. 287).

And if years of ignorant assumption have convinced policymakers that cost-sharing can reduce unnecessary utilization and/or hold down social insurance costs, it will require more than impassioned rhetoric on behalf of the disenfranchised poor to reverse the pattern.

Appendix 1

Study of Effects of Cost Sharing in the Medicaid Program

Position Statements

After preliminary investigation, it seems safe to list the following statements as facts which reflect, in general, the current state of knowledge about the effects of cost sharing and the need for additional study. Unless there is serious objection to any of these points, they will be taken as given for purposes of discussion during the meeting to be held October 22, 1971, in Washington. While additional statements might also have been listed, this limited group was selected in the hope that they, at least, would serve as a departure point and basis of agreement for deliberations.

1. There is a widespread belief on a priori grounds that cost-sharing mechanisms can and do have a significant impact if applied to a medical program.
2. There is a significant divergence of opinion as to the nature of this impact (i.e., whether it has its most important influence on program cost, utilization patterns or general health of the group).
3. There are serious disagreements as to the desirability of cost-sharing mechanisms, particularly with respect to their impact on low income groups.
4. There are no adequate data available at present to indicate what the introduction of *any* cost-sharing approach would do under the Medicaid program.
5. The limited empirical evidence which has been collected with respect to cost-sharing has been inconclusive, contradictory and generally based on results with insurance programs under which few, if any, medically indigent have been included.
6. A number of specific weaknesses of most past investigations in this field can be listed:
   a. unavailability of data from an appropriate control population;
   b. failure to ascertain the relationship between changes in total cost of care for the relevant population and changes in program or plan costs;
   c. little effort to distinguish between the effects of various types or combinations of cost-sharing mechanisms, e.g., deductibles, percentage participation (coinsurance) clauses; and

   d. focus on a single parameter without adequate attention to other effects, e.g., where the objective has been reduction in plan costs, costs have been measured without regard to evaluation of utilization patterns or overall health of the covered group.
 7. The lack of good baseline data on existing patterns of utilization of health services by the Medicaid target population represents a major challenge in conducting the present study.
 8. It is possible to generate data which will permit more scientific evaluation of the effects of cost sharing.
 9. Regardless of a priori attitudes on the merits of cost sharing, hard data are essential to sound policy and program decisions.
10. Time is of the essence in conducting this study because of the enormous political and social pressures for early action in the health care field.

Appendix 2

Study of Effects of Cost Sharing in the Medicaid Program

Potential Areas of Investigation

The following potential areas of investigation have been identified for study under the above topic. In order to facilitate maximum productivity from the meeting in Washington on October 22, 1971, we would appreciate it if you would:

   a. make whatever refinements and/or additions to this list which you feel are appropriate;
   b. rank the list in order of importance and likelihood of obtaining definitive research findings within two to three years; and
   c. return your list as soon as possible so that a composite ranking of items can be prepared to guide the discussion on October 22.

Suggested areas of investigation (amended):

1. impact of uniform deductible(s) on the utilization of various services;
2. impact of uniform deductible(s) on program costs;
3. impact of deductible(s) of various sizes on a given service;
4. impact of deductible(s) of various sizes on program costs;
5. impact of deductible(s) on various groupings of program eligibles, e.g., well, worried-well . . . ;
6. impact of uniform co-pay (percentage participation) clause(s) on the utilization of various services;
7. impact of uniform co-pay clause(s) on program cost;
8. impact of co-pay clause(s) of various sizes on a given service;
9. impact of co-pay clause(s) of various sizes on program costs;
10. impact of co-pay clauses on various groupings of program eligibles;
11. implications of varying the magnitude of a cost sharing provision by consumer income level within a program;
12. investigation of the short- versus long-term effects of all of the above on utilization, program costs and health status of the target population;
13. investigation of the potential viability of cost-sharing techniques other than co-pay and deductibles, e.g., can the provider be made to share costs?
14. impact of various cost-sharing mechanisms on providers' ordering of services;
15. impact of various cost-sharing mechanisms on providers' willingness to participate in program;
16. impact of cost-sharing provisions on providers' charges for various services;
17. applicability of available data to Medicaid eligibles;
18. examination of current patterns and level of health-care utilization by Medicaid eligibles;
19. examination of factors influencing patterns and level of health-care utilization by Medicaid eligibles;

20. examination of attitudes of Medicaid eligibles toward the imposition of cost sharing; and
21. what techniques other than cost sharing, if any, may be substituted to achieve similar objectives without altering program eligibility or benefits?

References

Beck, R. G.
  1972   "The impact of co-payment on poor families' use of physicians' services: The Saskatchewan case." Unpublished paper, July.
Chester, T. E.
  1972   "The effects of copayments and charges on the utilisation of health care: A comparative survey of the European situation." Unpublished paper, December.
Dickerson, O. D.
  1959   "Overutilization in health insurance." The Journal of Insurance 26 (Spring): 65–72.
Dolfman, M. L.
  1972   "The impact of Medicaid on utilization at Philadelphia General Hospital." Unpublished paper, June.
Glaser, William A.
  1970   Paying the Doctor: Systems of Remuneration and Their Effects. Baltimore: The Johns Hopkins Press.
Hall, Charles P., Jr.
  1966   "Deductibles in health insurance: An evaluation." The Journal of Risk and Insurance 23 (June): 262.
Hall, Charles P., Jr., et al.
  1972   "The effects of cost-sharing in the Medicaid program." Interim report, Unpublished, April 14.
Hall, Charles P., Jr., et al.
  1971   "The effects of cost-sharing in the Medicaid program." Progress report, Unpublished, December 20.
Munts, Raymond
  1967   Bargaining for Health. Madison: The University of Wisconsin Press.

Pollack, Jerome
   1957   "Major medical expense insurance: An evaluation." Ameri-
           can Journal of Public Health 47 (January): 322–334.
Scitovsky, A. A. *and* N. M. Snyder
   1972   "Effect of coinsurance on use of physician services." Social
           Security Bulletin 35 (June): 3–19.
Source Book of Health Insurance Data
   1972   New York: Health Insurance Institute.
Trowbridge, Charles L.
   1972   "Quantity-price relationships in health insurance." Actuari-
           al Note 79 (November), U.S. Department of Health, Edu-
           cation, and Welfare publication number (SSA) 73-11507
Williams, C. Arthur, Jr.
   1953   "The deductible in medical expense insurance." Journal of
           the American Association of University Teachers of Insur-
           ance 20 (March): 107–115.
Zelten, Robert A.
   1972   "The impact of cost-sharing on the utilization of health
           services." Unpublished paper, January.
Zelten, Robert A., R. D. Eilers, *and* William L. Kissick
   1972   "Physician reaction to cost-sharing for the poor." Unpub-
           lished paper, June.

Physicians

as Guiders of

Health Services Use

PAUL M. GERTMAN

It is frequently said that the physician is the key decisionmaker in the health-service system. One authority recently commented: "Most observers agree that once the patient has made initial contact with the medical care system, the physician becomes the principal decisionmaker and allocator of medical resources. He, in effect, decides how much and what types of additional medical services the patient should receive" (Shortell, 1972:2). If there is agreement with such statements, then it would seem that the physician's role as a guide to the use of health services would have priority in any discussion of health policy.

Yet the impact of physicians' decisions on the use of medical services and the reasoning behind them has been subject to relatively little scientific investigation or analysis. There is no real body of research literature specifically directed at the question. The following discussions will therefore be aimed at briefly reviewing four selected areas of physicians' actions and reasoning, some implications and trends of each, how their interactions may affect health-services utilization, and some questions for future research. The objective will not be to present a comprehensive analysis—nor is it possible to do so—but rather to provide a few perspectives on how the physician may guide health-services utilization.

362

Ambulatory Medical Care: Physician Direction

In a single year, patient contacts with physicians number about one billion. The premise, both explicit and implicit, in many discussions and analyses of ambulatory utilization-pattern dynamics is that patients' initiation of demand is and will continue to be the dominant force in determining patient-physician contacts. Examination, however, of some of the information about ambulatory practice and of trends in medical care should raise some questions about the validity of that premise.

To explore the current and future role of the physician in determining utilization, some data on physician visit rates and their relationship to incidence of illness are presented, and a few studies on referral patterns and patient disposition practices are then reviewed. In 1970, there was a national average of 4.6 physician visits per person (White, 1972). White and his colleagues (1961) estimated from national data sources that in each month seven hundred fifty out of every one thousand adults will recognize and recall an episode of illness or injury; two hundred fifty of the one thousand will consult a physician at least once during the month, and five will be referred to another physician. More recently, Richardson (1971) studied ambulatory use of physicians' services in response to illness episodes of a low-income population in Brooklyn served by a neighborhood health center operated by the Office of Economic Development. In his study, seventy-four percent of the patients with an illness episode contacted a physician. Although the figures at first seem dissimilar, in the low-income group only thirty-four percent recalled an episode of illness, and thus a corrected rate of physicians' visits for the total sample interviewed might be estimated to be approximately twenty-five percent.

The physician's role in directing ambulatory health-services utilization can be examined from two different perspectives—how the patient came to the physician and what disposition the physician made after the initial contact. Preliminary results from the United States samples of the World Health Organization/International

Collaborative Study of Medical Care Use (Kohn, 1973) indicate that approximately 28 percent of all ambulatory patient-physician contacts were scheduled or initiated by the physician. Recent data collected by Mushlin and Barr (1973) at the Columbia Medical Plan—a prepaid group practice affiliated with Johns Hopkins— showed that 47.2 percent of the visits were initiated by practitioners. Investigations of specialist practice referral sources also showed a substantial degree of physician-initiation. In a study of 4,608 "new" patients seen by internists in New York State, Johnson and his colleagues (1965) found that 63.6 percent were self-referred or referred by someone other than a physician, 18.2 percent were referred by general practitioners, 17.1 percent were referred by specialists, and in 1.1 percent of the cases, the source of referral was not determined; the total referral by physicians thus amounted to 35.3 percent.

Creditor and Creditor (1972), in examining the referral sources of 2,090 new patients seen in the private practices of specialists at the Michael Reese Hospital in Chicago, found that 53.7 percent were self and lay referrals (4.3 percent and 49.4 percent, respectively), 27.3 percent were referrals from other specialists or staff of the Michael Reese Hospital, 15.2 percent were from outside medical providers, and 4.4 percent were referrals from other sources.

After the patient has seen the physician for the first time, the latter can either (a) recommend no further care and discharge him; (b) continue to provide care by seeing him again; or (c) recommend care from another provider.

It is then that the physician probably directs almost totally the utilization of further physician services. Richardson's study (1971) indicated that 52 percent of initial patient visits led to a recommendation for a revisit. Initial results from the World Health Organization/International Collaborative Study of Medical Care Use (Kohn, 1973) show that of all persons who had a medical contact in a two-week recall period, 53 percent were scheduled for a revisit or referred to another physician. In Johnson et al.'s (1965) study of internists' "new" patients, almost 85 percent were directed to seek additional physician services; 55.3 percent were given further appointments with the same physician, 18.5 percent were returned to their referring physician for followup care, and 11.1 percent were referred to another specialist. Last and White (1969), studying the content of five primary or general practices located in Vermont, found that over a three-month period each patient illness "condition" resulted in an average of 1.5 physician contacts, which may be interpolated as a 50 percent revisit rate.

The general issue of how economic factors, particularly in the aggregate, affect utilization of physician services is beyond the intent of this paper. With respect, however, to the preceding discussion, one tangential issue might be briefly considered: "Does the physician consciously schedule unnecessary revisits, referrals, or tests to increase his personal financial gain?" Although there are no "hard" data that answer the question, the following speculative thinking might be considered.

First, it is self-evident that all physicians, to some degree, practice medicine to earn money, although most observers would agree that this is not usually the incentive affecting the manner in which they practice and their direction of patient consumption of medical services. Based on the studies mentioned earlier, a large part of a physician's income in ambulatory practice is derived either from revisits that he has directly initiated or from referrals of other medical care providers.

Second, in an ambulatory practice, a physician is essentially selling his time, and thus a significant incentive to schedule unnecessary patient visits might be expected only if there were less than one hundred percent demand for his time. Most information points, however, to a marked excess in today's ambulatory health-care marketplace of demand for physician services over supply. Recent survey data from the American Medical Association (Walsh, 1972) show that average total patient visits per week for all physicians was 132.5, with average office visits numbering 95.5 per week and average hospital visits 38.3; the general practitioner in a nonmetropolitan area averaged 210.8 patient visits per week. Salaries for employed physicians have escalated to the point where some organizations are offering over $75,000 a year to doctors just out of residency training. Discussions with physicians newly established in private practice related to primary care indicates that within six months of setting up shop they are so busy that they are turning away patients. Thus, at the current time, it does not appear that the average physician needs to or does schedule unnecessary visits to increase his income. This limited exposition does not deal, of course, with the issue that the overall demand pattern may have been so "revved-up" by medical practitioners in the past that the individual physician no longer has to act in a consciously self-serving fashion.

Another relatively unexplored area of what may be unnecessary medical-services utilization that might be affected by a physician's interest in personal gain is the ordering of ancillary services in his own office. A recent study by Childs and Hunter (1972) found that physicians providing direct X-ray services to their patients ordered diagnostic radiography for almost twice as many patients as did physicians who referred patients to radiologists for all X-rays. Additionally, the pattern of X-ray work ordered by a physician varied independently of the patient characteristics studied. The authors raised, with appropriate caveats, the following point: "We assume that a physician providing direct X-ray services owned, or had equivalent economic interest in, radiographic or fluoroscopic apparatus and that he operated it in his office. This economic interest would include the capital investment in the apparatus and the income that its use would generate. The physician with X-ray apparatus, therefore, would be motivated to use that apparatus in order to amortize the capital cost as well as to produce income."

There may be other explanations for their findings. A possible one is simply that once the physician has bought a piece of diagnostic equipment, he tends to use it frequently, not primarily to recover the capital investment or increase his income but simply because it is at hand. Bailey (1970) argues that since most ancillary services are available from other "firms" that specialize in them and since he finds that "the individual physician's productivity is not affected by possessing such equipment," the decision to produce the services internally should and can be analyzed separately from the basic decision of whether to order tests at all. That is another area for future investigation of the effect of physician behavior on medical utilization and one that may have some direct implications for attempts to control and regulate physician office fees.

One special aspect of patient disposition is the referral of patients from one physician to another. Williams et al. (1960;1961) in North Carolina found that only 3 percent of the patients seen in general practice were referred to other physicians. Last and White's (1969) study of Vermont general practices showed that the mean referral rate for both specialist and diagnostic examinations was 11.2 for every 1,000 visits or approximately 1.1 percent. The studies suggest that most primary practitioners were attempting to handle the vast majority of their patients' problems without recourse to referral. Evaluations by Peterson et al. (1956) and Clute (1963) of general practitioners in North Carolina and Eastern Canada were both highly critical of the lack of referral. Clute felt that 30 percent of the physicians saw and treated patients who should have been referred to specialists.

Referral rates between specialists appear to be considerably higher than those of general practitioners. In a study of an average week's practice by internists in the Chicago area, Shortell (1972) found that approximately 9 percent of all patient visits led to a referral to another physician. Penchansky and Fox (1970) in a study of prepaid group practice physicians learned that, on the average, 7 percent of the patients seen by urban internists and 9.5 percent of those seen by suburban internists were referred to other physicians. In the study by Johnson et al. (1969), New York internists referred 11.1 percent of their "new" patients to another physician. Given the general similarity of the results, it may be estimated that approximately 10 percent of patient contacts with an internal medicine specialist lead to a referral to another specialist.

The massive increases of future physicians currently in the medical education pipeline and the projected disappearance of general practitioner training make it probable that by the late 1980's American medical practice will consist almost entirely of specialty practice. Thus, it is likely that physician-to-physician referrals will be an increasing factor in determining the overall causal patterns of ambulatory health use.

Several other factors that may tend to increase the relative role of physician guidance in utilization practices are efforts to increase preventive-services utilization, to make health systems more comprehensive, and to increase patient compliance. All involve a more aggressive approach by practitioners to initiate ambulatory-service contacts, both from the outset and in followup care. Therefore, at some future time, a crosscut utilization survey of ambulatory visits may well show that the large majority are initiated by physicians (or other health practitioners) rather than by patients. Finally, one might speculate on the effect that might have on attempts to control patient initiation of services through economic mechanisms, such as deductibles and coinsurance.

Hospital Admissions

In 1971 there were more than thirty million community hospital admissions and expenditures of over twenty-nine billion dollars on hospital care (Cooper and Worthington, 1973). Since 1950 the average expenses per patient per hospital day have risen sixfold. The rise represents not only inflation and changes in hospital care but also a rise from 110.9 to 147.6 admissions per one thousand population per year (Source Book of Health Insurance Data, 1972–73, 1972). The issue of hospital utilization and costs ranks as the priority health-policy problem for public officials.

Physicians are almost totally responsible both legally and functionally for admission of a patient to a hospital, the care he is given, and the length of stay. Research about the physician's role has been largely concerned with the effect of practice organization on admission rates and with the variation in length of hospital stay. Most studies in the former category in recent years have focused on the lower admission rates of prepaid group practices compared with fee-for-service practice (Anderson and Sheatsley, 1959; Densen et al., 1962; 1960; Klarman, 1963; Perrott, 1971; Shapiro and Brindle, 1969). With the exception, however, of a study of federal employees under multiple-option plans (Perrott, 1971), few of the studies to date have large comparable populations and none have adequate measures of "out-of-plan" hospital use. With respect to the individual physician's role, there is no study that has tried to determine whether differences in admission rates are due to variations in patients' disease problems or to variations in physician behavior when faced with similar patient problems. Many studies have also been done on the wide variations in average length of stay for similar disease problems and for variations from physician to physician (McNerney et al., 1962; Hearman, 1964; Jones, 1964; Acheson and Feldstein, 1964; Riedel and Fitzpatrick, 1964).

In a recent study of Indiana Blue Cross-Blue Shield data, Praiss found that " . . . there tends to exist a pattern of providing patient care, as indicated by the length of hospitalization, which is relatively consistent within individual physicians regardless of the hospitals in which he practices, or of patient age group or, to a lesser degree, of the patient condition category" (1971:ii).

The Social Security Administration Medicare Analysis of Days of Care (MADOC) shows that average length of hospital stay in the Northeastern United States is approximately twice as long as that of the West Coast. Regional practice variations are often referred to (although Praiss's data indicate that there are also intraregional physician-related variations) but no explanation is given. Conceptually, it is hard to find a plausible explanation for the differences in physician behavior. United States medical education is highly standardized (compared with other forms of education), and there is significant national migration of physicians. In short, the information to date raises more questions than it answers. A key future research question must be: "What causes the variations in length of stay?"

The only major work exploring physician-decision rationales for hospital admission is Anderson and Sheatsley's study, *Hospital Use: A Survey of Patient and Physician Decisions* (1967). Their findings on a sample of 1,628 general admissions are thus worth reviewing in some detail. Their survey (see Fig. 1) indicated that

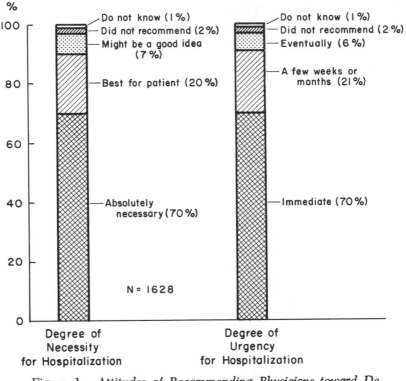

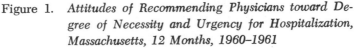

Figure 1. *Attitudes of Recommending Physicians toward Degree of Necessity and Urgency for Hospitalization,
Massachusetts, 12 Months, 1960–1961*

SOURCE: Anderson and Sheatsley (1967).

physicians believed that ninety-seven percent of the admissions
were medically warranted and also that ninety-seven percent of the
cases would either immediately, in the near future, or eventually require admission. Additionally, they felt that only three percent of
medical and four percent of surgical admissions could have been
treated equally well outside the hospital (see Fig. 2). Even with respect to "diagnostic" admissions, physicians reported that only eight
percent could have been treated just as well on the outside. Since
the study was made in 1961, one wonders whether, with the advent

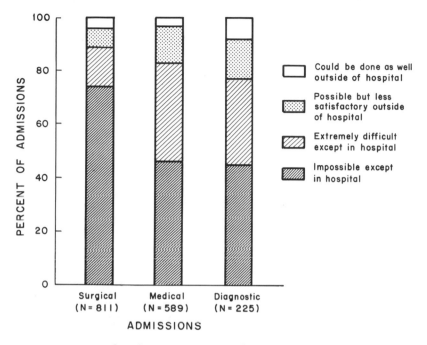

Figure 2.   *Classification of Hospital Admissions by Possibility of Outside Treatment, Massachusetts, 12 Months, 1960–1961*

SOURCE: Anderson and Sheatsley (1967).

of Medicare and utilization-review requirements, even these low figures of "unnecessary" admission would be disclosed by physicians today. Another interesting finding was that different sources of payment had no apparent effect on the physician's determination of either the necessity for admission or the length of hospital stay. Clearly, much more probing is needed of the casual dynamics of physician-directed utilization of hospital services. Since the advent of Medicare, however, with its denial of reimbursement for medically "unnecessary" admissions, physicians may be reluctant to disclose information that would increase our understanding of their rationale in hospital-admission decisions.

Medical Decision Practices

The most important factors in understanding the physician's role as a guide to health-services use and the dynamic impact physicians have on overall utilization patterns are the medical-decision concepts upon which diagnosis and treatment are based.

Ledley and Lusted (1959) in their classic paper, "The Reasoning Foundations of Medical Diagnosis," point out that a medical diagnosis is basically a probabilistic determination under conditions of uncertainty because diagnosis "can rarely be made with absolute certainty." Simplistically, in trying to determine between "wellness" and "sickness," a physician can take one of four actions:

(1) dismiss a patient as "well" when the patient is actually *well;*

(2) dismiss a patient as "well" when the patient is actually *sick;*

(3) treat (or continue to investigate) a patient as "sick" when the patient is actually *sick;* or

(4) treat a patient as "sick" when the patient is actually *well.*

Statisticians would label the second decision (i.e., rejecting a hypothesis that is true) as a "type 1" error, and the fourth decision (i.e., accepting a hypothesis that is false) as a "type 2" error.

The single largest element in a physician's judgment affecting medical-services utilization is his desire to avoid committing a type 1 error. Scheff (1963:97–107) made the following comment on that point: "Although there is some sentiment against type 2 errors (unnecessary surgery, for instance) it has nothing like the force and urgency of the sentiment against type 1 errors. A physician who dismisses a patient who subsequently dies of a disease that should have been detected is not only subject to legal action for negligence . . . but also to moral condemnation from his colleagues and from his own conscience. . . . Nothing resembling this amount of moral and legal suasion is brought to bear for committing a type 2 error. Indeed, this error is sometimes seen as sound clinical practice, indicating a healthily conservative approach to medicine." Thus, it is probable that type 2 errors far outnumber type 1 errors in medical practice. A study by Garland (1959), for example, of 14,887 X-ray diagnoses of tuberculosis, found 1,216 false positive readings (type 2 errors) in contrast to only 24 false negative readings (type 1 errors)—a ratio of over 50 to 1.

Even the availability of "hard" data to guide decisionmaking may have little influence on physician behavior. Bell and Loop (1971), for example, published an excellent analysis of clinical criteria for determining whether skull X-rays should be taken in cases of trauma. Use of their "high-yield" criteria would detect ninety-nine percent of all skull fractures and would eliminate the need for doing thirty percent of all X-rays currently performed for suspected skull fractures. Those criteria might save 320,000 persons each year from X-ray exposure and reduce medical-care expenditures by fifteen million dollars a year. When the data from the study were presented, however, to the senior resident staff of a major municipal teaching hospital (who make the decisions on ordering X-rays), every single house-officer stated that he would still continue to order X-rays for all patients who were in the "low yield" category because they could not take the one percent chance of missing a skull fracture!

The implicit and overriding decision norm—"When in doubt, suspect illness and treat (or follow) the patient"—produces a consistent bias for physicians to direct patients to utilize, and overutilize, their own services, hospital services, tests, ancillary services, medication, etc. Although the effect of the bias may be difficult to measure in an individual case, its aggregate impact on health-services utilization is probably enormous.

Ironically perhaps, the more "concerned" or "humanistic" physician may have a greater tendency to commit type 2 errors that lead to higher utilization costs than the "poor" doctor. While the latter may dismiss a patient having vague symptoms with a five-dollar prescription for tranquilizers, the former may schedule multiple tests and followup appointments that cost hundreds of dollars.

An area of great concern related to overtreatment has been the issue of unnecessary surgery. The concern is warranted because, of all general classes of physician procedures, surgery is the one that carries the greatest concomitant risk of death—even when a patient is well. Bunker (1970), Lewis (1969), and others (Anderson and Feldman, 1956; Cope, 1965) have pointed out that there are significant geographic (see Table 1) and socioeconomic variations in rates of surgical procedures. Once again, a solid medical rationale for the wide variation in rates of surgery for procedures like tonsillectomies and herniorrhapies is hard to find. Some critics of the analyses point out that while the U.S. has a greater rate of mastectomies than England and Wales, it also has a higher rate of five-and-ten-year survivals among women who have undergone the procedure.

Another effect of type 2 errors is to unnecessarily put patients in a "sick" role. One study by Bergman and Stamm (1967) illustrates a form of potentially negative results. They screened twenty-five thousand school medical records in Seattle, Washington, for children with heart murmurs. Of one hundred ten positive records, ninety-three chidren were examined; eighteen children had murmurs and organic disease, and seventy-five either had functional murmurs without organic disease or had no murmurs and no organic disease. Thirty of the seventy-five children without disease (or thirty-two percent of the total sample) were found, however, to be psychologically or physically restricted as a consequence of having been labeled as having cardiac disease.

In summary, the implicit decision norm in medical practice—to avoid the error of not detecting and/or treating a patient's illness —strongly influences the direction of health-services utilization. Additionally, it has several serious negative consequences. First, it produces a consistent bias for physicians to overutilize services. Second, to the sorrow of social scientists, it may make aggregate cost-benefit planning and allocation of medical services practically impossible. Finally, it often tends to obscure the potentially harmful effects to an individual of type 2 errors—particularly the serious hazards involved with some diagnostic procedures and therapeutic regimens, and the danger of having a well person entering a "sick" role and becoming eventually disabled or even developing organic disease.

TABLE 1 Comparative Rates for Selected Operations: the United States and England and Wales

RATE/1,000,000 POPULATION

OPERATION	USA (1965)		England & Wales (1966)	
	Male	*Female*	*Male*	*Female*
Thyroidectomy	9.8	68.5	8.7	42.3
Inguinal herniorrhaphy	508.0	51.1	294.0	29.2
Appendectomy	217.0	180.0	220.7	223.5
Cholecystectomy	94.5	273.0	32.2	89.9
All operations on eye	220.0	223.0	180.6	193.0
Extraction of lens	65.3	82.5	47.2	69.1
Tonsillectomy with or without adenoidectomy	637.0	641.0	322.7	321.9
Adenoidectomy without tonsillectomy	20.7	15.2	49.9	35.6
Hemorrhoidectomy	162.0	137.0	60.5	31.4
Circumcision	96.7		110.0	
Hysterectomy (including subtotal, total & vaginal)		516.0		213.2
All operations on breast	10.9	278.0	5.8	171.7
Partial mastectomy	6.5	196.0	3.0	100.6
Complete (simple) mastectomy		15.0	1.8	27.2
Radical mastectomy		51.0	0.5	25.1
Other operations on breast	4.4	16.0	0.5	18.8

Source: Bunker (1970).

Quality of Care

Increasing attention in recent years has been given to the measurement and regulation of the quality of care rendered by physicians. That concern has now been officially expressed in the establishment of Professional Standards Review Organizations (PSRO's) under section 249F of the 1972 Amendments to the Social Security Act (P.L. 92-603). The purpose of the PSRO's, as defined in the law, is " . . . to promote the effective, efficient, and economical delivery of health care services of proper quality . . . through the application of suitable procedures . . . [so] that services for which payment may be made . . . will conform to appropriate professional standards for the provision of health care. . . ." Additionally, it states that each PSRO " . . . shall apply professionally developed norms of care, diagnosis, and treatment based upon typical patterns of practice in its regions (including typical lengths-of-stay for institutional care by age and diagnosis) as principal points of evaluation and review."

The implications are serious both for the physicians—how they will direct utilization of health services—and for the health of patients. Additionally, it has two potentially paradoxical aspects: First, it does not recognize that there can be marked trade-offs between "economy and efficiency" on one hand and "effectiveness and proper quality" on the other. Second, it virtually institutionalizes existing regional variations in care and length of hospital stay, for which (as discussed earlier) there is almost no logical scientific or medical basis.

If the PSRO's function along the line that the federally funded prototype EMCRO's (Experimental Medical Care Review Organizations) have, they may well increase total utilization of health services. The "norms of care" concept has been translated by many of the organizations into the establishment of specific criteria of services that should be rendered for a defined diagnostic condition. Thus, any one physician who does not provide all the services outlined by a "minimal" criteria set will be judged to have rendered poor quality of care. The result will be to establish a floor of utilization for all patients that may be higher than current average utilization. Payne and Lyons (1972) in a study of medical care in Hawaii found that their criteria showed an underprovision (or underutilization) of indicated services of about twenty-five percent.

Another "process" criteria approach, particularly with respect to hospital care, has been to establish "maximal" service criteria, above which no reimbursement would be given. Unfortunately, that approach may produce a tendency for physicians to give or order all services that could be reimbursed; one study (Gertman, 1971) of such a maximal criteria set estimated that it could produce a thirty to fifty percent rise in hospital costs. Additionally, many observers are concerned that such criteria will force upon physicians a rigid uniformity in the provision of services.

Finally, studies by Brook and Stevenson (1970), Brook (1972a), Williamson et al. (1968), and others (Starfield and Scheff, 1971; Codman, 1916) raise serious doubts whether criteria of "good" medical-care process can validly and reliably be related to measures of "good" end results (or outcomes) of care. In a recent review of the research evidence for the Office of the Secretary of Health, Education, and Welfare, Brook made the following conclusion: "The assessment of quality of care based on process data must be dependent on physician judgment in terms of either establishing a list of process criteria statements, reading the medical record, or reading a case abstract. In terms of the studies noted above, this judgment is likely to include many tests and procedures whose benefit in preventing future impairment is questionable. *The end product of a system assessing process is likely to be higher medical care costs without major improvement in the health of the population*" (1972b:25).

Summary

The interacting effects of the factors discussed in this paper are likely to have a considerable and unidirectional impact on the utilization of health services. More care in the future is likely to be initiated at the direction of physicians, rather than by consumers. Initiation of care by physicians will tend to be biased towards overutilization because of a desire to avoid type 1 decision errors. And finally, despite an implicit bias to overutilize, we may have a national regulatory system that will set even higher patterns of health-service utilization. It seems that increasing physician guidance of health-care use in the United States, based on what little we currently know about the behavior of physicians and their rationale for medical utilization decisions, could drive national health-care expenditures to undreamed-of levels (particularly if financing is liberalized under a form of national health insurance).

Therefore, if our society wishes to have control over utilization of health care, it seems imperative to develop a better understanding of the mysterious behavior of that key decisionmaker—the physician—and the rationale he employs in guiding the use of health services.

References

Acheson, E. D. *and* M. S. Feldstein
  1964   "Duration of stay in hospital for normal maternity care."
          British Journal of Medicine 2: 95–99.
Anderson, O. W. *and* J. J. Feldman
  1956   Family Medical Costs and Voluntary Health Insurance: A
          Nationwide Survey. New York: McGraw-Hill Book Company.
Anderson, O. W. *and* P. B. Sheatsley
  1959   Comprehensive Medical Insurance: A Study of Costs, Use,
          and Attitudes Under Two Plans, Research Series No. 9.
          Chicago: University of Chicago, Center for Health Administration Studies.
  1967   Hospital Use: A Survey of Patient and Physician Decisions,
          Research Series No. 24. Chicago: University of Chicago,
          Center for Health Administration Studies.
Bailey, R. M.
  1970   "Economies of scale in medical practice." Pp. 255–273 in

Klarman, H. E. *and* H. H. Jaszl (eds.), Empirical Studies in Health Economics. Baltimore: The Johns Hopkins Press.

Bell, R. S. *and* J. W. Loop
1971　"The utility and futility of radiographic skull examinations for trauma." New England Journal of Medicine 284: 236–239.

Bergman, A. B. *and* S. F. Stamm
1967　"The morbidity of cardiac non-disease in school children." New England Journal of Medicine 276: 1008–1013.

Brook, R. H.
1972a　A Study of Methodological Problems Associated with Assessment of Quality of Care. Baltimore: Johns Hopkins University, Department of Medical Care and Hospitals.
1972b　"The quality of medical care received by poor people: A proposition paper." Unpublished paper.

Brook, R. H. *and* R. L. Stevenson
1970　"Effectiveness of patient care in an emergency room." New England Journal of Medicine 283: 904–907.

Bunker, J. P.
1970　"Surgical manpower: A comparison of operations and surgeons in the United States and in England and Wales." New England Journal of Medicine 282 (January 15): 135–144.

Childs, A. W. *and* E. E. Hunter
1972　"Non-medical factors influencing use of diagnostic X-rays by physicians." Medical Care 10: 333–334.

Clute, K. F.
1963　The General Practitioner: A Study of Medical Education and Practice in Ontario and Nova Scotia. Toronto: University of Toronto Press.

Codman, E. A.
1916　A Study of Hospital Efficiency: The First Five Years. Boston: Thomas Todd Company.

Cooper, B. S. *and* N. L. Worthington
1973　"National health expenditures, 1929–1972." Social Security Bulletin 36: 3–19.

Cope, O.
1965　"Unnecessary surgery and technical competence: Irreconcilables in the graduate training of a surgeon." American Journal of Surgery 110: 119–123.

Creditor, M. C. *and* U. K. Creditor
　　1972　　"The ecology of an urban voluntary hospital: 2. The referral chain." Medical Care 10: 88–92.

Densen, P. M., et al.
　　1960　　"Prepaid medical care and hospital utilization in a dual choice situation." American Journal of Public Health 50: 1710–1726.
　　1962　　"Prepaid medical care and hospital utilization: Comparison of a group practice and self-insurance situation." Hospitals 36: 63–68.

Garland, L. H.
　　1959　　"Studies on the accuracy of diagnostic procedures." American Journal of Roent. 82: 25–38.

Gertman, P. M.
　　1971　　"Effect of process criteria on hospital costs: A working paper." Washington, D.C.: President's Advisory Council on Management Improvement.

Hearman, M. A.
　　1964　　"How long in hospital." Lancet 2: 539–541.

Jones, F. A.
　　1964　　"Length of stay in hospital." Lancet 1: 321–322.

Johnson, A. C., H. H. Kroeger, I. Altman, D. A. Clark, *and* C. G. Sheps
　　1965　　"The office practice of internists: III. Characteristics of patients." Journal of the American Medical Association 193 (September 13): 916–922.

Klarman, H. E.
　　1963　　"Effect of prepaid group practice on hospital use." Public Health Reports 17: 955–965.

Kohn, R.
　　1973　　Personal Communication.

Last, J. M. *and* K. L. White
　　1969　　"The content of medical care in primary practice." Medical Care 7: 41–48.

Ledley, R. S. *and* L. B. Lusted
　　1959　　"Reasoning foundations of medical diagnosis." Science 130: 9–21.

Lewis, C. E.
　　1969　　"Variations in the incidence of surgery." New England Journal of Medicine 281: 880–884.

McNerney, W. J., et al.
  1962   Hospitals and Medical Economics. Chicago: Hospital Research and Educational Trust.
Mushlin, A. I. *and* D. Barr
  1973   Personal Communication.
Payne, B. G. *and* T. F. Lyons
  1972   "Methods of evaluating and improving personal medical care quality: Office case study." Ann Arbor: University of Michigan, February.
Penchansky, R. *and* D. Fox
  1970   "Frequency of referral and patient characteristics in group practice." Medical Care 8: 368–385.
Perrott, G. S.
  1971   "The federal employees health benefits program: Enrollment and utilization of health services—1961–1968." Washington, D.C.: Government Printing Office.
Peterson, W., et al.
  1956   "An analytical study of North Carolina general practice." Journal of Medical Education 31 (Part 2): 121.
Praiss, J.
  1971   A Study of the Variations in the Use of Hospital Services Within the Practices of Individual Physicians. Baltimore: Johns Hopkins University, Department of Medical Care and Hospitals.
Richardson, W. C.
  1971   Ambulatory Use of Physician Services in Response to Illness Episodes in a Low-Income Neighborhood, Research Series No. 29. Chicago: University of Chicago, Center for Health Administration Studies.
Riedel, D. C. *and* T. B. Fitzpatrick
  1964   Patterns of Patient Care. Ann Arbor: University of Michigan.
Scheff, T. J.
  1963   "Decision rules, types of errors, and their consequences in medical diagnosis." Behavioral Science 8: 97–107.
Shapiro, S. *and* J. Brindle
  1969   "Serving Medicaid eligibles." American Journal of Public Health 59: 635–641.

Shortell, S. M.
    1972   A Model of Physician Referral Behavior: A Test of Ex-
              change Theory in Medical Practice, Research Series No.
              31. Chicago: University of Chicago, Center for Health Ad-
              ministration Studies.
Source Book of Health Insurance Data 1972–1973
    1972   New York: Health Insurance Institute.
Starfield, B. *and* D. Scheff
    1971   Assessment of Patient Care: Process and Outcome. Balti-
              more: Johns Hopkins University, Department of Medical
              Care and Hospitals.
Walsh, R. J.
    1972   Socioeconomic Issues of Health. Chicago: American Medi-
              cal Association, Center for Health Services Research and
              Development.
White, E. L.
    1972   "Current estimates from the Health Interview Survey, United
              States, 1970." Vital and Health Statistics 10 (72).
White, K. L., T. F. Williams, *and* B. G. Greenberg
    1961   "The ecology of medical care." New England Journal of
              Medicine 265: 885–892.
Williams, T. F., K. L. White, L. P. Andrews, E. Diamond, B. G. Green-
      berg, A. A. Hamrick, *and* E. A. Hunter
    1960   "Patient referral to a university clinic: Patterns in a rural
              state." American Journal of Public Health 50: 1493.
Williams, T. F., K. L. White, W. L. Fleming, *and* B. G. Greenberg
    1961   "The referral process in medical care and the university
              clinic's role." Journal of Medical Education 36: 899–907.
Williamson, J. W., J. Mitchell, *and* S. Kreider
    1968   Outcomes of Medical Care: A Study of Heart Failure
              Management in Emergency Rooms. Baltimore: Johns Hop-
              kins University, Department of Medical Care and Hospi-
              tals.

Directions
for Health Services
Research

Directions for
Health Services Research

SELMA J. MUSHKIN

Are the incentives right for the individual and his family when they are making choices about health care? Or are their choices distorted by third-party payments, tax savings, governmental health services? And to what extent? Perhaps more important still is the question of how incentives of proposed new programs will work. Will they improve care, encourage disease prevention, make care more uniform for poor and rich? Or will they raise prices and make more burdensome, rather than less, the cost of serious illness?

The current policy debates center on forms of health insurance and relative costs. There are, however, personal and family characteristics that encourage (or discourage) care that could avert diseases. It was the thesis of the 1973 Milbank Memorial Fund-sponsored Round Table that demand for health care depends upon psychological, biological, ethical, economic, and social incentives, and that response to each incentive varies according to the stage of illness or "wellness." The preliminary study given to the subject in the papers presented at the Conference support that hypothesis but identify additional characteristics that warrant separate consideration and more intensive research. The research base on which to design consumer incentives appears to be thin despite the oft repeated statements on the importance of understanding those incentives in developing new methods for financing or organizing health care.

The Conference sought to identify the incentives that increase, decrease, or direct demand only from the perspective of the consumer. Incentives that influence providers of health services and the production of such resources as technology, manpower, and health facilities—i.e., the supply side—were ignored. Thus, a companion effort is needed in those areas if we are to understand better the types of incentives facing providers, including incentives governing the pricing of care and delivery of care. The discussions, however, did not omit entirely that important guide to consumer demand—the "advice of the physician." Clearly, demand is governed in large measure by the health practitioners.

The mechanisms that are the governing incentives of producer demand differ from those that determine consumer demand. Different stages of illness undoubtedly trigger different responses from health personnel, but other factors, including interactive behavior of providers, affect costing, the using of health resources, fee schedule setting, patient and third-party billing, and responsiveness to patient and family. Types of interactions are diagrammed in Table 1.

The Need to Emphasize Incentives

Why at this time is the incentive structure so important? One reason lies in the mounting percentage of the gross national product that health care has claimed. Another is uncertain relief from high medical bills that the large resource commitments of the past have achieved. A third is the way in which incentives enter into the basic debate about processes and direction of public policy in the period ahead.

Shares of the GNP

The proportion of national resources claimed by health care has been increasing, despite the high GNP growth rates at current prices. Part of the explanation lies not in the comparatively greater growth of resources for health but in the comparative rise of prices for health care. During the past two decades, medical prices in the

TABLE 1   Producer Incentives in Health Care

Types of Producer Interactions	Factors and Incentives Affecting Interactions [a]	Impacts on Final Price	Impacts on Consumer Use
Provider response to patient			
Provider to non-institutional provider (by type)			
Provider to institution (by type)			
Insurer to non-institutional providers			
Insurer to institution			
Provider and institution to health agencies			
Provider and institution to other agencies			
Insurer to public agencies			
Insurer to insurer			
Training and educational institutions to provider			
Training and educational institutions to hospital			

[a] Both positive and negative (e.g., cost reimbursement, malpractice suits, professional ethics, public standards).

United States have risen more rapidly than any other component of the Consumer Price Index. In fact, from 1950–1972, the rise was almost double that of the total index.

The rise in the share of the GNP going for health care is not confined to the United States. European nations have experienced a similar growth. Nor is the comparative rise in medical care prices unique to this country. Indeed, the comparative intercountry experience could provide a natural experiment for determining whether incentive structures are greatly distorted by methods of social insurance protection against medical care costs.

Protection Against Higher Costs

Despite efforts in the United States to even out costs of medical care by private insurance against the risk of illness, and public protection for the high risk groups such as the aged, some families are without protection. For those who have coverage, it is often restricted to care in hospitals. Thus, high medical care costs still remain a potential burden, even for those who are covered, and may be made even more burdensome by higher prices.

Studies by Densen et al. (1960; 1962) and others have shown that higher hospital use is a consequence of current insurance practices, with their concentration on inhospital care, including inhospital physician care. Thus, the demand for hospital care tends to be higher than it would be without that incentive. How does the price of care at the time of illness affect other uses of health resources? Do persons demand more private-room care and private nursing in the hospital because the basic rate of semiprivate accommodations is met by insurance? If the price for care is reduced for those with insurance and the demand is price elastic, one would tend to assume a higher quantity of services would be demanded, increasing the pressure on limited supplies of health care.

Health insurance is not just a different way of paying for a given flow of hospital services; it is, in addition, a service called "protection against the risk" of medical care bills, or protection against having to reduce other family living expenses or against added personal debt. That service and the demand for it have risen markedly, and almost everyone is now covered by hospital insurance. The cost of insurance itself increases the cost of health services.

Public Policy Choices

The Conference's focus on incentives, however, was due primarily to the debate on public policy and concern about health insurance, a concern sharpened by the experience with Medicare and Medicaid. National health insurance coverage has been proposed; under several versions, the scope of protection would be increased and some protection provided for people who have none. Unless the rise in demand for health care expected as a consequence is controlled in some way that takes the place of present price constraints, medical care prices could rise even faster than they have in the past. Furthermore, if the insurance is less than complete, individuals could find themselves worse off than before despite the insurance protection. Some aged persons, for example, find their medical care costs higher after Medicare than before. Other approaches would limit medical insurance for example to costs above a determined percent of income, e.g., five percent. Efforts also are directed to altering supplies of services and keeping demand more nearly in line with supply.

Whatever the changes proposed, the incentives structure has come to be regarded as of major importance in the public policy debate.

Incentives, by Stage of Illness

The emphasis of the Round Table on the variation in determinants of consumer demand according to stage of illness highlighted the need for new research on preventive care, on acute and emergency care, chronic illness, rehabilitation, and terminal care. Special importance was given to the factors that determine behavior for positive health, termed the stage of "preprevention." The discussion made clear that the research done by Densen et al. (1960; 1962), Feldstein (1971a; 1971b), Davis and Foster (1972: chapter 1), Scitovsky and Snyder (1972), and others (Phelps and Newhouse, 1972) marks only a small beginning to understanding the existing structure of incentives both private and public in determining consumer demand. Existing research fails to differentiate incentives by stage of illness. The development of appropriate incentive systems to promote effective, equitable, and efficient achievement of health objectives requires that differences in responses by stage of illness be understood.

Price deterrents and other incentives work differently at the various stages of care. While the papers for the Round Table identified the importance of stage of illness, much additional research is required to understand the modus operandi of the system of consumer incentives at present for each stage and to determine what changes in incentives are needed.

Disaggregation by stage of illness points strongly also to a new emphasis on age differences in the use of health services. Under-standing of behavior toward health care policies requires that age of the patient be taken into account. Responses differ on use of care in terminal illness, for example, when the patient is one day old, thirty years old, or ninety. While use rates for hospital, physician services and dental care traditionally are documented by age, the impact of prepayment coverage and family budget price on use by age has received far less attention. Repeated recommendation for such research was made at the Conference.

The research questions identified by the participants may be classified in terms of motivational determinants, socioeconomic factors, policy directives, and program feedbacks. Despite the length of the lists, they are not intended to be complete. The series of research questions that are classified below may be redefined as a series of hypotheses for study.

I. *Motivational Determinants*

1. What individual, family, and community qualities and circumstances encourage health promotion behavior, such as proper nutrition, recreation?

2. What genetic factors and family disease experience deter or stimulate health promotion?

3. What kinds of persons under what circumstances seek to enlarge disability or death risks and thus avoid preventive health care?

4. What motivates what types of consumers (or deters them) from, among other things, using such services as TB screening, pap smears, periodic health examinations?

5. Would full coverage of health services alter the use of care at the various stages of illness in a differentiated way?

6. How do price elasticities of demand for services change at the various stages of illness?

7. What are the cross elasticities of price between complementary and substitute health services of all kinds?

8. What are the structures and processes that underlie consumer selection of place of care in acute and in emergency care cases?

9. How do the employer and employment environment contribute to place of care and use rates?

10. What are the personal, family, and community patterns that contribute to those selections?

11. What are the psychological and sociological motivations that lead to care in chronic cases?

12. What are the responses to price, place of care, and provider attitudes of those with chronic illnesses in their nonacute phases?

13. What incentives operate in selecting, completing, and maintaining rehabilitation and restorative health?

14. How can demand for rehabilitative services best be predicted?

15. What are the determinants (medical, psychological, social, ethical, etc.) of health care use in terminal cases?

16. What are the behavior patterns that increase the risk of premature death?

17. What are the taboos that restrict understanding of the use of medical care for the terminally ill?

II. Socioeconomic Factors

1. Is behavior different toward preventive health care and also toward terminal care for the rich and the poor?

2. Are different qualities of care sought by different socioeconomic classes? Are these quality differences dependent on price?

3. What are the roles of place and structure of care in use of health services by persons from minority groups?

4. What are the chief deterrents to care for target groups? What is known about methods of overcoming those deterrents?

5. How do differences in socioeconomic conditions relate to differences in behavior on nutrition, recreation, and other actions that can promote health?

6. What are the socioeconomic determinants of disease avoidance behavior?

7. What kinds of incentives have been tried to promote avoidance behavior for high risk groups? With what full conse-

quences as to costs and gains? For what income and social groups?

8. How do differences in prices for qualities of services affect use by income groups and regions?

9. How does the system cope with the "problem" patient? Are disincentives varied by income and social classes?

10. What are the patient and family health consequences of alternate methods of providing care at the various stages of illness for different socioeconomic groups?

11. How do different routes of access to care by socioeconomic groups affect outcomes of care?

12. What are the measured differences in quality of care now provided, by income group?

13. To what extent do central city health-care facilities contribute to concentration of minority population in that center?

14. What characteristics of urban areas promote equality (or inequality) in health status? Are those characteristics the same for all age groups?

15. What are the comparative costs (and prices for consumers) of care at the various stages of illness by type of disease, by age, and by income and place of residence?

16. What are the income distribution impacts over a period of a generation or so of chronic disease care that is life saving?

17. Who uses rehabilitation services by age, income status, prior employment and nature of impairment?

18. How do high use rates and high costs of terminal care differ by socioeconomic status?

19. What is the income elasticity of terminal illness expenditures? And how does this compare to nonterminal illness?

III. Policy Directives

1. What kinds of external stimuli, such as advertising, influence promotion of health behavior and use of care?

2. How do medical facilities, services, and publicity impact on health promotion behavior and use of care?

3. What are the roles of the schools, employers, and health agencies in influencing consumer behavior? What is the role of housing authorities in influencing consumer behavior toward health?

4. What is known about family rules and law enforcement practices that achieve avoidance of premature death and disability? How can more widespread use of "the best" practices be encouraged? What practices work best with high risk groups?

5. What are the legal protections against undue governmental controls that are designed to reduce health hazards (e.g., sterilization of chronically blind)?

6. What timetable for health and dental examinations is cost effective (e.g., six months, two years)? How does the timetable vary by age, sex, geographic location? How do such findings come to be communicated to consumers?

7. What services (transportation, educational) support health care?

8. What are the costs of environmental health risks to consumers of health care? What are means to encourage public response that can lower risks?

9. What share of resources goes for care at the various stages of illness?

10. How can consumer groups encourage efficient, equitable care?

11. What types of institutions (local clinics, hospitals, etc.) can best serve consumers at various stages of disease?

12. What is the experience with types of services designed to encourage appropriate selections of kinds of care required (e.g., ambulance-call screening, "action" lines)?

13. What are the methods of identifying use rates of various kinds of care by time of day, week, season and of matching services to provide the right amount at the right time?

14. Do the current incentives achieve the lowest cost care consistent with consumer quality requirements?

15. What are the known differences in outcome (length of in-

tervals of work or other normal activity) in care attributable to differences in types and in quality of services? At what comparative cost differences?

16. Is policy direction sufficiently discriminating on approaches to services by age of patient? What are the factors that contribute to such differences?

17. How should degrees of disability be defined for rehabilitative care?

18. How should uncertainty be dealt with in compensating disability?

19. What are the cost-benefit relations for different degrees of rehabilitative care?

20. What share of nonviolent deaths are in hospitals or in other institutions? And what are the factors that lead to the choice of an institutional setting?

21. What types of services increase the costs of care for the dying? What are the service contents differences when standarized for nature of illness?

22. What is essentially known about informing the patient about a terminal disease and the chances of prolonging life?

23. What are the criteria to apply to quality services for the dying?

IV. Feedbacks

1. What are feedbacks in "fear" and "stress" of health promotion and disease avoidance publicity efforts?

2. What are the consequences in terms of personal and family health of high pressure preventive health campaigns?

3. Are there differences in individual patient outcome attributable to differences in services? How do those differences impact on standards and guidelines?

4. Are there differences in family health status attributable to differences in the way health services for the acutely ill are provided?

5. How does the care of the terminally ill affect the volume

and quality of hospital services for the population generally?

6. Would special health services for the dying such as psychological counseling improve general quality of care in the
hospital?

7. How do the location, quality, and quantity of services for
the terminally ill influence the health of members of the
family by age and family relationships?

Policy Goals and Research

The direction of additional study may be considered from another perspective starting with major health goals.

The selected goals from the consumer viewpoint include the following:

1. enlarging consumer choice;
2. strengthening the consumer voice in decision making;
3. improving the response of the system to consumer needs;
4. improving collective decision making (or public choice);
and
5. improving the equity of services among groups.

Various optional ways of implementing those goals are presented along with research questions that need further exploration in
order to provide vital information for policy choice.

1. To enlarge consumer choice
   —broaden the scope of choice among all types of health
   services in hospital and out
   —broaden choices among all classes of family consumption
   —reduce the current distortions in choice in favor of hospital care
   —reduce the distortions in choice between health care and
   other goods.

Study would hardly suggest that a return be made to full market decisions in health care on a pay-as-you-go basis in order to constrain health services within budget limits. The research that has been done in the past has essentially concentrated on altering payment methods yet within a market system. But too little attention has been given to how public choice can be collectively designed to permit a balancing of choices of services by consumers.

The demand for health services, as has been indicated by Schottland (1974), depends on the agency auspices under which the services are provided. In California, a person who needs cornea transplant may arrange its financing through the welfare department under the auspices of the blind prevention program, or through county or city hospital as a "charity" or a Medicaid patient, or through the state rehabilitation program as part of the federal-state vocational rehabilitation programs. Alternatively, private hospitalization might be used paid by insurance carriers. Clientele tend to be different for each of the service choices. What determines the choice of place and type of facility selected by the individual and the different program auspices under which governmental health services are provided? Study would help identify these differences and the consequences, if any, for quality of care.

2. To strengthen the consumer voice in decision making
    —broaden consumer participation in group decisions, including decisions of health providers, e.g., hospitals, health maintenance organizations
    —provide better information on the types of health care in the community, including information on alternate providers, alternate costs, alternate insurances, and quality of care
    —give the patient more information about the risk and benefits of treatments for his dissease problems and about certainty or uncertainty about diagnosis and prognosis
    —establish grievance procedures governing relationships between patient groups and providers to develop rules governing quality and quantity of provider service and to establish legal means of contesting or questioning departures from such rules

—deepen understanding of the probability of prolonging life, getting well, reducing pain, and reducing the number of days lost from ordinary activity as a consequence of following optional methods of treatments

—establish procedures for removing barriers to consumer representation

—reinforce competitive practices in providing health care

—focus consumer efforts on those procedures which are most likely to yield favorable changes.

To achieve a consumer voice in health decision, a range of research studies is needed. High on the list of research priorities are studies that would facilitate informed choice about methods of gaining a consumer voice. Is consumer representation in a neighborhood health center a better way of gaining an effective consumer voice than is participation of a neighborhood health aide as a member of a medical team? Or is the neighborhood law center the better way?

Among the kinds of research studies required are those that address the possibility of the development of a law of health care grievances analogous to the grievance procedure in labor-industry relations. Such an approach requires an understanding of those aspects of health care which lend themselves to collective bargaining by groups such as unions and cooperatives, with organized providers such as HMOs. In the research, "units" for bargaining would have to be designed and tested and approaches developed to "regulations" that could be set forth as a developing body of consumer law on health.

That difficult question of defining and quantifying risk and benefits of treatments for diseases must be researched if consumers are to have the information they need to make informed choices. What we now know about courses of treatment and risk of such treatment requires documentation in a type of "consumer report." Benefits of treatment arrayed for each treatment modality and in accord with consumer criteria of quality medical care would have to be determined for each disease.

A number of other questions require assessment that look to-

ward evaluation of existing health measures asking: How do those
methods work in achieving the purposes of a strengthened consumer voice? What do each of these processes suggest as to new methods of gaining consumer voice? The kinds of questions that might
be addressed are these:

>What incentives could foster consumer representation in
>health care decision?
>
>What experiments on processes of consumer representation
>might be designed on the basis of the findings of the evalua-
>tions that have been made?
>
>What criteria have been used in judging consumer represen-
>tation techniques? Do they lend themselves to health care
>evaluations?
>
>What has been the experience in the funding of consumer
>advocates in terms of the criteria established?
>
>Does consumer participation serve as a health education
>measure improving health care utilization? And through
>what processes can improved use be achieved?

3. To improve the response of the system to consumer needs
   —decentralize care, so that decisions on resource allocation
   in the neighborhood would be made by the consumer
   —establish ombudsmen procedures for gaining hearings on
   rules that impair flexible adjustment to meet individual needs
   —build into the system new health workers who will combine health resources for the patient, and strengthen communication links between patients and provider
   —strengthen consumer-group processes for challenging inadequate medical services such as long delays in emergency
   room care
   —provide means for changing the place of care when a special facility would improve the patient's chances for recovery
   —create new competitive producing units for care among
   which consumers may choose.

We need to pursue a number of questions in gaining the knowledge required to achieve the goal of responsiveness of the system
and measure that response.

Among the major gaps in research is the inadequacy of information on the effect of various methods for gaining consumer representation on the outcomes sought by such representation, namely, greater responsiveness to the different consumer needs. Do consumers of health services in neighborhood health centers more nearly get the kind of services they seek in terms of both quantity and quality than consumers who use other health services? Do the children in families using neighborhood health centers, for example, fare better in terms of preventive services or not?

The methods that have been formulated to achieve the purpose of consumer response have at best been partially evaluated, including such devices as the ombudsmen, the neighborhood health workers, the neighborhood health clinic, and the use of neighborhood legal aids to establish rules and standards.

Evaluation requires criteria for measurement of quantity and quality. Quality of care has multiple characteristics. Not all individuals presumably view quality in the same way. These differences are not well understood. There could be a quality of medical care to give an extreme case, for example, that takes individuals over a threshold of acceptability. The care may be sharply at variance with daily mode of living. Excess care may generate fear or other behavior that is not conducive to recovery.

Rules designed by institutions often disregard individuals and their families. Almost all of us without regard to income have little means to bend those rules because of the mystique of medicine. For the poor, the incapacity to cope with institutional rules is particularly great. Personal and family stress originates often in uncertainties or lack of easy communication. The research that has been done on stress and health underscores the need to re-examine the structure of health care to make the system more responsive to the patient and to his family. It may be that present "rules" enlarge health problems in some cases rather than provide cures.

Among the questions for which additional study seems relevant are these:

> How can differences in quality of care sought by consumers be defined in a functional way that takes account of differences in individual characteristics?

How can differences in quality of care sought by consumers be organized operationally, e.g., self-care facilities, midwifery?

What groups tend to seek out and respond to information about services in terms of quantity, quality, type, and place? Is the existing system by which individuals receive information about health care working efficiently?

What groups are not reached by usual information channels?

How can communication be achieved for those who are not literate or who do not read? Is the TV soap opera a good communication device? Is behavior changed?

What is the neighborhood response to various levels of health workers ranging from the resident physician to the neighborhood outreach worker? What do these evaluations suggest as to the most effective way of reaching and responding to the groups who are poor in the city? And in the rural areas?

What is the experience with services that refer individuals to health care at their request?

4. To improve collective decision making (or public choice)
   —more adequate measurement of health care outputs in relation to public purpose
   —design of measures of health services productivity
   —a better understanding of how the totality of public services contribute to human development, e.g., to what extent is housing a substitute for child health care, or proper feeding of mothers a substitute for education of the mentally retarded
   —an understanding of how the timing and sequences of health care (e.g., vaccinations) can affect consumer behavior, and what kinds of incentives help to alter inefficient timing
   —knowledge of the determinants and process of public action
   —an understanding of process of building creativity and change into public decision making.

First, outputs of health care must be better understood if the success of incentive structures is to be measured. Probing of outcome measurements is still rudimentary. Reductions in death, disability, and debility rates are used most frequently as outcome measures in public programs, and "debility" has yet to be defined in a quantifiable form. Positive measures—measures of "wellness" and quality of health—remain an important subject for new research. Moreover, specific criteria are required to evaluate specific programs—in lead poisoning prevention, for example, the criteria are reduction in the number of mentally retarded or reduction in the number and proportion of two- and three-year-olds with "undue" body burdens of lead. Economists have focused their measures of success on additions to work-force and lifetime earnings values. But personal attributes such as dignity, self-esteem, reduced tension, and internal-external control are also outputs of health services. Also important is a better understanding of the importance of reduction in pain and the degree of certainty or uncertainty of prognosis. Biases in counts of output also must be understood.

The research questions on payoff require collaboration among agencies with divided responsibility for reducing disease and achieving better health. Program interactions are many. Much new empirical work is needed on interaction effects between the various determinants of use and agencies contributing to that use. How are cooperative efforts to be achieved on flows of services that are connected to particular persons and families?

Multiple-agency administrations are fraught with problems of overlaps and duplications and, even more difficult administratively, with problems of fragmentation of responsibility. Though attention has been given to addressing the question of consumer choice and the responsiveness of health practitioners to consumers, the need is also for a better understanding of design and implementation of collaborative administrative undertakings to achieve identified outcomes in response to the public. Especially urgent is the understanding of the interaction of health care, nutrition, education, housing, and income maintenance.

Second, public service impacts on personal development must

be defined. The problem's boundaries must be defined as a preliminary step in analysis. Joint products and joint costs need to be identified, and, in general, a better understanding needs to be reached of what works in combination to produce quality in human advance. Much of program performance hinges on an understanding of human development in its multifaceted dimensions. Single-track disciplines, narrowly viewed, cannot provide a guide to understanding incentives that achieve or deter the achievement of public policy purposes. Sociology, ethics, law, psychology—all play a part in human behavior and determine response to change. Quality of life measurement is not exclusively an economic issue.

Third, the timing and sequences of health care should be the subject of research to guide the design of a consumer incentive structure on policy. What is the time frame for dealing with a health problem? Should incentives be designed to alter the timing of some health services? What would be the effect on outcomes for human development? Perhaps immunizations, for example, should be encouraged later, or possibly earlier, than they are now. What would the consequences be in terms of costs and health? Can some health problems be subjected to a five-year plan, or is such a timetable unproductive? How should a time factor be built into an incentive structure? What kinds of incentives would help to change inefficient time sequency?

Fourth, for those concerned with developing better information in support of policy decision, a number of specific questions on "How to do it" require answers that take full account of varied disciplinary research that can guide political debate.

> What are the specific criteria to be applied in measuring health program results? For which programs?
> What are the measurement problems, and how are they to be met?
> What types of data on measurement can be collected routinely? What kinds require special collections? At what level of accuracy?
> What program policies are to be compared in assessing pro-

gram options? For what age groups? For what illness categories?

IIow is the search for alternatives to be carried out?

How are costs to be defined and particular programs costed?

How broad should the perspective be in explaining and analyzing trade-offs? (In assessing economic gains, what account should be taken of unemployment and the potential availability of job access for groups in the population? Or to turn the question about: how, for example, does health care, especially "cosmetic" medicine, affect employability?) How is the information compiled and analyzed to be presented so as to gain interaction with policy officials?

The basic research task is to find ways to make governmental budgeting and planning for health care work well. This task requires a better knowledge of how demand for care arises and how it can best be met. As we have noted, this demand presumably responds to various social, financial, governmental, and psychological incentives. But what those incentives are, how they react and interreact on consumer demand, and—much more important for the current policy debate—how they can be redesigned to produce a more efficient and equitable health delivery system, are all factors which are incompletely understood.

5. To improve equity in health care
   —clarify equity goals in health care
   —provide access to health services appropriate to low income group needs
   —redesign delivery systems to make access rules more flexible
   —strengthen basic income maintenance measures
   —make uniform public protections after taking account of income variations
   —give priority to health services directed to special problems of prior neglect, e.g., lead poisoning prevention, in-

ner ear infections, alcoholism of American Indians, drug
dependence.

Two aspects of equity require further assessment along with a
better understanding of whether different kinds of incentives work
better for some groups than others. Those aspects are distribution
and quality.

Before those aspects can be measured, it is necessary to consider the very basic questions of whether or not services and care
can produce "equal health." The seeking of health care for the poor
and the design of incentives to improve their health status assumes
that health care does make a difference. Does health care matter in
achieving the basic output of better health or reduced illness? Research so far, however, provides no definitive answer on the causal
connection between medical care and "health"; on the contrary,
some important research studies challenge any causal connection.

Furthermore, a recent study (Luft, 1972: chapter 2, page 18)
states, at least tentatively, that the most important disease pathologies are probably distributed independent of income:

> If careful distinctions are made among several aspects of
> poor health, and the income-social class data are recognized to
> include, in some cases, the *effects* of poor health, then some
> tentative conclusions can be drawn from the literature. It ap-
> pears that, for most of the currently important diseases in the
> United States, there is no pronounced income gradient, while
> occupation may have an effect on injuries and some of the less
> common diseases.

However, research has established that there are types of impairments that indicate special needs on the basis of past neglect.
Among them are hearing and vision difficulties that often are cor-
rectable. Do more poor children than children from middle-income
families go to school with uncorrected hearing and vision defects?
How are the families to be encouraged to seek corrective care? It
may prove useful to assemble, more systematically than has been
done before, information on diseases and impairments in the population that indicate medical neglect, and to test the operation of op-

tional programs and incentives experimentally. Some of these medi-
cal-neglect items might be put together in an index of potentially
corrective health care. A set of corrective health-care indexes applied to health program performance could become part of account-
ability testing and measurement of success of incentive systems.

In short, the Round Table, far from concluding that there are
no major inequalities in health status, leaned toward the idea that
our current methods of measuring health status need to be revised.

The first aspect of equity in health care concerns the distribution of care and access. Many of the critical problems of inequity in
access to care are those of poor distribution of facilities and services
around the country. They are omitted here in the discussion of consumer incentives, since distribution usually reflects the impacts of
incentives upon the providers of care. These factors are not, of
course, without consequence to the consumer.

There are other aspects of unequal geographic access that might
well be covered. They, in turn, are questions of differences and
similarities in consumer behavior in different areas of the nation.
There are indications that consumer preferences for health care depend on factors that vary with geography. Such geographic variations make difficult single solutions that are efficient for, say, a single health insurance plan. The design of improved incentive policies
would be easier if more were known about regional differences in
use rates of health services and about regional income and price
elasticities of demand. Not only are aggregate data of interest but
also data on differences in perspective with respect to preventive
care, emergency care, and other levels of care. The urban-rural variation suggests that persons from rural areas delay care but use it
for longer periods. Their attitudes toward health care may differ
sharply from those of city dwellers. The topic is far from new, but
an updated look at rural-urban variations in health care use is needed.

Far more important in the current policy debate is the question
of distribution of services between rich and poor and between suburb and center city. The most recent survey indicates no substantial
difference in physician visits by income class (U.S. Department of
Health, Education, and Welfare, National Center for Health Statis-

tics, 1972: table 2). The percentage of persons seeking physicians' services differed little; the average days of hospital care per person were reported to be higher rather than lower in the lower-income group (U.S. Department of Health, Education, and Welfare, National Center for Health Statistics, unpublished data, 1972). But there is indeed evidence that persons in need of care are not receiving it. Care is costly to reach for some even within a city; and the costs include lost wages, transportation, and frequently just painful exertion. Sometimes little incentive exists to seek care. The lack of self-esteem and "control" capacity points in that direction. Furthermore, quality of care may not be to the individual's taste; it often involves treatment that the patient does not like and yet cannot change or even find a way of discussing.

The experience with such centers could shed light on how to design incentives to overcome target group problems with access to care. Some questions that could be examined include:

> Did the closeness of neighborhood health centers work as an incentive for use?
> Did use rates go up in the city, or did they go down?
> To what factors should the change in access be attributed?
> Was health better as a consequence?

Various arrangements such as those encouraged by the OEO programs for homemaker services, visiting nurses, and a variety of other social arrangements, influence the demand for health services to low-income groups. These arrangements should be re-evaluated in accord with the consumer criteria developed on quantity and quality of care.

A second aspect of equity is quality of care. At this time in the nation's history with emphasis on greater equalitarianism, public policy that seeks to gain greater equality indirectly through health care, or education, is being replaced by more direct income policy. The hypothesis is being advanced even more strongly that higher family cash income through public income maintenance is the essential means toward improved health status and a higher quality of care. Experimentally designed studies on income compared with services should throw light on this vital policy issue. For instance, does greater purchasing power necessarily mean the delivery of higher quality care, or are there other more pertinent determinants of quality?

It is often claimed that standard setting is the major determinant of quality, since regulations have been especially important in achieving fairness for target groups. Densen (1973) in particular has emphasized that more scientific data are needed on the effects of different quality of care on health. He wrote:

> . . . it need not, indeed must not, be inevitable that we fail to recognize the arbitrariness of some of the decisions and neglect to initiate the necessary health service research to provide the solid scientific underpinning which is necessary to insure that standard setting really does protect the interests of the people.

For the poor, the question of incentives for quality care is especially important. As indicated earlier, poor people lack the capacity to negotiate their own way through the medical hierarchy and gain bending of the rules when necessary.

Much medical experimental research will be needed to support standards on quality of care that can guide providers and encourage consumers to demand optimum quality. However, such a research design may be tricky.

Is there indeed a basis for scientific experimentation on quality components and on incentives for optimum quality care? Certainly components of the questions can be identified and examined. For example, the stress-illness consequences of long, uninformed waits for a spouse in a clinic or hospital could be studied with consequences for the policies that produce such waits.

In addition to a better scientific basis for medical standards and expert opinion on high quality care, there are standards of quality that are consumer-oriented, and, therefore, more subjective. Quality controls are too often discussed without consideration of consumer or patient attitudes on what constitutes quality. Quality requirements as defined might encompass not only the technical quality of the care but the degree of kindness, warmth, time spent in explanation of diagnosis and prognosis, waiting time, referrals to assistance, responsiveness of providers to patient's and to family queries, and understanding of family stresses. But how are such quality requirements to be measured? There is a true urgency to come to grips with such problems, for legal contests on the quality of care under the equal protection clause of the Constitution are now underway. Such legal reviews demand new measurements of care more discriminating than mere death rates. The penalty of the lawsuit and the publicity generated by that suit become incentives for change.

Financing of Health Care

Most health financing structures involve incentives to provide rather than use health services, but the structures are not without consequences for the consumer. Obviously, direct payment by the consumer is no incentive to seek care. The possibility of high medical bills can delay or even deny care. In short, direct patient payments do affect demand in many ways that should, of course, be studied further.

But today, with the debate on national health insurance and other proposals, there is an urgency to research other forms of financing not involving direct patient payment. Traditional options in this area include tax financing of care in either public or private facilities through such programs as Medicare, Medicaid, military health and veterans benefits; insurance prepayment through personal or employer plans; and post-treatment payments through various disability or rehabilitation plans. These "third-party" payment plans, although serving mainly to encourage the provision of health services to selected groups or subscribers, have consequences on the consumer. Some foster better health, but that objective may be undermined in other proposals.

The major question concerns the consequences to the consumer of third-party systems. The very definition of what constitutes a reimbursable outlay for care cannot help but influence the kind of services received by consumers. More than the issue of hospital as opposed to nonhospital care is involved. Transportation connected with health care may be included as a reimbursable expense. Coverage of dental surgery may be included. One possibility is for providers to define the services within the context of the "allowable"; another is to exclude the care, with consequences for the patient. A dual system of reimbursement—Medicaid and Medicare, for example—can also have an impact on quality of care, as can facilities encouraged by reimbursement but structured to care only for the poor. One hypothesis suggests that services for the poor over time breed poor services.

Third-party payment also removes the checks and controls on the use of health services. The earlier practice of fee payment at the time of receipt of services presumably provided better yet unduly harsh control. Third-party bill-payers, however, have little control over the quantity and quality of services for which they pay. Distorted use of those services easiest to administer is another result of prepayment plans, but this may be corrected by comprehensive insurance with a wider range of health services, or by an amended hospital insurance package that introduces price signals for part of the care.

We are not likely to return to the notion of payment at the time of service because of the hardships that such a system produced. Nor are we likely to move toward postpayment plans that seem to lessen the burden by calling for installment payments for services rendered; this is not only because of the financial hazards to the patient and his family, but also because of the uncertainty of payment it means for providers.

Much research has been focused on the financial arrangements for health care and more particularly on third-party payments or prepayment devices. Many optional methods of prepayment have been analyzed. But research is still needed to understand better (1) the full range of determinants in seeking health care and the way in which behavior patterns of families and patients, and of providers in their response to families and patients, can be changed, or (2) optionally, the means to insure that demand signals are real and are not distorted unintentionally by governmental act or insurance companies.

Previous research has produced numerous proposals to cut costs by such measures as HMOs, limited-care facilities, home-health services, public utility price controls. Analysis of the various options not only in terms of cost but in terms of patient care is necessary. A number of ways to cut cost could be designed, if that is the sole objective, but some of them would be hazardous to the health of the nation. The objective of low cost for high quality is harder to reach.

Among the issues that require further study are those that impact on new organizational modes. Two examples of study questions are given below:

Health Maintenance Organizations (HMOs)
> What are the incentives for consumer enrollment in HMOs? What kinds of information would reduce consumer resistances to participation in group practice medicine? Is reduced risk of surgery an incentive to joining?
>
> Do preventive services encourage HMO participation? Is quality control within HMOs an incentive?
>
> What information about HMO operation is to be provided to consumers? How are the data to be organized and distributed?
>
> What kinds of consumer responses may be expected to provider behavior under per capita payment arrangements? How can HMOs in a community be made competitive with each other?
>
> How are HMO benefits to be marketed?
>
> What are some other by-products of separation of payment from service decision?
>
> How do differences in night-hours care and home visit practices influence HMO enrollments?

Home Health Services
> What are the incentives for use of home-health care?
>
> What are the resistances to home-health care?
>
> What kinds of information about home-health services would induce shifts to care in the home?

What kinds of provider care in the home would encourage use of home-health services?

What are the family and patient resistances to care in the home?

What kinds of changes in information, payment, or provider behavior would reverse current practices?

Would ready transportation services to clinic and hospital improve use of home-health care?

Would professional emergency services encourage use of home-health care?

It also has been proposed that special tax provisions relating to medical care deductions be dropped from the income tax. At present, the taxpayer who itemizes his deductions can subtract from adjusted gross income the following: fifty percent of any medical insurance premium up to one hundred and fifty dollars, plus defined medical care costs in excess of three percent of adjusted gross income. Included in defined medical care costs are expenses for drugs and medicines in excess of one percent of adjusted gross income and also medical insurance premiums in excess of one hundred and fifty dollars. Furthermore, employer contributions to health insurance are not defined as income of the individual taxpayer. These provisions encourage the taxpayer to spend more on formal medical care than he perhaps otherwise would and, presumably, encourage also the acquisition of health insurance. Discussion of the impact of the present tax provisions is based on a series of assumptions that call for substantial added fact gathering and an understanding of the way in which the tax incentives work.

The current deduction of half the health insurance premium was introduced to encourage the purchase of insurance and to remove the incentive under the earlier tax laws to be self-insured. Under the earlier laws, the cost of medical care could be deducted when amounts exceeded three percent of income without distinguishing between health insurance premiums and all other medical care. Thus, for the high-income taxpayer, the government shared in the high medical care bills by taxpayer saving; in effect a coinsurance arrangement was operative.

The change was made to encourage insurance rather than out-of-pocket payment of direct medical expenses. The present tax deduction system is thought by some to be badly designed because it encourages insurance against routine medical expenses within the one hundred and fifty dollar ceiling and self-insurance against catastrophic medical bills in excess of three percent of income.

What we understand too little is how the tax provisions affect various groups in the population, particularly when expenses are categorized by disease and stage of illness. The subsidy represented by tax deductions and exclusions from taxable income accrues mainly to the higher-income taxpayer, with the value increasing with higher marginal tax rates in the upper income brackets. Approximately a third of the $3.5 billion revenue loss is estimated to accrue to those with annual incomes of $15,000 and over and less than fifteen percent to those with incomes under $5,000. What proportion of the total deduction is claimed by those with catastrophic illness? Some part of that amount represents terminal illness costs, costs of care of children with burns, and so on. We should anticipate repercussions and hardships if action is taken to exclude medical care deductions. We need information on those hardship categories. What share of deductions represent uninsured nursing-home care, particularly for the aged, or services in extended-care facilities? What would be the resulting tax equity if the deductions were uniformly removed?

But with the nation moving urgently toward major rearrangements in health financing, more than mere proposing must be done. We need trial programs in which some of the concepts of financing are in fact worked through for demonstration purposes. The vital replication of such demonstrations is difficult but necessary to insure that results are valid. Experimentation with health insurance providing cash reimbursement is relatively simple. More complex are trial experiments with control groups, in which uniform services are provided that permit comparative results. Services are hard to keep uniform. Price adjustment may be necessary for such trials and for judging costs across state and community lines implying a new research on local area price indexes.

Experience with varied forms of health protection in other nations provides in effect an experimental laboratory within which to ask: What part of this experience is relevant for program policy in the U.S.? What are the differences in use, the effect on health status, the cost under the various arrangements?

Evaluation of foreign programs can, in effect, provide a short-cut to the knowledge that is needed now. However, to use effectively the financial experience of foreign systems in designing optional programs in the U.S., comparative costs have to be measured along with comparative use rates. One further step is required—namely, formulation of a standard basket of health goods that could be used to develop an inter-country price index. Services that are important for understanding U.S. health finances might be given special weight. The package or bundle of services should be defined and then priced in the currency of each nation. Such a plan would not be any more difficult, conceptually, than is medical care pricing in the U.S.; collection of the data could be inexpensive.

A brief summary of the kinds of questions such new research on financing should consider in the light of the foreign experience, including experiences in such countries as Hungary, Poland, Rumania, U.S.S.R. are these:

1. Do hesitation fees (or coinsurance features) at what rates make a difference in use? What groups are affected?
2. What has been the demand response to public utility rules or administered prices on health care?
3. When payment methods "charging what the traffic will bear" change, do consumer reactions to medical fees change? Under what circumstances?
4. What have been consumer responses to administrative price controls? Have these controls been understood? Or do the third-party systems effectively obscure direct prices and budgetary choices?
5. What kinds of subsidies, negative prices, or other incentive forms would encourage more efficient use and lower costs?
6. What kinds of subsidies, negative prices, or other incentive

forms encourage unions and other consumer groups to
keep use and costs down?

7. What kinds of coinsurance and hesitation payments would
make health care use more effective?

8. Do employer payments and selection of coverage by industry and unions weaken the voice of the final consumer?

9. What control mechanisms are used to ration care when
prices are not used? What are the results, for what types
and stages of illness?

10. Are use differences and methods of finance reflected in
variations in health status?

11. What experiments abroad with methods of financing are especially relevant to United States' policies?

Of the two major aspects of health care—finance and health
service organization—the response of consumers in the past has
been mainly the result of price structures and the changes brought
about by third-party payments. Demands on organizational change
have been structured primarily through unions and other organized
groups. As more research is done to understand the response, its
conditions and characteristics, increasing emphasis undoubtedly will
be put on trial programs, experimentally executed. Out of such experiments may come a better design for financing and organization
in the future.

References

Davis, K. *and* R. W. Foster
    1972   Community Hospitals: Inflation in the Premedical Period.
            Research Report, Office of Research and Statistics, Social
            Security Administration, U.S. Department of Health, Edu-
            cation, and Welfare. Washington, D.C.: Government Print-
            ing Office.
Densen, Paul M.
    1973   Standard Setting, Monitoring, and Health Services Re-
            search. Paper prepared for Symposium on Health Care Re-
            search, University of Calgary, Calgary, Alberta, May 29
            (processed).

Densen, Paul M., et al.

    1960   "Prepaid medical care and hospital utilization in a dual choice situation." American Journal of Public Health 50 (November): 1710–1726.

    1962   "Prepaid medical care and hospital utilization, comparison of a group practice and self-insurance situation." Hospitals 36 (November 16): 65.

Feldstein, M. S.

    1971a   "Hospital cost inflation. A study of nonprofit price dynamics." American Economic Review 61: 853–872.

    1971b   "A new approach to national health insurance." Public Interest 23: 93–105.

Luft, Harold

    1972   Poverty and Health: An Empirical Investigation of the Economic Interaction. Doctoral dissertation, Harvard University (processed).

Phelps, Charles E. *and* Joseph P. Newhouse

    1972   Coinsurance and the Demand for Medical Services. Santa Monica: The RAND Corporation (R-964-OEO).

Schottland, Charles I.

    1974   Personal communication (January).

Scitovsky, Anna A. *and* Nelda Snyder

    1972   "Effect of coinsurance on use of physician services." Social Security Bulletin 35 (June): 3–19.

U.S. Department of Health, Education, and Welfare, National Center for Health Statistics

    1964   Hospital Discharges per 1000 Population July 1963–June 1964. NCHS Series 10, No. 30.

    1972   Physician Visits and Interval since Last Visit U.S. 1969. NCHS Series 10, No. 75.

Index

Accessibility: of health care system, 44, 307–308, 313, 324, 405

Accidents: automobile, 5, 7, 12, 18, 20, 154, 164, 186; home and alcohol, 7; risk predictors, 27; and dislocation, 62; and ambulance calls, 99; and death, 186, 188; expenses, 191

Activity: limitation and chronic illness, 116, 117, 118, 119–120, 122–123, 126, 144, 145; of disabled, 155; and terminal illness, 185; limitation and increase in illness, 246; rejection of well role, 253

Acute illness, 49, 114, 115, 118, 121, 126n, 140, 143, 145, 146

"Addictive" users, 14

Adults: nondrinkers, 14; health education, 21; and dangers of alcohol, 24; income and use of care, 141

Advertising: alcoholic beverages, 7, 11; cigarette, 8–10, 11; antismoking, 22; and rehabilitation, 167, 169–170

Age: and car accidents, 5; and smoking, 25; as constraint variable, 71; and use of screening, 78, 79; and ambulance service, 97, 99; and use of emergency room, 100, 102, 103; and chronic illness, 118, 120, 121, 145; and rate of depreciation in health capital, 125, 127n, 132; and use of care, 140, 141–142, 146, 226, 390; and disability, 156–157; and rehabilitation, 161, 162; and terminal illness, 188, 190, 193; and perception of symptoms, 254; and surveys of satisfaction, 311, 312, 313

Aged. *See* Elderly

Alcohol: use of, 3; and government, 11, 12; and driving, 13, 15, 20, 25; pricing effects, 16; prohibition, 17–18, 19; per capita consumption,

18–19; education efforts, 20, 21; dangers of, 24; intervention strategy, 24

Alcohol abuse. *See* Drinking, excessive

Alcoholic beverage industry, 7, 10–11

Alcoholics Anonymous, 14, 15, 19

Alcoholism, 6–7, 8, 10, 19, 20, 266

Alienation, and use of medical services, 40, 41, 44, 46, 48, 51, 272–275, 282

Altruism, 280–281

Ambulance services, 91, 97–99

Ambulatory care: coverage of, 50, 95, 234; in emergency room, 100, 106; physical rehabilitation, 162; physician's direction, 363–368

Ambulatory problems, and societal environment, 178

American Academy of Pediatrics, 323

American Cancer Society, 51; antismoking campaigns, 17, 20, 23

American Medical Association, and health legislation, 311

Ancillary services, 103, 366

Anglo-Saxon Protestants, and symptoms, 255

Anomie, 39, 51

Antenatal services, 65, 70, 73

Antismoking, 17, 22, 24, 25–26, 28

Architecture, 40–41, 51

Atlanta, Ga., 354

Automotive industries, 10–11

Autonomy of physicians, 315, 316, 319, 320, 324

Aversive therapy, and smoking, 19

Baltimore, Md., 95

Barriers: to behavioral change, 10–14; to health care, 40, 42–44, 51, 107, 336, 337, 342, 355; to rehabilitation services, 162–164, 178; to curtailment of treatment, 206